Language, Text and Context

This wide-ranging collection of essays focuses on the principle of contextualization as it applies to the interpretation, description, theorizing and reading of literary and non-literary texts. The collection aims to reveal the interdependencies between theory, analysis, text and context by challenging the myth that stylistics entails a fundamental separation of text from context, linguistic description from descriptive interpretation, or language from situation.

Stylisticians have particular expertise in the form, function and structure of language in discourse which far from 'delimiting' the text can be usefully applied to interpretive approaches in literature. The essays cover a historically diverse set of texts from Puttenham to Colemanballs and a number of language-sensitive topics: from postmodernism, genre and newspaper representations to irony, gender and narrative. This challenging collection demonstrates the vitality and diversity of current practices of stylistic analysis and offers a variety of language-orientated ways into the reading and unmasking of texts.

The INTERFACE Series

> A linguist deaf to the poetic function of language and a literary scholar indifferent to linguistic problems and unconversant with linguistic methods, are equally flagrant anachronisms.
>
> (Roman Jakobson)

This statement, made over twenty-five years ago, is no less relevant today, and 'flagrant anachronisms' still abound. The aim of the INTERFACE series is to examine topics at the 'interface' of language studies and literary criticism and in so doing to build bridges between these traditionally divided disciplines.

Already published in the series

NARRATIVE
A Critical Linguistic Introduction
Michael J. Toolan

LANGUAGE, LITERATURE AND CRITICAL PRACTICE
Ways of Analysing Text
David Birch

LITERATURE, LANGUAGE AND CHANGE
Ruth Waterhouse and John Stephens

LITERARY STUDIES IN ACTION
Alan Durant and Nigel Fabb

LANGUAGE IN POPULAR FICTION
Walter Nash

THE LANGUAGE OF JOKES
Analysing verbal play
Delia Chiaro

The series editor
Ronald Carter is Professor of Modern English Language at the University of Nottingham and was National Coordinator of the 'Language in the National Curriculum' Project (LINC) from 1989 to 1992.

Language, Text and Context

Essays in stylistics

Edited by Michael Toolan

London and New York

First published in 1992 by
Routledge
11 New Fetter Lane, London EC4P 4EE

Simultaneously published in the USA and Canada
by Routledge
a division of Routledge, Chapman and Hall, Inc.
29 West 35th Street, New York, NY 10001

Typeset in 10/12pt Times by
Selectmove Ltd, London.
Printed in Great Britain by
Clays Ltd, St Ives plc.

British Library Cataloguing in Publication Data
  Language, text and context. – (Interface)
  I. Toolan, Michael J.   II. Series
  801.95

Library of Congress Cataloging in Publication Data
Language, text and context / [edited by] Michael Toolan.
  p.   cm. — (Interface)
  Includes bibliographical references and index.
  1. Discourse analysis. 2. Context (linguistics). 3. Language and
languages—Style. I. Toolan, Michael J. II. Series: Interface (London,
England)
P302.S79 1992
401′.41—dc20   91–31696

ISBN 0–415–056462
    0–415–069955 pbk

Contents

Series editor's introduction to the Interface series

There have been many books published this century which have been devoted to the interface of language and literary studies. This is the first series of books devoted to this area commissioned by a major international publisher; it is the first time a group of writers have addressed themselves to issues at the interface of language and literature; and it is the first time an international professional association has worked closely with a publisher to establish such a venture. It is the purpose of this general introduction to the series to outline some of the main guiding principles underlying the books in the series.

The first principle adopted is one of not foreclosing on the many possibilities for the integration of language and literature studies. There are many ways in which the study of language and literature can be combined and many different theoretical, practical and curricular objectives to be realized. Obviously, a close relationship with the aims and methods of descriptive linguistics will play a prominent part, so readers will encounter some detailed analysis of language in places. In keeping with a goal of much work in this field, writers will try to make their analysis sufficiently replicable for other analysts to see how they have arrived at the interpretative decisions they have reached and to allow others to reproduce their methods on the same or on other texts. But linguistic science does not have a monopoly in methodology and description any more than linguists can have sole possession of insights into language and its workings. Some contributors to the series adopt quite rigorous linguistic procedures; others proceed less rigorously but no less revealingly. All are, however, united by a belief that detailed scrutiny of the role of language in literary texts can be mutually enriching to language and literary studies.

Series of books are usually written to an overall formula or design. In the case of the Interface series this was considered to be not entirely appropriate. This is for the reasons given above, but also because, as the first series of its kind, it would be wrong to suggest that there are formulaic modes by which integration can be achieved. The fact that all the books address themselves to the integration of language and literature in any case imparts a natural and organic unity to the series. Thus, some of the books in this series will provide descriptive overviews, others will offer detailed case studies of a particular topic, others will involve single author studies, and some will be more pedagogically oriented.

This range of design and procedure means that a wide variety of audiences is envisaged for the series as a whole, though, of course, individual books are necessarily quite specifically targeted. The general level of exposition presumes quite advanced students of language and literature. Approximately, this level covers students of English language and literature (though not exclusively English) at senior high-school/upper sixth form level to university students in their first or second year of study. Many of the books in the series are designed to be used by students. Some may serve as course books – these will normally contain exercises and suggestions for further work as well as glossaries and graded bibliographies which point the student towards further reading. Some books are also designed to be used by teachers for their own reading and updating, and to supplement courses; in some cases, specific questions of pedagogic theory, teaching procedure and methodology at the interface of language and literature are addressed.

From a pedagogic point of view it is the case in many parts of the world that students focus on literary texts, especially in the mother tongue, before undertaking any formal study of the language. With this fact in mind, contributors to the series have attempted to gloss all new technical terms and to assume on the part of their readers little or no previous knowledge of linguistics or formal language studies. They see no merit in not being detailed and explicit about what they describe in the linguistic properties of texts; but they recognize that formal language study can seem forbidding if it is not properly introduced.

A further characteristic of the series is that the authors engage in a direct relationship with their readers. The overall style of writing is informal and there is above all an attempt to lighten the usual style of academic discourse. In some cases this extends to the way in which notes and guidance for further work are presented. In all cases, the style adopted by authors is judged to be that most appropriate to the mediation of their chosen subject matter.

We now come to two major points of principle which underlie the conceptual scheme for the series. One is that the term 'literature' cannot be defined in isolation from an expression of ideology. In fact, no academic study, and certainly no description of the language of texts, can be neutral and objective, for the sociocultural positioning of the analyst will mean that the description is unavoidably political. Contributors to the series recognize and, in so far as this accords with the aims of each book, attempt to explore the role of ideology at the interface of language and literature. Second, most writers also prefer the term 'literatures' to a singular notion of literature. Some replace 'literature' altogether with the neutral term 'text'. It is for this reason that readers will not find exclusive discussions of the literary language of canonical literary texts; instead the linguistic heterogeneity of literature and the permeation of many discourses with what is conventionally thought of as poetic or literary language will be a focus. This means that in places as much space can be devoted to examples of word play in jokes, newspaper editorials, advertisements, historical writing, or a popular thriller as to a sonnet by Shakespeare or a passage from Jane Austen. It is also important to stress how the term 'literature' itself is historically variable and how different social and cultural assumptions can condition what is regarded as literature. In this respect the role of linguistic and literary theory is vital. It is an aim of the series to be constantly alert to new developments in the description and theory of texts.

Finally, as series editor, I have to underline the partnership and co-operation of the whole enterprise of the Interface series and acknowledge the advice and assistance received at many stages from the PALA Committee and from Routledge. In turn, we are all fortunate to have the benefit of three associate editors with considerable collective depth of experience in this field in different parts of the world: Professor Roger Fowler, Professor Mary Louise Pratt, Professor Michael Halliday. In spite of their own individual orientations, I am sure that all concerned with the series would want to endorse the statement by Roman Jakobson made over twenty-five years ago but which is no less relevant today:

A linguist deaf to the poetic function of language and a literary scholar indifferent to linguistic problems and unconversant with linguistic methods, are equally flagrant anachronisms.

The volume *Language, Text, and Context* is unique in the way in which work in stylistics, socially oriented linguistics, and literary and cultural theory are integrated. The contributors show a consistent awareness that the discipline of stylistics must move forward, in particular, by directly addressing issues of styles and contexts. For too long literary stylistic analyses have tended to be founded on a text-immanent view of language with consequent universalist readings of the selected, usually canonical, texts. As techniques of description were refined such idealizations were, of course, necessary and understandable but the challenge for the 1990s is to show how systematic analysis of the language of all texts can be related to contextual patterns, particularly those which are social and historical in origin. The task is a complex and ambitious one. This book, edited by Michael Toolan – a previous contributor to the Interface series – points the way authoritatively and accessibly.

Tables and figures

Notes on contributors

Brian McHale teaches and researches in the Porter Institute for Poetics and Semiotics of Tel Aviv University. His research interests include contemporary poetry and poetics, and postmodernism. He is the author of *Postmodernist Fiction* (1987), and Assistant Editor of the journal *Poetics Today*.

George Dillon, of the English Department of the University of Washington, has published extensively in semantics, stylistics, discourse analysis, and rhetorical theory. His latest book, *Contending Rhetorics* (forthcoming), is on writing and argumentation in the academic disciplines.

Gill Francis and **Anneliese Kramer-Dahl** both teach at the National University of Singapore, in the Department of English Language and Literature, and the English Language Proficiency Unit, respectively. Both have research interests in systemic linguistics, and in the application of that linguistics to written texts and the process of writing.

Eugene Kintgen, of the English Department of Indiana University, has written on reader-response approaches to critical interpretation of texts, culminating in his book *The Perception of Poetry*. More recently his research has been on Elizabethan literature, and the factors affecting its contemporary reception.

Anne Waldron Neumann's research interests include the application of stylistics to the eighteenth- and nineteenth-century English novel, narratology, and contemporary South African literature in English. She teaches in the English Department of Ohio State University, and has completed a book manuscript on Austen's style.

Norman Macleod teaches in the Department of English Language of the University of Edinburgh. His research interests include pragmatics and literary stylistics, both of which are areas in which he has published; he has also written extensively on Kingsley Amis's style.

Marie Paule Hastert and **Jean Jacques Weber** both teach in the Département des Lettres et des Sciences Humaines of the University of Luxembourg. Dr Weber's research and publications address the semantic and pragmatic factors involved in the construction of literary narratives.

Formerly at the University of Strathclyde, **Sara Mills** has recently moved to the Department of English of Loughborough University. Her research interests include feminism and the linguistic analysis of the ideology within texts; she is author of *Discourses of Difference* and a co-author of *Ways of Reading* (both forthcoming).

Kate Clark graduated in English Langauge and Literature from Liverpool University in 1987. Since then she had been working in Palestine, returning recently to England where she is studying Arabic and is active in the Women's movement and in Middle East solidarity work.

Rukmini Bhaya Nair has research interests ranging from child language and pragmatics to postcolonial literature and theory. Her book entitled *The Story in Conversation* is forthcoming. She teaches in the Centre for Linguistics and English, Jawaharlal Nehru University.

Geoffrey Leech has published numerous books on English language and linguistics, including (with M. Short) *Style in Fiction* (1981) and *Principles of Pragmatics* (1983). He is a co-author of *A Comprehensive Grammar of the English Language* (1985), and is Professor of English Linguistics and Modern English Language in the University of Lancaster.

Paul Simpson teaches in the Department of English Language and Literature of the University of Liverpool, and has published articles in stylistics (particularly on Flann O'Brien) and the sociolinguistics of narrative. He is also editor of *Liverpool Papers in Language and Discourse*.

Michael Toolan is in the English Department of the University of Washington, Seattle. He has published widely in stylistics, most recently authoring *The Stylistics of Fiction* (1990).

Preface and acknowledgements

The thematic focus for this collection is the principle of contextual-ization. These essays show a variety of stylisticians considering the contextualizations that ground interpretation, description, theorizing and reading, as they see relevant. In this way we hope to dispel the myth that stylistics envisages and rests upon certain radical binarisms – the text vs. the context; and linguistic description vs. discourse interpretation. There are interdependencies between theory, analysis, text and situation, which require acknowledgement and exploration. Stylisticians have a particular expertise with the form, function and structure of language in discourse, and this should never (have) become unfashionable. If we have been displaced, in the pantheon of approaches to literature, by feminist, new historicist, Marxist and psychoanalytic perspectives, then this in part reflects a misunderstanding of stylistics – as purely formalist, treating the text as autonomous, 'delimited', and so on. On the contrary, there is nothing to prevent – and much to recommend – incorporating literary linguistic procedures into the prosecution of those and other interpretative contextualizations.

All these essays address literary topics, broadly understood, but some concentrate on some stylistic phenomenon in a single text while others consider a principle or technique as it applies to a range of texts. All demonstrate the vitality and diversity of current practices of stylistic analysis; all show an awareness of and engagement with theories and frameworks other than those simply in the mainstream of orthodox linguistics. They should make suggestive, challenging and even inspiring reading.

I have supplied a preface to each of the chapters. These prefaces are partly an introduction, partly a foreword, and partly an afterword to the essay that follows. I try to specify what I see as the main concerns and arguments of each essay, but I additionally hazard some reactions to those concerns and arguments, mentioning connections with other approaches included here or influential in contemporary literary linguistics. These prefaces are, then, fairly speculative, and attempt to chip into the conversation between the author and the reader, in a spirit of dialogism.

The essays have been grouped into four parts, but in a highly provisional spirit. The cross-linkages are numerous: Bhaya Nair's chapter is certainly about the strategic representation of men and marriage and cultural values, rather than solely about women, so could fit in Part II; Simpson's on Colemanballs is clearly a dissection of an unintentionally hilarious 'fashion of speaking', so could fit in Part I, and so on. Nevertheless, I believe the essays within each part do more particularly speak to one another, or to some shared preoccupations, than to the remainder, as I attempt to indicate in my prefaces.

My thanks go to all the contributors, who generously made their work available, and bore with delays in editing and compiling.

Acknowledgement is due to the copyright holders and publishers for their permission to reprint the following: 'Metamorphosis', from *As We Know* by John Ashbery. Copyright © 1979 John Ashbery. Used by permission of Viking Penguin, a division of Penguin Books USA Inc.; and of Carcanet Press Ltd, UK. 'Live Acts', from *American Poetry Since 1970 Up Late*, second edition, © 1989. Edited by Andrei Codrescu. Reprinted with permission of Four Walls Eight Windows. 'Of Movement Towards a Natural Place', from *Wound Response* (1974) as reprinted in *Poems* (Agneau 2, Edinburgh and London, 1982), p. 221, copyright © 1974, 1982 J. H. Prynne. Reprinted with permission of the author. A bird's-eye view axonometric drawing of the Gehry house, Santa Monica, from *The Architecture of Frank Gehry* (1986), used by permission of Mr Gehry. 'Valentine', from *Selected Poems 1954–1982*, copyright © 1985 John Fuller. Reprinted by permission of Martin Secker & Warburg Ltd.

Part I

Situated fashions of speaking and writing: from nonsense to common sense

Editor's preface

Brian McHale, who has written extensively on postmodernism as an artistic and literary phenomenon, considers what it might mean to view postmodernist poetry as 'nonsense' – in a positive rather than pejorative sense of that term. Significantly, the question of context is directly relevant here: as McHale reminds us, readers – and language-users generally – are ordinarily remarkably resourceful in the business of contextualizing seeming gobbledegook, random lines, and so on. Our sense-making, or framing of signs, may be characterized as integrative acts at three most basic levels: in terms of the world, the voice or speaker, and the overarching theme that a poem invokes for a reader. Attentive to such levels or criteria, we are immensely creative at adducing some hospitable semantic environment, within which the 'word-salad' will appear to be at least a semi-coherent verbal meal. Accordingly, 'making nonsense' is no small achievement, and greater acknowledgement needs to be paid here to the 'making' aspect. To make nonsense, as in postmodern poetry, is carefully to block our interpretative acts of naturalizing conceptualization; postmodernist nonsense is 'antiabsorptive' discourse. We are driven back, by such poems as those by Berryman and Prynne which McHale discusses, to reference to that unsatisfactory device of the theorist, the 'no (integrated) context' context.

As Stewart (1979) has argued, a culture's nonsense is defined and understood in relation to its sense: the one is a construction whose perception is made possible by the concomitant postulation of the other. *Mutatis mutandis*, analogous remarks apply also to two other hierarchized binary pairs relevant here: text and context, and the literal and metaphorical. Indeed the interrelations between these binarisms are numerous and provocative. Certainly, the path from text/context to metaphor/literal is relatively direct, once two further pairs are invoked: figure/ground, vehicle/tenor. And clearly what makes all these viable at all are the structuralist prerequisites, perceived difference, perceived relation.

But as McHale shows, all this business-as-usual is noticeably disrupted in postmodernism, where we have no great confidence as to which elements (in a poem, for example) are literal, which are metaphorical, or what is figure and what is ground. The one pair that might seem most stable here is that of text and context, but as indicated, context seems impossible to retrieve at all satisfactorily. The consequence, uncanny though it may appear at first consideration, is that even the category we label 'text' becomes provisional or attenuated: we read the text before us, but experience a diminished confidence as to whether this is a single text, the real text, the whole text, or 'really a text'. Ever intent on rationalizing, the analyst confronted by this discoursal mess may take the predictable absorptive step of declaring 'Yes, the text is a mess, but that "being/doing mess" is the point, is the theme.' Such a manoeuvre is considered by McHale when he explores the degree to which his selected poems work as metapoetry: poetry about poetry, and particularly, poetry that displays and rejects the mystificatory powers of 'normal' language. Again, though, this is rather a thin conclusion, still only a negative definition of such writing, in terms of what it is not, rather than a positive valuation in terms of what it actually is.

McHale proposes, as a richer solution, that these postmodern poems be seen in the context of architect Frank Gehry's extraordinary 'postmodernist' house, which comprises a traditional cottage structure wrapped in a heterogeneity of modern shapes, materials, and junk. Both house and poems are attempts at a 'cognitive mapping' of the postmodern world. Both are maps less in the familiar aesthetic sense of models or representations of, say, a psyche or way of living; but in the more innovative sense of signposts along a possible way, a possible direction, for the reader to engage with dialogically and interactively (perhaps more compass than map). Teasing out the contrast is not easy, but it may be worth reflecting on the difference between consulting a map in a study (where we think of looking at a map of Germany as looking *at* Germany), and using a map in the course of an actual journey, already begun. In the latter case, the map may be a helpful guide (though it may equally be a distraction or hindrance) but it will hardly be so without the active efforts of the mapreader.

It is significant, also, that McHale's essay – even while addressing the most contemporary topic of postmodernism – finds insight on matters of nonsense and context in the brilliant work of a theorist of an earlier age, William Empson (together with the equally brilliant work, cut short by her untimely death, of a theorist of our own age, Veronica Forrest-Thomson). In particular, Empson's *Seven Types of Ambiguity*, together with the work of, for example, Bally, Spitzer, and Jakobson, constitute a canon of pathbreaking, issue-confronting texts in stylistics.

1 Making (non)sense of postmodernist poetry

Brian McHale

> We do not want more poems about everyday life; there are enough
> and more than enough poems that do that; but never today enough
> Dada poems.
>
> (Forrest-Thomson 1978)

TALKING NONSENSE

Accusations of nonsense put literary people on the defensive. 'This is
not nonsense talk', writes Marjorie Perloff (1987: 231), defensively, of
a passage from a poem she admires by the postmodernist 'language'
poet Charles Bernstein. She is right to get defensive, for the passage
in question (from a poem called 'Dysraphism') certainly *looks* like
nonsense, and a sustainable charge of nonsense is normally fatal
to a poem's claims on our serious readerly attention. A stronger
defence, however, would have involved turning the accusation into
a description, that is, admitting the charge of nonsense while denying
that the label 'nonsense' must inevitably be pejorative. 'Nonsense'
can just as well identify a valuable, and valued, quality. It has
functioned that way historically, and not only in marginalized poetry
('children's classics': Dodgson, Lear), but, more pertinently, in
Russian futurist *zaum* and Dada poetry. Many postmodernist poems
might appropriately be described as 'neo-Dada' or 'nonsense', and
part of the process by which we might come to understand why
such poems could be worth writing and reading involves coming to
understand the possible uses and value of nonsense.[1] In recognition
of this, the present essay uses the term 'nonsense' neither pejoratively
nor dismissively, but as a neutral descriptive category.

Why might one value nonsense? First, nonsense, far from being only
too easy to fall into, as one might infer from the pejorative contexts
of the term's use, proves to be quite difficult to make. This is because

readers or hearers of sentences are such resourceful sense-makers, able to extract sense from the least tractable materials. Anecdotal evidence of such resourcefulness is to be found, for instance, in Stanley Fish's by now notorious experiment in which well-drilled students of religious poetry were able to develop a plausible interpretation for a cryptic (to all appearances nonsensical) pseudo-poem – in fact a list of linguists' names left on the blackboard from a previous class (Fish 1980: 322–37).[2]

Philosophers of language and philosophically oriented linguists often assume that certain grammatically well-formed expressions are 'inherently nonsensical', e.g. 'Colorless green ideas sleep furiously'. But J. F. Ross has persuasively argued that, on the contrary, 'there is no grammatically well-formed string of words that is in all environments semantically impossible or semantically unacceptable. . . . Something is nonsense only relative to an environment' (Ross 1981: 55). Consequently, nonsense arises only when extraordinary efforts are made to render an environment semantically inhospitable to sense: 'Meaninglessness [i.e. nonsense] occurs only when meaning is environmentally *prevented*' (172).

If this is so, and nonsense really is as difficult to produce as Ross contends, and as Fish's experiment seems to corroborate, then it might be valued precisely for this quality of difficulty surmounted. Of course, the value attached to difficulty surmounted is not by any means a universal; it is, we might suppose, a modernist value, but not necessarily a postmodernist value. In any case, the evidence of nonsense's difficulty would lead us, at the very least, to assume that nonsense must be motivated; in other words, it would lead us to ask why, if nonsense is so difficult to achieve, would someone have bothered to produce it?

Second, nonsense might be valued precisely for the light it throws on its antithesis: sense-making. Nonsense yields valuable insight into how sense is made, giving us access to the sense-making process in a way, perhaps, that nothing else can. This is because of the intimate relationship between nonsense and common sense: nonsense depends on common sense. 'Our ways of making nonsense will depend upon our ways of making common sense', writes Susan Stewart (1979: viii); 'the nature of nonsense will always be contingent upon the nature of its corresponding common sense' (51). 'Where there is a common sense, there will be a common nonsense' (52); consequently, 'There will be as many varieties of nonsense as there are varieties of sense' (16). Now this is, in effect, a negative value: nonsense is to be valued for what it tells us about what it is not. Whether it can acquire some positive value in its own right, and if so what, is a question to which we shall return later.

The best and most economical way to investigate how nonsense is made and common sense resisted in postmodernist poetry is to analyse specific texts. Thus, the bulk of this chapter will be devoted to readings of three poems: John Ashbery's 'Metamorphosis' (1979); J. H. Prynne's 'Of Movement Towards a Natural Place' (1974); and Charles Bernstein's 'Live Acts' (1986). But before we can undertake these readings, we will need to equip ourselves with an appropriate descriptive apparatus, one designed to capture Stewart's insight into the dependency of nonsense on common sense. We will need, in other words, to give some account of how we typically make sense of difficult or obscure poetry, as a preliminary to accounting for how we fail to make sense of postmodernist nonsense poetry.

MAKING SENSE

The most attractive and persuasive account of sense-making I know of, for all its incompleteness and eccentricities, is the one proposed by Veronica Forrest-Thomson (1978; see also Forrest-Thomson 1971, 1972, and 1973). Her approach to literary intelligibility might be characterized as a 'strong misreading' of William Empson, especially the Empson of *Seven Types of Ambiguity*.[3] What in particular Forrest-Thomson retains from Empson is his emphasis on the reader's resourcefulness in rationalizing (Forrest-Thomson says 'naturalizing') the text's semantic anomalies, cruxes, and 'ambiguities' (in Empson's extended sense of the term).

How do we make poems, especially 'difficult' or 'obscure' or apparently 'nonsensical' poems, intelligible?[4] We do so, according to Forrest-Thomson, by identifying pertinent levels (we might just as properly say frames) of coherence or integration. Identifying a level of coherence or integration (or what Forrest-Thomson somewhat anomalously calls an 'image-complex') enables us 'to assimilate features of various kinds, to distinguish the relevant from the irrelevant, and to control the importation of external contexts' (1978: xii). In other words, it enables us to integrate a range of features, both semantic and non-semantic,[5] under the same explanatory rubric; it enables us to establish, relative to this rubric, a hierarchy or priority of features, some of them judged to be relevant, others irrelevant; and, finally, it enables us to decide which, if any, external frames of reference (in the sense of Hrushovski 1979, 1984a, and 1984b) might relevantly be referred to.

The actual frames or levels of coherence which might be pertinent to specific poems are, of course, very various, but we can propose three basic frame types or conventional levels of integration which have served readers well in their naturalizations of (at least) western poetry since (at least) the Renaissance.

1 The level of world, which Forrest-Thomson calls the 'empirical image-complex'. This involves the reader's reconstructing a situation, scene, event, etc., at the extreme limit an entire cosmology.
2 The level of voice, Forrest-Thomson's 'discursive image-complex'. At this level the reader reconstructs for the poem a 'speaker' or source persona, in some cases a more or less fully personified 'character', in others a supra-personal or conventional source, a register, discourse, or level of style keyed to a specific genre or topic.
3 The level of theme, Forrest-Thomson's 'thematic synthesis'.[6] This involves identifying an 'idea' sufficiently abstract to allow for the assimilation of other local 'ideas' identified in the text.[7]

In reading most poems, all three frames come into play and interact; in some types of poetry, one frame is clearly dominant (e.g. 'world' in topographical-descriptive poetry, or 'voice' in dramatic monologue poems), the others subordinate (or inapplicable). In the process of naturalizing or rationalizing poems, 'feedback loops' typically function among these three levels: thus, the identification of a world (situation, scene, event) helps us to integrate a speaker at the level of voice, and vice versa; identification of a speaker helps us to integrate a situation at the level of world; while identification of a theme may guide us in reconstructing a world and/or a voice, and vice versa; reconstruction of a world, a voice, and/or the interaction between them, may guide us in identifying a theme.

Forrest-Thomson's approach to sense-making in terms of the assimilation of textual features at different levels of coherence finds interesting corroboration in the work of others who have investigated these processes from other perspectives. For example, J. F. Ross has proposed an account of disambiguation and semantic coherence whereby the relatively intransigent words in a sentence (the ones whose range of meanings is most narrowly prescribed) coerce (or 'dominate', to use Ross's own term) the less intransigent words, weeding out their irrelevant meanings ('differentiating' them, as Ross puts it) and assimilating these words to the semantic context (Ross 1981; cf. Thompson and Thompson 1987). This, it seems to me, amounts to a version of Forrest-Thomson's account of assimilation and hierarchies of relevance and irrelevance, but pitched at the sentence-level rather than, like Forrest-Thomson's, at the text-level. Similarly, Alex McHoul's (1982) 'Cumulex' exercise tends to corroborate not only Forrest-Thomson's general approach, but even the levels of coherence which she specifies. In grappling with a semantically diffuse and enigmatic text (in fact, a synthetic 'pseudo-poem'), McHoul's student readers construct 'scenes' or fragments of a world (1982: 22, 30), often importing external frames of reference to 'flesh out' these world-fragments (32); they try to identify voices or personas, and routinely assume that the text has been 'authored', that is, that it emanates from a single source and intention (18, 29); and above all, they strive for thematic synthesis, easily the most conspicuous and dynamic of the sense-making operations they apply.

If Forrest-Thomson is, as we have noted, a faithful Empsonian in her general orientation towards sense-making, she nevertheless parts company with him at one important juncture. For Empson, the resolvability of semantic anomalies is a positive value; texts which successfully resist rational resolution are described as 'decadent', and are said to 'misuse' ambiguity (1947: 165, 160). Empson's negative valuation of unresolvable ambiguities is explained by his anxiety about control: texts which do not contextually limit or constrain ambiguity give the reader too much interpretative freedom. Forrest-Thomson exactly reverses Empson's valuation. Where he regards the resolvability of semantic cruxes as the mark of poetic success, she regards it as a measure of overly facile sense-making, premature or 'bad' naturalization; while the texts which in Empson's view 'misuse' ambiguity Forrest-Thomson regards as encouraging suspended or 'good' naturalization.

The poet Charles Bernstein, who has read Forrest-Thomson as carefully and sympathetically as she has read Empson, proposes a concept of 'absorption' to cover much the same ground as Forrest-Thomson's assimilation and levels of coherence. Texts may be 'absorptive' in two interrelated senses: they absorb diverse materials, that is, they integrate or assimilate them and make them cohere, in roughly Forrest-Thomson's sense; and in the process of absorbing materials they may also absorb the reader, in the sense of engrossing or fascinating him or her. Bernstein describes approvingly a range of 'antiabsorptive' strategies by which his postmodernist contemporaries' poems counteract the absorptive tendencies of sense-making.[8] These strategies might just as readily be called nonsense strategies, and it is their operation, and the resistance they present to the operations of sense-making, that we will observe in action in the analyses which follow.[9]

BUILDING WORLDS

Some working hypothesis about the reconstructed world of a poetic text is often essential for distinguishing between the two frames of reference whose interaction constitutes a metaphor (see Hrushovski 1984a; McHale 1987: 133–47). Metaphor is not always or inevitably signalled grammatically, so in many cases we must operate with a semantic hypothesis about which frame is 'present' and 'literal' (i.e. the tenor of the metaphor) and which is 'absent' and 'figurative' (i.e. its vehicle). This hypothesis about the reconstructed world establishes the literal frame; any anomaly or deviation within that frame must be processed as metaphor. This is the operation we apply when making sense of elliptical metaphor, e.g. Imagist juxtaposition. Consider the paradigmatic case of Pound's 'In a Station of the Metro'. Here the literal frame is established (as in many poems) by semantic coherence between the text's title and its first line ('The apparition of these faces in the crowd'); consequently the anomalous second line ('Petals on a wet, black bough') must be understood as the vehicle of a metaphor.[10] It is this operation of contextualization, or what Forrest-Thomson calls naturalization, that rescues metaphor from nonsense: 'Metaphors make "common sense" so long as they are taken as metaphors and contextualized as such' (Stewart 1979: 35). Without a working world-hypothesis to distinguish the literal from the figurative frame, the tenor from the vehicle, metaphor lapses into nonsensical literalness: 'In nonsense, metaphor "runs rampant" until there is wall-to-wall metaphor and thus wall-to-wall literalness' (ibid.).

In John Ashbery's 'Metamorphosis' (see Appendix 1 for the full text), unlike in the case of 'In a Station of the Metro', the title offers little help in establishing a world-hypothesis. Is there any discernible scene or situation? We can identify certain fragments of landscape: 'The barges and light they conflict with against/ The sweep of low-lying, cattle-sheared hills' (ll. 17–18); 'the unmapped sky over the sunset' (l. 40). Perhaps we can guess at a bucolic setting, on the strength of such details as the hammock and the straw (l. 31). Perhaps, too, we detect a literal event involving a ladder (perhaps a fall from one? ll. 43–4). Having identified such fragments, however, we remain unable to integrate them into a single scene, or, alternatively, to motivate their selection and juxtaposition.

Worse, some of these world-fragments are just as likely to function figuratively (as the vehicles of metaphors) as they are to function literally. This evidently is the case with the first landscape fragment, which seems to belong to the figurative frame of a kind of epic simile:

> . . . the nutty context isn't just there on a page
> But rolling toward you like a pig just over
> The barges and light they conflict with against
> The sweep of low-lying, cattle-sheared hills,
> Our plight in progress.
>
> (ll. 15–19)

On the other hand, the sunset-scene fragment and the event involving the ladder seem likely to belong to literary allusions, i.e. to what Forrest-Thomson would call 'discursive images' as distinct from 'empirical' ones. If the 'stitches' of l. 38 are the antecedent for the pronoun 'they' of l. 39 (but pronoun antecedence is notoriously elusive in Ashbery), then this entire passage would seem to make a witty, revisionist allusion to the paradigmatically modernist figure at the beginning of Eliot's 'Prufrock':

> . . . the stitches ceased to make sense.
> They climb now, gravely, with each day's decline
> Farther into the unmapped sky over the sunset
> And prolong it indelicately.
>
> (ll. 38–41)

> Let us go then, you and I,
> When the evening is spread out against the sky
> Like a patient etherised upon a table [.]
> ('The Love Song of J. Alfred Prufrock', ll. 1–3)

The event involving the ladder would seem to allude either to the famous final proposition (6.54) of Wittgenstein's *Tractatus*, or (if we allow the fragmentary bucolic context to exert some pressure) to Robert Frost's 'After Apple Picking'; or conceivably, of course, to both at once. In any case, the world of 'Metamorphosis', minimal as it is, disperses into metaphor and allusion, and we find integration at this level fatally blocked.

In the case of J. H. Prynne's 'Of Movement Towards a Natural Place' (see Appendix 2 for the full text), once again the poem's title proves to be unhelpful. However, here we might have recourse to the title of the volume in which this poem originally appeared: *Wound Response*. This, like much of the diction of the poem 'Of Movement', is ambiguous between two frames of reference, that of medical pathology and that of the emotional life, where terms such as hurt, wound, bruise, etc. function as long-dead metaphors. Which of these frames is literal, which figurative in 'Of Movement'? When we read 'Remorse is a pathology' (l. 11), or 'the/ input of "blame" [. . .] patters like scar tissue' (ll. 12–13), syntax seems decisively to disambiguate whatever potential ambiguity there might be in the diction. What we have before us, it would appear, is a species of metaphysical conceit: the emotion of remorse (the literal frame) is being elaborately compared to a physical wound (the figurative frame).

If the discourse of medical pathology is conclusively figurative, can we identify a literal scene, a situation, characters? A *day* is specified (the one on which the event for which someone is remorseful occurred? l. 1); so are a *he* and a *she*. Certain events, presumably literal, seem to be narrated: 'He sees his left wrist rise to tell him the time' (l. 9); 'she tells/ him by a shout down the staircase' (ll. 25–6). But the literalness of this fragmentary situation proves to be problematic; for, apart from the unambiguously metaphorical expressions in ll. 11–13, cited above, the vehicle of this presumed conceit is syntactically out of control, free-floating, as it were. This free-floating medical discourse threatens to overwhelm the fragments of the (hypothetical) literal world, exerting contextual pressure which tends to convert 'remorse', and consequently the fragmentary scenes and characters evidently associated with it, into figures of speech for literal situations in the realm of medical pathology. We are left with two competing literal frames, each seeking to subordinate the other as figurative vehicle to its own tenor. This is, in other words, precisely a case of the type of Empsonian ambiguity in which two worlds or universes of discourse are juxtaposed and neither dominates the other, so that each world functions reciprocally as a metaphor of the other (Empson 1947: 211–12, 217–18; cf. McHale 1987: 133–7).

As unstable as the world is in 'Of Movement', it is, if possible, even less stable in Charles Bernstein's 'Live Acts' (see Appendix 3 for the full text). Here again we might start with the title in order tentatively to establish a level of integration. The 'live' of 'Live Acts' presumably indicates a stage performance in contrast to a filmed or videotaped one. Nowadays the likeliest context for such an expression might be one in which it referred to topless or nude dancers, or even 'live' sexual acts on stage. Perhaps the title is a 'found' text, citing a newspaper advertisement or a sign outside a nightclub, thus evoking the external frame of reference of urban red-light districts.

Equipped with this working world-hypothesis, we might scan the text for segments that could be construed as corroborating it. 'You want always the other' (l. 1) and 'another person' (l. 3) might be construed as referring to sexual cruising. Perhaps the 'encounter,/ in which I hold you' (ll. 5–6) is a sexual encounter; if so, then 'a passion made of cups' (l. 6) might qualify it as a drunken encounter. Are 'Crayons of immaculate warmth' (l. 7) phallic symbols? Is 'this purpose alone' (l. 8) the sex act itself? No doubt we could continue in this vein to the end of the text, isolating likely segments and manhandling them semantically until they made an approximate fit with our working hypothesis. But clearly there is a good deal of strain involved, and eventually our hypothesis begins to buckle under it. Moreover, we can only proceed in this way at the cost of ignoring the segments which resist assimilation to our world-hypothesis: for instance, the baffling, fragmentary phrases of ll. 2–5, or the opaque metaphor of ll. 6–7.

Suppose we return to the title for reorientation. This time we might note its grammatical ambiguity: 'live' could be either adjective or verb, its vowel changing value accordingly; 'acts', similarly, could be either plural noun or verb. This double ambiguity yields four possible combinations for the phrase, some of them less grammatical than others, no doubt, but all construable if we want badly enough to construe them. In short, this is hardly a stable foundation on which to attempt to construct a world. The very title of 'Live Acts' neatly exemplifies the quality of 'confused dominance' which Bernstein himself has ascribed to his poetry (Perelman 1985: 17).

TRACING VOICES

Failing to integrate these texts at the level of world, we shift to the level of voice. Here we ask not 'What world is this?' but 'Who speaks?' In other words, can a consistent 'voice', register, discourse, or level of style be discerned, on the basis of which the image of a 'speaker', a persona, could be reconstructed? If so, we might then be able to loop back to the level of world to construct a speech situation, a fragment of world for that persona to inhabit. Alternatively, if no single consistent voice can be identified, can the juxtapositions of voices, registers, discourses and/or styles in the text be motivated in terms of some reconstructed image of interacting speakers? Lacking such a motivating hypothesis, the discourse must lapse into discontinuity, and, as Susan Stewart writes, 'The more extreme the discontinuities of discourse, the more nonsensical the discourse' (1979: 158).

Stylistically, Ashbery's 'Metamorphosis' is schizophrenic: its stylistic profile is distinctly dissimilar in the two halves of the poem. Its first half, running from the beginning to l. 22 (i.e. the first two verse paragraphs), is comprised of (at least) three juxtaposed registers:

1 an archaic register, functioning as a marker of 'high style' or 'poetical' language: 'Its pleasaunce an urn' (l. 3), the poetical 'O' in the apostrophe ('O marauding beast', l. 4) and emotive outburst ('O farewell grief and welcome joy!', l. 11), the pseudo-Shakespearian iambs of ll. 12–13 ('Yet stay,/ Say how we are to be delivered' etc.), 'blessed decoction' (l. 21), and so on.
2 American colloquialisms: 'Around the clock' (l. 6), 'a breather' (l. 7), 'Gosh!' (l. 11; the colloquial equivalent of the poetical 'O'), 'nutty' (l. 15), and so on.
3 a parody of formal written language, perhaps of bureaucratese or of an academic/pedantic register: 'Testimonials/ To its not enduring crispness notwithstanding' (l. 8), and so on.

To complicate the stylistic situation further, throughout these first two verse paragraphs certain segments seem to owe a double stylistic allegiance. For instance, the words 'term' and 'elect' in the phrase, 'And for what term/ Should I elect you . . . ?' (ll. 3–4), certainly evoke the register of contemporary electoral politics (and thus perhaps cohere with the bureaucratese of ll. 7–8). But there are also competing archaic senses for these words: 'term', in the sense of goal, end, object (an obsolete or rare usage, according to the *OED*);[11] 'elect', in the sense of pick out, choose (again, obsolete according to the *OED*). Similarly, 'the fair content' (l. 13) could be construed in an archaic sense, as 'con*tent*', accenting the second syllable (the accent favoured by the iambic scansion of this line), meaning a satisfaction, pleasure, or source of satisfaction;[12] or of course it could be construed in a more modern sense, with the accent on the first syllable, as '*con*tent', a thing contained, especially contained in a text.[13] In all these cases we have instances of what J. F. Ross calls 'conflicting dominance'. Context pulls, or pushes, these words in conflicting directions, causing the entire passage to hover indecisively between different registers and different senses:

> Equivocation caused by conflicting dominant environmental
> factors generates nonsense because it can prevent sense . . . the
> words can join together in twos and threes but not *all* together
> . . . there is no one scheme pattern in which the *whole* sentence
> can be linked together, even inconsistently, because one of the
> words behaves like a duck-rabbit picture, jumping to one scheme
> as it hooks to one word and to another as it hooks to the next.
> Because dominating words *capture* a common word the sentence
> is torn apart.
>
> (Ross 1981: 172–3)

The effect, as Susan Stewart writes, is that of 'a text that splits
itself into simultaneous texts with every step' (1979: 162; cf. Empson
1947: 180–9, 111, 124).

By contrast, the second half of 'Metamorphosis' (its third and fourth
verse paragraphs, ll. 23–48) is distinctly more homogeneous in style.
Here the stylistic strategy involves not the juxtaposition of competing
registers, as in the first half, but a proliferation of intertextual
allusions. We have already noted certain probable allusions to Eliot's
'Prufrock' (ll. 38–41), and to Wittgenstein's *Tractatus* and/or Frost's
'After Apple Picking' (ll. 43–4). There is at least one other, in ll.
45–8:

> . . . you
> Had built the colossal staircase in my flesh that armies
> Were using now, their command a curse
> As all my living swept by, the flags curved with stars.

The allusion here would seem to be to a recurrent Renaissance sonnet
conceit, that of love as an army occupying the lover's body. The
locus classicus is Petrarch's 'Sonnetto in Vita', 91; English versions
include both Wyatt's and Surrey's respective translations of this
sonnet (Wyatt, 'The long love that in my thought doth harbor';
Surrey, 'Love, that doth reign and live within my thought').

Thus, each half of 'Metamorphosis' separately resists integration in
terms of a consistent voice or persona, the first half by multiplying
and juxtaposing registers, the second half by multiplying intertextual
allusions. Furthermore, the two halves, with their distinctly different
stylistic strategies, resist integration with one another. It is almost
as if 'Metamorphosis' were a hybrid text consisting of two separate
poems collaged together. Finally, even after we have fully taken into
account the heterogeneity of this text, a certain unassimilable residue
still remains, a froth of verbal junk on the surface of the poem. We

encounter certain infelicities, inexplicable but evidently deliberate, reminiscent of Joyce's 'Eumaeus' chapter, of Gertrude Stein, or of Donald Barthelme (see McHale 1987: 151–6): 'The barges and light they conflict with against' (l. 17), 'Us and our vigilance who [that?]' (l. 26), 'wherever straw was' (l. 31), 'got abated' (l. 43), and so on. There are also instances of Ashbery's trademark pronouns lacking specifiable antecedents (*he*, l. 25; *it*, l. 32; *it*, l. 36; etc.), as well as a number of semantically ungainly mixed metaphors (ll. 19–21, 24–5). All these incidental infelicities seem to function to block assimilation of the language of 'Metamorphosis' to any voice or register or speaker-position whatsoever; they are intractably 'antiabsorptive' elements, in Bernstein's sense.

If 'Metamorphosis' is a stylistic collage, defying integration in terms of a single consistent voice or speaker, then Prynne's 'Of Movement Towards a Natural Place' is even more radically plurivocal, approaching the condition of a macaronic text. Literally a tissue of quotations, some of them explicitly marked, others not, it includes two quoted passages (ll. 6–7, 18–20) that would seem to belong to medical or scientific discourse; several words or phrases ('nothing much', l. 3; 'blame', l. 13; 'excited', l. 17) set off by quotation marks as though someone were disavowing responsibility for them (but who, and why?); an italicized phrase in Latin (ll. 22–3), source unknown;[14] another passage (ll. 17–18) italicized rather than placed between quotation marks, for no apparent reason; and a quoted passage (ll. 24–5) which lacks quotation marks, so that one cannot be certain where exactly the quoted material begins or (especially) where it ends.

At the very least, then, this is a highly diversified text, from the point of view of 'who speaks' in it. Like 'Metamorphosis', it is also a text of juxtaposed and competing registers. It is saturated, as we have already seen, with language from the register of medicine, in particular medical pathology: 'the/ bruise . . . drains' (ll. 2–3), 'neural space' (l. 5), 'white rate' (i.e. white blood-cell count, l. 10), 'scar tissue' (l. 13), 'contre-coup' (l. 20),[15] 'neuroleptic' (i.e. able to reduce nervous tension, tranquillizing, l. 24), 'plaque' (i.e. blood-platelet, l. 28), 'blood levels' (l. 29), 'immune reflection' (l. 30), etc. Cohering with this medical register is a scattering of more generally scientific (or quasi-scientific) diction: 'damage control' (l. 10), 'expanded time-display' (l. 12), 'depletes/ the input' (ll. 12–13), 'flux link' (l. 15), 'cognition' (l. 23), 'granular' (l. 24), etc. In addition there are two deictic phrases – 'at top left' (l. 2), 'top right' (l. 16) – which might be construed as captions to a picture or diagram (perhaps, in this context, from a medical textbook?).

Juxtaposed with this technical medical and scientific discourse we find a register of everyday vocabulary from the semantic fields of the emotions and moral judgement: e.g. 'recall' (ll. 1, 4, 25), 'moral' (ll. 1, 21), 'false' (l. 4), 'remorse' (l. 11), 'blame' (l. 13), 'intentions' (l. 14), 'need' (l. 25), 'benevolence' (l. 27), 'charity' (l. 27), etc. As in the case of 'Metamorphosis', there are a number of instances of conflicting dominance, words or phrases for which two registers in effect 'compete'. Competition arises between medical discourse and everyday discourse, as we have already seen, over such terms as 'hurt', 'bruise', 'cut', 'excitement, excited', and, particularly strikingly, over the ambiguously moral/electrical term 'charge' ('His recall is false but the charge/ is still there', ll. 4–5). Or consider the fragment 'What mean square error' (l. 11). Each word here (apart from 'what') owes a double stylistic allegiance.[16]

In addition to this competition between technical medical and everyday moral or emotional discourse, 'Of Movement' is also the site of competition between medical discourse and conventionally lyrical, poetic discourse. 'Pearly blue with a/ touch of crimson' (ll. 5–6) is both a poetic image and, perhaps, a medical description (as in a coroner's report, say?). 'Godly suffusion' (l. 22) and 'starry and granular' (l. 24) seem similarly to collapse into one the medical or scientific and the poetic. Most striking of all is the phrase, 'at the same white rate' (l. 10). A fragment of medical discourse, this phrase seems also to allude to Dylan Thomas's 'The Force that through the Green Fuse Drives the Flower' (1934):

. . .
And I am dumb to tell the crooked rose
My youth is bent by the same wintry fever.
. . .

(ll. 4–5)

And I am dumb to mouth unto my veins
How at the mountain spring the same mouth sucks.

(ll. 9–10)

. . .
And I am dumb to tell the lover's tomb
How at my sheet goes the same crooked worm.

(ll. 19–20)

Intertextual allusion here serves to intensify the conflict of dominance between the two discourses.

Who speaks in 'Of Movement Towards a Natural Place'? A

multitude, and, consequently, no one in particular. 'The macaronic', writes Susan Stewart,

> does not effect a synthesis – it is a simultaneity of examinable elements, a conjunction that, like all nonsensical simultaneity, is the sum of its parts and no more. Its movement is perpetual but not hierarchical; it does not rise to a conclusion, it simply keeps going.
>
> (1979: 166)

Charles Bernstein aspires, he says, to write a 'multidiscourse text' – 'a work that would involve many different types & styles & modes of language in the same "hyperspace". Such a textual practice would have a dialogic or polylogic rather than monologic method' (1986: 227). 'Live Acts' would seem to be a poem in which Bernstein undertakes to produce the multidiscursive, polylogical text to which he aspires. Stylistically highly heterogeneous, 'Live Acts' is a patchwork or mosaic of discourses, some of them traceable to specific discourse practices in the everyday world, others elusive or untraceable. It features, as we have already noted, a passage (ll. 2–5) of conspicuously non-fluent, abstract language characterized by a proliferation of 'floating' prepositions and fragmentary prepositional phrases. This passage offers the same resistance to 'absorption' as the deliberate infelicities we observed in Ashbery's 'Metamorphosis'. Do we detect here a parody of academic or pedantic discourse, perhaps, or of bureaucratese? Next (ll. 7–8) we encounter what seems to be a parody of the densely figurative language typical of, say, Shakespearian poetry, or that of high modernism (e.g. Hart Crane?). Having reached this lyrical peak, the text promptly (ll. 10–11) stages a bathetic collapse into American colloquialism, reminiscent of similar collapses in 'Metamorphosis':

> . . . Essentially a hypnotic referral, like
> I can't get with you on that, buzzes by real fast . . .

The latter half of 'Live Acts' is characterized by a kind of lexical exhibitionism, a display of various forms of lexical playfulness and innovation, as though the text were reflecting metalinguistically on the potential for innovation in the English lexicon itself. Thus we find, for instance, the phrase 'aquafloral hideaway' (l. 12), a kind of demonstration of the capacities for word-formation in English, the first word (a nonce-formation modelled on aquacade, aquadrama, aquadrome, etc.) exploiting latinate lexical resources, the second ('hideaway') exploiting Anglo-Saxon resources. Similarly, the word 'pigeoning' (l. 14) seems designed to demonstrate the freedom to change a word's grammatical function: from the noun 'pigeon' we are free to coin a verb, 'to pigeon',[17] hence the gerund form 'pigeoning'. 'Owns', in the phrase, 'the/ answer which never owns what it's really about' (ll. 14–15), illustrates verbal polysemy, ambiguity in the classic Empsonian sense: in this context, 'owns' may mean either (or both) 'to possess' and 'to admit, acknowledge, confess'. Finally, the phrase 'Gum sole shoes' (l. 16) seems to lay bare the process of etymological derivation: from gum sole shoes, or galoshes, in which (presumably) the wearer can move stealthily about, we derive (at any rate according to this etymology) the American colloquial 'gumshoe', for detective, someone for whom moving stealthily about is a professional skill.

By mingling in this way heterogeneous, elusive discourses – untraceable echoes, parodies and pastiches, forms of lexical exhibitionism – 'Live Acts' effectively frustrates integration at the level of voice. Resistance to the category of 'voice' in poetry is a major ideological position of the so-called 'language' poets, including Bernstein.[18] Both in their many polemical writings and manifestos and through their own poetic practice, the 'language' poets expose and critique the ideological underpinnings of 'voice', its implications of a centred, unified self and of full authorial presence in the poem. 'The voice of the poet', writes Bernstein in one of his polemical texts,

> is an easy way of contextualizing poetry so that it can be more readily understood (indiscriminately plugged into) as listening to someone talking in their distinctive manner (i.e., listen for the person beyond or underneath the poem); but this theatricalization does not necessarily do the individual poem any service & has the tendency to reduce the body of a poet's work to little more than personality
>
> (Bernstein and Andrews 1984: 41).

In articulating this principle, Bernstein makes explicit what is implicit not only in 'Live Acts' and other 'language' poets' texts, but also in texts like Ashbery's 'Metamorphosis' and Prynne's 'Of Movement Towards a Natural Place': namely, the text's resistance to assimilation to any single unifying speaker, speaking-position, or speech situation.

ABSTRACTING THEMES

Having failed to integrate these texts at the levels of world and voice, we shift next to the level of theme. Integrating at this level involves identifying thematic rubrics of appropriate scope and importance;

collecting textual segments and features capable of being interpreted in terms of these rubrics; and allowing textual evidence to act upon themes and themes to act upon textual evidence, dialectically, to achieve an ever-tighter feedback loop and what Forrest-Thomson calls a 'thematic synthesis'.[19]

A thematic synthesis of Ashbery's 'Metamorphosis' might begin with the metaphor in ll.4–5: 'O marauding beast of Self-consciousness'. This supplies an appropriately large abstraction, a good candidate for thematic integration. Next we could return once more to the poem's title. Coherent with nothing at the level of world, the title 'Metamorphosis' perhaps ought to be understood more abstractly, as naming a theme. Thus we might propose a working thematic hypothesis: 'Metamorphosis' is 'about' the metamorphosis of self-consciousness, that is, change in the quality or degree of self-consciousness from, say, lesser to greater, or from none to some. This is at least a plausible theme for a poem, if for no other reason, because it belongs to the postromantic repertoire of privileged poetic themes. In other words, according to our hypothesis, 'Metamorphosis' instantiates the familiar thematic *topos* of the 'fall' from innocence into experience.

Scanning the text, we readily identify corroborating evidence for this theme. The entire poem is structured around a 'now' vs. 'then' opposition: the present-tense verbs of its first half (recurring briefly in ll. 37–9) contrast with the past-tense verbs of the second half. This contrast of tenses can be construed as corresponding to an opposition between anxious self-consciousness (the poem's 'now') and a lost pastoral idyll (its 'then'). Evidently the loss of this state of pastoral innocence has been a painful one (as the fall-from-innocence *topos* prescribes): 'The penchant for growing . . ./ Has left us bereft' (ll. 23–4). 'Just then/ It [what?] all turned the corner into a tiny want ad' (ll. 35–6): perhaps this can be read as a metaphor (somewhat trivializing and ironic in tone) for the transition from innocence to experience. If the 'fall' into self-consciousness involves erotic experience (as it often does in poems belonging to this *topos*), then that might explain the allusion to the Petrarcan conceit of the 'colossal staircase in my flesh' (ll. 45–8), and perhaps even make sense of the mysterious fall from the ladder (ll. 41–6), which can now be understood as a metaphor for the (erotic) fall from innocence.

If the evidence for this reading seems thin, we only need to shift our ground somewhat to make our reading more comprehensive. So far we have been considering the theme of self-consciousness as it applies to a human self (the poet's persona, presumably); but this theme can easily be transferred from the poet's persona to the poem itself. Thus we broaden the theme of heightened self-consciousness to include the theme of poetic self-consciousness or self-reflexiveness; in other words, we can undertake to read 'Metamorphosis' as a poem about itself, a metapoem. Now it may seem odd to treat self-reflexiveness as a poetic theme of the same order as the fall-from-innocence theme. Surely metapoetry is one of the strategies for short-circuiting thematic synthesis and suspending sense-making? Not so; although there is a tendency among critics suspicious of 'meaning' (including Forrest-Thomson, who should have known better) to treat 'metapoetry' as somehow not a 'meaning' or theme, but rather an escape from or transcendence of thematics, somehow 'beyond' thematic integration. In fact, however, metapoetry must be recognized as just another potential theme at the thematic level of integration; indeed, it is the privileged theme of much recent (including postmodernist) poetic practice.

Corroboration for this self-reflexive reading of 'Metamorphosis' abounds. There are the foregrounded words with a metalinguistic meaning: 'content' (accent on the first syllable, l. 13), 'context' (l. 15), 'term' (l. 3). There is what seems to be an invitation to the reader to edit the text: 'You can take that out' (l. 9). There are the locutions that can be construed as referring to the poem's own discontinuity and heterogeneity: its 'nutty context' (l. 15), the 'crevasses/ In between sections of feeling' (ll. 19–20), even the 'stitches' which have 'ceased to make sense' (l. 38). In this context we need also to take into account the allusions to forms of conceited writing, modernist ('Prufrock') and Renaissance (Petrarcan sonneteering).

One could carry this self-reflexive reading even further. As we observed above (p. 15), 'Metamorphosis' is stylistically schizophrenic, its violently heterogeneous, compact, and disjunctive first half (ll. 1–22) contrasting sharply with a second half (ll. 23–46) which is more homogeneous, continuous, and expansive. Now, one widely accepted account of John Ashbery's poetic development ascribes to him a kind of mid-career poetic conversion experience, when he abandons the violently disjunctive poetry of his early phase (e.g. *The Tennis Court Oath* 1962) for a more homogeneous, continuous and accessible style, as exemplified by his most widely acclaimed poem, 'Self-Portrait in a Convex Mirror' (1975). In the light of this narrative, it would be tempting to try reading 'Metamorphosis' as a kind of *mise-en-abyme* or allegory of Ashbery's poetic career. Such a reading would effectively collapse into one the theme of the personal 'fall' into self-consciousness and the metapoetic theme, achieving a total thematic synthesis of the text.

A total thematic synthesis, yes; but at what cost? The cost can perhaps be calculated if we turn briefly to Prynne's 'Of Movement'. Here, too, a thematic rubric is made available to us – the theme, let's say, of remorse – and here, too, that theme collapses readily into the theme of metapoetry. 'Remorse', we read, 'is a pathology' (l. 11); so far so good. But only turn the corner of the abruptly enjambed line, and the theme veers around: 'Remorse is a pathology/ of syntax'. This seems to be a clear instruction to read metapoetically, seeking evidence of the poem's reflection upon itself.

Such corroboration is not far to seek. 'Of Movement', as we already know, is a tissue of quotations, and quotation always signals some degree of metalinguistic or metapoetic reflection. It is as if specimens of language were being displayed, as if our attention were being directed to bits of language *as* language. One instance of quotation, in particular, as much as announces the metalinguistic function of quotation in this text: 'the/ bruise is glossed by "nothing much"' (ll. 2–3). Other segments of the text seem capable of being construed metapoetically – 'it makes sense right at the contre-coup' (l. 20), 'immune reflection' (l. 30) – as does, of course, the (possibly) parodic allusion to Dylan Thomas's 'The Force that through the Green Fuse' (l. 10; see above, p. 18).

But finally, once we have marshalled all our evidence, picking through the text for segments that could be ranged under the rubric 'poetry about poetry', how fully have we accounted for the poem? Not very fully; neither in the case of 'Of Movement' nor in that of 'Metamorphosis' does the theme of metapoetry come near to exhausting the material of the poem. The supposed 'total thematic synthesis' turns out to leave much in these poems unmotivated and unexplained. Too little of these texts has been made relevant, too large a residue of 'irrelevance' remains.

In the case of Bernstein's 'Live Acts', a metapoetic reading seems also to be solicited, if only by default. In the absence of any other likely candidates for an integrating theme for this poem, we focus on its metalinguistic features, such as its exhibition of lexical innovation, described above (viz. 'aquafloral hideaway', 'pigeoning', 'gum sole shoes', etc.), or its deictic words ('this purpose alone', l. 8; 'These projects alone', l. 18), which can be understood as referring self-reflexively to the text itself.[20] In this case, however, a further context of interpretation is made available, extra-textually, through Bernstein's polemical and programmatic writings and the writings of his fellow 'language' poets. These 'ancillary' writings supply us with a key, if we choose to use it, to an interpretation of the 'language' poets' practice of metapoetry.

By their own account, the 'language' poets produce the kinds of texts they do – texts which resist integration or absorption and which reflect metapoetically on their own language – in order to deconstruct contemporary linguistic practices, exposing the ideological bases of such practices and pointing the way to the development of subversive counter-practices. Bernstein himself, for instance, writes, describing fellow-writers of 'nonabsorbable or antiabsorptive works':

> For these writers,
> there has been a useful
> questioning of what we are normally
> asked to be absorbed into, &
> an outright rejection of any accommodation
> with or assimilation into this 'bourgeois'
> space. . . .
> . . . For such
> writers, the project is to wake
> us from the hypnosis of absorption.

(Bernstein 1987: 39)

In other words, we are invited by the 'language' writers themselves to motivate their works in terms of a highly abstract, high-powered political intention, generally neo-Marxist in orientation.[21] And indeed, once we have been given this political 'key' to interpretation, it becomes hard *not* to motivate the 'language' poets' nonsense politically. Nor are Ashbery and Prynne, poets unaffiliated with the 'language' group, immune from such a reading, as witness Keith Cohen's (1980) attempt to ascribe to Ashbery the political intention of 'dismantling . . . bourgeois discourse'.

The question remains, however, whether a thematic synthesis in terms of a demystificatory and subversive political programme is any more satisfactory than a synthesis in terms of 'poetry about poetry'. I think not. If the metapoetic reading leaves too much unaccounted for, too large a residue of 'irrelevance', this 'political' reading has the opposite problem: it allows for too *little* irrelevance, reducing everything to relevance. The 'language' poets' account of their own texts seems, in other words, too monolithic and over-determined, not fine-grained enough to account for textual details, tending to flatten and reduce poems to a single reiterated message – an interpretative steamroller where something more like a set of dentists' drills seems called for.

Furthermore, when we read postmodernist poetry as the critique and demystification of current language practices, we continue to value it *negatively*, for what it tells us about what it is *not*. Nonsense, as Susan Stewart never tires of repeating, functions to expose common sense as ideology, as a cultural product and alibi rather than what it pretends to be, 'second nature' (Stewart 1979: 49–50, 88–9, 200–1, 206 and *passim*). Even if we grant that the postmodernist nonsense of such poets as Ashbery, Prynne, Bernstein, and Bernstein's fellow 'language' poets functions in just this way, this leaves us, paradoxically, focusing on the common sense which has been demystified and discarding the nonsense which has served as our serviceable (but disposable) tool of demystification.

Is there no way postmodernist nonsense can be valued for itself, apart from its function as a tool of demystification? Andrew Ross, one of the critics who endorses the 'language' poets' political self-interpretation, has wrestled with this problem.[22] He writes:

> what is foregrounded by these experiments . . . is the *language system* itself and its otherwise transparent methods of circulating meaning (while the easy Luddism of smashing this system of language relations is replaced by the practice of constructing new relations within the system). . . . this is no celebration of the utopian reader, free to produce meanings at will, in response to the open invitation of canonical post-structuralism. Nor is it the celebration of a liberationary, utopian language, like the surrealists' discourse of contradictions. The construction of a future, utopian or otherwise, lies instead . . . in the *shock* of recognizing the fully systematic domination of the present.
>
> (1988: 373)

If I read him correctly, Ross is straining here to ascribe some positive ('utopian') value to the 'language' poets' nonsense – and failing in the attempt. The best he can do is assert that it is not merely destructive of the current language system (not some 'easy Luddism'), but that neither is it constructively utopian in the mistaken way of 'canonical post-structuralism' or surrealism. But when he tries to specify how postmodernist nonsense is constructive, he can only do so (once again) negatively: it involves the recognition of the 'fully systematic domination' of contemporary language practices; that is, as Stewart might say, it demystifies common sense, it tells us about what it is not. Ross asserts that the 'language' poets construct 'new relations' within the language system, without being able to specify what these new relations might be. Can we find some sounder basis for valuing postmodernist nonsense?

COGNITIVE MAPPING

A renegade Empsonian, Veronica Forrest-Thomson (as we have seen) values poetry precisely for the ways in which it frustrates sense-making. A superior poem, for her, is one which blocks integration and suspends naturalization almost successfully. 'Almost', because ultimately these blockages and suspensions will be resolved at some higher level of naturalization; the whole art of poetry (and of reading poetry) lies, for Forrest-Thomson, not in not naturalizing at all, but in not naturalizing *prematurely*.[23] Charles Bernstein, too, sees the antiabsorptive strategies of his own and others' poetry less as an end in themselves than as a means to the end of some higher-level absorption:

> In my poems, I
> frequently use opaque & nonabsorbable
> elements, digressions &
> interruptions, as part of a technological
> arsenal to create a more powerful
> ('souped up')
> absorption than possible with traditional,
> & blander, absorptive techniques.
>
> (1987: 38)

According to this account, the purpose of blocking absorption at one level is to effect a shift in absorption's 'plane of engagement', achieving thereby a 'redirected absorption' (Bernstein 1987: 56, 57).

But what might such higher-level naturalization or redirected absorption look like? We know what it is not: it is not a reconstructed world, not an integrated voice or speaker, not a thematic synthesis; but if it is none of these things, how are we to describe it in positive terms? In several places in his writings Bernstein himself gropes towards a description of the kind of higher synthesis he has in mind for his poetry. His most successful and most interesting solution, though a somewhat elusive one, is to describe writing as 'mapping', not in the familiar sense of a mapping of the writer's consciousness, but rather a mapping *for* the reader:

Writing as a map for the reader to read into, to interpolate from the space of the page out onto a projected field of 'thinking'. . . . So that the meaning of the text is constituted only in collaboration with the reader's active construction of this hypertext. . . . The conception of a text as a map or model whose final constitution requires the reader's active response is a theory of reading. This concept of reading extends beyond the text into the world, into the realm of reading human culture.

(Bernstein 1986: 234–6)

To a certain extent this is only a formulation of the increased involvement of the reader in the reconstruction of difficult texts like Bernstein's own, and as such is hardly a novel idea. But Bernstein seems to have something more in mind by this metaphor of mapping, and it is worth considering for a moment what that might be.

Mapping as a projection 'into the realm of reading human culture': there is an intriguing connection here with Fredric Jameson's recent elaboration (Jameson 1984, 1988) of a notion of 'cognitive mapping'. This notion arises in the context of his discussion of the postmodern problem of how we are to represent to ourselves the world-system in which we live. That world-system, the system of late or multinational capitalism, is of a complexity and ubiquity that defy our best efforts to grasp and master it imaginatively. But if we cannot represent the late-capitalist world-system to ourselves – this is Jameson's ultimate concern – what hope can we have of imagining ways to resist and change it? Current forms of picturing this world-system[24] are inadequate to our needs because they undertake to model the world-system at the level of content and theme alone, while what is really required is formal innovation which would make modelling possible at the level of form (Jameson 1988: 356). What is needed, says Jameson, borrowing a term from the urbanist Kevin Lynch, is a new 'cognitive mapping' of the postmodern world.

One of Jameson's examples (Jameson 1987) of the kind of cognitive mapping he has in mind is a piece of postmodernist architecture, namely the house that the architect Frank Gehry built for himself and his family in Santa Monica in 1979 (see Appendix 4 for an axonometric drawing of the Gehry House). The core of the house is a cottage in the traditional vernacular style, around which the new house has been 'wrapped'. The new house partly absorbs the original house, partly 'preserves' or 'displays' it as if in a museum; the new house in a sense places the old one between quotation marks. The materials are wildly heterogeneous: high-modernist materials and forms (e.g. a perfect glass cube, which, however, has been tilted disconcertingly on to one edge) are juxtaposed with the *ad hoc* materials of 'cheapskate architecture' (corrugated metal, chain-link fencing), and both these kinds of materials are juxtaposed with the traditional building materials of the original cottage. The wrapping of one house around another creates a disquieting interior space (or, Jameson says, 'hyperspace').

Philip Johnson and Mark Wigley (1988) have characterized the Gehry House as 'deconstructivist architecture'; it might even more appropriately be described as nonsense architecture.[25] Jameson urges us to think of it as an attempt to model or to allegorize the social space of the postmodern USA.[26] The Gehry House is a cognitive map, but a map in four dimensions, incorporating, in addition to the three dimensions of its architectural space, the fourth of time: the duration of lived experience in and of the house, which maps the experience of living in the space of postmodern society. The Gehry House, Jameson concludes in a striking turn of phrase, constitutes 'the attempt to think a material thought'.[27]

Let me propose, then, that we try to think of postmodernist nonsense poems, counterparts of Gehry's postmodernist nonsense architecture, as so many attempts at a 'cognitive mapping' of the postmodern world.[28] Just as the Gehry House 'quotes' and displays the original vernacular house, so postmodernist poems like 'Metamorphosis', 'Of Movement Towards a Natural Place', and 'Live Acts' quote and display 'poetry', both through parodic literary allusions or pastiches and through foregrounded features of 'literary language' (lineation, metre, figurative language, apostrophe, etc.). Just as the Gehry House abruptly juxtaposes the most heterogeneous building materials, so these poems juxtapose technical registers, colloquial language, bureaucratese – in short, a sampling of the discourses which circulate in our world, as well as bits of verbal residue or junk, intractably antiabsorptive elements. Just as the wrapping of one structure around another in the Gehry House creates a disquieting interior space, so too do these postmodernist poems. There is, first of all, the reconstructed space of the worlds of these poems: fragmentary, discontinuous, flipping back and forth between literal and figurative. Second, there is their chaotic linguistic 'space', the echo-chamber in which discourses resound and mingle without our being able to assimilate them to any single unitary speaker or speaking-position. Third, there is the space of logical paradox created by these texts' reflection on their own language and mode of existence.[29]

Finally, just as the Gehry House, through its disjunctive and troubling deployment of spaces and materials, seems to aspire to think a material thought about postmodern society, so, I want to suggest, do these poems. They might be read as, in effect, 'translations' of the architectural discourse of the Gehry House into verbal discourse.[30] These poems aspire, as Bernstein says, to project on to the world of human culture a map for the reader to read himself or herself into, a cognitive tool for finding our ways – and for finding our 'selves'? – in the hyperspace of postmodern culture:

> . . . These projects alone contain
> the person, binding up in an unlimited way what
> otherwise goes unexpressed.

NOTES

1   On the relation of postmodernist 'language' poetry, in particular to both Futurist *zaum* (trans-sense poetry) and Dadaist nonsense, see Hartley 1989: 8–16. The Dada connection was first seriously explored, to my knowledge, by Paul Carroll in his reading of John Ashbery's 'Leaving the Atocha Station' (in Carroll 1968).

2   For further 'experimental' corroboration of a sort, see Alex McHoul's report of the 'Cumulex' exercise he conducted with a class of student readers. Confronted with 'a set of randomly culled lines' (McHoul 1982: 17) – the first lines of fourteen randomly chosen poems by Pierre Reverdy, presented as a single 'naturally-occurring' poem – McHoul's readers were able to produce commentaries which ingeniously made sense and coherence of the pseudo-poem. 'The attribution of "meaninglessness"', McHoul concludes (1982: 29–30), 'was very much a last resort for readers. Instead, they would go to lengths in order to search out meanings . . . if these were not instantly available to them.'

3   Forrest-Thomson, writes Charles Bernstein in a manifesto-poem which is in part an appreciation of her work, 'carries Empson's criticism one step further than Empson was willing to go' (1987: 66 n. 2).

4   In the account that follows I have somewhat systematized what, in Forrest-Thomson's own account, is at best only partially systematic.

5   This distinction between semantic and non-semantic features, which is intrinsic to Forrest-Thomson's account, is contested by Bernstein (1987: 6–13), for whom all features, including phonological and graphological features, are semantic.

6   Forrest-Thomson treats 'thematic synthesis' as the highest level of coherence, the *telos* towards which reading inevitably tends. I want to weaken its status, and instead to treat thematic integration as on a par with other levels, at least in theory; but Forrest-Thomson is right, of course, in so far as thematic synthesis has often been the *telos* of integration in practice.

7   Some will no doubt want to propose other levels of coherence, claiming for them an applicability at least as broad as that of the three levels specified here. Genre, for example, might seem a strong candidate

for inclusion in this scheme. I would want to argue, however, that a genre is less a level of integration in itself than a configuration spread over these three levels. A sonnet, for instance, is, apart from its verse-form, characterized by (a) a conventional situation, (b) a conventional/supra-personal speaker, (c) a repertoire of (Petrarcan) themes e.g. 'immortalization through poetry'.

8   Ross also describes certain strategies by which sense may be resisted or prevented. These are, generally: (a) conflict of dominance i.e. unresolvable semantic cruxes or ambiguities such as those in Empson's types five, six and seven; and (b) lack of dominance, presumably the sort of abstractness and indeterminacy we find in Ashbery's poetry (Ross 1981: 172–3; cf. Thompson and Thompson 1987: 134).

9   Both Elizabeth Sewell and Susan Stewart have described how nonsense resists semantic integration and 'absorption' in Bernstein's sense. See, e.g., Sewell 1952: 56, 98, 144, 149, 154; Stewart 1979: 166 and *passim*.

10   To confirm this analysis, try the experiment of changing the poem's title to 'In an Orchard': the effect is to invert the tenor/vehicle hierarchy of the text.

11   The assonance of 'term' and 'urn' perhaps has the effect of binding 'term' to the archaic context of 'Its pleasaunce an urn' (l. 3), and thus partly disambiguating its register.

12   Cf. 'pleasaunce' (l. 3), meaning the condition of being pleased; the action of pleasing; a pleasing trick or pleasantry; all obsolete, archaic, and/or poetic usages, according to the *OED*.

13   Cf. 'context' (l. 15), which echoes 'content' in both its form and its (literary-critical) register, and thus perhaps partly disambiguates its register. Cf. Bernstein's analysis of 'content' (in the double sense of *content* and con*tent*) in an Emily Dickinson lyric (1987: 18).

14   This phrase translates roughly as, 'the whole soul [or being] in every organ of its body'.

15   According to the *OED*, a 'contre-coup' is the effect of a blow, e.g. injury or fracture, produced exactly opposite or at some distance from the part actually struck; cf. 'on both sides', l. 21.

16   'Mean' can have the sense of inferior, low, ignoble, small-minded, stingy, all terms of moral opprobrium, or alternatively it can have the sense of arithmetical mean; 'square' can mean just, equitable, honest, honourable, upright, solid, steady, reliable, and so on, but also, a number multiplied by itself, or measurement based on square units; 'error', a mistake or transgression, but also, the mathematical quantity by which a result differs from an accurate determination.

17   The verb 'to pigeon' means, according to the *OED*, either 'to swindle, cheat [at cards]', or 'to send a message by messenger-pigeon'; or perhaps it is short for 'to pigeon-hole'.

18   For surveys, with special attention to the issue of 'voice', see Bartlett 1986, Perloff 1987, McGann 1988, Hartley 1989.

19   This account of thematic synthesis is based partly on insights to be found in Alex McHoul's (1982) report on his 'Cumulex' exercise. The student participants in McHoul's exercise started the synthesizing process by identifying early lines of the sample poetic text as 'keys' to thematic integration, anticipations of patterns which could be expected to emerge

as the text unfolded (1982: 17, 31). Thematic synthesis was then able to operate both prospectively and retrospectively, later segments being construed sometimes as altering, sometimes as corroborating the meanings of earlier ones (1982: 19, 20, and *passim*). General rubrics were sought which would encompass several more particularized themes (1982: 26). A principle of 'mutuality of evidence and pattern', McHoul observes (1982: 11, 21, 3), governed the entire process: that is, the emerging patterns were made to underwrite the reading assigned to any particular line, while, conversely, the readings of particular lines were used to confirm the patterns.

20 In the manner of Shakespearian sonnet couplets, e.g. 'So long as men can breathe, or eyes can see, / So long lives *this*, and *this* gives life to thee' (sonnet 18); 'So, till the judgement that yourself arise,/ You live in *this*, and dwell in lovers' eyes' (sonnet 55); cf. also sonnets 74, 107. (Emphasis added.)

21 It should be noted, however, that Bernstein is himself somewhat sceptical of the claims of neo-Marxist discourse to occupy an 'Archimedean point of absolutely greater vantage', relative to all other interpretative discourses (1986: 363–82).

22 So, too, has George Hartley, somewhat inconclusively, in his exemplary discussion of Steve McCaffery's poetry (1989: 82–3).

23 See, e.g., Forrest-Thomson's exemplary readings of Prynne's 'Of Sanguine Fire' (1978: 47–51, 142–6) and Ashbery's 'They Dream only of America' and other texts from *The Tennis Court Oath* (1978: 154–9).

24 Jameson mentions three: social-scientific discourse, which he considers to be unusable for the purposes of the imagination (but see the transcript of the ensuing debate over this point, Jameson 1988: 358); the cybernetic model or metaphor; and the thematics of paranoia and conspiracy characteristic of contemporary US art fiction (e.g. the so-called 'systems' novels of Pynchon, DeLillo, McElroy, Gaddis, and others.)

25 Just as verbal nonsense (at least by Susan Stewart's account of it) depends upon common sense and serves to expose the ideological underpinnings of common sense, so, according to Johnson and Wigley (1988: 17), do the distortions of deconstructivist architecture serve to expose the imperfection inherent in modernist 'pure form'.

26 Johnson and Wigley's (1988) reading of deconstructivist architecture, including the Gehry House, converges with Jameson's at a number of points, with the major difference that Wigley is actively hostile to any suggestion that this architecture 'maps' the culture around it; its sole context, by his account, is the architectural tradition, especially the modernist purist tradition, which it deconstructs.

27 Interestingly, Elizabeth Sewell, in her seminal account of literary nonsense, suggests that the next step beyond nonsense would be (though she does not say so in so many words) something like the attempt to think a material thought; except that the medium in which she imagines such an attempt might be made is not architecture but dance; Sewell 1952: 188–9, 192.

28 This proposal has already been advanced by George Hartley (1989: 52), though left undeveloped by him.

29 The connection between self-reflexiveness and spatial paradox is made explicit by John Barth's story 'Frame-Tale', a text printed on a Mobius strip which runs, in an endless loop, 'Once upon a time there was a story that began once upon a time there was a story that began' etc., etc.

30 'Translation' into other media and genres is also possible: into musical discourse (e.g. the postmodernist music of John Zorn's *The Big Gundown* and *Spillane*), into the discourse of prose fiction (e.g. the postmodernist disjunctive novels of William Burroughs or Kathy Acker), into cinematic discourse (e.g. the postmodernist films of Hans-Jürgen Syberberg), into theatrical discourse (e.g. the postmodernist 'operas' of Robert Wilson), etc.

APPENDIX 1

Metamorphosis

John Ashbery. From *As We Know* (1979)

1   The long project, its candling arm
2   Come over, shrinks into still-disparate darkness,
3   Its pleasaunce an urn. And for what term
4   Should I elect you, O marauding beast of
5   Self-consciousness? When it is you,
6   Around the clock, I stand next to and consult?
7   You without a breather? Testimonials
8   To its not enduring crispness notwithstanding,
9   You can take that out. It needs to be shaken in the light.

10 To be delivered again to its shining arm –
11 O farewell grief and welcome joy! Gosh! So
12 Unexpected too, with much else. Yet stay,
13 Say how we are to be delivered from the fair content
14 If all is in accord with the morning – no prisms out of order –
15 And the nutty context isn't just there on a page.
16 But rolling toward you like a pig just over
17 The barges and light they conflict with against
18 The sweep of low-lying, cattle-sheared hills,
19 Our plight in progress. We can't stand the crevasses
20 In between sections of feeling, but knowing
21 They come once more is a blessed decoction –
22 Is their recessed cry.

23 The penchant for growing and giving
24 Has left us bereft, and intrigued, for behind the screen

25 Of whatever vanity he chose to skate on, it was
26 Us and our vigilance who outlined the act for us.
27 We were perhaps afraid, and less purposefully benevolent
28 Because the chair was placed outside, the chair
29 No one would come to sit in, except the storm,
30 If it ever came. No shame, meanwhile,
31 To sit in the hammock, or wherever straw was
32 To see it and acclaim the differences as they were born.

33 And we were drunk as flowers
34 That should someday be, or could be,
35 We weren't keeping track, but just then
36 It all turned the corner into a tiny want ad:
37 Someone with something to sell someone
38 And the stitches ceased to make sense.
39 They climb now, gravely, with each day's decline
40 Farther into the unmapped sky over the sunset
41 And prolong it indelicately. With maps and whips
42 You came eagerly, we were obedient, and then, just then
43 The real big dark business got abated, and I
44 Awoke stretched out on a ladder lying on the cold ground,
45 Too upset and confused to imagine how you
46 Had built the colossal staircase in my flesh that armies
47 Were using now, their command a curse
48 As all my living swept by, the flags curved with stars.

APPENDIX 2

Of Movement Towards a Natural Place

J. H. Prynne. From *Poems* (1982)

1 See him recall the day by moral trace, a squint
2 to cross-fire shewing fear of hurt at top left; the
3 bruise is glossed by 'nothing much' but drains
4 to deep excitement. His recall is false but the charge
5 is still there in neural space, pearly blue with a
6 touch of crimson. 'By this I mean a distribution
7 of neurons . . . some topologically preserved transform',
8 upon his lips curious white flakes, like thin snow.
9 He sees his left wrist rise to tell him the time,
10 to set damage control at the same white rate.

11   What mean square error. Remorse is a pathology of
12   syntax, the expanded time-display depletes the
13   input of 'blame' which patters like scar tissue.
14   First intentions are cleanest: no paint on the nail
15   cancels the flux link. Then the sun comes out
16   (top right) and local numbness starts to spread, still
17   he is 'excited' because in part shadow. *Not will*
18   *but chance* the plants claim but tremble, 'a
19   detecting mechanism must integrate across that
20   population'; it makes sense right at the contre-coup.

21   So the trace was moral but on both sides, as formerly
22   the moment of godly suffusion: *anima tota in singulis*
23   *membris sui corporis*. The warmth of cognition not
24   yet neuroleptic but starry and granular. The more
25   you recall what you call the need for it, she tells
26   him by a shout down the staircase. You call it
27   your lost benevolence (little room for charity),
28   and he rises like a plaque to the sun. Up there the
29   blood levels of the counter-self come into beat
30   by immune reflection, by night lines above the cut:

31   Only at the rim does the day tremble and shine.

APPENDIX 3

Live Acts

Charles Bernstein. Taken from Codrescu (1987)

1   Impossible outside you want always the other. A continual
2   recapitulation, & capture all that, against which our redaction
3   of sundry, promise, another person, fills all the
4   conversion of that into, which intersects a continual
5   revulsion of, against, concepts, encounter,
6   in which I hold you, a passion made of cups, amidst
7   frowns. Crayons of immaculate warmth ensnare our
8   somnambulance to this purpose alone.
9   The closer we look, the greater the distance from which
10   we look back. Essentially a hypnotic referral, like
11   I can't get with you on that, buzzes by real fast, shoots
12   up from some one or other aquafloral hideaway,

13 emerging into air. Or what we can't, the gentleman who
14 prefers a Soviet flag, floats, pigeoning the
15 answer which never owns what it's really about.
16 Gum sole shoes. The one that's there all the
17 time. An arbitrary policy, filled with noise, & yet
18 believable all the same. These projects alone contain
19 the person, binding up in an unlimited way what
20 otherwise goes unexpressed.

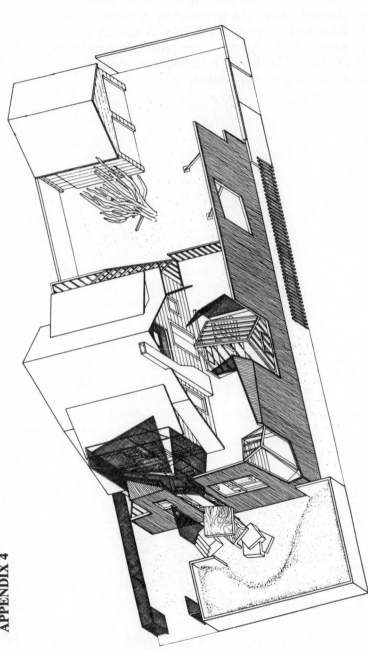

Bird's-eye view axonometric drawing of the Gehry House, Santa Monica, CA.

Source: *Frank Gehry: Buildings and Projects*, New York, Rizzoli/Minneapolis: Walker Art Center, 1986: 37.

Editor's preface

One of the interesting topics George Dillon touches upon, and invites
further study of, in this suggestive review of the differing contractual
relations that may be involved in variant ways of addressing insiders
to a discourse community (here, linguists), is the question whether
academic or professional authority can co-habit with irony. The
discoursal styles of Chomsky and Fillmore – two eminent linguistic
theorists of the past quarter century – are compared by means of
introductory passages of their writing which are taken as representative of their distinct styles of intervention or participation in the
'conversation' of leading-edge linguistic theory. Each in his own
way can be seen 'doing' certain of the interactional maxims (such as
modesty, tact, quality and quantity) that are also a focus of attention
in Leech's chapter in this volume.

Another way of capturing the contrast between the Chomsky and
Fillmore texts is in terms of certainty vs provisionality: Chomsky
quietly declares total confidence in the *theory* of his kind of linguistics
(that is to say, in the coherence and centrality and importance of the
basic questions his research addresses), and simply acknowledges –
even insists upon – the provisionality of the current government and
binding modelling or representation of answers to those questions.
Fillmore, however, expresses considerable uncertainty as to what the
overarching or foundational theory should be (implies that to have a
core of key theoretical questions would be premature), but embraces
the provisional contingent activity of text-interpretation.

And Fillmore clearly contrasts with Chomsky in his (however
fleeting) uses of irony, a mode of discourse which always implies
some degree of resistance to the stance of on-record, face-value,
objectified assertion. The contrast between non-ironic (Chomsky)
and ironic (again, no matter how slightly) modes perhaps leads
back to an opposition between belief and scepticism. The non-ironic

modest master-language of Chomsky is expressive of unshakeable belief, while discourse at all ironized as is Fillmore's is expressive of a declared uncertainty as to the essential foundational status of whatever assumptions or claims are made. Similarly, notice the ironizing effect, the is-it-or-isn't-it? question raised by Dillon's own use of quotation marks around the word *work*. Clearly there are dangers, in terms of affect, in pronounced forms of either ironic or non-ironic style: the former may be received as excessively arch, playful or incoherent ('the speaker has no firm position on anything'), the latter may be received as the language of the autodidact – which is why the modesty markers in Chomsky's text are so important.

This in turn may well be one of the bases for Dillon's conclusion that, though surely more 'outsider-friendly' than Chomsky's text, Fillmore's style may be less compelling, to the typical outsider, in terms of judgements of authoritativeness, and mastery. I use the term 'mastery' here somewhat speculatively: it might be worth pursuing the notion that styles that contrast in the way Chomsky's and Fillmore's do reflect more patriarchal vs. feminist modes of discourse. Intuitively, to me, the subject positions assumed by Chomsky and Fillmore, and allotted to their readers, seem quite different (in the Althusserian terms elaborated in Sara Mills's essay in this collection).

2 Insider reading and linguistic form
Contextual knowledge and the reading of linguistic discourse

George Dillon

We do not think of academic (or scholarly) writing and reading as being strongly affected by context, or, rather, we think of such endeavour as being set within well-defined conventions. It is often taken as lying at a pole opposite that of casual conversation – as maximally unsituated, impersonal in its appeals, and hence as the prototype of literacy (as opposed to orality) or text (as opposed to utterance). While academic discourse typically does not rely on particular personal knowledge (or 'presence') between writer and reader to make its case or to guide interpretation, much academic discourse addresses an audience of experts and concerns a topic which is timely to that audience in a way non-experts can only guess at. I will use the term insider to refer to experts (players), but also to other members of a disciplinary discourse community who might be conceived of as avid fans – readers who keep track of the state of the discipline in order to report it in lectures, refer to it in publications, and gossip about it in coffee rooms, conferences, and cocktail parties. 'Insiders' thus include both the *esoteric* and the *exoteric* audiences for an academic/scientific article described by Greg Myers – both the immediate circle of fellow researchers and the more disinterested disciplinary audience (Myers 1989a). Both of these audiences are insiders, as distinct from the audiences for textbooks or popularized (*Scientific American/American Scholar*) writing.

Insider reading is very unlike that assumed by a communication model built around the transmission of information or even the demonstrating of a case to a relatively passively receptive reader. Insiders have large funds of special information about other relevant claims, received opinion, and previous positions of the writer; in addition, they have an interest in the matter under discussion: they themselves have positions against which they test the argument, and their reading is inclined to test, challenge, and counter what is claimed. Charles Bazerman (1988) has distinguished differences in the level of interest insiders may take in scientific articles, principally the different purposes of adding to their background knowledge vs. mobilizing aspects of the article for their own immediate work. There is an obvious over-simplification here – 'insiderhood' is clearly a matter of degree – but I hope the reader will allow it for the time being in order to get a question and some cases on the table. Insiders, I am claiming, are privy to a much richer sense of context for a piece of academic writing than outsiders, and they are interested professionally and personally in reading critically in ways outsiders are not. They are in a position to evaluate what is said in terms of what is alluded to, obliquely touched on, or even unsaid. How might one make that claim specific enough to develop and explore? How might insiders read particular texts, or even paragraphs, or sentences, differently? Gregory Coulomb and Joseph Williams (1985) found that expert readers sometimes preferred and were able to assimilate paragraphs whose textual structure was less signalled and felt to be confusing, jargon ridden, and incoherent to non-experts. Pushing even further, what is the relation of those readings to the linguistic form of the texts or sentences themselves? Do insiders respond differently to passives and nominalizations with omitted agency? Or lexical choice? Or metaphor or irony? And, running the level of magnification up to the limit, can one go beyond analysing the registers or collective decorums of academic/scientific writing to discussing the individual choices and effects achieved in the style of particular scholars?

These questions are so phrased to acknowledge the increasingly general view that reading is non-deterministic, which is to say that particular linguistically identified features of a text function at most as triggers for constructive activity on the reader's part. Thus far there is agreement, but controversies have arisen over about the last twenty years as to what makes a particular linguistic feature a trigger and what it triggers. Before discussing certain extracts from texts, it is well to examine some of the well-known answers to these questions that have been entertained in the past, notably those discussed by Stanley Fish, Roger Fowler *et al.*, Kenneth Burke, and the (largely British) social studies of discourse, here represented by Nigel Gilbert and Michael Mulkay.

The view that I am associating with Fish is not one that he holds, but one that he criticized in 'What is stylistics and why are they saying such terrible things about it?' (reprinted in Fish 1980). This is broadly the view that linguistic form, especially syntactic constructions, sets off certain psycholinguistic processes that yield, ultimately, well-formed semantic representations for sentences. This view underlay the earlier applications of generative grammar to stylistic analysis and was often described in fairly deterministic language ('when we process a passive sentence with a deleted agent, we restore it to normal active form and assign a referent to the dummy (or 'someone') agent, etc.) Fish noted a certain looseness and lack of consensus, however, in the accounts of how syntactic form affected (or impeded) the 'recovery' of meaning, and concluded that this version of 'stylistics' was neither as scientifically grounded nor as compelling as it purported to be. Unlike subsequent theories, this one made no place for differences of knowledge, interest, attitude, or interpretation on the part of readers; the effect of syntactic form and stylistic choice was regarded as unconscious, obligatory, and automatic – 'hard-wired', to use Jerry Fodor's metaphor. The model did provide an explicit procedure for identifying triggers via grammatical analysis (e.g. a 'missing' element), and it was often esteemed for advancing stylistics beyond the impressionism and subjectivity of old-fashioned critical practice, where the noting of significant features of linguistic form seemed to depend on the intuition and tact of the refined critic – on his say-so, in a word.

A similar 'linguistic' motivation was claimed by Roger Fowler, Bob Hodge, Gunter Kress, and Tony Trew for their check-list of features the 'critical linguist' should examine in any given text. It is similar in that it incorporates some of the notions of generative grammar (and older grammars as well) about passives and nominalizations, but extends the list using speech act theory and Hallidayan systemic linguistics to include transitivity, modality, and cohesion, and some old/new ideas about lexical categorization. Although the list of potential triggers and features to be checked in a text are drawn from linguistic theories, Fowler *et al.* emphasize that critical linguistics is an interpretatively guided practice which is looking for 'social meanings': 'Interpretation is the process of recovering the social meanings expressed in discourse by analysing the linguistic structures in the light of their interactional and wider social contexts' (1979: 196). The significance of the linguistic features, that is, is not that they have set psycholinguistic processes to work that determine the individual's experience of a text; rather, they provide a student with ways of interrogating a text to locate its ideological power.

Getting their categories from linguistics is useful for Fowler *et al.* for two reasons: the categories are apparently independent of any ideology and they are simply inherent in human discourse. There is nothing obviously theory-dependent about asking 'is the matter represented as an action, and if so, who is the agent?' And they suggest that such a thorough interrogation of a text will lead the students to a clearer grasp of the text's ideological power (over them, mostly). There does not seem to be any place for differentiating outsider interpretations from insider ones; this is principally because the texts they are examining are those addressed to the general public and oriented towards regulating behaviour and shaping opinion. And indeed, they do not appear to think interpretations will vary significantly; the 'light' of 'interactional and wider social contexts' is the plain light of day which shines equally on 'us' all. Put more directly, the 'knowledge' of the social context the student needs is basically the view of contemporary Britain as a rather highly stratified class society with democratic, egalitarian ideals and run by a powerful, coherent Establishment intent on maintaining its hegemony. An expert with a more developed and detailed theory of all that would not necessarily spot things in, say, swimming-pool regulations that Fowler *et al.* missed, or look more deeply or differently into them.

Kenneth Burke's schema for interrogating and comparing texts – his pentad of act, agent, agency, scene, and purpose – is not usually discussed in surveys of linguistic stylistics, but it has proved of considerable use to social scientists who want to discuss how writing shapes our understanding of actions and motives (Burke 1950). These five categories are basic to understanding, Burke maintains, but are not categories of linguistic analysis or any other formal system. Rather, they are substantive, though one might add they bear a considerable resemblance to the categories of case grammar and some of the more recent California hybrids of linguistic/conceptual structure such as 'space grammar'. Hence they do not lead to specifying formally identifiable 'triggers', but they do focus analysis on a text's handling of topics close to the heart of more linguistically guided critics such as Fowler *et al.* and some of the transformationalists – topics such as how particular actions are staged in terms of agents and agency and the constraints and possibilities furnished by the scene in which they act. Burke tries to set up a grid of possibilities (a grammar of motives) from which particular philosophies, ideologies, and ways of looking at actions make choices, so that, for example, one may speak of phenomena associated with teenage pregnancy or drinking-driving as the result of the acts of individual agents or as the result of agency manifesting itself through scene (what might be very roughly called the social science perspective). Burke also is not concerned with expert discourses, and hence does not raise the insider/outsider distinction of readers and reading, though his dramatistic scheme has been applied to writing in social science by, for example, Gusfield (1981). Though, as noted, the pentad cannot be very readily made to generate a check-list of linguistic features – potential triggers – it does work to make visible aspects of a text that would otherwise perhaps pass unremarked. It does, in other words, promote the initial move of stylistic analysis, which is to look at a text askance, or to make the writing opaque.

Like Burke, the 'discourse analysts' Nigel Gilbert and Michael Mulkay do not directly derive their analytic categories from linguistic theory. Their method of making visible aspects of scientists' discourse is to contrast two 'repertoires' (the empiricist and the contingent), which they find characteristic of scientists' published research and oral interviews, respectively. These two repertoires are styles or modes of account-giving, 'stories' scientists tell of the doing of science. They contrast in several ways clustering around the placement of agency in the scientific activity. Characterizing the empiricist repertoire, they say

> Neither the author's own involvement with or commitment to a particular analytical position nor his social ties with those whose work he favours are mentioned. Laboratory work is characterised in a highly conventionalised manner, as instances of impersonal, procedural routines which are generally applicable and universally effective. Although the content of experimental papers clearly depends on the experimenters' actions and judgements, such papers are overwhelmingly written in an impersonal style, with overt references to the authors' actions and judgements kept to a minimum. By adopting these kinds of linguistic features, authors construct texts in which the physical world seems regularly to speak, and sometimes to act, for itself. Empiricist discourse is organised in a manner which denies its character as an interpretative product and which denies that its author's actions are relevant to its content.

> (Gilbert and Mulkay 1984)

'Denies', one might note, is a strong word, suggesting that there is some obfuscation at work; that the impersonal empiricist repertoire renders invisible the engagement of the scientist as a situated social actor does not directly constitute denial (or ellipsis, or deletion) of that engagement. Gilbert and Mulkay do not rely solely on bald assertion of those social and personal dimensions, however, for they find them foregrounded in the contingent repertoire – the style of account-giving manifested in interviews with them:

> Its guiding principle is in direct opposition to that of the empiricist repertoire in that it enables speakers to depict professional actions and beliefs as being significantly influenced by variable factors outside the realm of empirical biochemical phenomena. When this repertoire is employed, scientists' actions are no longer depicted as generic responses to the realities of the natural world, but as the activities and judgements of specific individuals acting on the basis of their personal inclinations and particular social positions.
>
> (1984: 57)

These repertoires, it should be noted, are bundles of stylistic, grammatical, and lexical features, and correspond very closely to what Whorf (1952) called a 'fashion of speaking'. That is, the features take on their value in part from the configuration of the whole, conceived of as a social practice. Officially, Gilbert and Mulkay claim that the two repertoires are simply two different kinds of account giving, and that they cannot pick out one or the other as the real story or true account, though, as we have noted above, their language frequently tips the balance in favour of the contingent accounts.

One might object to Gilbert and Mulkay that these two repertoires do not base their differences on different conceptualizations of doing science (i.e. do not make us think about it one way or the other), but, rather, on differences of audience, occasion, purpose, and medium. Experimental reports are written communications with other experts; the interviews, by contrast, are given to sociologists with no expert knowledge of biochemistry and might be expected to foreground the human drama, especially as elicited by questions. Gilbert and Mulkay attempt to defend themselves against this criticism, principally by arguing that scientists' humour illustrates a kind of keeping of double books on their endeavour and a tension between their human situatedness and the impersonal decorum of the experimental report.

Gilbert and Mulkay's work poses the insider/outsider opposition in a particularly pointed way, as most analyses of scientists' discourse do. When they read the experimental reports, they are definitely outsiders and cannot read them in the same way as the scientists, even if they wished to. Their descriptions of the way the language works is the way it works for them. It is likely, for example, that the working expert would be able to recognize the laboratory routines described in an article, fill in many details and qualifications, and summon the necessary grains of salt. Similarly, the scientists' interviews are intended for non-experts, and one could imagine yet a third repertoire of 'bench talk' which might be unintelligible to outsiders. In fact, one doesn't even have to imagine it: goodly sections of Michael Lynch's transcripts (1985) are virtually inaccessible even with his photographs, diagrams, and extensive glosses. (Some of that talk is not account-giving, of course, but some of it is.)

Another problematic aspect of Gilbert and Mulkay's approach is that they have no place for individual, stylistic variation. Experimental reports are of course highly formated, but do they really eliminate stylistic variation entirely? Tracing the successive drafts of one report with Karin Knorr-Cetina (1981), one would have to suppose not, though the procedures of revision and review make 'authorship' far more complex than the standard picture of the solitary scholar sitting in his or her study. And again, the insider problem arises, as the stylistic options might not be accessible to one not thoroughly versed in reading and writing what is called, after all, 'the literature'.

I am pressing these points fairly hard because they are bringing me to the cases I will use to test these approaches and assumptions about linguistic form and readers' experiences. The academic discourse I will examine is one that should be familiar to anyone who has reached this point in this chapter, namely linguistics, and in particular linguistic theory (rather than experimental reports, which, as we all know, are not common in linguistics). As I cast about for samples of linguistic theorizing I was struck by how much of it was first delivered as lectures to audiences of linguists, participants in institutes, and other interested members of the academic public. None the less, there are certain features of Chomsky's writings that are relatively constant over professional lectures (e.g. *Lectures on Government and Binding*), public lectures (e.g. *Rules and Representations*), and linguistic monographs (*Aspects of the Theory of Syntax*). And, to anticipate slightly, these are features of impersonality and objectivity; 'linguistic theorizing' appears almost an autonomous, self-sustaining activity, despite (or because of) the speaker's major, not to say dominating, role in it. To foreground these features, I will employ many of the categories discussed above, and in addition use the stylistic analyst's oldest device, comparison with another theorist's texts delivered on similar occasions, namely those of Charles J. Fillmore, and I will construct a quasi-fictional expert reader reading with a kind of subvocalized commentary and debate.

I will take my sample of Chomsky's style of theorizing from the beginning of a fairly short monograph, *Some Concepts and Consequences of the Theory of Government and Binding* (1982). The 'Introductory Comments' begin:

> I would like to sketch some features of an approach to linguistic theory that has been slowly coming into focus in the past few years and that has considerable promise, I believe. Because of the crucial roles played by the notions of government and binding, the approach is sometimes called *government-binding (GB) theory*. I will refer to it by that name here, though it develops directly and without a radical break from earlier work in transformational generative grammar, in particular, from research that falls within the framework of the Extended Standard Theory (EST).

Outsiders, equipped with no more than some scheme of grammatical analysis, would note the relative impersonality ('an approach', 'earlier work', 'sometimes called') and the location of agency or at least activity in the approach and related abstractions ('notions', 'research') rather than human agents ('coming into focus', 'playing crucial roles', 'develops', 'falls'). They might generalize that all this intellectual activity is portrayed as relatively autonomous – as a vibrant, exciting swirl of activity not under anyone's direction or control. They might also note that Chomsky seems a little uncomfortable with the perhaps trendy but slightly inaccurate name for the theory, but is willing to go along with it as a good sport and member of the community.

Insiders, however, may well have read *Lectures on Government and Binding* published, after much pre-print circulation, the year before the MIT Press edition, and may remember that its opening paragraph includes the sentence

> In the course of this discussion, I will consider a number of conceptual and empirical problems that arise in a theory of the GB type and will suggest a somewhat different approach that assigns a more central role to the notion of government; let us call the alternative approach that will be developed here a 'government-binding (GB) theory' for expository purposes.

In short, Chomsky is the 'sometimes caller' of his own coming-into-focus approach which doesn't just happen to develop out of TGG and fall within the EST, all entities named and instigated by him. Insiders would not be bamboozled as to what is afoot in the slightest.[1]

Outsiders would, I think, find the next paragraph simply puzzling:

The concepts and principles of GB theory are fairly simple, and it should be possible to present an elementary and systematic exposition of them, presupposing very little. I have not undertaken that task here. Rather, the presentation is more exploratory, with successive revisions as the discussion proceeds.

Why, outsiders might wonder, mention that 'it should be possible' to give an elementary account, and then announce you are not doing it? Again, one could add examples to the list of preferred impersonals ('the presentation is', 'successive revisions'). Perhaps, they might think, Chomsky is warning the less initiated that, though short, the book is not the simple exposition that they might be hoping for.

Insiders would recognize the method of Chomsky's *Aspects of the Theory of Syntax*, and of most of Chomsky's subsequent theoretical writings: pursuing generality in a formulation and then assessing it in relation to other constructions, revising the initial formulation so as to 'capture' more generalization, and so on. In these writings, it is sometimes hard to be sure what the final model is – the one that could be given simple and systematic exposition. Theorizing with Chomsky is like walking down a carpet that is constantly rolling up behind you. In a sense, then, such an exposition would be premature, since we don't know whether we have yet found the truly elementary principles. It is not that he simply disdains to do it, but that such an exposition would immediately have to be thrown out; with Chomsky, it is not the theory but the theorizing that matters, which appears to be the burden of the following sentences:

> As concepts and principles become simpler, argument and inference tend to become more complex – a consequence that is naturally very much to be welcomed. We hope that it will ultimately be possible to derive complex properties of particular natural languages, and even to determine the full core grammar of a language with all of its empirical consequences, by setting the parameters of general linguistic theory (universal grammar, UG) in one of the permissible ways. While this goal should always have been an obvious one, it is only quite recently that the task could actually be considered in a serious way, a development that is in my opinion a sign of significant progress in linguistic theory.[2]

The first sentence of this paragraph might well strike outsiders like a hallucinated fortune cookie, even before they get to the clause after the dash. 'Naturally'? To some degree, the outsider might hope, the second sentence will step down the generality and suggest an application to linguistic theory, but to see how, one has to know the basic terms of GB theory, as well as its 'permissible' options. The third sentence is breath-taking in its impersonality (obvious to whom, considered by whom, development by whom?). The answer, the insider knows, is 'to anyone who has thought about syntactic theory for as long as and in just the way that Chomsky has'. What has enabled its consideration? Chomsky's new posing of the goal. What is the serious way? Chomsky's recent 'work' in GB theory and 'work' inspired by it. The outsider might suppose anything from 'the end of the war' to 'funding by the Sloan or MacArthur Foundation'. So much distance does Chomsky put between himself and his work that he can have an 'opinion' assessing its value which does not seem extraordinarily self-congratulatory! Actually, on my analysis, nobody would think that Chomsky is deviously blowing his own horn here: the outsider wouldn't know enough, and the insider, at least the sympathetic one, would take the rather different meaning that Chomsky believes he has attained a major turning point or breakthrough in his theorizing and has developed the concepts and techniques ('in a serious way') to set off a new wave of grammatical theory. In retrospect, I think it is safe to say he was right.

> 'So you see,' the insider says, 'it all hangs together as a very close and subtle account, albeit displaced, of the nature and magnitude of the changes Chomsky is making in his theory(ies).'
> 'I always prefer coherence to chaos,' the outsider replies, 'and I am willing to believe, though I do not fully understand. How can I learn to read Chomsky as you do?'
> 'I think you have to ask experts how they read him, or take a seminar. In grammatical theory.'

To some degree, Chomsky's tactics of minimizing his own agency in the formation and direction of linguistic theory can be viewed as his preferred choices from the available means of creating a suitable modesty for scientific discourse as outlined by Greg Myers. The general preference for modesty would include also the personal hedges ('I think', 'in my opinion') and understated praise ('considerable promise'). Indeed, these passages are reminiscent of the opening sentences of one of the most famous and discussed papers of modern science:

> We wish to suggest a structure for the salt of deoxyribose nucleic acid (D.N.A.). This structure has novel features which are of considerable biological interest.

Myers develops his theory of politeness in scientific writing from Penelope Brown and Stephen Levinson's account (1978) of face preservation in interaction, an account that correlates the amount and kind of 'redressive action' a speaker engages in with the magnitude of the threat to the other's positive and negative face wants. Proclaiming a new set of rules for syntactic theorizing is quite face-threatening to other scholars, and thus there arises an ironic consequence or implicature from extreme gestures of modesty that what one is claiming is of vital importance.

The lectures and writings of Charles J. Fillmore provide a rather different model of 'doing modesty' in which the knowing and discoursing subject is very much in the foreground, as are the alternative scholarly approaches which that subject engages in dia-logue and debate. Here is the beginning of a published series of four lectures originally delivered to the 1975 Linguistics Institute. They bear the general title 'Topics in lexical semantics':

> My task in these lectures is to offer an informal and intuitive approach to the description of word meaning and text meaning. My main goal is that of presenting a uniform conceptual framework for discussing the meanings of words, the construction of sentence readings, the interpretation of texts, and the processes of express-ion and comprehension.

> (Fillmore 1977: 76)

This opening amounts to a very carefully worded contract with the reader, and I think it is patently so even to the outsider, someone just familiar enough with linguistics or related disciplines to recognize that 'informal and intuitive' promise just the lowest degree of linguistic theorizing. The shift in the next sentence from 'task' to 'goal' raises the stakes somewhat in a fairly recognizable *gradatio* beginning with 'word meaning' and ascending all the way to the 'processes of expression and comprehension'. The paragraph thus marks out a space of theorizing from the task of description (which he doubtless will fulfil) to the goal of a uniform and comprehensive theory (which he may attain).

The next paragraph then presents an argument that such a goal is what will raise his treatment of the questions above other previous and current scholarly ones:

> I believe that the linguist, in his consideration of a number of issues in semantic theory, can profit from the exercise of examining these issues within a larger view of language production and language comprehension. Previous traditions of semantic analysis

have tended to be limited in their subject matter because of their commitment to lesser goals. Some linguists – Coseriu, for example – have gone to great pains to ensure that they are limiting themselves to what is exclusively and purely linguistic, free of contamination from knowledge about cultures, belief systems, or facts about the world. The anthropological or so-called cognitive semantics tradition has concentrated on the discovery and display of systems of discriminations in taxonomies (etc.).

(ibid.)

These sentences exhibit a straightforward topic/comment chain of development: what do I mean by 'lesser goals'? Well. . . . And the list continues with structuralist traditions, generativist traditions, and a final contrast with his own concern with a 'larger theory of language processing'. (Note here too the finicky concern with the 'names of approaches' – a common trope of linguistic theorizing, though in this case the questionable terminology is not covertly self-referential but a usage some anthropologists had promoted. That, and the information that Coseriu was a Romanian linguist little known in America then or now, though of some reputation in Europe, are the only 'insider' glosses I can provide.)

With that traditional scholarly preamble, Fillmore launches into his discussion:

I would like to begin my discussion with an examination of the various steps in the comprehension process. One pastime indulged in by people working in text interpretation is that of choosing or inventing some text that offers particularly serious problems for the theory and challenging each other to show what can be done with it. The result of such demonstrations is usually – and justly – a sense of gloom about the prospects of an ultimate theory of texts. Since my interest, for now, is in discovering the steps in the interpretation process, without worrying too much about how in the end everything can be accounted for, I offer my example of a particularly troublesome text in good conscience. I do not pretend to be ready to talk about the final form of the correct theory.

(1977: 77)

Here a tonal shift into light irony is noticeable. It is sometimes said irony is an insider device, in that one cannot appreciate its aptness unless one can recognize the values and attitudes being mocked, and implicitly shares the underlying values of the writer. The second sentence juxtaposes the usual notion of linguistic discoursing as 'work' with the indulging of the pastime of coming up with 'stumper' texts – a pastime, but not a harmless one, as it frequently produces depression and dismay. The insider may be able to think of instances – say in artificial intelligence – but the outsider will have to take that report on trust. Fillmore uses it to lead up to his own complex little text, which he can introduce 'in good conscience' for reasons he explains not once but twice – he is not trying to depress everyone with the problems his passage would pose for an integrated, explicit, comprehensive processing model, and in fact he is too modest to claim to have one. The insider is perhaps quick to recognize that as a theorist, Fillmore should have such a model, and hence see that he is making a virtue of his defect, or may be pretending to do so. The careful contract of the first paragraph is now recast as a cat-and-mouse game with the reader: will Fillmore's little example illuminate processing in some depth and generality or just be another conundrum to cause a finite processing algorithm to jam? The insider can construct a slightly different subtext here, however, in so far as he or she might suspect Fillmore is opposing premature model building – model building, that is, which is slapped together before the rich and subtle range of facts to be modelled have even been described and inventoried. Notice that Fillmore is essentially dealing with the same question as Chomsky in the passages quoted above, namely, taking a position on where linguists' efforts are best directed in the area under discussion; but Fillmore proposes to persuade by rather teasingly offering an example of how to do it rather than invoking metatheoretical reflections on theory construction. Thus his own motives, acts of selection, and attitude towards his discourse become crucial dramatizations of doing good semantics: intuition, not methodology, is one of the principle sources of his authority. Two others are his erudite grasp of relevant scholarship in related fields and his tact and judgement – crucial qualities in hermeneutic endeavour. (Fillmore can be even more self-dramatizing in less formal settings, as in his wonderfully self-deprecating Georgetown Round Table paper 'Some problems for case grammar': see Fillmore 1971.)

The overall effect of this personalizing and dramatization of linguistic enquiry, I think, is to blur the line between outsider and insider, to make the discourse more accessible to less 'advanced' or initiated readers. Insiders can annotate the discourse, and appreciate the justness of its characterizations, but they do not possess keys to unlock subtexts as they do with Chomsky's introductions. This very accessibility may limit the authority of Fillmore's discourse, of course, in so far as (protestations notwithstanding) authority is accorded to the capacity to mystify and suggest behind the scenes arcana and a vast, impersonal, autonomous world of scholarly 'work'.

'Well, but I thought you were going to discuss styles of scholarly writing in linguistics, yet you end up talking about different conceptions of what knowledge is in linguistics and how it is produced and reproduced in readers.'

'But that is what style enacts – in this context.'

NOTES

1 For outsiders, it may be worth recording that these abbreviations stand for Transformational Generative Grammar and Extended Standard Theory.
2 N. Chomsky, *Lectures on Government and Binding* (Dordrecht: Foris, 1981).

Editor's preface

Whether or not scientist-writers such as Stephen Jay Gould and Oliver Sacks are populist is debatable; that they are popular, with enormous readerships from all manner of class and educational backgrounds, is not. How do they do it, and what is it, in fact, that they do? These questions are among those of interest to Gill Francis and Anneliese Kramer-Dahl in their textual analysis of Oliver Sacks's manner of narrating a case history. Sacks is a neuropsychologist, writing discursive and reflective commentaries on those dysfunctional individuals he has encountered in his professional practice. But he writes in a noticeably personal and experiential way, quite different from the established genres of science report. Using systemic linguistic categories in their description, and making copious comparisons between a Sacks essay and a standard case-history report, Francis and Kramer-Dahl specify the chief lexicogrammatical features which arguably do three things: set Sacks's writing apart from mainstream neuropsychological discourse, are constitutive of its unique appeal, and reflect and express Sacks's distinctive views of epistemology and appropriate procedure in the treatment of people who are neuropsychologically impaired.

Stylistic analyses of poems and prose fiction using Halliday's grammatical descriptions of the ideational, interpersonal, and textual components of English text have flourished for some years. Francis and Kramer-Dahl's work breaks new ground in its careful inclusion of a number of Hallidayan requirements: it is attentive to genre constraints and assumptions (indeed this is one of the chapter's themes); it is deeply comparative; it takes up the challenge facing text linguistics, to be as delicate and detailed as possible in analysis; and – relatedly – it is exemplary in its use of both quantitative and qualitative measures in the analytical task. The authors go beyond the preliminary count of types of transitivity processes in the passages compared, where distributions at first glance seem quite similar. An early example of this is their analysis of process types used in the two texts to describe the stage of interaction where the patient is being examined: superficial process-type similarities are noted, but Francis and Kramer-Dahl then explore the kinds of roles the two patients fill in those seemingly similar processes. Here, sharp contrasts are revealed, answering to intuitive judgements of the contrasts in the styles of case-historiography – the genre-observance of Kertesz, the genre-breaking of Sacks.

As this reference to 'genre-breaking' might imply, the following chapter provokes reflection on fundamental issues in discourse analysis, over and above questions concerning the applications of systemic grammar and the precise nature of Oliver Sacks's style. Perhaps most intriguing is the question which lurks behind genre-comparative studies, namely, 'What is a genre?' In part, the answer must be that any genre is an institutionalized and conventionalized contextualization, i.e. a set of 'received' verdicts as to what the proper context (of participants, setting, goals, etc.) is, within which to interpret a given text. But beyond this response lie further questions as to why and how such powerful determinate contextualizations come into being, how they can be revised or flouted, and how their suitability to their supposed tasks can be assessed.

It is therefore fitting that in their conclusion Francis and Kramer-Dahl highlight the relevance of Bakhtinian concepts to their subject-matter, pointing out the heteroglossic and hybridizing nature of Sacks's writing – representative of all cross-generic writing – which attempts to fuse or draw upon the inherently counterposed voices and styles of impersonal science and humane story-telling. At one point in the essay (p. 63) the authors suggest that 'the homely nature of these tests enables Sacks to ignore the standards of objectivity' – which might be viewed as a carnivalizing acceptance of Sacks's own Bakhtinian carnivalizing of scientific method. But Sacks's homely circumventions, as Francis and Kramer-Dahl show, are also genre-shaping, and the crux here is ideological as well as procedural; the homely tests both raise and ignore concerns for objectivity, replicability, comparability. Mainstream scientists will ask: what is the genre of scientific writing there for in the first place? Are not written reports of scientific experiments and studies powerfully geared to the establishing of testable and inspectable knowledge, and the confirmation or refutation of operationalized hypotheses? If Sacks does not want to be viewed as totally removed from the realm of rational scientific enquiry, is he attempting to have it both ways, wanting lay readers to trust that, if needed, he can do things the standard Kertesz way? The question then becomes, can he and his neo-genre get away with it? Will his intelligent lay readership accept and respect, as explanatory, 'No face was seen as a "thou"' and such locutions? Or will they press for something closer to Kertesz's seemingly much less interpretative 'she could not pick out her sister'?

3 Grammaticalizing the medical case history

Gill Francis and Anneliese Kramer-Dahl

INTRODUCTION

Several years ago, in a paper for *The American Scholar*, Clifford Geertz reflected on the vast amount of what he called 'genre blurring', or 'jumbling of discourse varieties', in recent academic life. As he sees it, there are a large number of writers and texts that escape any clear definition and location on the academic map. They have emerged not simply as a result of 'another redrawing' of the boundaries between one discipline and another; instead they reflect a radical 'alteration of the very principles of mapping' (Geertz 1983: 20).

The work of the writers Geertz mentions are a useful resource for the linguist interested in non-conventional registers and genres. Some of their texts have their origins in the natural sciences, among them the 'scientific discussions posing as belles-lettres' of Lewis Thomas and Loren Eiseley, and the 'methodological polemics got up as personal memoirs' of James Watson (ibid.). It is almost certain that if Geertz had written his essay a few years later, he would also have included the recent writings of neuropsychologist Oliver Sacks in his list of 'blurred-genre' texts. Sacks's major works, for instance, *The Man who Mistook His Wife for a Hat* and *Awakenings*, can be seen variously as collections of biographical anecdotes, as short stories and as medical case studies. One's difficulties with categorizing and locating these texts begin in the library.

Why does Sacks write the way he does? Is his innovative treatment of genre indeed motivated, as Geertz would claim, by epistemological necessity, by a radical rethinking of what it means to practise and write medicine? Or is he merely attempting, as his detractors suggest, to 'accommodate' his more technical, specialist texts to a much wider readership?

If we examine the literature, albeit scarce, on science

popularization, we find that the major generic and lexicogrammatical features of 'popular' texts also characterize Sacks's work. According to rhetorician Fahnestock (1986), popularizations, when compared to professional science reports, typically undergo a genre shift from the 'forensic' to the 'epideictic'; that is, from discourse whose main purpose is to validate its claims, to discourse whose primary aim is to celebrate the uniqueness of its topic (1986: 278). One could easily see Sacks's texts as making that, and only that, epideictic appeal. A glance at his introductory remarks in *The Man who Mistook His Wife for a Hat* reveals that, by emphasizing the strangeness and awesomeness of his subject, he is consciously appealing to a 'general' readership. Moreover, by describing his patients as 'travellers to unimaginable lands – lands of which we would otherwise have no idea or conception' (1985: xi), and likening his text to Osler's *Arabian Nights*, he is, at least superficially, rejecting mainstream professional case studies in favour of popular 'human-and-wonder appeal' storytelling.

Similarly, Myers's study of science popularization, informed by work on the sociology of science, sheds some light on Sacks's writing. Myers argues that the popular account of scientific activity is different from, and incompatible with, its professional counterpart. Professional reports recount what he calls (rather misleadingly) the 'narrative of science', because they 'follow the argument of the scientist, arrange time into a parallel series of simultaneous events all supporting their claim' (1989b: 2), and demonstrate the need for scientific expertise and mediation. Popularizations, on the other hand, tell 'the narrative of nature', in which the encounter between scientist and nature is chronologically dramatized and scientific artifice is intentionally downplayed. Myers's characterization of popular articles also applies to Sacks. Here it is the encounter between doctor and patient, doctor and disease, which is chronologically dramatized. Sacks occupies centre-stage as the chronicler; he presents himself as empathetic 'Dr Sacks', testing casually and conversationally, speculating freely, entering his patients' worlds, and single-handedly solving the mysteries of their diseases.

But does Sacks really abandon 'the narrative of neuroscience' – to adapt Myers's term – for the personal narratives of his encounters with his patients? If we look at the title story of his collection *The Man who Mistook His Wife for a Hat*, we can see that he attempts to maintain a close connection with scientific activity: for example, he engages in debates with other scientists about the values of the dominant neuroscientific establishment. In fact, we are cautioned that 'Dr P.'s' story is not being told merely for its own sake; rather, his condition is a metaphor for 'our' professional condition:

> Our cognitive sciences are themselves suffering from an agnosia
> essentially similar to Dr P.'s. Dr P. may therefore serve as a
> warning and a parable – of what happens to a science which eschews
> the judgmental, the particular, the personal, and becomes entirely
> abstract and computational.
>
> (1985: 19)

Sacks's self-reflective remark brings us back to where we began.
Geertz views his blurred genres as emerging out of necessity, for
ideological reasons; they are not just attempts to be innovative or
to appeal to the general reader. Similarly, Sacks's novel texts are not
only popularizations: they also represent his attempt to communicate
his unusual vision of neuroscientific practice. Neuropsychology, as
he points out, is a discipline on the borderline between the natural
and the human sciences. Therefore it must retain its scientific
rigour, and at the same time 'restore the human subject at its
centre' (1985: x). Part of doing this may be to evolve a way of
communicating specialized knowledge which is accessible to a wide
general readership. The scientist's text should not simply contribute
another turn in the ongoing discourse of the discipline, but participate
in what Michael Oakeshott has termed 'the conversation of mankind'
(see Bruffee 1984).

In this paper we will examine the title piece of *The Man who Mistook
His Wife for a Hat*, a 'clinical tale', to use Sacks's expression, about
Dr P., who suffers from a particular kind of visual agnosia. We will
show how Sacks's linguistic choices, and the interplay between them,
reflect his beliefs about neurologically afflicted human beings, their
conditions, and the relationships between them and their physicians.
We will also compare this text with a text which is more representative
of the writing of current dominant neuropsychology; for it is with such
'standard' texts that Sacks's clinical tales carry on an intertextual
dialogue, questioning the ideology that they encode. The text we
have chosen for comparison is entitled 'Visual agnosia: the dual
deficit of perception and recognition', a case report published in
Cortex (1979), which is a professional journal of neuropsychology.
The writer, Andrew Kertesz, is referred to by Sacks himself as one
who 'has an unrivalled knowledge of the world literature on the subject
and has . . . published some extremely detailed studies of patients with
such agnosias' (1985: 20).

Following Halliday (1985), we will explore how the lexicogrammatical patterns of both texts realize the metafunctional options available

on the semantic level, and how these, in their turn, realize the options available in the larger context of culture. We will deal separately with the three metafunctions – ideational, textual and interpersonal – in order to 'understand why the texts mean what they do' (Halliday 1988: ix), but we will endeavour not to lose sight of the ways in which these functions interact. Only with, to quote Hasan, 'the combined calibration' (1988: 53) of all metafunctions can a text's special personality be shaped.

THE IDEATIONAL METAFUNCTION

The experiential component

Let us turn first to the experiential function. How is experience, both of the 'outside' world and of the inner world of consciousness, encoded in these two texts? In attempting to answer this question, we will at times examine each text as a whole, and at others concentrate on four excerpts (reproduced in the Appendix), selected from the texts because of similarities in function, 'content' or both.

Types of process and participant

Initially we look at the process types chosen by Sacks and Kertesz to introduce the history of the patient prior to their consultations with the two specialists (see Table 3.1).

Table 3.1 Process types – patient's history prior to consultation (Excerpt 1)

	Material	Mental	Verbal	Behavioural	Relational	Existential
Sacks	8	8	3	2	11	2
Kertesz	7	6	3	1	11	–

Notice that the distribution of processes is strikingly similar. However, we still get the impression that the world of events and relations prior to the text's time is significantly different in each case (see Appendix, Excerpt 1). Dr P. has an immediate presence in the drama about to take place: he is granted a definite, almost caricatured personality: that of a likeable and cultured man, interacting nuttily but harmlessly with those around him. Kertesz's account of his '41-year-old woman', on the other hand, is dry and factual: he details her accident briefly, including only minimal personal information ('Prior to her accident, she worked as a nurse's aide, and was considered bright by her family') and the results of the preliminary neurological investigations. She herself, the woman at the centre, does not come through; we cannot imagine her.

In order to explain how these different impressions are created, the participant roles associated with the processes have to be examined. First, Sacks's Dr P. assumes an *-er* role (Hasan 1985) in the majority of the processes in which he participates. For instance, he took the initiative to 'consult an ophthalmologist', after which he 'came to me' (Dr Sacks). He himself is capable of observing and evaluating his reactions, for example: 'These odd mistakes were laughed off as jokes, not least by Dr P. himself.'

Kertesz's patient, on the other hand, plays *-ed* roles in all the mental processes, half of the material and a third of the verbal processes in which she is involved. Her *-er* roles in the few clauses in which she does participate actively are also noteworthy. In all the material processes, the goals she acts upon are inanimate ('obstacles', 'doorknobs', etc.); in the two verbal processes no receiver is mentioned, and in all the other instances she is cast as the carrier of relations – a role which is near the bottom of Hasan's scale of dynamism (1985: 46).

What contributes further to our differing perceptions of the two patients is that Dr P. is never alone as an *-er* participant: a corresponding *-ed* participant is explicitly stated whenever he assumes this role. Conversely, an *-er* participant is involved whenever he is cast in an *-ed* role. Kertesz, on the other hand, chooses to cast his patient in *-ed* roles without mentioning a corresponding *-er* participant: there is no evidence of interaction. For example: 'She was institutionalised because of poor memory' and 'She was discovered to have severe visual agnosia.' Even in the complex-transitive clause '[She] was considered bright by her family', Kertesz's embedding of the relational process within the mental one tones down what would otherwise have been a positive attribution; compare this with Sacks's 'Dr P. was a musician of distinction'.

Relational processes in the two passages, although identical in number, can be clearly distinguished by the nature of their attributes. A selection of these processes from Excerpt 1 is presented:

Relational processes – patient's history prior to consultation (Excerpt 1)

Sacks
Dr P. was *a musician of distinction* . . .
[he was] *well-known for many years as a singer* . . .

[he would] be *astounded* when they did not reply.
[he had] *a quirky sense of humour* . . .
His musical powers were *as dazzling as ever* . . .

Kertesz
[she] was *in a serious automobile accident in October 1965* . . .
[she] was *unconscious* for 18 days . . .
She had *linear fractures of the right frontal, parietal and temporal
bones.*
Her deficits appeared to be *essentially stable.*
Neurological examination was *essentially negative.*

Sacks's choice of largely evaluative, 'subjective' attributes is as
intentional as Kertesz's neutral, 'objective' ones. In Sacks's own
words 'there is something quite fundamental which is missing in
the "objective" styleless style *de rigueur* in neurology' (1983: 207).
According to him, Kertesz gives us only the cold hard facts – the
patient's biodata; there is no 'colour, warmth, no residue of the living
experience' (ibid.). Almost any of the features attached to Kertesz's
patient could 'as well apply to a rat as a human being' (Sacks 1985:
x). Kertesz, of course, would not see it this way: his lexical choices are
not intended to be judged according to the criteria of literary stylistics.

Let us look now at some of the processes involved in the next
section of each paper – the examination of the patient and the
reporting of tests and their results (see Appendix, Excerpts 2 and 3).
Throughout this section, whenever Kertesz's patient is actor, what she
does is overwhelmingly mechanical, never creative: write, copy, trace,
draw, match, sort, point to, and perform (in the sense of 'achieve
a particular score'). Similarly, as the sayer of verbal processes, she
typically lists, names, and repeats in response to stimuli. (There is one
exceptional occurrence of 'say', followed by her only direct locution.)
Moreover, she is the constant receiver of sayer-less messages and
sayer of receiver-less ones, and seems to exist in a world where close
contact with other sayer-less messages she receives are commands to
perform actions within tests – for example 'she was asked to keep
her head straight'. There are no questions inviting her creative verbal
response or encouraging her interaction.

Dr P., on the other hand, is involved in creative action: between
tests he is pictured carrying out activities such as dressing, singing,
humming, moving, eating and starting ('on the cakes'). He also
participates actively and creatively in verbal processes: he announces,
exclaims, confirms, asks, and replies, often with an accompanying
speech projection.

Table 3.2 Process types – examination of patient

	Material	Mental	Verbal	Behavioural	Relational	Existential
Familiar faces (and five related tests in Kertesz) (Excerpt 2)						
Sacks	3	12	1	7	5	4
Kertesz	9	10	2	1	5	–
Memory and verbal intelligence (Excerpt 3)						
Sacks	2	8	9	1	5	1
Kertesz	2	9	–	1	16	–

Let us now look at one set of tests which is similar in both texts. They both include accounts of the specialist's exploration of his patient's reactions to familiar faces, and of his or her memory and verbal intelligence. Table 3.2 shows the patterns chosen; in Kertesz these are fairly representative of his tests and results. In Kertesz's tests-and-results section we encounter a highly stabilized, almost behaviourist universe, in which the patient is objectified as a receiver of stimuli, while the specialist (usually unidentified) carries out a series of established tests to measure her reactions. The procedure is routine; there is no improvisation and no mention of the mental processes of the researcher. This accounts for the quick, rather monotonous alternation between two types of process: material transactions, in which the patient is usually the understood recipient of the stimulus/goal, and mental/cognitive reactions. The minimal transitivity structure in most of the forty-two test accounts is

1 X was/were presented/used
2 She recognized/performed etc. (*or* she did not/could not recognize/ perform) n out of X.

In these processes the goal, X, is typically prescribed test stimuli, such as 'large capital block letters', 'six primary colours', and 'line drawings of common objects'. This information, however cryptic it may seem to outsiders, is relevant to Kertesz's audience of fellow-experts, showing them that all the testing conditions have been conscientiously and rigorously observed and that the results are quantifiable and reproducible. We are even told about the tests which could *not* be performed – for example: 'Elithorn mazes could not be performed, as the patient was unable to proceed beyond the demonstration items.'

Behaviour, then, is tested by Kertesz in an enormous variety of ways, and the patient, the behaver, is led like a circus animal through her whole 'performance' (a non-accidental pun). She is faceless and characterless, crowded out of the situation – and the text – by batteries of tests. The researcher, too, has disappeared into the tests: he has become merely an administrator. There is no speculation, no dialogue, no confrontation, no argument. The Discussion section is, indeed, a quite separate section of the paper.

Sacks, on the other hand, breaks away from this constrained rhetorical universe in a number of ways. Instead of confronting his patient with routine tests, he takes the initiative and improvises, thus giving at least the illusion that the examination is a natural, unplanned encounter. He does not say how many of the standard tests he has carried out; instead he reports apparently improvised experiments done with roses, gloves, magazines, and other everyday paraphernalia. The homely nature of these 'tests' enables Sacks to ignore the standards of 'objectivity' observed by other researchers, since no neuroscientist would be able to reproduce his tests in laboratory conditions. Notice the unconventional stimuli participating in the following, from Excerpt 3:

> I asked him to imagine [entering one of our local squares] from the north side, . . . and [to] tell me the buildings he might pass as he walked.

and

> Thinking of the almost hallucinatory intensity with which Tolstoy visualises and animates his characters, I questioned Dr P. about *Anna Karenina*.

Moreover, description and interpretation are never kept apart. Each of Dr P.'s reactions immediately leads Sacks to speculate about the mind that produced it. Compare Kertesz's accurate, strictly result-orientated report: 'From a live line-up of 2 very familiar persons and 6 strangers, she could not pick out her sister or the examiner' with Sacks's much more involved and interpretative account of Dr P.'s reaction to similar photographs:

> For he approached these faces – even of those near and dear – as if they were abstract puzzles or tests. He did not *relate* to them, he did not *behold*. No face was familiar to him, *seen* as a 'thou', being just *identified* as a set of features, an 'it'.[1]

(Excerpt 2)

Here, the four mental process clauses all refer to the same experience – the one which Kertesz succinctly encodes as 'pick out' – rephrasing it in increasingly interpretative, metaphysical terms. (This rephrasing, and the foregrounding of the interpersonal achieved by these gradually intensifying parallel structures will be discussed later.)

The Memory and Verbal Intelligence excerpts (Excerpts 3) differ most crucially in their distribution of relational processes (sixteen in Kertesz as opposed to only five in Sacks). Reporting the results of the Wechsler Memory Scale Form I, a set of tests measuring particular cognitive abilities, Kertesz repeatedly uses the ideational structure 'X was Y' where X usually encodes, in nominalized form, the aspect being tested, and the attributes Y are again largely figures, measurements, or estimations like 'very poor' and 'within normal limits', the meanings of which are clearly established and hence known by other experts.

Kertesz, then, relates his patient's experiences *incongruently*, a technical term used to describe, for example, the encoding of processes as nouns rather than as verbs (see Halliday 1985: 321ff. for a full explanation). The relations thus encoded are typically static, timeless and 'possessed', such as: '*Auditory association learning* was also very poor' and '*Her recall of digits* forward was within normal limits, but *memory for digits backwards* was very poor.' Of the sixteen relational processes in this excerpt, eight involve nominalized carriers. Of these, only two nominalizations retain traces of the patient as senser in the form of the possessive pronoun; the remaining six omit such encoding entirely.

Such nominalization is of course typical of scientific writing, and is necessary for the accumulation of shared meanings within the discourse community. Nevertheless, the consistent emphasis on objects rather than processes, attribution and classification rather than events, affects our perception of the *patient*, who is presented less as a person than as an experimental resource (see Kress 1988 for a similar interpretation).

Sacks, on the other hand, encodes his patient's reactions congruently and dynamically; they are personal human experiences. This is how he records Dr P.'s responses to his questions about *Anna Karenina*:

> He *could remember* incidents without difficulty, . . . but completely *omitted* visual characteristics, visual narrative or scenes. He *remembered* the words of the characters, but not their faces . . . he *could quote* . . . the original visual descriptions.

Such congruence between processes and the recounting of them is conscious and deliberate on Sacks's part. In his view, it is the very depersonalization of the patient apparent in Kertesz, her reduction to an 'it', that neuropsychology must avoid. For, as he puts it: 'here [in neuropsychology] the patient's personhood is essentially involved, and the study of identity and disease cannot be disjoined' (1985: x).

Let us turn now to the last part of each text, and compare the processes and participants in the excerpt from Sacks's speculative Postscript with those of Kertesz's Discussion. The process types are set out in Table 3.3.

Table 3.3 Process types – Postscript and Discussion sections (Excerpt 4)

	Material	Mental	Verbal	Behavioural	Relational	Existential
Sacks	4	9	3	7	15	–
Kertesz	1	3	3	–	25	3

The larger number of relational processes in the Kertesz excerpt is motivated by what he sees the job of the Discussion to be, given the established science-reporting format. In this section he must draw inferences from his evidence and show how it fits in with, and extends, the existing body of knowledge within his research community. Hence the most recurring type of clause contains an identifying process with an additional agency feature which Halliday calls *caused modalities* (1985: 153). Verbs like indicate, suggest, and point to are repeatedly used, and their agent/assigner is typically an aspect of the central patient's condition or that of other 'cases' with the same or similar symptoms, problems or deficits. There is also a value/medium, usually a fact, expressed clausally or through nominalization. Examples (see Excerpt 4) are:

Her 'Witzelsucht', or jocularity, tendency to perseverate, and failure of sorting by categories all indicate frontal lobe involvement.

and

That a callosal lesion is not necessary to visual agnosia is suggested by the unique case of Albert, Soffer, Silverberg and Reches.

Sacks, however, does not share Kertesz's communal, consensus-seeking concerns. He ventures into metatheoretical speculation which is critical of the scientific establishment. In fact, as we have mentioned, he goes as far as to use the case of Dr P. to argue against the status quo of neuroscience, making use of many of the ideational features which Martin (1985, 1986) sees as characteristic of hortatory exposition. One of the principle *-er* roles is *we*, evidently including fellow-members of the discipline who, like Kertesz, are caught up in its conventions. *We*, as neurologists, are engaged in such destructive material processes as deleting and reducing, the goals of which are positive metaphysical concepts like the concrete, the real, and feeling. Moreover, neurology and psychology gain life in order to enter the debate: they become sayers – they speak, they talk – and sensers – they suffer. Unlike Kertesz's Discussion, the nominalized participants in Sacks are few, and when Sacks does nominalize he prefers *-ing* forms – judging, feeling, classifying, and categorizing, which Martin ranks as the most active on his cline of dynamism for nominalizations: they 'retain a sense of something going on' (1986: 242).

Finally, if we look specifically at the roles involving the researcher throughout each text, we see that Kertesz himself (and/or his colleagues) is a participant only once, where the pronoun *we* is used. In other cases, we can infer that where the patient is the receiver of a verbal process, Kertesz is the sayer, and where she is the goal or recipient of a material process, he is the actor. However, he is always suppressed, largely through the use of the passive voice. His persona is that of the traditional, disengaged researcher, characterized by Bazerman as one who 'assimilate[s] bits, follow[s] rules, . . . and add[s his] bit to an encyclopedia of behavior of subjects without subjectivity' (1988: 275), without participating in the processes or the resulting texts.

It is this persona that Sacks tries to overthrow in his work. He portrays himself not as a follower of established procedures in accordance with the expectations of research-paper requirements, but as an on-the-spot decision-maker who relies heavily on his 'feel' for a situation. This is reflected in the transitivity patterns throughout the text, with Sacks himself as actor, senser, and sayer in an appreciable proportion of the processes.

Circumstantials

In his metatheoretical speculations, Sacks characterizes mainstream neuropsychology as 'mechanical', as reducing its subject-matter to the basic question 'What exactly is the case with regard to this, at this particular time and place?' (1983: 204). Kertesz unwittingly demonstrates just how astute Sacks's characterization is, especially in his tests-and-results section. Here, in each of the forty-two test accounts, all the circumstances are specified:

In 1970, the E.E.G. showed more prominent theta activity and occasional sharp wave activity *in the left parietotemporal region* and some irregular theta activity was seen in *the right parietal region*, as well. *In 1971*, high voltage theta activity and some sharp wave activity was seen *from both temporal and parietal areas*. Again, this was more prominent *from the left parietotemporal region*, with phase reversals *in this area*.

Moreover, the most important inscription in the text, a table which presents a long series of test results, consists exclusively of numerical answers to when and how much questions.

Sacks attempts to be accurate in a different way and about different things. Faithful to his claim that 'the disease–the man–the world go together, and cannot be considered separately as things-in-themselves' (1983: 206), he takes great pains to capture the atmosphere of Dr P.'s 'familiar habitat' – recalling '*fin de siècle* Berlin' – by means of various location and direction circumstantials, often thematized. Even more striking is the frequency of his comparative manner adverbials, particularly the 'as if' clauses which he uses to give an impression of Dr P.'s curious reactions:

> He was . . . confabulating non-existent features, *as if the absence of features in the actual picture had driven him to imagine the river and the coloured parasols*.

Unlike Kertesz, who reports only the patient's reactions that are quantifiable and precise, Sacks seeks here to describe reactions that are novel and can only be partially understood. To arrive at the best available explanation, he looks for affinities with more familiar phenomena, expressing the resemblances in similes and other figurative language.

Ideation and discourse structure

Finally, it is worth noting that in Kertesz's text, which follows the format prescribed for research reports, the major divisions – Introduction, patient's background, tests-and-results and Discussion – are supported by divisions in the ideational structure as well, as the patient is foregrounded in a particular role in each one of them as summarized below:

In Sacks's text, there is far less correlation between structure and ideation, mainly because there is little separation between 'facts' and inference-drawing. Because of the self-reflective and hortatory

Typical processes associated with the patient in Kertesz

structural element	process types	role of patient
Introduction	relational	carrier (1 instance)
Background	relational	carrier, phenomenon
Tests and results	material, verbal, mental	recipient, receiver, sayer, senser
Discussion	verbal, mental, relational	deleted, or embedded in nominalized process

nature of the Postscript, however, Dr P. surfaces less frequently as a participant; when he does, it is in comparative clauses in which his actions, perceptions and states are likened to those of classical neurology.

The logical component

The logical metafunction is concerned with the structure of the clause-complex and the relationships between clauses. A major difference between our two texts is revealed by means of a simple word-count and clause-count. The texts are roughly the same length – Kertesz around 5,900 words and Sacks around 5,400. Yet there are far more clauses in Sacks than Kertesz – 662 as opposed to 474, or 40 per cent more. There are also 40 per cent more themes in Sacks than in Kertesz – the proportion of themeless clauses is roughly the same (see Table 3.4).

Table 3.4 Number of clauses in the Sacks and Kertesz samples

	Total	Main(themeless/ellipted)		Subordinate(themeless/ellipted)	
Sacks	662	494	(88)	168	(70)
		(total themeless: 158)			
Kertesz	474	332	(28)	142	(78)
		(total themeless: 106)			

The figures in the table reflect the fact that Sacks has more clause-complexes than Kertesz and, more important, that the clause-complexes tend to contain more clauses. In other words, while Kertesz is lexically denser, Sacks is grammatically more intricate. It is noteworthy that, while the ratio of main to subordinate clauses is roughly the same in both texts, the ratio of main to subordinate themeless clauses (including ellipted themes) is different. In Sacks 56 per cent of the themeless clauses are main clauses, indicating a predominance of co-ordinated paratactically related clauses with ellipted themes. In Kertesz, on the other hand, only 26 per cent of the themeless clauses are main clauses, indicating a preponderance of hypotactic -*ing* clauses with no subjects.

As Halliday (1985) has pointed out, the intricacy favoured by Sacks is typical of spoken language, and hence it is no accident that he chooses this approach to his readers. The frequent use of conjoined paratactic clauses, with ellipted themes, is also a feature of speech as well as of narrative genres – again this reflects Sacks's aims. Dillon (1981: 59) discusses people's deep-seated preference for narrative, for 'thinking of things according to the pattern of human actions'. Sacks's spoken narrative is iconic: it reproduces, or purports to, the sequence of things as they happened, thereby drawing the reader into the plot.

Closely connected with this is the frequency of the paratactic projection of direct quoted dialogue in Sacks. He turns his examination into an amicable dialogue with Dr P., continuously switching roles with him as sayer and receiver of verbal processes. This seems to be a deliberate encoding of his wish to establish 'a direct and human confrontation, an "I–Thou" relation' (1983: 204) with his patient. The dialogue allows the main characters to 'speak for themselves', portraying them as autonomous actors, rather than mere puppets. There is also a dramatic motive: the many pages of dialogue tend to give the impression that what is reported is a complete record of what went on, the whole story. It conveys a sense of immediacy (which must be the only reason that Sacks reconstructs even the ophthalmologist's wording – see Excerpt 1).

Kertesz, on the other hand, uses hypotactic projection throughout. Except for one brief exchange, the patient's responses are projected 'indirectly' or, more often, summarized in clauses where she is no longer the subject. For example: 'On the paired association task, only the easy items were recalled.' This conveys the impression that she has no autonomy; Kertesz has appropriated her, and is her sole spokesperson. This is, of course, standard practice in research reports.

Another 'spoken' feature of Sacks is his liking for apposition and parentheses, sometimes emerging as very intricate structures. For example:

the downfall of judgment (whether in specific realms, as with Dr P., or more generally, as in patients with Korsakov's or frontal-lobe syndromes)

and

These [Dr P.'s eyes], instead of looking, gazing, at me, 'taking me in', in the normal way, made sudden strange fixations – on my nose, on my right ear, down to my chin, up to my right eye – as if noting (even studying) these individual features, but not seeing my whole face, its changing expressions, 'me', as a whole.

On the whole, such structures convey the impression that Sacks is moving in uncharted territory, where terms have yet to be defined. We see him groping towards the words he wants, explaining those which remain inexact, qualifying his overstatements, adding asides. The effect is curiously 'spoken' because it is usually in speech that we witness this process of formulating meanings. Hence it also seems highly interactive, as we, the readers, are drawn into the quest. Clearly this feature also has interpersonal meaning, as will be discussed later.

Kertesz, on the other hand, prefers to use co-ordination, embedded prepositional phrases, and defining relative clauses to expand his noun-phrases:

An excellent illustration of the difference between her drawing and copying . . .

and

Anyone who has had the opportunity to observe a patient with this striking inability to recognise objects visually, yet give an immediate and accurate response when they are touching or hearing the same stimulus . . .

Where he does use apposition, it does not convey any impression of groping for meanings.

The 'spoken' narrative motive also explains Sacks's choice of so-called periodic clauses and other suspensive patterns, where the completion of the message is delayed. In contrast, Kertesz prefers cumulative structures, where expansions serve to fill in details after the message has been outlined.

The effect of the suspensive structures preferred by Sacks is again to involve the reader – we are always waiting to find out what happens 'next'. Such structures may occur within clause-complexes and larger stretches of text as well as clauses: Halliday, writing of Tennyson, uses the terms 'dynamic' and 'choreographic': 'you cannot foresee the ending from the beginning, nor recover the beginning by looking at the end' (1988: 38).

Suspensive structures are extremely varied, with delaying material lodged, for example, before the subject or between subject and verb.

There is also the 'not/but' pattern, which is preferred by Sacks but not used at all by Kertesz. In its suspensive use, the reader finds out what something is *not* before discovering what it is. As Dillon (1981) points out, however, the difference may be only apparent, because saying what is *not* usually helps to define what *is*, hence the structure delays positive statement but may fairly directly lead one into it – it is implicit definition. An example from Sacks is:

> 'There's *nothing* the matter with your eyes', the doctor concluded. '*But* there is trouble with the visual parts of your brain. You *don't* need my help, [instead] you must see a neurologist.'

These structures are typical of hortatory exposition; they prepare the reader to accept the inevitability of what *is*. Sacks's use of negation, however, is not limited to such structures, as Table 3.5 shows.

Table 3.5 Negative particles in the Sacks and Kertesz samples

Negation	Sacks	Kertesz
not	51	32
*n't	9	2
no	27	8
never	7	3
nothing	7	–
no-one/nobody	2	–
neither	1	1
nor	3	1
none	2	–
Total:	109	47

As can be seen, there is far more negation of all types in Sacks than in Kertesz, and again it seems to have a dramatic, persuasive function. Halliday (1988: 38), in his discussion of Tennyson, refers to 'deautomised grammar, the meanings that are created by the grammar outside the control of the semantics', such that although negatives may cancel each other out, their effect remains. Perhaps the piling up of negatives in Sacks is a powerful latent pattern, encoding his fundamental despair over Dr P.'s case and hence over the state of the neurological establishment. This interpretation is reinforced by the way the negations are foregrounded in parallel structures:

> he recognised *nobody*: *neither* his family, *nor* his colleagues, *nor* his pupils, *nor* himself.

But for Dr P. there was *no* persona in this sense – *no* outward persona, and *no* person within.

and

whereas Dr P. was *not* fighting, did *not* know what was lost, did *not* indeed know that anything was lost.

THE TEXTUAL METAFUNCTION

The textual metafunction draws on the meanings of the other metafunctions and assigns second-order values to them. Thus ideational – and interpersonal – components are *ordered* as theme or rheme, *focused* as given or new, and *identified* as known or unknown.

Method of development: 'typical' choice of theme

One aspect of thematization is 'method of development' – how writers typically select certain participants (human and otherwise) as theme at different points in the text. These participants, as they group, disappear and re-group, provide a shifting framework which establishes for the reader what the text is about. From this point of view it is clear that the Sacks and Kertesz texts are only superficially about the same thing. Below we have summarized the ways in which the patient is thematized in the two sample texts.

Patient as theme

Sacks			
	Dr P.	24	
	he	113	
	you	7	(in dialogue)
	I	8	(in dialogue)
	a lovely man	1	
Total		153	

Kertesz			
	she	78	
	you	1	(in dialogue)
	patient	13	
	woman	1	
	case	2	
Total		95	

(excluding ellipted themes)

In numerical terms, the picture is very similar – both texts, not surprisingly, are clearly *about* the patient – who accounts for 30 per cent of the theme-heads in Sacks, and for 26 per cent in Kertesz. The resemblance ends here, however. First, the range of lexis used for reference to these individuals is different: in Sacks's long dialogues, the identification is naturally exophoric: 'you' and 'I'; elsewhere the themes are often 'Dr P.' Kertesz, on the other hand, avoids dialogue, does not name his patient and prefers 'the patient' and 'this case' as non-pronominal terms of reference. There is also a tie-up, here, between theme and transitivity. Kertesz's patient is thematized as a *passive subject* in 11 of the 95 'patient' themes. In a further 14 clauses she is thematized as participant in a *not* process: the messages here are about what she 'could not' do. In yet a further 13, she is thematized in clauses about negatively marked processes like forgetting, misinterpreting, perseverating, and confabulating. The text then is essentially about a passive, negative, repetitive person; this is the typical point of departure, the framework within which the case is presented. In Sacks, on the other hand, Dr P. is never asked, or observed, to do anything – he is never thematized as a passive subject. And as we have seen, he is depicted in positive, day-to-day activities, not simply as the recipient of tests.

What about the rest of the themes? Some interesting points emerge if we consider *who* is typically thematized other than the patient. In Sacks, a major thematic participant is Dr Sacks himself, generally referred to as 'I' but occasionally as 'you' by the patient in dialogue – he accounts for a further 71 themes (14 per cent). This text is about the doctor as much as it is about the patient, which reflects Sacks's expressed beliefs about disease and treatment, about the necessity for direct confrontation between the worlds of physicians and patients (1983: 204). The alternation of 'I' and 'Dr P.' (or 'he') themes in the text (see the first part of Excerpt 3, for example) seems to echo this confrontation. In Kertesz, on the other hand, there is no 'I'; the writer/researcher does not emerge as a person.

In Sacks, in addition, there is a total of thirteen thematizations of the pronoun *we*; in three instances this refers to various combinations of Dr Sacks, Dr P. and Mrs P., but in the majority of cases 'we' means the neurological establishment – Sacks and his colleagues. In some instances it *also* seems more inclusive – 'you and I', all of us, the interested and worried 'we' who read this text.

Altogether, then, 'I', 'you' and 'we' themes, with various referents (and one instance of 'the interested reader') account for eighty-five (17 per cent) of the total themes of the Sacks text. In Kertesz, on the other hand, there are only two such themes (one 'we'; one 'you'), and neither includes the reader. This again points to a very fundamental difference between the two texts. Sacks conveys the impression of involvement and concern which he wishes to share with the reader, while Kertesz's rigorous 'objectivity' is detached and dispassionate: he presents only the observable, properly collected and reproducible facts, and their least contentious implications.

Nominalized and 'abstract' themes

Where Sacks prefers personal pronoun and other 'human' themes, the majority of the themes in Kertesz are nominalizations and abstractions; in other words, they are *incongruent* realizations of meanings in grammar. J. R. Martin discusses this in terms of the semiotic 'distance' between a text and what it describes – the more nominalized the text, 'the less iconic the relation between grammatical structures and the events to which they refer' (1986: 241). He classifies nominalizations under six headings, ranging from the 'more active' *-ing* clauses, through derived and underived verbal nouns to 'abstractions'.

If we compare the themes of Sacks's Postscript with those of Kertesz's Discussion, we find that no less that 65 per cent of Kertesz's themes are nominalized abstractions, compared to only 27 per cent in Sacks. (This includes only lexicalized nominalizations: pronoun-themes have been ignored.) This difference, incidentally, is in spite of the fact that Sacks's speculative Postscript contains more nominalizations than his previous sections. A short representative selection from Kertesz is listed below.

Nominalizations as theme in Kertesz
1 The relative uniformity of success in the identification by pointing on auditory stimulation
2 The improvement of visual recognition with auditory verbal stimulus
3 Relative sparing of visual identification with auditory stimulus
4 The association of prosopagnosia and visual agnosia
5 Restriction of visual attention to a single object and apraxia of visual fixation
6 Alteration in adaptation rate and visual efficiency
7 The fluctuation of visual function in our patient
8 The nature of frequent confabulatory responses, often form confusions

9 The frequency of severe amnestic deficit in visual agnosia
10 Her 'Witzelsucht', or jocularity, tendency to perseverate, and
    failure of sorting by categories

Kertesz not only uses far more nominalizations than Sacks, but they
are lengthier and tend to contain embedded prepositional phrases.
He also uses classifiers and noun-compounds whose meanings have
either been established in the course of the text or are known to his
specialist readers. These long nominalized themes are a vital resource
for encapsulating and aligning given information. Yet, although they
are informative in Martin's sense, they do not necessarily inform the
lay reader – their informativeness depends on advanced specialist
knowledge.

If we look in more detail at the nominalized themes in Kertesz's
Discussion, we see that perhaps half of them are problems, failures,
difficulties, and disturbances. In fact, such 'deficits' account for about
17 per cent of the themes in the text as a whole. Moreover, in many
cases the deficit is not preceded by 'her', making it seem curiously
detached and reified: 'the difficulty integrating visual stimuli', 'the
recognition difficulty in the naming mode', and so on. In Sacks
there are seven or eight 'deficit' themes at most; elsewhere (1985)
he deliberately rejects the idea that case histories are primarily about
what is *wrong* with a patient. Far too little attention, he says, is paid
to what has remained intact in spite of the patient's neurological
condition.

Closely connected with the thematizing of 'deficits' in Kertesz's
Discussion is the large number of 'tests and testing' themes, which
cluster in the earlier tests-and-results section. These account for about
22 per cent of the total themes in the text – and this excludes the
numerous sub-headings, which are themselves thematic.

Their frequency reflects the fact that for Kertesz, as we have seen,
the tests are crucial; they are what the report is about, and for its
readers their number and nature is known information. The results,
of course, are unknown, and usually presented as new. In Sacks's
terms, this emphasis on tests is typical of 'classical', 'mechanistic'
neurology. Our tests, he says (1985), are ridiculously inadequate,
designed not merely to uncover deficits, but to *decompose* the patient
into functions and deficits. In Sacks's text, predictably therefore, test
items are rarely thematized; his case stories are not about tests any
more than they are about deficits, and neither is typically selected as
the point of departure for the message.

'Special' thematic structures

A further difference between the two texts is that Sacks tends to use thematic structures associated with persuasive argumentation. These are themes which order and focus information in marked ways – a short selection is listed below

'Special' themes in Sacks
1   *What had been funny, or farcical, in relation to the movie*, was tragic in relation to real life.
2   . . . and yet *it is precisely the downfall of judgement (whether in specific realms, as with Dr P., or more generally, as in patients with Korsakov's or frontal-lobe syndromes . . .)* which constitutes the essence of so many neuropsychological disorders.
3   *All of these* [card faces] he identified instantly,
4   For *not only did Dr P.* increasingly fail to see faces, but *he* saw faces . . .
5   *What a lovely man*, I thought to myself.

In Kertesz, such 'special themes' are altogether absent. The vast majority of his themes coincide with subjects, the only marked ones being the occasional prepositional phrase or hypotactic clause. Again the reason for this must be sought in his perception of the genre – in the rigorously 'objective', painstaking and complete account of test results and their implications, there is no room for overt mediation and persuasion. This is not to say that Kertesz does not intend to persuade, but rather that he feels constrained to allow the 'facts' to speak for themselves. Hence he relies on 'standard' information-ordering resources of the language to signal importance and relevance.

Theme and discourse structure

Looking now at the global structure of the texts, we find that in both, the method of development changes along with the broad divisions between sections. In Kertesz this is particularly noticeable; for example the patient is thematized continually in the first sections but disappears almost completely from the themes of the Discussion, where nominalizations and abstractions take over. In Sacks, the patient is thematized far less often in the Postscript than elsewhere, but since Sacks does not separate 'facts' from theory as rigidly as Kertesz, the correlation between typical theme and discourse structure is far less clear.

We also considered the incidence of marked themes, in order to see whether these are frequently found at the boundaries between structural elements, as Fries (1991) suggests. We found that this is clearly the case in Sacks, whose marked themes serve to orientate the reader with respect to particular sections, both global and local. For example, the last clause of Excerpt 1 is 'And so, *as a result of this referral*, Dr P. came to me.' The prepositional phrase summarizes and encapsulates the whole of the first section through the text-referent 'this referral', and directs the reader towards the focus of new information not only for this clause but for the whole of the following section, which is about what happened when Dr P. 'came to me' – i.e. went to Sacks for consultation (the section we have dubbed 'tests-and-results' in the foregoing discussion).

Section boundaries are also signalled by clauses which, by analogy, function thematically within the section (Fries 1983). For example, the first clause in Sacks's Postscript is '*How* should one interpret Dr P.'s peculiar inability to interpret, to judge, a glove as a glove?' This question sets the scene for the whole of the speculative discussion that follows.

In Kertesz, on the other hand, section boundaries are never signalled by marked themes – we see no systematic relationship between marked themes and any structural element. This is in spite of the fact that in other respects (explicit headings, processes and participants, method of development) Kertesz's sections are more clearly delineated than Sacks's. The explanation for this would have to be sought in terms of the writer's cognitive processes: we have mentioned earlier that Sacks's text is more 'literary' and more consciously constructed than Kertesz's, but there is no space here to explore the point further.

THE INTERPERSONAL METAFUNCTION

The interpersonal metafunction is concerned with interaction between the writer of the text and its intended audience, and, as Halliday (1985) points out, it carries a heavy semantic load. Its lexicogrammatical resources are those of mood and the associated patterns of modality, intensification, and other evaluative devices, realized prosodically throughout the text.

Mood

The mood component is important in the realization of role relationships between addresser and addressee. According to Hasan (1985:
41), mood selections are also pertinent to the question of involvement
and detachment. There are two relationships which are relevant to
our texts: that negotiated between writer and reader and, embedded
within it, the relationship between specialist and patient. Both dyads,
as Martin argues (1986: 244), tend to establish asymmetrical status
relations.

In the case of Kertesz, predictably, we find such asymmetry. He
re-encodes the standard role relationships: he is expert physician
with his patient and expert writer with his readers. In the entire
text only two clauses are non-declarative, one a *wh-* and the other a
yes/no interrogative – the only exchanges that are actually projected
in 'direct speech'. Elsewhere, Kertesz appropriates his patient's
responses through 'indirect' speech and thought projection – all
realized declaratively. The writer–reader relationship is similarly
asymmetrical: Kertesz sees his task as primarily that of imparting
information which will maintain and reinforce the scientific status
quo, adding one uncontentious brick to the vast edifice. This again is
in accordance with the interpersonal rhetoric of professional science
reporting.

Sacks, on the other hand, attempts to defuse the asymmetrical,
disengaged relationships between doctor and patient, writer and
reader. This is partially achieved through selections from the mood
system. Of the 662 clauses in his text, 65 (10 per cent) are non-
declarative. Of these, 54 are interrogative and the remainder are
imperative and exclamative. As suggested earlier, the doctor–patient
dialogue thus encoded has an iconic function: it instantiates the
direct confrontation to which Sacks aspires. The interactive episodes
display a recurring pattern. Sacks, in his 'doctor' role, initiates most
sequences with a *wh-* interrogative like 'What is this?' (indicating an
object). The exchanges that follow are highly elliptical: usually the
mood block is omitted and there is a good deal of tossing back and
forth of the *wh-* item.

Throughout Sacks's text, then, the recurring question–answer
patterns, both projected and 'rhetorical', project the image of a
doctor whose final diagnosis emerges from a dialogic encounter
between himself and his patient, in the course of which he tests and
revises his own cognitive processes and tries to develop new modes
of enquiry. Through the externalization of his internal dialogue,

he casts his audience in a role similar to his own; he takes us along as co-enquirers in his professional deliberations. Similarly, the audience is given a taste of his helplessness and frustration in the face of the insoluble. With him, we have to try to make sense of Dr P.'s mysterious, seemingly paradoxical behaviour. Thus, with him, we puzzle: 'How could he, on the one hand, mistake his wife for a hat and, on the other, function . . . as a teacher at the Music School?'

Modality and other types of evaluation

The resources for evaluating the experiential content of the discourse are very varied: they include modality expressions, evaluative epithets and intensifiers, connotative meanings, and parallel arrangements of clauses. Together with mood selections all these are, to quote Halliday, 'strung throughout the clause as a continuous motif or colouring' (1979: 66); they often occur simultaneously and thus their effect is cumulative.

Modality, in our texts, primarily involves degrees of probability and degrees of usuality. In Kertesz's tests-and-results section, he makes use of a large number of usuality expressions, especially modal adjuncts like often, frequently, and usually. Probability expressions are rare, due to the fact that his evidence-gathering techniques are highly standardized and his results quantifiable.

In his Discussion section, the ratio of usuality to probability is reversed, and probability predominates. 'Caused modality' verbs like suggest (ten occurrences) and indicate (seven) are very frequent, as are may and could. Kertesz's tentative authorial stance represents a choice to shape his text according to the modes of argumentation current within the discipline. It reflects both the delimited nature of his contribution to neurological research and his anticipation of detailed criticism.

Sacks's authorial position is a very different one: his task is to convince his audience not simply of the validity of a specific claim, but of the necessity for an entirely new perspective. Hence he must make his presence much more strongly felt, and must launch his criticism of the establishment with force and certainty. This accounts for the sparseness of modulation in the Postscript: where modality is selected the modal adjuncts are extreme in value (high or low rather than median): always, never, precisely, and of course. For example, '*Of course*, the brain *is* a machine and a computer', and others in the Appendix, Excerpt 4.

However, the very modality which is missing from the hortatory Postscript is (in stark reversal of the situation in Kertesz) much in evidence throughout the earlier narrative. Here there is uncertainty everywhere, which crystallizes whenever Sacks, in his dialogue with himself/the reader, tries to make sense of Dr P.'s unusual behaviour.

Evaluation is also encoded in emotive lexis and grammatical intensification devices such as exclamatives and rhetorical questions. References to Dr P. are strongly evaluative, with a shift, as the narrative unfolds, from admiration of his genius to mourning his condition. The following clauses illustrate the shift:

. . . he had a wonderful musical cortex.
What had been funny, or farcical, in relation to the movie, was tragic in relation to real life.
This wall of paintings was a tragic pathological exhibition, which belonged to neurology, not art.

Finally, intensity – particularly in the Postscript – is also achieved through grammatical parallelism, a characteristic feature of political and other hortatory discourse. The emphatic, interactive effect of rhetorical questions, for instance, is often increased through their serial arrangement and parallel structure. Likewise, phrasal parallels are strategically ordered, as in the negation clauses mentioned above (p. 71).

These overtly evaluative and intensive devices are not found in the Kertesz text.

CONCLUSION: SACKS AND THE ROMANTICIZATION OF SCIENCE

In this discussion, we have explored the systematic lexicogrammatical features of the two texts at clause level, looking at the choices made by the two writers to encode meanings. We will end by looking at the texts in terms of how they participate in the formulation of genres, defined by Kress as 'codings of relations between participants in social occasions' (1988: 137).

Let us consider Kertesz's case report from the point of view of genre. We find that just as the lexicogrammar tends towards the 'written', maintaining maximal distance from the reader, so its generic structure as a whole is as far as possible from the structure of the activity sequence it encodes. The macrostructural staging into unconnected sections is highly prescribed – Introduction, tests-and-results and Discussion (with an attached Summary, or abstract).

The same applies to its very technical lexis, which includes many acronyms and abbreviations, and its economical citation format, which succinctly demonstrates the incrementalism of the literature. Similarly prescribed are the accompanying inscriptions, which take the form of tables and photographs whose reading demands knowledge of interpretative procedures. Thus Kertesz's text constructs an audience of fellow experts, who share specialized and highly codified knowledge and who agree on the nature of appropriate subjects to investigate, appropriate procedures for gathering evidence and appropriate ways of interpreting this evidence in the light of existing knowledge. However much Kertesz may – and does – disagree with the interpretations of individual researchers, he is in full epistemological agreement with them as to the goals of the enterprise of neuropsychology.

Sacks's stance is radically different. His view of professional case reports is that their rigour and exactness may be useful in the construction of hypotheses about neurological conditions, but they can never convey the 'experience of the person, as he faces, and struggles to survive, his disease' (1985: x). In order to capture that experience, a dramatic and biographical presentation is called for. Hence Sacks returns to a generic form that is 'much nearer the bone' (Halliday 1986) and which mirrors much more closely the actual sequence of experiences than the professional case report. In fact, he re-creates one of the most elementary types of staging: in his own words 'that universal and prehistorical tradition by which patients have always told their stories to doctors: the tale' (1985: x). The resulting text issues in constructions similar to those of Freud and, later, Luria: empathetic yet systematic uncoverings of the conceptual world in which Dr P. lives.

But Sacks does not merely return to that earlier, archetypal form, nor does he simply see himself as renouncing the procedures for knowing and writing that are current in conventional neurology. In 1985 he speaks lyrically of 'the medicine of the future, a perfectly rational yet practical medicine, and an utterly beautiful and elemental "existential" medicine', which are 'calling to be conjoined'. His aim has been 'the fusion of the scientific and "romantic" penetrations' into what Aleksandr R. Luria has called 'romantic science'. In his attempt to make the scientific and romantic meet, he creates a heteroglossic text in which two 'languages' illuminate one another: his scientific community's rigorous mode of observation and discovery, on the one hand, and on the other, the traditional story-telling mode. The latter, however, is prior: 'science' is neatly embedded in story-telling, as these two passages illustrate:

Again he mentioned only those buildings that were on the right side, although these were the very buildings he had omitted before. Those he had 'seen' internally before were not mentioned now: presumably they were no longer 'seen'. It was evident that his difficulties with leftness, his visual field deficits, were as much internal as external, bisecting his visual memory and imagination.

How should one interpret Dr P.'s peculiar inability to interpret, to judge, a glove as a glove? Manifestly, here, he could not make a cognitive judgement, though he was prolific in the production of cognitive hypotheses. A judgement is intuitive, personal, comprehensive and concrete – we 'see' how things stand in relation to one another and oneself. It was precisely this seeing, this relating, that Dr P. lacked.

The first passage shows Sacks primarily as the clinical psychologist, using objective, rigorous modes of observation and precise, technical wording. The second portrays him as the empathetic interpreter, who can use his clinical observations in the pursuit of an understanding of his patient's 'struggling relation to the world' (1983: 208). Both, however, are iconic, retaining elements of the real-time sequencing of the archetypal doctor–patient encounter.

More complex still is what Bakhtin would call 'hybridization', which he defines as 'a single utterance containing mixed within it two utterances, two speech manners, two styles, two semantic and axiological belief systems' (1981: 304). To give just one example:

Dr P.'s temporal lobes were obviously intact: he had a wonderful musical cortex. What, I wondered, was going on in his parietal and occipital lobes, especially in those areas where visual processing occurred?

The effect of putting these two languages into direct dialogue is intentionally humorous, but it may also be seen as a serious attempt to bridge the gap between distant and near experience, between scientific and 'everyday' knowledge, and between specialized and everyday audiences. We can perhaps say the same of Sacks as Halliday says of Tennyson: that with his grammar he constructs 'a semiotic universe' at the intersection between science and art (1988: 44).

We must conclude, however, on a note of caution. It is easy to stress Sacks's mastery of his chosen genre, which is arguably a true and original generic mutation. True, he argues convincingly for a more human way of writing science. Nevertheless we cannot help but judge his defence of Dr P. as premature and feeble. After all, Kertesz studied his 'remarkable patient' for ten and a half years before writing his pedestrian yet thorough account. Sacks, on the other hand (*if* we are to believe him), flashed his 'neurological kit', listened awhile, looked closely into his patient's curiously malfunctioning eyes, came up with his penetrating diagnoses, and was then satisfied to write his story without ever seeing Dr P. again – a fact he admits quite nonchalantly. He compensates by saying that he 'often wonders' about Dr P., which is in keeping with the 'parable' schema and the timelessness of its message.

It is also true that Sacks appears as the doctor-friend, the epitome of empathy and patience. But, on close reading, there are perceptible weaknesses in his position. He comes across as paternalistic and somewhat condescending; he glamorizes the strangeness of Dr P.'s affliction, and insists rather too much on his own exceptional caring for the human being behind the fascinating neurological case. His insistence may do much for Dr P. as a functioning 'I', but it devalues him as a *patient*, as someone who has a debilitating and worsening neurological condition. We wonder how Dr P. felt when he heard Sacks's almost careless answer to his final, for him existential, question:

> 'Well, Dr Sacks', he said to me. 'You find me an interesting case, I perceive. Can you tell me what you find wrong, make recommendations?'
>
> 'I can't tell you what I find wrong', I replied, 'but I'll say what I find right. You are a wonderful musician, and music is your life. What I would prescribe, in a case such as yours, is a life which consists entirely of music. Music has been the centre, now make it the whole, of your life.'

The romantic, impractical flippancy of this answer will be apparent to anyone who has had any direct contact with neurological problems on the scale of Dr P.'s, and even more so to those who have to take care of such sufferers – in particular 'The Wife who is Mistaken for a Hat'.

NOTE

1   Here, and elsewhere in the extracts, the emphasis is added.

APPENDIX

Excerpt 1 – Sacks

Dr P. was a musician of distinction, well-known for many years as a singer, and then, at the local School of Music, as a teacher. It was here, in relation to his students, that certain strange problems were first observed. Sometimes a student would present himself, and Dr P. would not recognise him; or, specifically, would not recognise his face. The moment the student spoke, he would be recognised by his voice. Such incidents multiplied, causing embarrassment, perplexity, fear – and, sometimes, comedy. For not only did Dr P. increasingly fail to see faces, but he saw faces when there were no faces to see: genially, Magoo-like, when in the street, he might pat the heads of water-hydrants and parking-meters, taking these to be the heads of children; he would amiably address carved knobs on the furniture, and be astounded when they did not reply. At first these odd mistakes were laughed off as jokes, not least by Dr P. himself. Had he not always had a quirky sense of humour, and been given to Zen-like paradoxes and jests? His musical powers were as dazzling as ever; he did not feel ill – he had never felt better; and the mistakes were so ludicrous – and so ingenious – that they could hardly be serious or betoken anything serious. The notion of there being 'something the matter' did not emerge until some three years later, when diabetes developed. Well aware that diabetes could affect his eyes, Dr P. consulted an ophthalmologist, who took a careful history, and examined his eyes closely. 'There's nothing the matter with your eyes', the doctor concluded. 'But there is trouble with the visual parts of your brain. You don't need my help, you must see a neurologist.' And so, as a result of this referral, Dr P. came to me.

Excerpt 1 – Kertesz

This 41-year-old woman (born in 1937) was in a serious automobile accident, in October, 1965, and was unconscious for 18 days, requiring a tracheotomy. She had linear fractures of the right frontal, parietal and temporal bones. Subsequently, she was observed to have severe memory impairment and difficulty naming objects. Prior to her accident, she worked as a nurse's aid, and was considered bright by her family.

She was discovered to have severe visual agnosia, in October, 1967, during a naming task, in the course of neurological assessment. She was institutionalized because of poor memory, at that time, and her behaviour did not suggest blindness. She avoided obstacles, reached for doorknobs and never stumbled on steps. She never complained about visual difficulty and, when asked about it directly, she would offer a denial or a confabulatory response. In the ensuing 10½ years, she was tested on 20 occasions. Her deficits appeared to be essentially stable.

Neurological examination was essentially negative, apart from her recent memory deficit and visual performance. Her visual acuity was difficult to determine because of her agnosia, but using the open E method, and the occasional correct letter identification, it was found to be 20/20 bilaterally. Several attempts to determine her visual fields resulted in variable field defects. At one point, homonymous hemianopia was questioned. She was noted to have difficulty fixating on the centre. Visual fields, in 1978, were still difficult to determine because of excessive adaptability to stimulation, resulting in a 'spiralling' defect, without hemianopia. Optokinetic nystagmus was present bilaterally, but decreased in amplitude and regularity to the right.

Excerpt 2 – Sacks

On the walls of the apartment there were photographs of his family, his colleagues, his pupils, himself. I gathered a pile of these together, and, with some misgivings, presented them to him. What had been funny, or farcical, in relation to the movie, was tragic in relation to real life. By and large, he recognized nobody: neither his family, nor his colleagues, nor his pupils, nor himself. He recognized a portrait of Einstein, because he picked up the characteristic hair and moustache; and the same thing happened with one or two other people. 'Ach, Paul!', he said, when shown a portrait of his brother. 'That square jaw, those big teeth, I would know Paul anywhere!' But was it Paul he recognized, or one or two of his features, on the basis of which he could make a reasonable guess as to the subject's identity? In the absence of the obvious 'markers', he was utterly lost. But it was not merely the cognition, the gnosis, at fault; there was something radically wrong with the whole way he proceeded. For he approached these faces – even of those near and dear – as if they were abstract puzzles or tests. He did not relate to them, he did not behold. No face was familiar to him, seen as a 'thou', being just identified as a set of features, an 'it'. Thus there was formal, but no trace of personal, gnosis. And with this went his indifference, or blindness, to expression. A face, to us, is a person looking out – we see, as it were, the person through his persona, the face. But for Dr P. there was no persona in this sense – no outward persona, and no person within.

Excerpt 2 – Kertesz

Presentation at an unusual angle, without kinesthetic clues

It was observed that the patient often rotated her head, to try to get a look at the objects from various angles. In order to control the variables of the angle of presentation and the number of visual clues, she was asked to keep her head straight, and then the objects were presented to her at an unusual angle; e.g. the hammer head on. She only recognized 4 out of 20 objects in this mode of presentation, but when the same objects were rotated in front of her immobile head, then 9 out of 20 were recognized.

Line drawings of objects, without kinesthetic clues

Line drawings of common objects, on 20 × 20 cards were used, with visual presentation only, without kinesthetic clues.

Line drawings with rotation and tracing

Subsequently rotating the cards or allowing her to trace the outlines did not improve recognition significantly.

Colours

Six primary colours (blue, red, green, yellow, brown, black) were presented, to avoid ambiguities. Colour recognition was better than for objects and letters, surpassed only by naming of body parts.

Letters

Large, capital, block letters were presented, in groups of six and individually.

Familiar faces

Photographs of 16 famous people, politicians, heads of state, actors etc., recognition of whom was expected for her educational level, were presented individually. She recognized only President Kennedy the first time, but not on subsequent occasions. From a live line-up of 2 very familiar persons and 6 strangers, she could not pick out her sister or the examiner, when they were silent and motionless. She could not tell if the persons were male or female or what they were wearing. However, earlier, she saw her sister walking at a distance of 50 metres and recognized her spontaneously. She recognized everybody familiar, by their voices, spontaneously.

Excerpt 3 – Sacks

The testing I had done so far told me nothing about Dr P.'s inner world. Was it possible that his visual memory and imagination were still intact? I asked him to imagine entering the square from the north side, to walk through it, in imagination or in memory, and tell me the buildings he might pass as he walked. He listed the buildings on his right side, but none of those on his left. I then asked him to imagine entering the square from the south. Again he mentioned only those buildings that were on the right side, although these were the very buildings he had omitted before. Those he had 'seen' internally before were not mentioned now; presumably they were no longer 'seen'. It was evident that his difficulties with leftness, his visual field defects, were as much internal as external, bisecting his visual memory and imagination.

What, at a higher level, of his internal visualisation? Thinking of the almost hallucinatory intensity with which Tolstoy visualises and animates his characters, I questioned Dr P. about *Anna Karenina*. He could remember incidents without difficulty, had an undiminished grasp of the plot, but completely omitted visual characteristics, visual narrative or scenes. He remembered the words of the characters, but not their faces; and though, when asked, he could quote, with his remarkable and almost verbatim memory, the original visual descriptions, these were, it became apparent, quite empty for him, and lacked sensorial, imaginal, or emotional reality. Thus there was an internal agnosia as well.

Excerpt 3 – Kertesz

Memory and verbal intelligence

Memory was formally tested in the Wechsler Memory Scale Form I, in December, 1967. She could not recall any items from 2 paragraph-length, short stories. Auditory association learning was also very poor. Her recall of digits forward was within normal limits but memory for digits backwards was very poor. Visual memory for designs was extremely poor. Reproduction consisted largely of fragmented displays of squares. She was poorly oriented in time and place, and although she had better memory for the names of more frequently seen persons, she would forget the occasional tester or therapist. Similar performance was obtained in 1969, when she had a memory quotient of 57. At that time, she mixed up the two stories, retaining 3 items from one and 1 from the other. She made only a few mistakes in mental control and was able to carry out serial addition of 3. Her digit forward was a surprising 8, but only 4 backwards. On the paired association task, only the easy items were recalled.

Her memory continued to be impaired in 1978: although she knew where she was, she thought it was 1977 and that Kennedy was the Prime Minister. The MQ was 59, unchanged from 1969, and in contrast to a verbal IQ of 88.

Excerpt 4 – Sacks

Neurology and psychology, curiously, though they talk of everything else, almost never talk of 'judgment' – and yet it is precisely the downfall of judgment (whether in specific realms, as with Dr P., or more generally, as in patients with Korsakov's or frontal-lobe syndromes) . . . which constitutes the essence of so many neuropsychological disorders. Judgment and identity may be casualties – but neuropsychology never speaks of them.

And yet, whether in a philosophic sense (Kant's sense), or an empirical and evolutionary sense, judgment is the most important faculty we have. An animal, or a man, may get on very well without 'abstract attitude', but will speedily perish if deprived of judgment. Judgment may be the first faculty of higher life or mind – yet it is ignored, or misinterpreted, by classical (computational) neurology. And if we wonder how such an absurdity can arise, we find it in the assumptions, or the evolution, of neurology itself. For classical neurology (like classical physics) has always been mechanical – from Hughlings Jackson's mechanical analogies to the computer analogies of today.

Of course, the brain is a machine and a computer – everything in classical neurology is correct. But our mental processes, which constitute our being and life, are not just abstract and mechanical, but personal, as well – and, as such, involve not just classifying and categorising, but continual judging and feeling also. If this is missing, we become computer-like, as Dr P. was. And, by the same token, if we delete feeling and judging, the personal, from the cognitive sciences, we reduce them to something as defective as Dr P. – and we reduce our apprehension of the concrete and real.

By a sort of comic and awful analogy, our current cognitive neurology and psychology resembles nothing so much as poor Dr P.! We need the concrete and real, as he did; and we fail to see this, as he failed to see it. Our cognitive sciences are themselves suffering from an agnosia essentially similar to Dr P.'s. Dr P. may then serve as a warning and a parable – of what happens to a science which eschews the judgmental, the particular, the personal, and becomes entirely abstract and computational.

Excerpt 4 – Kertesz

The nature of frequent confabulatory responses, often from confusions, also points to perceptual clues being misinterpreted. This is in agreement with Geschwind's (1965) interpretation that confabulation may represent a response of the disconnected speech area to incomplete information. Perception, in fact, seems to take place but it is disconnected (not passive) from visual memory by an associative defect. This patient had a severe and persistent amnestic syndrome, an often observed phenomenon with visual agnosia (Benson *et al.* 1974; Lhermite and Beauvois 1973). This feature underlines the importance of memory in visual perception. The significance of visual-limbic connections has been recognized since the temporal lobectomies in monkeys by Kluver and Bucy (1937) and has been emphasized in man (1974). The frequency of severe amnestic deficit in visual agnosia is almost certainly more than an anatomical coincidence, occasioned by the same blood supply to the occipital and inferior temporal regions. The rich visual-limbic connections also support the inseparable role recent memory and retrieval mechanisms play in perception, evidenced from behavioural observations in this and other patients. Even though many cases of visual agnosia are associated with an amnestic syndrome, this cannot be blamed for the failure to recognize visually presented material, as this never happens in severe cases of Korsakov's syndrome alone. The relatively low scores in the formal intelligence tests of this patient are related to specific deficits, such as memory loss and her frontal lobe damage. Her 'Witzelsucht', or jocularity, tendency to perseverate, and failure of sorting by categories, all indicate frontal lobe involvement, which was indicated by the C.T. scan, as well. Behaviourally, she did not resemble dementia at all, as she was very quick to use non-visual clues for recognition.

The lesions, in cases of visual agnosia, are most often bilateral, with parieto-occipital, occipito-temporal and callosal lesions, in combination. That a callosal lesion is not necessary to visual agnosia is suggested by the unique case of Albert, Soffer, Silverberg and Reches (1978). There are some cases, where only the dominant occipital lobe and the splenium of the corpus callosum are affected. These patients usually have adequate visual perception, as evidenced by preservation of copying, and therefore, fall in the category of associative visual agnosia. Cases with documented apperceptive visual agnosia and prosopagnosia often have right hemisphere damage, as well. A study by Warrington and Taylor (1973) indicated that deficits in the right parietal-occipital lobes were responsible for impairment on a task where objects had to be identified on an unconventional view. It was postulated that 'Gestalt formation' was intact but 'perceptual classification' was impaired in these patients. Visual agnosia, related to bilateral parieto-occipital lesions and their temporal connections, is a complex deficit; it incorporates, as in this case, other entities, such as simultanagnosia (Wolpert), optic ataxia (Balint's syndrome), prosopagnosia, visual static agnosia (Botez) and alexia without agraphia (Balint 1909; Botez *et al.* 1964; Wolpert 1924).

Editor's preface

Eugene Kintgen undertakes an exercise in forensic reconstruction, elaborating an Identikit portrait of the counterpart, in the Elizabethan era, of modern stylistics, on the basis of the ways certain influential Elizabethan rhetoricians write about writing. He proceeds from the assumption that we can get a sense of the mainstream Elizabethan view of language and style from their own comments and practices of reading. To begin with, he shows how the Elizabethan idea of 'method' approximates quite closely to what we now term 'interpretative conventions', a grammar that will guide the looking for whatever we then see.

The kind of stylistics Kintgen identifies as that of the Elizabethans, on the basis of influential treatises and handbooks of rhetoric and good writing such as those of Puttenham (his *Arte of English Poesie*), Palsgrave, and Harvey (in whose writings we find uncanny congruences with modern proposals, from Jakobson, Ohmann, and others), is 'check-list stylistics'. Check-list stylistics assumes writing can be annotated, or produced, by reference to menus of notional word-types (native/foreign/inkhorn/addressed to the ear/addressed to the mind/addressed to both ear and mind/courtly or vulgar, etc.), by reference to cautionary questions concerning the syntax (is this syntactically truly English, or Latinized?), and review of the schemes and tropes used. He concludes with a simple, dismaying observation that encapsulates a source of puzzlement and frustration that extends far into the work of style-study – and writing classes of all kinds – of today as of the past:

> Puttenham clearly knows what to examine [when examining style], and how to examine it, but he never explains how to put it all together.

What seems most striking in all this is the untroubled adherence to received opinions in matters of style and rhetoric (the great 'giver' here is Cicero): Kintgen finds little evidence of the troubled, reflexive critique of the assumptions – in short, little analysis – underpinning Puttenham *et al.*'s attention to word-types and figures. When Puttenham teaches that high matters require high figures, base things need a low manner of utterance, it is evident that the common-sense view is so common or so dominant that doubts (without which explanations, accountings, are unnecessary) simply do not – or perhaps may not – arise.

What is overwhelmingly evident here, and from our perspective perhaps rather constraining (given the diversity of publishing media, verbally mediated cultural documents and documentation, and so on – the sheer breadth and heterogeneity of literacy, and discoursal production and reproduction), may be the sense of the unthinkability (or better, and more properly Whorfian) the habit of not-considering, of the ideological motivations for the unquestioned, most sensible, modes and techniques for rhetorical effectiveness. It is hard to think of contemporary analogues for such *closed* literary communities – Stanley Fish's concept of interpretative communities notwithstanding. No doubt there are coteries today as ever, akin to the closed circle of court poets, euphuists, and so on; but the readership cannot ordinarily be so closed: there are no sharp exclusions today as to who may read an author's work, to anything like the same degree as in the sixteenth century. Relatedly, *a* common sense, a homogeneity of culture, a singleness of perspective and value is unravelling in today's more open societies as never before. One response to this is postmodernist poetry; another – more panicky? – is E. D. Hirsch's version of cultural literacy.

4   Reconstructing the interpretative conventions of Elizabethan readers

Eugene R. Kintgen

Stanley Fish's continued saturation bombing of stylistics – the phrase is Barbara Herrnstein Smith's, but he proudly adopts it at the beginning of 'What is stylistics and why are they saying such terrible things about it?' (1980, part II: 247) – has, it seems to me, the unexpected and so far unexploited effect of suggesting a way to reconstruct what stylistics would have been like in earlier periods. Fish's argument, it will be remembered, is that

> formal patterns are themselves the products of interpretation and that therefore there is no such thing as a formal pattern, at least in the sense necessary for the practice of stylistics: that is, no pattern that one can observe before interpretation is hazarded and which therefore can be used to prefer one interpretation to another.
>
> (1980: 267)

This is saturation bombing, to be sure, but we may suspect that the bombs are only water balloons; since Fish uses 'interpretation' in an extremely extended sense to indicate the process by which external events receive an internal representation, we have to assume that all perception, literary or otherwise, requires it. Once we admit that stylistics prefers a particular kind of interpretation – one using the categories made available by the other interpretative discipline of linguistics – we are in the same position as any other literary (or perceptual) approach: we utilize perceptual or interpretative strategies to make sense of experience (see Smit 1988). This need not cause any particular anxiety, since, as Fish says, 'like it or not, interpretation is the only game in town' (1980: 355), and we can continue to play the version we like. We lose, perhaps, a sense of privilege, a sense that linguistic categories are somehow more basic in language than others, but even a brief consideration of how the linguistic categories used in stylistic studies come and go – where are the word counts or transformational histories of yesteryear? – suggests that Fish is entirely correct.

The unexpected bonus from his argument is that once we acknowledge that our own research is guided by strategies that are constructed rather than natural, we can identify similar strategies used by others. Fish himself has provided a contemporary study in his articles about stylistics, and Jonathan Culler provides others. My own current interest is in reading in Elizabethan England, and so I would like to suggest that even though there is no evidence of stylisticians active then, we can reconstruct what one would have been like by identifying the interpretative strategies available at the time that would have made linguistic categories noticeable. Although the concept of interpretative strategies was in fact available to the Elizabethans, it is not strictly necessary for them to have articulated the concept to have profited from its use: Fish and Culler demonstrate that contemporary writers use interpretative strategies they probably could not explain or justify, just as speakers use grammatical rules that are tacit. After presenting some evidence that such strategies were familiar to the Elizabethans, I will consider a number of sources of information about how the Elizabethans viewed language and style and from their comments derive some of their interpretative conventions.

During the sixteenth century, and especially after the works of Ramus and Taleaus became popular, the idea of *method* became central to many undertakings, academic and otherwise. In *Francis Bacon, Discovery and the Art of Discourse*, Lisa Jardine argues that Bacon

> held particularly strongly the view that all search for knowledge is dominated and controlled by certain universally applicable organizing procedures. As I shall show, *method*, the study of such procedures, had, during the sixteenth century, become an increasingly central topic in dialectic. As a topic in dialectic, *method* in theory covers both the investigatory procedures which reveal new knowledge . . . and procedures for selecting and arranging existing information for purposes of communication and instruction.
>
> (1974: 2)

Method was not limited to academic enquiry; it was applicable to many fields, including – of all things – travel, the example I will use. In the dedication of his translation of Albertus Meierus's *Certaine briefe and speciall instructions for gentlemen, merchants, students . . . marriners, &c. Employed in seruice abroad, or anie way occasioned to conuerse in the kingdomes, and gouerments of forren Princes* (STC 17784, 1589), Philip Jones touches in passing on the great importance of *method*:

> There is no man, although but of meane and ordinary insight in the state of things, that is ignorant of the great necessity and commoditie of Methods, and directions to men of all qualities: insomuch that whoever undertaketh any course or profession without it, are like the foolish youth, that would needs prove a Latinist without his grammar, or to the mad Architect, which went about to set up a house without his rule and compasse, both whose beginnings were confused, and their conclusions ridiculous.

Methods are necessary because untutored observation is unprofitable, as was the case with the son of the wise man of Naples, who returned from his travels to report 'that he had seen men, women, wals, houses, woods, and medowes, but of the state, manners, lawes, government, and natures of the people, his simple wit could make no reasonable answere'. Method – in this case, method in travelling – provides a means whereby

> the thicke mistes of ignorance, and harde conception will soone be scattered, and the same conuerted into a quicke sight, and illumination of the senses, so that the traueller (although in that course a Nouice) after his ranginges and peregrinations, shall retire him selfe a man of skill.

The actual method employed in this book is simple enough: it consists of well over two hundred questions for the traveller to answer about everything ranging from the location and topography of the place visited to its political, economic, and ecclesiastical government and its literature, history, and chronicles.

But more important for my purposes than the specific method is the testimony it provides of how widespread such a conception was, and how similar it was to something like Culler's notion of literary competence. Jones's linguistic reference is suggestive: just as a grammar of Latin is necessary for the Latinist, so a grammar of travelling is necessary for the traveller. Grammar, the first part of the *trivium*, or basic course of study, provides the prototype for other disciplines; linguistics then as now the bellwether. Knowledge, whether linguistic or topographical, can be expressed as a sequence of rules or instructions (or even questions) that guide comprehension. And as now, we can propose a slight extension of linguistic enquiry to stylistics.

George Puttenham, in *The Arte of English Poesie*, makes a distinction between speech and style that is not entirely dissimilar to the current one between competence and performance:

> Speach is not naturall to man sauing for his onely habilitie to speake, and that he is by kynde apt to vter all his conceits with sounds and voyces diuersified many maner of wayes . . . then as to the forme and action of his speach, it commeth to him by arte and teaching, and by vse or exercise.
>
> ([1589] 1936: 143–4)

Speech, or as we would say, language, is natural to humans; what they do with their natural ability – the form and action (i.e. effect) they give it, are the result of art and practice. In an earlier discussion of poetry among the ancients and the moderns, Puttenham clarifies what he means by an art:

> Then as there was no art in the world till by experience found out: so if Poesie be now an Art, & of al antiquitie hath bene among the Greeks and Latines, & yet were none, vntill by studious persons fashioned and reduced into a method of rules & precepts, then no doubt may there be the like with vs. And if th'art of Poesie be but a skill appertaining to vtterance, why may not the same be with vs aswel as with them, our language being no less copious pithie and significatiue then theirs. . . . If againe Art be but a certaine order of rules prescribed by reason, and gathered by experience, why should not Poesie be a vulgar Art with vs aswell as with the Greeks and Latines, our language admitting no fewer rules and nice diuersities then theirs?
>
> ([1589] 1936: 5)

As is apparent, the main thrust of his argument is that an art of poetry is as reasonable for English as for Latin and Greek, but along the way he illuminates the relation between speech, art, and exercise. Language is governed by rules; the ones he is contemplating are rules of Latin explained in the grammar every schoolboy studied, but the conception is not dissimilar to our own. Following these rules, and guided by their own reason, some speakers discover that their speech, or some forms of it at any rate, is particularly effective, moving, or pleasing: it has a particular 'action'. By practice (exercise) these speakers perfect these forms of speech; the art they have thus perfected consists of a certain order of rules they tacitly follow in their productions. Other 'studious persons' (e.g. Aristotle and others in the great rhetorical tradition) study this special speech and derive their own rules for it, reducing it to 'a method of rules and precepts' which can then be made available to students. Still later, other 'studious persons' may try to recover both the rules and precepts that had been articulated and those that were followed only tacitly.

The two aspects of method Jardine distinguishes are evident in these examples: Bacon and Meierus are more interested in discovering new knowledge, while Puttenham is concerned with communicating received knowledge to a new audience – he claimed that his chief purpose in writing the treatise was 'for the learning of Ladies and young Gentlewomen, or idle courtiers, desirous to become skilful in their owne mother tongue, and for their private recreation to make now & then ditties of pleasure' ([1589] 1936: 158). In both cases, there is agreement that the method can be formalized, whether by means of a series of questions, as Meierus did, with a prose explanation of the applicable rules, as with Puttenham, or by means of the dendritic schemata that Ramus and his followers popularized, which bear an interesting resemblance to the trees of transformational grammar, and a positively uncanny one to the systems of polysystemic grammar.

Having (I hope) established that a *method* of stylistics would not have been foreign to the Elizabethan mentality, I would now like to turn to the stylistics itself. Though there are many references in Elizabethan works to style, they are not very useful in defining an Elizabethan stylistics, for two reasons. First, they were very general, usually referring to the three styles – Puttenham colloquially calls them high, mean, and base – that were fit, by the theory of *decorum*, for three different kinds of subject matter. Puttenham is fuller in his discussion of style than most other writers, so he goes on to distinguish 'other humors or qualities of stile, as the plaine and obscure, the rough and smoth, the facill and hard, the plentifull and barraine, the rude and eloquent, the strong and feeble, the vehement and cold stiles' (149). His definition of style itself is extended, echoing ancient conceptions (Willcock and Walker 1936: l xxix) and anticipating more modern ones like those of Buffon and Ohmann:

> Stile is a constant & continuall phrase or tenour of speaking and writing, extending to the whole tale or processe of the poeme or historie, and not properly to any piece or member of a tale: but is of words speeches and sentences together, a certaine contriued forme and qualitie, many times naturall to the writer, many times his peculiar by election and arte, and such as either he keepeth by skill, or holdeth by ignorance, and will not or peradventure cannot easily alter into any other. . . . And because this continuall course

and manner of writing or speech sheweth the matter and disposition of the writers minde, more than one or few words or sentences can shew, therefore there be that haue called stile, the image of man, for man is but his minde, and as his minde is tempered and qualified, so are his speeches and language at large, and his inward conceits be the metall of his minde, and his manner of vtterance the very warp & woofe of his conceits.

(148)

But even this very full consideration of style remains general: never is there presented anything like a method, a check-list, a set of rules for either achieving or recognizing a style.

The second reason that Elizabethan discussions of style are not very helpful is that 'instruction in style had become, for all practical purposes, instruction in using figures of speech' (Hudson 1935: xvii). Rhetoric books abounded, whether the Susenbrotus used in grammar schools or the various vernacular versions available, but they dealt only with rhetoric and not with the other components of style. And they were written for the writer or speaker, not the auditor or reader, as Hudson indicates when he says that the instruction was in 'using' the figures of speech.

We can circumvent both these problems, I think, by approaching the subject in a slightly different way. First, even though most of the rhetorics instructed the reader in the use of figures of speech, they can also be read as a method of reading: that is, a set of rules or check-list of what to notice in reading. Educational practice in grammar schools warrants this conversion, since the students were constantly drilled in rhetorical analysis of standard texts, and they thus first learned to recognize the figures they later learned to use (see Baldwin 1944). Even Puttenham recognizes this close connection when he claims that his instructions are 'not vnnecessary for all such as be willing themselves to become good makers in the vulgar, or to be able to iudge of other mens makings' (159): production and judgement rely on the same concepts. Second, instead of limiting ourselves to what the rhetorics say about style, we can look at other sources for information about the qualities of language that would be noticed. In the rest of this chapter I would like to use two main sources to triangulate the question of style, one from the academic tradition – Gabriel Harvey's *Ciceronianus* – and one from the popular tradition – Puttenham. Other popular works will be included as relevant.

Although the original aim of rhetoric was to produce orators, by the Elizabethan age prowess in rhetoric was being demonstrated both in speaking and in writing; indeed, public lectures were often published, sometimes only after careful revision. An example of this is Gabriel Harvey's *Ciceronianus*, which was delivered (in Latin) at Cambridge in 1576 and then published in London a year later. In it, Harvey, a praelector in rhetoric at Cambridge, presented his conception of the perfect orator (or writer). Probably more for rhetorical effect than autobiographical accuracy, he recounts how his early pleasure in reading Cicero had been heightened by reading Petrus Ramus' own *Ciceronianus*, a book which convinced him to study not only Cicero's 'latinity but his resources of wisdom and factual matter' ([1577] 1945: 73). Harvey's *Ciceronianus* is thus a thoroughly Ramistic introduction to the kind of study that allows one to appreciate, and thus imitate, Cicero (Wilson 1945: 18–30): 'Let us select as an everlasting model for imitation whatever in him is distinguished and admirable, whatever delights either the ear or the mind or has a view to some noble end' (85). The Ciceronian reader will be equally attentive to arguments (the traditional province of dialectic) and their presentation (the province of rhetoric):

> Let us return, then, dear Cantabrigians, to that interrupted but not abandoned exercise of Ciceronian exegesis. . . . Let us make rhetoric the expositor of the oratorical embellishments and the arts which belong to its school, and dialectic the expositor of invention and arrangement.

(85, 87)

Harvey's main argument is that attentive readers should pay attention to both style and argument, but he is most illuminating for our purposes when he recounts his earlier (and now abandoned) emphasis on the ornaments of style, for here he outlines what he, and presumably many others, considered most important in a style:

> Why should I tell how great and simon-pure a Ciceronian I was at that time in the choice of every single word, in the composition and structure of sentences, in the discriminating use of cases and tenses, in the symmetry of cut-and-dried phrases, in the shaping of sentence-divisions and clauses, in the rhythmical measuring of periods, in the variety and smoothness of clausulae, in the careful and elaborate multiplication of all sorts of refinements?

(85)

He proceeds to give examples of opening formulae for speeches and letters ('And yet, Although'), syntactic connectives ('While . . . yet',

'again and again'), the set phrases ('for how many people would
have done that?' 'I am wont to think it very strange'), and even the
abbreviations he affected ('for "Jupiter Optimus Maximus", from
whose very name in those days I derived marvellous refreshment,
I wrote according to the ancient and consecrated custom IVP') (63,
65).

His conversion has convinced him that matter is as important as
manner, but there are still many who content themselves with

> merely pointing out . . . the ornaments of tropes and the embellish-
> ments of figures . . .: 'This is a notable repetition; this is an
> elegant agnomination; this is an appropriate transfer; this is an
> illustrious and splendid translation'. . . . If they can occasionally
> press home the same points with Greek terminology as well, . . . if
> they can interweave and accumulate some other Greek words that
> are not exactly common; why, they straightway think they have
> unstoppered all the scent-bottles of Aristotle and Hermogenes,
> and have provoked not just one city's applause but universal
> admiration.
>
> (87)

I don't want to identify hypothetical Elizabethan stylisticians with
the very people Harvey excoriates, but even if his criticism is
exaggerated, it suggests what many readers were likely to think of as
the elements of style. First, and most important, was diction: Harvey
refers to 'some men, not ineloquent in [his] opinion and exceedingly
eloquent in their own, who think that everything depends on their
jotting down in a diary proper words, figurative words, synonyms,
phrases, epithets, differences, contraries, similes, and a few notable
maxims' (91) – and we can be relatively sure that readers (at least
the ones with public school and university training) were extremely
sensitive to the nuances of word choice. He characterizes his pre-
conversion self as

> a man more careful than Perionius himself in the choice of words
> . . . and if any words did not quite suit him – and there certainly
> were very many such – fastidiously reiterating at every single use
> of them an 'if I may so say', or 'so to speak', or 'if it is permissible
> to use this word'.
>
> (65)

In short, he

> valued words more than content, language more than thought, the

one art of speaking more than the thousand subjects of knowledge
. . . [he] believed that the bone and sinew of imitation lay in [his]
ability to choose as many brilliant and elegant words as possible,
to reduce them into order, and to connect them together in a
rhythmical period.

(69)

Each word had a history (remember Harvey is dealing with
Latin) that the educated reader knew: Harvey admits that before
his conversion, he

immediately took offense if any syllable chanced to drop from
anyone's lips that had not been originally borrowed from my [I
retain the original pronoun to convey the flavour of the phrase]
Cicero. And so [he] rejected some words as causing hiatus; others
[he] denounced as obsolete; others [he] weeded out as jejune; in
some [he] thought [he] detected roughness and a sort of cacophony

(69)

but after reading Ramus, he becomes convinced that other classic
Latin writers also offer elements worthy of emulation:

I also saw that from them I must borrow, with due regard to the
purity of Latin style, whatever was Ciceronian in them, and Ramus
interprets 'Ciceronian' to mean excellent and in conformity with
the most careful usage of speech and thought'.

(71)

English words, of course, did not have the same history, but the
qualities Harvey objected to in unclassical Latinisms – obsolescence,
jejuneness, roughness, cacophony – could also be identified and
objected to in English words. And English words did have a kind
of history, since they could be identified as native or borrowed, and
if borrowed, they could be interrogated for their utility. In his chapter
on language, Puttenham echoes Harvey in advising the fledgling poets
for whom he wrote the book to use language which is 'naturall, pure,
and the vsuall of his countrey', that is, the language of the court ('the
vsuall speach of the Court, and that of London and the shires lying
about London within lx. miles, and not much aboue' ([1589] 1936:
145). He inveighs against 'inkhorn terms',

which corruption hath bene occasioned chiefly by the peeuish
affection . . . of clerks and scholars or secretaries long since,
who not content with the vsual Normane or Saxon word, would
conuert the very Latine and Greeke word into vulgar French, as

to say innumerable for innombrable.

(117)

But even they can be admitted if they are useful or mellifluous: *method, placation, assubtling, compendious*, for example, are admitted on the former basis, *penetrate*, on the latter (there are other terms to express the meaning, 'but not so well sounding' (147)). Many other words of Latin or French origin, however, were 'not so well allowed': '*audacious*, for bold: *facunditie*, for eloquence: *egregious*, for great or notable: *implete*, for replenished: *attemptat*, for attempt: *compatible*, for agreeable in nature, and many more' (147).

It is sometimes difficult to understand the specific grounds of Puttenham's objections to particular words, and since he ends his chapter by quoting Horace to the effect that 'use and custom' are the 'onely vmpiers of speach' (148), full understanding is probably not necessary. But he does suggest how Harvey's attention to Latin diction could be translated into the vernacular: nonnative words become the counterparts to unCiceronian diction, and just as unCiceronian words can be admitted if they are excellent and conform to the most careful usage of speech and thought, nonnative ones that are useful, harmonious, and current in the right circles can be accepted. This suggests the kind of attention a stylistician would give to the diction of a piece: identifying the native and nonnative words, deciding whether the nonnative ones were affectations (inkhornisms), and judging whether they were obsolete, jejune, rough, or cacophonous.

Having identified the choice of words, the Elizabethan rhetorician would next move to study their use. The rhetorical tradition normally distinguished three kinds of figures, as Thomas Wilson explains in *The Arte of Rhetorique* (1553), a book its most recent editor calls 'the first comprehensive rhetorical treatise in English and also the most popular work of this kind in sixteenth-century England' (Derrick 1982: lxiii):

> There are three kinds of figures, the one is when the nature of wordes is chaunged from one signification to an other called a trope of the Grecians: The other serveth for woordes when they are not chaunged by nature, but only altered by speaking, called of the Grecians a Scheme: The third is when by deversity of invention, a sentence is many ways spoken, and also matters are amplified by heapynge examples, by dilatynge argumentes, by comparing thynges together, by similitudes, by contraries, and

by divers other like, called by Tullie Exornacion of sentences, or coloures of Rhetorique.

(341)

Other arrangements were of course possible, and Puttenham, ever mindful that his audience was popular rather than academic, divides them rather differently into auricular figures, which affect only the ear; sensable ones, which affect the mind; and sententious, which affect both the ear and the mind (159–60). The last category corresponds with Wilson's third category, but otherwise they do not, and in each of his groupings Puttenham devotes a section to figures that pertain to single words and another dealing with the figures pertaining to whole clauses.

Puttenham's auricular figures for single words are of minimal importance, dealing with the addition or deletion of sounds from words, as *endanger* for *danger*, *goldylocks* for *goldlocks*, *remembren* for *remember*, *twixt* for *betwixt*, *tane* for *taken*, and *morn* for *morning* (181–2). Of the sensable figures involving single words, the most important is metaphor, but the baker's dozen that Puttenham provides also includes metonymy, synecdoche, onomatopoeia, and litotes. One of Puttenham's innovations is the translation of these terms into English – if he had retained only the original Latin and Greek names 'it would haue appeared a little too scholasticall for our makers, and a peece of worke more fit for clerkes then for Courtiers for whose instruction this trauaile is taken' (158) – and so he dubs them 'transport', 'misnamer', 'quick conceit', 'new namer', and 'moderator', respectively (178–85).

Our reconstructed Elizabethan stylistician would thus look at two aspects of the diction of the piece being studied: the word choice, and the ways in which the chosen words are used. After dealing with the individual words, syntax would be considered. We have seen Harvey's favourite schemes to assure the proper Ciceronian balance in Latin, but when the language was English there were two related considerations, paralleling the two topics in diction. The first was clearly recognized by John Palsgrave: too many

> haue by their greatte studye . . . so moche prouffyted in the Latyne tongue, that . . . they can wryte an Epistle ryght latyn lyke, and therto speake latyne, . . . yet . . . they be not able to expresse theyr conceyte in theyr vulgar tonge, ne be not suffycyente, perfectly to open the diuersities of phrases betwene our tonge and the latyn.

(1937: 6)

Palsgrave's explanation of this is hardly likely to win the approbation of linguists today – he identifies the causes as 'the rude language vsed in their natiue countreyes' and the lack of 'occasions to be conuersaunte in suche places . . . as the pureste englysshe is spoken' (6) – but he does identify a very real problem for students whose entire education had been in a foreign language: how would they know how to translate what they had learned about Latin into useful advice about English? Palsgrave provides an answer in his edition of *Acolastus*, a play in Latin composed for the schoolroom in 1529 by William Fullonius. Palsgrave's 'ecphrasis', as he calls it, supplements 'the comedye of Acolastus translated into oure englysshe tongue, after suche maner as chylderne are taught in the grammar schole, first worde for worde, as the latyne lyeth, and afterwarde accordynge to the sence and meaning of the latin sentences', with marginal notes indicating 'Adages, metaphores, sentences, or other fygures poeticall or rhetoricall'. He does not actually provide a word-for-word translation, as the following brief example will show, but he is as good as his word in providing alternative versions: the ecphrasis on the first words of the third scene, 'NVnc quod futurum est, colligo' is 'Nowe gather I together the thinge that shal be hereafter .i. nowe reason I or coniecte [conjecture] with my selfe, the thynge which is to come' (47), and he notes in the margin that 'quod futurum est colligere' is, as explained on the title page, a 'phrase, that is to say, kynd of spekyng vsed of the latyns, whiche we vse not in our tonge, but by other wordes, expresse the sayde latyn maners of spekinge'. One may wonder whether Palsgrave's rendering of the Latin phrase into English in this case does much to advance the cause of English prose style, but his book is remarkable for its clear statement of the problem learners faced in translating their knowledge of Latin syntax and phraseology into something acceptable in English.

Having considered the extent to which the syntax was English rather than Latin, our stylistician would turn to the means that had been used to beautify it, that is, to the auricular and sensable figures Puttenham identifies as applying to clauses or sentences. These are primarily the schemes; Puttenham identifies 21 auricular and 12 sensable figures, including zeugma (the 'single supply'), parenthesis (the 'interferer') homoioteleuton (the 'like loose'), polysyndeton (the 'coople clause'), hendiadys (the 'figure of twins'), allegoria (the 'false semblant'), ironia (the 'dry mock'), and so on. More important, perhaps, are what he identifies as the figures 'sententious' or 'rhetoricall', which appeal both to the ear and to the mind:

And your figures rhetoricall, besides their remembered ordinarie vertues, that is, sententiousness, & copious amplification, or enlargement of language, doe also conteine a certaine sweet and melodious manner of speech, in which respect, they may, after a sort, be said *auricular*: because the ear is no lesse rauished with their currant tune, than the mind is with their sententiousnes.

(196–7)

Here he includes anaphora (the 'figure of report'), antistophe (the 'counterturn'), symploche (the figure of 'replie'), ploche (the 'dou-bler'), and some two dozen more before he modulates into the figures of amplification (which will be discussed below).

These figures, so recondite to us, were second nature to the Elizabethans: 'A well-educated modern reader may confess without shame to momentary confusion between *Hypozeuxis* and *Hypozeugma*, but to his Elizabethan prototype the categories of the figures were, like the multiplication tables, a part of his foundations' (Willcock and Walker 1936: lxxix). Jonathan Culler is certainly right when he claims that 'the repertoire of rhetorical figures serves as a set of instructions which readers can apply when they encounter a problem in the text' (1981: 181), but he unnecessarily limits his discussion to tropes and to the translations required to naturalize them. From the point of view of stylistics, the unproblematical, if it is typical and recurrent, is just as important, and the Elizabethan reader, we may assume, enjoyed rhetorical analysis of all kinds of effects. In particular, the schemes, by emphasizing various forms of repetition or its avoidance, provide a practical method of identifying Jakobson's poetic function, which 'projects the principle of equivalence from the axis of selection into the axis of combination' (1960: 358).

The specific kind of analysis attention to schemes and tropes would lead to is not often explained (at least not outside the classroom where, if we believe Harvey, the emphasis was primarily on identification), but we may take a comment by John Hoskyns in *Directions for Speech and Style*, a manuscript written to provide practical stylistic advice for a young member of the Temple, as exemplary. Discussing parison ('an even gait of sentences answering each other in measures interchangeably' ([1599] 1935: 37), he quotes 'Rather seek to obtain that constantly by courtesy which you cannot assuredly enjoy by violence' and comments, 'verb to verb, adverb to adverb, and substantive to substantive' (38).

Finally would come attention to the means by which the topic itself is augmented or expanded. 'To amplify and illustrate are two the chiefest ornaments of eloquence', says Hoskyns, who then goes on to provide specific means for both (17). Here, however, we get away from language proper and into schemes of invention which allow more detailed exploration of the subject at hand, as for example by division, when the topic is broken into its constituents and each treated separately. Instead of saying, 'He put the town to the sword', Hoskyns suggests

> He neither saved the young men, as pitying the unripe flower of their youth, nor the aged men, as respecting their gravity, nor children, as pardoning their weakness, nor women, as having compassion on their sex; soldier, clergyman, citizen, armed or unarmed, resisting or submitting, – all within the town destroyed with the fury of that bloody execution.
>
> (22)

The similarity to invention is clearly underlined when Hoskins goes on to say 'Note that your divisions here are taken from age, profession, sex, habit, or behavior, and so from many circumstances' (23). With this, we are back to Harvey's insistence that the matter must be examined along with the manner.

What kind of stylistics, then, do we reconstruct for the Elizabethan age? It is a kind that I think of as check-list stylistics, familiar from Walker Gibson's 'Tough, Sweet, and Stuffy' or Leech and Short's more recent *Style in Fiction* (1981) characterized by a list of elements to check for in a text. Puttenham in fact provides just such a check-list in his 'Table of the Chapters in this booke, and euery thing in them conteyned' (309), which indexes not only the chapters, but also all the figures he discusses. All stylistics is of course reducible to this variety – if we follow Fish, all interpretation or perception is similarly reducible – but these examples are more overt than most others in actually providing the check-lists. For the Elizabethans, the elements would have been primarily the characteristics of words and the schemes and tropes in which they were used. Grammar, as far as I can tell, was assumed to be too elementary to merit more than passing comment as such, but we can identify various aspects of it in the discussions of the time. Attention to phonology is evident in Puttenham's auricular figures; to morphology, in such figures as homioteleuton and others that identified repetition of morphemes, as well as in word choice (Harvey copied Cicero in refusing to use the barbarisms *specierum* and *speciebus* ([1589] 1936: 67); and to syntax in the various figures and schemes that assured rhetorical balance.

Like the moderns who identify elements of style, but are less successful in showing how these elements are combined into style itself, the Elizabethans – at least as seen through the work of Puttenham (which may not be typical) – would have had no explicit method for developing the specific comments they made on particular passages into a characterization of the style as a whole. Puttenham clearly knows what to examine, and how to examine it, but he never explains how to put it all together:

> matter[s] stately and high . . . require a stile to be lift vp and aduanced by choyse of wordes, phrases, sentences, and figures, high, loftie, eloquent, & magnifik in proportion: so be the meane matters, to be caried with all wordes and speaches of smothnesse and pleasant moderation, & finally the base things to be holden within their teder, by a low, myld, and simple maner of vtterance, creeping rather then clyming, & marching rather than mounting upwardes, with the wings of stately subiects and stile.
>
> (152)

Words, phrases, sentences, and figures – these are what an Elizabethan stylistician would have noticed, and unlike us, he would have done so in the complacent and common-sensical belief that they were actually present in the text.

Part II
Strategic styles

Editor's preface

Anne Neumann shows that the seemingly highly 'literary' vehicle of free indirect discourse is, *contra* Banfield (1982), not at all categorically confined to the literary (see also Short 1988): in this area as in others probed before (creative metaphor, ambiguity, fictionality) literary language is not categorically distinct from non-literary. Neumann operates with a broad functional notion of free indirect discourse (FID), rather than a formal one (the latter might stipulate pronoun- or tense-shift, and lack of framing 'she said/thought' clause). The advantage of a functionalist view is that, at the outset, it aligns the analyst and the readers. As readers, an immediate consideration – however this may be attended to or neglected – is the question of attributing the utterances we encounter to probable sources. With every utterance the question of who is responsible for this formulation must arise. Our 'default' assumptions may be that direct or indirect discourse adjoined to a framing 'inquit' clause ('Mrs Bennet said') is the responsibility of the named speaker; and that all other utterances are ordinarily the responsibility of the narrator. Neumann notes, however, that discourse sometimes occurs which, though 'unframed', seems more likely to be attributable to some character rather than the narrator. Neumann's definition allows for – even guarantees – differences in readers' judgements as to whether particular textual instances are FID or not, and reflects a healthy shift in the literature on this topic, away from essentialist tendencies to treat and pursue FID as an objectivist thing. FID is our rhetorical name for a strategy or tendency, not a thing; it names – in the best structuralist traditions – a relationally determined space which lies outside both narrative and speech. And the strategy itself must be understood as a narrational means to some authorial end: the fictional construction and display of empathy, irony, satire, contradiction, psychopathology, paranoia, compassionating (Toolan 1990), or other effect.

FID as a topic is of importance not least for the consequences and resistances it raises to and for speech-act theory (and its range of subsidiary distinctions: performatives, indirect speech acts, illocution vs. perlocution, felicity conditions, intentionality, conventionality). Wherever we suspect FID to be in play, we override the default performative readings which attribute whatever is uttered, unambiguously, to narrator or character: 'I, the narrator/character, hereby declare. . . .'

Topics of related interest to Neumann include the role of the language of and about moral behaviour and sentiments, in a novel partly intended as a form of moral instruction. In such an undertaking, as Neumann notes, 'Language becomes an instrument of judgement and correction when it is used to remember and describe both actual and ideal behaviour so discrepancies can be discerned and thereafter eliminated' (see p. 125). Furthermore, the novel of moral precepts, as Neumann shows, draws very heavily on characters' and readers' powers of recollection and comparison of previous words and deeds with present ones. In all this, citation and quotation are an important means of giving evidence, so as to challenge or confirm the present behaviour of individuals.

In Bakhtinian terms we might speak of undeclared quotation as a means by which past discourse can be embedded in present discourse, traversing and confronting its representations of character and world. (Undeclared quotation also compels the reader to effect a recontextualization of the utterances so used, in a new situation with distinct circumstances, so that a revised assessment of both the former context and the present one is involved.) Neumann's further thesis is that characters in eighteenth-century Richardsonian fiction are models, in their appropriations and recyclings and re-inspections of each others' prior utterances, for readers of the time, who were expected to participate in a parallel activity of recycling and review. (The western archetype for such appropriations and recyclings – attributed and unattributed – in the service of moral education is surely the Bible, with its numberless dialogic echoes, particularly between the Old and New Testaments.)

5 Free indirect discourse in the eighteenth-century English novel: speakable or unspeakable?

The example of *Sir Charles Grandison*

Anne Waldron Neumann

This essay has several purposes. It confirms that free indirect discourse is indeed 'double-voiced' (as in Bakhtin, 1984: 190) but suggests that this double voice is not unique to literary narrative. It therefore also counters the tendency to seek linguistic differences between fictional, literary narratives, and other kinds of discourse. It demonstrates what has been neglected – that free indirect discourse is already widespread in eighteenth-century fiction. Since I argue too that free indirect discourse is often easily identifiable and attributable in eighteenth-century fiction, my essay implies that, though the ambiguity of free indirect discourse may be its most intriguing feature, free indirect discourse, even in later fiction, is not always undecidable. Finally, as I discuss free indirect discourse in one particular eighteenth-century novel, *Sir Charles Grandison*, I suggest why reported discourse in general is so prevalent in this novel and others like it – why it supports the novel's moral endeavour. The way characters in this and similar novels remember and quote from each other, with or without attribution, suggests how some eighteenth-century novelists *hoped* to be remembered and assimilated by readers – indeed, how readers do sometimes remember and assimilate their reading.

According to most definitions, free (as opposed to tagged) indirect discourse quotes speech or thought indirectly but omits the tag or inquit – the 'John said' or 'Jane thought' – that both identifies what follows as quotation and attributes it to a particular source. Like tagged indirect discourse, free indirect discourse shifts pronouns and verbs to fit the quoting speaker's perspective but, typically, retains any other indicators of the here-and-now of the quoted speaker as well as independent-clause word order. Below are typical examples (following Chatman 1978) of tagged and free direct and indirect discourse. Note that free *in*direct discourse, hereafter FID, comprises both free indirect thought and free indirect speech (to see what free indirect thought looks like, substitute 'John asked *himself*' for 'John asked Jane' in the examples below). In this essay, however, I shall discuss only free indirect speech, out of which, I hypothesize, free indirect thought evolved. (Moreover, I shall ignore a distinction between free *direct* discourse and free *in*direct discourse as immaterial to the following argument.)

tagged direct discourse:	John asked Jane, 'Shall I come here to see you tomorrow?'
free direct discourse:	Shall I come here to see you tomorrow?
tagged indirect discourse:	John asked Jane whether he should go there to see her the next day.
free indirect discourse:	Should he come here to see her tomorrow?

In prose fiction, the narrator's FID – that is, unattributed quotation of a character by the narrator – can, because of the shifted tenses and pronouns, often be mistaken for objective narration. Correctly identifying and attributing FID is important, however, in so far as it is possible, because it determines who sees and who speaks in the given passage, the factors determining point of view in fiction.

I refine the above definition in my 1986 article on FID in Jane Austen's *Pride and Prejudice*. In that article, I suggest we define FID as any sentence containing words not explicitly attributed as quotation (or at least not as quotation from a specified source) but likely to originate with a character rather than with the narrator, or with some character other than the quoting character. Bakhtin describes this kind of quotation in 'Discourse in the novel':

> The speech of another is introduced . . . in *concealed form*, that is, without any of the *formal* markers usually accompanying such speech, whether direct or indirect.

> The division of voices and languages takes place . . . often within the limits of a simple sentence. . . . Frequently . . . even one and the same word will belong simultaneously to two languages, two belief systems.
>
> (Bakhtin, 1981: 303, 305)

I stress that characters as well as narrator quote in this way in Austen's fiction. And I identify two kinds of FID in Austen. First, what I call 'words-and-phrases' FID quotes only isolated words or phrases of a character's locution; such quotation is, as Bakhtin's theory elsewhere predicts, often satiric (Bakhtin [Volosinov] 1973: 130–1). In Austen and in later novelists, it usually quotes speech rather than thought. It seems especially typical of eighteenth-century fiction, however, where it is sometimes sympathetic. Second, what I call 'whole-sentence' FID back-shifts a whole sentence of quoted discourse (as in the above example) to form all or most of a quoting sentence; Austen and later novelists use this mode, often sympathetically rather than satirically, for the free indirect quotation of thought as well as of speech. This last of the many possible kinds of FID – the sympathetic (rather than satiric) quotation by the narrator (rather than another character) of whole sentences (rather than words or phrases) of a character's thought (rather than speech) – is typical of the romantic novel and contributed to an earlier German view of FID as stemming from an imaginative identification between writer and characters so extreme that, according to one early theorist, the writer 'inwardly experiences' what the characters experience (quoted in Pascal 1977: 22); hence the German name for FID, *erlebte Rede* or 'experienced discourse' (for a summary of this view of FID, see Pascal 1977: 22–30). This earlier view may inspire Banfield's definition of FID as represented consciousness and similar attempts to see free indirect thought as linguistically distinguishable from free indirect speech (Banfield 1982). Another purpose of this essay is to suggest that my broader definition of FID is more useful, however, embracing, as it does, eighteenth-century as well as nineteenth- and twentieth-century practice.

What does my broader definition of FID imply? In particular, what follows from defining FID as any words plausibly identifiable as quotation that are not explicitly attributed as quotation? I argued in my 1986 article that if a sentence without attribution can plausibly be read as indirectly quoted discourse, then according to my definition it *is* FID: that is, I *call* it FID. Readers may question the plausibility and reject the identification as quotation without attribution in specific instances, but the category of FID thus defined remains available. I also argued that though my definition thus allows for the ambiguity we usually associate with FID, it also acknowledges that not every instance of FID is equally ambiguous. Context defines which words are quoted and whose words they are more unambiguously in some instances of FID than in others. In what I call 'definite' FID, for example, we feel sure which words are quoted and from whom, often because we have seen them explicitly quoted before, with attribution.

In 'almost definite' FID, on the other hand (arguably the most common kind of FID in Austen), the case for identifying a passage as quotation can be very strongly made, perhaps because we 'know' by some means that a character said or thought something at a particular moment in the story, and a sentence at the appropriate point in the narrative strikes us as translating back into what that character would typically say or think in that situation. In '*in*definite' FID, finally, we may not know whether to attribute particular utterances to the narrator, or to a character, or even to which character, or, if we can identify the character to associate with the viewpoint expressed, we may not know whether the sentence renders words he or she actually *does* speak or think now, or only reports what he or she *might* say or think, now or another time.

Whether FID originated in real life or in literature has been much debated. The first linguists to identify and describe this mode of reported discourse found examples in literature (Goethe and Austen are often cited as among the earliest exemplars in German and English), but disagreed on whether or not FID originated in everyday speech (for a summary of this early debate, see Pascal 1977: 18–19; for more recently opposed viewpoints, see Chatman 1978: 80–1 and Banfield 1982: 231). Clearly only narrators can quote characters' *thoughts*. But, that the characters of eighteenth-century fiction use FID to quote each other's speech as often as narrators do in itself strongly suggests that FID is possible in everyday speech and may have originated there (at least readers could imitate fiction by using FID in conversation). FID by characters is often easily identifiable in these novels. First, when a character quotes another character without attribution, we may recognize the quotation because it was quoted previously by the narrator with attribution. Second, eighteenth-century novels sometimes use italics to identify this re-quoted material for the novel's readers (like modern quotation-marks-within-quotation-marks). This variation on FID – FID with italics – still has no inquit or attributing clause, however, and readers – though they see which words are quoted – must still decide who is quoted (other characters, who cannot 'see' the italics, presumably hear an intonation that implies quotation). FID with italics in eighteenth-century fiction supports the 'double-voice' theory by modelling visibly how the subjective and evaluative expressions of one character can interweave with those of another. The way eighteenth-century fictional characters quote without attribution suggests how we might read unattributed quotation by eighteenth-century narrators *and* how we might recognize and interpret FID in Austen and later novelists after the convention of italics has begun to disappear.

My examples of FID in eighteenth-century fiction will, for co-herence and brevity, all be drawn from Samuel Richardson's *Sir Charles Grandison* (1753). I make this less familiar choice for several reasons. In Jane Austen's *Northanger Abbey* (1818), Isabella Thorpe, an ardent reader of Gothic romances, supposes the heroine's mother, as a typical member of the older generation, must condemn novels. 'No, she does not', Catherine Morland exclaims, 'She very often reads Sir Charles Grandison' (*Northanger Abbey* p. 41). Austen's joke about the high moral tone of Richardson's now least read novel – implying that the entire eighteenth century had produced only one novel Mrs Morland thoroughly approves – testifies equally to *Sir Charles Grandison*'s enormous earlier appeal: after all, not only does Mrs Morland approve of *Grandison*; she seems to be always actually *reading* it. Though the novel's seven-volume length may partly account for Mrs Morland's constant devotion, the novel did have tremendous realistic and romantic interest for its eighteenth- and early nineteenth-century readers, including Austen herself: 'Every circumstance narrated in Sir Charles Grandison, all that was ever said or done in the cedar parlour, was familiar to her', wrote Austen's nephew, 'and the wedding days of [Harriet and Charlotte] were as well remembered as if they had been living friends' (Austen Leigh 1906: 84). I have chosen *Grandison* in part, therefore, because it influenced not only readers but also authors – not least Austen, who was herself so influential, and who is so often considered the inventor of FID in the English novel.

In fact, Richardson meant *Grandison* to be innovative and influen-tial: in his final novel, he set out to demonstrate to his contemporaries that fiction could hold interest even though its hero was a 'TRULY GOOD MAN' (3.462). The novel was meant to be as exemplary as its hero – both moral and appealing. How, precisely, did Richardson hope not only to inculcate morality but also to appeal to readers? *Grandison*, like Richardson's earlier *Pamela* (1740) and *Clarissa* (1747–8), is a '*HISTORY . . . IN A SERIES OF LETTERS Published from the ORIGINALS*'. Moreover, the novel's letters primarily describe the social gatherings its contemporaries called 'conversation pieces'. Richardson justifies *Grandison*'s many con-versations, correspondents, and characters – a preface lists fifty 'Principal Persons' (1.5) – as offering moral lessons that also entertain: 'it is hoped the Variety of Characters and Conversations necessarily introduced into so large a Correspondence, as these Volumes contain, will enliven as well as instruct' (1.4). *Grandison*'s many conversations and characters are justified not only by morality and by truth-to-life but also by immediacy and romantic interest. And a principal element in both the realism and emotional appeal of Richardson's novels – and in their length – Richardson called 'writing to the moment':

> The Nature of Familiar Letters, written, as it were, to the *Moment*, while the Heart is agitated by Hopes and Fears, on Events undecided, must plead an Excuse for the Bulk of a Collection of this Kind. Mere Facts and Characters might be comprised in a much smaller Compass: But, would they be equally interesting?

(1.4)

Or, as Charlotte, the hero's lively and satirical younger sister, writes in a letter to the heroine, 'I love, Harriet, to write to the moment; that's a knack I had from you and my brother: And be sure to continue it, on every occasion: No *pathetic* without it!' (3.24). The italics of Charlotte's '*pathetic*' reflect her ambivalence about romantic interest and suggest her preference for the satiric and realistic. Indeed, her own lively and satirical letters (like her character) demonstrate the 'enliven[ing]' (1.4) rather than the '*pathetic*' appeal of 'writ[ing] to the moment' and also add greatly to *Grandison*'s realistic appeal.

Grandison is literature, in short, that attempts in part to preserve the flavour of real life. It may seem paradoxical to cite literary examples when arguing that FID can exist outside literature. But, since *Grandison* is an epistolary novel, it consists entirely of – that is, it imitates or it *claims* to imitate, at least – everyday *written* language. And the 'conversation pieces' its letters purport to transcribe claim to imitate everyday *spoken* language. Since these letters and the conversations they recount contain many examples of FID, and since an epistolary novel has no heterodiegetic narrator, *Grandison* demonstrates incontrovertibly that the double-voice theory of reported discourse does not depend on a narrator for its second voice.

I quote at length a conversation transcribed by the lively and satirical Charlotte in a letter to the more romantic Harriet. (The modern edition I quote from preserves the italics of the first edition, which Richardson printed himself; italics in Charlotte's letter we understand as rendering in print her handwritten underlining.) Charlotte's report illustrates the prodigious memories Richardson imagines for his characters. It also shows how FID can vary in *Grandison*. In her letter to Harriet, Charlotte quotes her elder sister and brother-in-law *and* herself using both whole-sentence and words-and-phrases FID satirically (indeed, Lord and Lady L. imply in this conversation that Charlotte ought to treat her new husband, Lord G., *less* satirically). Though I identify and discuss in square brackets the kinds of reported discourse Charlotte's letter contains, reading the conversation first without my bracketed comments will indicate how fluent it is.

Lady L. told me, I [Charlotte] might be the happiest creature in the world, *if* – and there was so good as to stop.

[Tagged indirect discourse with concluding comment; this indirect discourse seems very 'direct', however, because Charlotte's italics suggest her sister's vocal emphasis.]

One of the happiest only, Lady L.! Who can be happier than you?

[Direct discourse because of the present tense and unshifted pronouns. It looks like *free* direct discourse because it has neither inquit nor quotation marks, but free direct discourse is rare in fiction, the new paragraph suggests a new speaker, and Richardson usually employs quotation marks only for quotation within quotation, so this is Richardson's normal mode of direct quotation, and we may therefore decide to class it with the more usual tagged variety.]

But I, said she, should neither *be* so, nor *deserve* to be so, *if* – Good of her again, to stop at *if*.

[Lady L. explains her own happiness in tagged direct discourse: this sentence has an inquit though no quotation marks. Note Charlotte's italics when she re-quotes her sister's *'if'* one last time in order to comment on it, however.]

We can't be all of one mind, replied I. I shall be wiser in time.

[Tagged direct discourse again.]

Where was poor Lord G. gone?

[FID – the past tense makes it indirect. A whole sentence in Charlotte's letter quotes a whole sentence of Lord or Lady L.'s speech: 'Where *is* poor Lord G. gone?']

Poor Lord G. is gone to seek his fortune, I believe.

[Charlotte quotes herself in direct discourse, but the sentence she quotes includes her own words-and-phrases FID – an example of how Richardson imagines FID might occur in conversation as well as correspondence: Charlotte quotes 'poor' ironically without being explicit that she is quoting (but note her italics). And 'seek his fortune' is her sarcastic response to another speaker's 'poor'.]

What did I mean?

[FID of whole sentences, rendering 'What do *you* mean?']

I told them the airs he had given himself; and that he was gone without leave, or notice of return.

[Tagged indirect discourse.]

He had served me right, *ab*-solutely right, Lord L. said.

[Also tagged indirect discourse, because of the inquit and the shifted tense and pronouns, but much more direct than the summary in the previous sentence: note that Charlotte not only repeats Lord L.'s repetition and his expressive '*ab*-solutely' but even the intonation with which he speaks that word.]

I believed so myself. Lord G. was a very good sort of man, and ought not to bear with me so much as he had done: But it would be kind in them, not to tell him what I had owned.

[Charlotte quotes *herself* in whole-sentence FID; try a version of the usual 'translation test': shift past tenses into present and 'them' into 'you'.] (2.437)

It is clear from this passage that indirect discourse was often very 'direct' in the eighteenth century. And, because Richardson's direct discourse also lacks quotation marks or even dashes, the boundary between his direct and indirect quotation is fluid. Indeed, indirect discourse in Richardson often violates today's boundaries: indirectly quoted questions have question marks or independent-clause word order, for instance. Perhaps whole-sentence FID evolved from this very direct indirect discourse by dropping the tag. Words-and-phrases FID, on the other hand, reminds us that, despite the grammatical shifts, sentences of indirect discourse typically contain words actually spoken by the quoted speaker (like Charlotte's '*ab*-solutely', which should be in quotation-marks-within-quotation-marks in a 'correct' version of Charlotte's letter). Note too the sarcastic emphasis with which Charlotte singles out isolated words or phrases from the discourse she quotes: '*Poor* Lord G.' or 'right, *ab*-solutely right'.

But FID is not restricted to satire, nor to Charlotte, in *Grandison*. More important, other characters in the novel use FID, and quotation in general, to reflect on the moral implications of someone else's discourse. We may understand this function of FID better when we examine, in the next quoted passages, a character who *fails* to reflect in this way. *Grandison*'s villain, Sir Hargrave Pollexfen, whose abduction of Harriet Byron introduces her to the rescuing hero, first makes to Harriet what he considers to be honourable addresses. Handsome, wealthy, and noble, he is so astonished by Harriet's refusal that he can only echo it in FID. As usual, Harriet's letter signals these echoes with italics:

> I thank you, Sir, for your good opinion of me; but I cannot encourage your addresses.
>
> You *cannot*, madam, *encourage my addresses*! . . . Good heaven!
>
> (1.83)

[I classify 'You *cannot*, madam, *encourage my addresses*' as FID – rather than free *direct* discourse – because it shifts the pronoun though not the verb tense.] Sir Hargrave presses Harriet to explain her objections, but Harriet, whose duty is not to correct Sir Hargrave (see 1.96), hesitates to explain her real reason:

> – *shall* I say? (Pardon me, Sir) You do not – You do not, hesitated I – hit my fancy – Pardon me, Sir.
>
> If pardon depends upon *my* breath, let me die if I do! – Not *hit your fancy*, madam! [And then he look'd upon himself all round] Not *hit your fancy*, madam!
>
> (1.84, Richardson's brackets)

Again, italics signal part of Sir Hargrave's echo of Harriet (he repeats her 'pardon' without italics). Sir Hargrave can only suppose Harriet's affections are already engaged:

> [W]hy then will you not say that you are engaged?
>
> If I own I *am*; perhaps it will not avail me: It will still much less, if I say I am *not*.
>
> *Avail* you! . . . But give me leave to say [and he reddened with anger] that my fortune, my descent, and my ardent affection for you, considered, it may not *dis*-avail you. Your relations will at least think so.
>
> (1.85, Richardson's brackets)

Note that the *second* time Sir Hargrave echoes Harriet's 'avail', italics on '*dis*' stress the contrast between his meaning and hers. When Sir Hargrave renews his addresses several days later, Harriet, pressed, finally names her real objection:

[W]hen he insisted upon my reasons for refusing him, I frankly told
him, tho' I owned it was with some reluctance, that I had not the
opinion of his morals that I must have of those of the man to whom
I gave my hand in marriage.

Of my *morals*, madam! (starting; and his colour went and came)
My *morals*, madam! – . . .

Indeed, Sir Hargrave, you must pardon me on *this* occasion, if I
repeat that I have not that opinion of your morals –

Very well, madam –

That I must have of those of the man on whose worthiness I must
build my hopes of *present* happiness, and to whose guidance intrust
my *future*. This, Sir, is a very material consideration with me, tho'
I am not fond of talking upon it, except on *proper* occasions, and
to *proper* persons. . . .

(1.96)

Note that Sir Hargrave's 'Very well, madam' interrupts Harriet,
suggesting that he believes she has finished speaking before she
has made her most important point about her hopes for earthly
and heavenly happiness. Using yet another typographic convention
for quotation-within-quotation, Harriet records Sir Hargrave's anger:

He walked about the room muttering, 'You have no opinion of
my morals' – By heaven, madam! – But I will bear it all – Yet,
'No opinion of my morals!' – I cannot bear that – . . . Mr Reeves
attended him to the door – Not like my morals, said he! – I have
enemies, Mr Reeves – 'Not like my morals!'

(1.96)

After abducting Harriet Byron, Sir Hargrave recalls these conversations. Harriet recalls them too. *And* she obviously expects her
correspondents to recall them. Recognizing that she is being quoted
even where Sir Hargrave does not remind her, Harriet uses italics to
alert her correspondents to her words within Sir Hargrave's discourse:

Ha, ha, ha, hah! What, my sweet Byron, I don't hit your *fancy*!
You don't like my morals! Laughing again. My lovely fly, said the
insulting wretch, . . . All your struggles will not *avail* you – Will not
avail you. That's a word of your own, you know.

(1.165; see also 1.152)

In both whole-sentence and words-and-phrases FID, Sir Hargrave
repeats without attribution the expressions that rankle about his
'*morals*' and Harriet's '*fancy*'; he retrospectively attributes '*avail*'

explicitly to her. Here, he both uses and mentions Harriet's discourse after the fact, no longer just echoes it immediately. Indeed, Sir Hargrave does *not* echo Harriet; that is, he does not quote her perfectly: Harriet's careful 'I have not that opinion of your morals . . . [t]hat I must have of those of the man on whose worthiness I must build my hopes of [earthly and heavenly] happiness' quickly becomes the less specific 'You have no opinion of my morals'. And Sir Hargrave's final *'You don't like my morals!'* trivializes Harriet's 'very material consideration' into mere 'lik[ing]', on a par with 'I don't hit your *fancy!*', which is how Sir Hargrave remembers Harriet earlier hoping to avoid more serious explanations. Sir Hargrave's inaccuracy suggests he neither understands nor feels Harriet's objection as he should. He may remember her words and quote them to some extent, but he does not take them to heart, and he will not be corrected by them.

In *Grandison*, Richardson is careful to have his rake repent, however, after the hero's goodness to him. In a letter to the Reverend Dr Bartlett, Sir Charles's tutor and mentor, the dying Sir Hargrave begs for comfort in his wretched final hours. His desire for consolation and repentance now necessitates the *words* he was so careless of earlier:

> [P]ut me in the way of repentance; and I shall then be happy. Draw me up, dear Sir, a Prayer, that shall include Confession. . . . You are a heavenly-minded man; give me words which may go to my heart; and tell me what I shall say to my God.
>
> (3.144)

If goodness begins with the desire to act well, then words that go to the heart will create that desire, Sir Hargrave implies, and thus promote goodness. And if goodness means acting on good intentions, then affirming those intentions in words may be an inducement to perform them. Sir Hargrave's plea for good words suggests how Richardson must imagine moral literature promotes goodness by means of language: might we describe Richardson's intention in *Grandison* as giving his *readers* words to go to their hearts and tell them what to say?

The importance of *words* in conveying the novel's moral sentiments partly explains *Grandison*'s great length; in Samuel Johnson's famous comment: 'Why, Sir, if you were to read Richardson for the story, your impatience would be so much fretted, that you would hang yourself. But you must read him for the sentiment, and consider the story as giving occasion to the sentiment' (quoted in *Grandison*, 507n;

Harris (in Richardson 1986) notes that in Richardson's *Collection of the Moral and Instructive Sentiments, Maxims, Cautions, and Reflections, Contained in the Histories of Pamela, Clarissa, and Sir Charles Grandison* (1755), 'sentiment' is equivalent to 'maxim').

The importance of words in conveying the novel's moral sentiments also explains how often and how accurately characters other than Sir Hargrave *do* remember and repeat each others' discourse: 'What a *rememberer* . . . is the heart! – Not a circumstance escapes it', Harriet exclaims in one of her letters (2.299). Of course, Richardson does not expect such a tenacious memory for exact phraseology from his heroine's readers: letter-writers must remember well enough to repeat; letter-*readers* need remember only well enough to recognize. And recognition is often prompted. For example, when Harriet ponders how she first heard from Sir Charles that his 'Compassion' though not his 'Honour' engages him to Clementina, the Italian noblewoman whose sanity may depend on marrying him (2.118 and 2.131), Harriet quotes Sir Charles's crucial words a *second* time for her cousin Lucy – her chief correspondent – because, she writes, 'You [Lucy] may not have my Letter at hand which relates that affecting address to me; and it is impossible for me, while I have memory, to forget them'. The reader, as well as Lucy, may not have Sir Charles's words 'at hand'; Harriet quotes from a previous volume in the early editions:

> He had just concluded his brief history of Clementina – 'And now, madam, what can I say? – Honour forbids me! – Yet honour bids me – Yet I cannot be unjust, ungenerous, *selfish*!'
>
> (2.387, originally vol. 4; quotes 2.132, originally vol. 3)

Harriet has been pondering these words since she first heard them. Her second sentence in the following passage quotes them in FID:

> But what means he by the word *selfish*! He *cannot be selfish*! – I comprehend not the meaning of this word – . . . This word confounds me, from a man that says nothing at random!
>
> (2.293)

In passages like these, Harriet displays her own memory and exercises that of her readers. She quotes to herself, as well as to her correspondents, using FID and other modes, in order to determine a word's meaning, certain it *is* meaningful. She is right that '*selfish*' is not 'random': Sir Charles uses it again in a conversation with the Countess Dowager of D., who wishes Harriet to marry her son and who therefore asks Sir Charles his intentions towards Harriet. Sir Charles, refusing to convert to Catholicism, has yet to learn whether he will be accepted as Clementina's husband. He explains his uncertainty to the Countess, who repeats it to Harriet in direct quotation:

> 'As I know not what will be the result of my journey abroad, I should think myself a very *selfish* man, and a very dishonourable one to *two* Ladies of equal delicacy and worthiness, if I sought to involve [Miss Byron] in my own uncertainties.'
>
> (2.383–4)

The embedding here – Harriet quotes, to Lucy, the Countess of D., who quotes, to Harriet, Sir Charles – testifies further to the importance of quotation to Richardson and to characters like Harriet. Able to remember and compare two texts, Harriet now hazards an interpretation of the crucial word:

> But, Lucy, tell me – May I, do you think, explain the meaning of the word SELFISH used by Sir Charles in the conclusion of the Library-conference at Colnebrooke (and which puzzled me then to make out) by his disclaiming of *selfishness* in the conversation with the Countess above-recited? If I may, what an opening of his heart does that word give in my favour, were he at liberty? Does it not look, my dear, as if his *Honour* checked him, when his *Love* would have prompted him to wish me to preserve my heart disengaged till his return from abroad? Nor let it be said, that it was dishonourable in him to have such a thought, as it was *checked* and *overcome*.
>
> (2.386–7)

Harriet, speculating that Sir Charles is torn between '*Honour*' and '*Love*', quotes in FID (with italics but without other attribution) the word Sir Charles does twice speak – '*Honour*' (2.387 and 2.383–4) – and hypothesizes the word he does *not* speak – '*Love*'. Harriet never doubts that Lucy is nearly as interested in such remembering and speculating as she is. And Lucy, remembering, feeling, and pondering all Harriet's dilemmas, is a model for Richardson's readers. We have seen how well Jane Austen, for one, remembered and felt *Grandison*'s events. This virtual memorizing was surely the sort of reading Richardson sought if his novel was to 'instruct' as well as 'enliven' (1.4).

That instruction always depends on memory is particularly apparent in a novel where character is judged and corrected by means of words. Language becomes an instrument of judgement and correction when it is used to remember and describe both actual and ideal behaviour so discrepancies can be discerned and thereafter eliminated. We observe

Sir Charles using language this way when he reminds himself that he *'cannot be selfish'*: Harriet too understands how Sir Charles, by using a language that is never 'random', has *'checked* and *overcome'* a potentially dishonourable wish.

Similarly, Sir Charles uses his correspondence with Dr Bartlett to check and overcome potential dishonour:

> I found the following questions often occur to me, and to be of the highest service in the conduct of my life – 'What account shall I give of this to Dr Bartlett?' 'How, were I to give way to *this* temptation, shall I report it to Dr Bartlett?' . . . Thus, madam, was Dr Bartlett in the place of a second conscience to me: And many a good thing did I do, many a bad one avoid, for having set up such a monitor over my conduct.
>
> (2.116)

If Dr Bartlett is 'a second conscience' to Sir Charles, Sir Charles also describes how Richardson must imagine a *first* conscience functions by means of language – how conduct is monitored by a verbal 'account' and motivated by words that go to our hearts and tell us what to say to our God.

Like many other eighteenth- and early nineteenth-century authors, Richardson hoped his novels would motivate as well as monitor, or 'enliven as well as instruct' (1.4) – enliven by displaying a variety of characters, and instruct by teaching readers how to assess them. Quoted discourse is central to both these projects. Quoting the discourse of his characters is how Richardson 'enlivens'. But quoted discourse also supports the novel's instruction in how to assess characters, as FID in particular demonstrates: FID implies that contemporary readers, like the characters this fiction depicts, expected, remembered, and recognized quoted and *re*-quoted discourse, *even without attribution*, because they had learned to judge and correct character by means of discourse and thus had a schema into which to assimilate it and thereby remember it.

The absence of attribution in FID not only demonstrates the familiarity and thus the prevalence and importance of quoted discourse in eighteenth- and early nineteenth-century fiction, however. It also has its own significance. Though FID neither identifies given words as quotation nor tells us to whom they should be attributed, it would serve little purpose in these didactic novels could we not, upon consideration, make that identification and attribution. (Again, the eighteenth-century typographic convention of italics signals which words are quotation but leaves us to infer which speaker.) Thus FID points to the language itself, rather than the speaker, to let us, at least momentarily, judge language apart from its speaker. It teaches us, that is, how to judge not *ad hominem* but objectively, by the discourse produced – by the behaviour it constitutes and the beliefs it reflects. On the other hand, by allowing us after consideration to make the correct attribution, FID also teaches us how language characterizes – or, in other words, identifies – its speaker: FID displays language separated from its speaker but demonstrates that language is still a basis for judging and characterizing.

The way characters in eighteenth-century fiction quote and discuss each others' discourse made them models for – if not mirrors of – how contemporary readers could, or did, quote and discuss their own conversations and reading. If actual contemporary conversations are unavailable to us, the way Richardson's characters quote and discuss each others' discourse in their conversations and in their letters, nevertheless mirrors how Richardson himself interacted through letters. And Richardson's letter-writing, in turn, can tell us much about his fictional practice. In an autobiographical letter to his Dutch translator, Johannes Stinstra, Richardson confided, 'From my earliest Youth, I had a Love of Letter-writing.' The earliest letter Richardson mentions was written in an assumed character and intended as moral correction:

> I was not Eleven Years old, when I wrote, spontaneously, a Letter to a Widow of near Fifty, who, pretending to a Zeal for Religion, . . . was continually fomenting Quarrels & Disturbances, by Backbiting & Scandal, among all her Acquaintance. I collected from ye Scripture Texts that made against her. Assuming the Stile and Address of a Person in Years, I exhorted her; I expostulated with her. But my Handwriting was known: I was challenged with it, & owned ye Boldness. . . . My Mother . . . commended my Principles, tho' she censured the Liberty taken.
>
> (*Letters*: 230–1)

Not only did Richardson in this letter 'Assum[e] the Stile and Address of a Person in Years' – that is, the address of a person in authority – but also he 'collected from ye Scripture Texts'. That is, he quoted authoritative, publicly available, widely recognizable moral maxims (so recognizable they may not have needed attribution) to reinforce the authority he 'Assum[ed]', as later he must have hoped his own moral maxims would be remembered, appropriated, and recognized by others. (As I noted, he even extracted and published separately the maxims from *Pamela*, *Clarissa*, and *Grandison*.)

Richardson was equally ready, however, to be 'exhorted' and 'expostulated with' himself by a person in authority. One of few 'Opportunities' for the 'Improvement of my Mind' as a printer's apprentice, Richardson wrote Stinstra, was 'a Correspondence with a Gentleman greatly my superior in Degree, & of ample Fortunes, who, had he lived, intended high things for me': 'He wrote well, [and] was a Master of ye Epistolary Style' (*Letters*: 229). Richardson, who seems to have had a singularly *public* notion of private correspondence, would have been as glad later to appropriate his older friend's actual letters as he was eager to have his own fictional letters appropriated:

> I could from them, had I been at Liberty, & had I at that time thought of writing as I have since done, have drawn great Helps: But many Years ago, all ye Letters that passed between us, by a particular Desire of his (lest they should ever be published) were committed to the Flames.
>
> (*Letters*: 229–30)

This private correspondence *in propria persona* suggests a possible model for Sir Charles's improving correspondence with his 'second conscience', Dr Bartlett. It remained private. But Richardson described to Stinstra other earlier letters that were written in an assumed character and designed for appropriation:

> As a bashful & not forward Boy, I was an early Favourite with all the young Women of Taste & Reading in the Neighbourhood. Half a Dozen of them when met to Work with their Needles, used, when they got a Book they liked, & thought I should, to borrow me to read to them; their Mothers sometimes with them; & both Mothers & Daughters used to be pleased with the Observations they put me upon making. I was not more than Thirteen when three of these young Women, unknown to each other, having an high Opinion of my Taciturnity, revealed to me their Love Secrets, in order to induce me to give them Copies to write after, or correct, for Answers to their Lovers Letters.
>
> (*Letters*: 231)

Stinstra, reading this passage, wondered whether Richardson had modelled his heroines on these young women. No, Richardson replied in a second letter, what 'this opportunity' did more generally was to 'point, as I may say, or lead my inquiries, as I grew up, into the knowledge of the female heart; and knowing something of that, I could not be an utter stranger to that of man' (*Letters*: 297). Richardson may have gained more than a knowledge of the female heart – or even the human heart – from this experience, however. Not surprisingly, given this early willingness to write letters designed to be quoted by others without being attributed to himself, Richardson, as a prosperous 50-year-old printer, agreed to compose a book of model letters 'on the useful concerns in common life' (*Letters*: 41). As he wrote to Stinstra,

> Two Booksellers, my particular Friends, entreated me to write for them, a little Volume of Letters, in a common Style, on such Subjects as might be of Use to those Country Readers who were unable to indite for themselves. Will it be any Harm, said I, in a Piece you want to be written so low, if we should instruct them how they should think & act in common Cases, as well as indite? They were the more urgent with me to begin the little Volume, for this Hint. I set about it, & in the Progress of it, [wrote] two or three Letters to instruct handsome Girls, who were obliged to go out to Service, . . . how to avoid the Snares that might be laid against their Virtue. . . . [H]ence sprung Pamela.
>
> (*Letters*: 232)

Hence sprung not only *Pamela*, of course, but also *Clarissa* and finally *Grandison*, nineteen volumes in all of popular and admired epistolary fiction. Moreover, as Richardson described himself to Stinstra, he was as indefatigable a correspondent in life as in fiction:

> I have been engaged in Epistolary Correspondencies, chiefly with Ladies. I am envied, Sir, for the Favour I stand in with near a Score of very admirable Women, some of them of Condition; all of them such as wd. do Credit to their Sex, & to the Commonwealth of Letters, did not their Modesty with-hold them from appearing in it. Yet with several of them, I have charming Contentions on different Parts of what I have written. Should I ever have the Pleasure to see you in England, I would shew you Volumes of Epistolary Correspondencies.
>
> (*Letters*: 234)

Within four years of writing to Stinstra in 1753, Richardson was hoping his correspondence might be more than a file of letters he could show individual visitors. Negotiations with a German publisher came to nothing over the issue of overcoming the 'Modesty' of his correspondents, but in 1757 Richardson wrote to his principal correspondent Lady Dorothy Bradshaigh that he had been striking out intimate passages from his copies of their letters partly because he wished to leave his correspondence to his family 'for their Instruction

& Delight' (*Letters*: 335) and partly, according to John Carroll, the editor of Richardson's selected letters, because he now expected that 'an edition of his correspondence would be called for after his death':

> Richardson's delicacy in expunging these passages is characteristic, but, just as characteristically, he had previously shown Lady Bradshaigh's letters to a few friends and reaped praise of her charming comments on the novels. The situation is typically Richardsonian; like his exemplary characters, he thought of private letters as sacred property, yet made free with them to select acquaintances.
>
> (*Letters*: 4)

Richardson's attitude is characteristic but not contradictory: private letters should be made public *because* they are sacred – sacred when they open a window on the human heart (to paraphrase a passage from Richardson's letters cited below). In *Clarissa*, the villain Lovelace tells the heroine that writing to a friend 'is writing from the heart (without the fetters prescribed by method or study)' (4.286). Lovelace forgets, however, that, in Richardson's world, letters *produced* 'without . . . study' will be studied by their *recipients* for what they reveal about the heart of the writer. Certainly, Richardson believed, letters in fiction reveal the human heart. He wrote to Sarah Fielding, for example, that he had reread 'with great pleasure' her *Familiar Letters Between the Principal Characters in David Simple* (which her brother Henry, perhaps remembering his rivalry with Richardson, had ungenerously prefaced: 'No one will contend that the epistolary style is in general the most proper to a Novelist; or that it hath been used by the best writers of this Kind' (quoted in *Letters*: 330n.)). '[I] found many new beauties in [it]', Richardson wrote:

> What a knowledge of the human heart! Well might a critical judge of writing say, as he did to me, that your late brother's knowledge of it was not (fine writer as he was) comparable to your's. His was but as the knowledge of the outside of a clock-work machine, while your's was that of all the finer springs and movements of the inside.
>
> (*Letters*: 330)

The views of this 'critical judge of writing' resemble Johnson's comparison of Henry Fielding not with his sister but with Richardson (see *Letters*: 330n.). Richardson believed that private letters may reveal the human heart in reality as well as in fiction. Indeed, he believed, *fictional* letters can reveal the heart of the real *reader* of an epistolary novel. How might this be possible? Not only did Richardson hope the 'charming Contentions' with his correspondents on different aspects of his novels would provide 'Instruction & Delight' to more than his immediate family and intimate friends. He also designed his novels to arouse just such 'charming Contentions' among his wider readership. He wrote of *Grandison*, for example:

> Many things are thrown out in the several Characters, on purpose to provoke friendly Debate; and perhaps as Trials of the Readers Judgment, Manners, Taste, Capacity. I have often sat by in Company, and been silently pleased with the Opportunity given me, by different Arguers, of looking into the Hearts of some of them, through Windows that at other times have been close shut up. This is an Advantage that will always be given by familiar Writing, and by Characters drawn from common Life.
>
> (*Letters*: 315–16)

The 'Advantage' Richardson sees in writing about 'familiar' subjects is that his readers, as this passage implies, can judge and will wish to debate the behaviour of *Grandison*'s true-to-life characters because the situations those characters find themselves in are also largely 'drawn from common Life'. In these debates, readers will open their hearts to each other and reveal, for possible admiration or correction, the principles on which they themselves act in similar situations of 'common Life'. And these principles will in turn be available to the listeners for appropriation or rejection. Thus *Grandison*'s moral lessons will be compounded as the novel is debated by its readers.

Richardson's own voluminous correspondence is rich in moral debates, often debates suggested by his novels. Since we have examined at length how Richardson imagines *Grandison*'s characters debate each other in their letters, and seen how he hoped *Grandison*'s readers would debate its characters in their conversations, it is worth noting, briefly at least, how he managed 'charming Contentions' in his own correspondence. Writing on Richardson's 'Epistolary Theory and Practice' in the introduction to his edition of Richardson's selected letters, John Carroll notes a particular device by which Richardson makes his letters into debates with his correspondents: 'In following his correspondents' leads he often quotes their observations at length before replying to them and thus turns the letters into dialogues' (in *Letters*: 33). These quotations are sometimes explicitly attributed and sometimes *not*, as, for example, when Lady Bradshaigh and Richardson debate learning in women. A brief sample of this debate must suffice (longer excerpts might show Lady Bradshaigh less conservative and Richardson somewhat more so than appears here). Discussion of the forms of quotation in this sample of Richardson's correspondence must be equally brief. According to A. L. Barbauld's arrangement of *The Correspondence of Samuel Richardson* (hereafter *Correspondence*), Lady Bradshaigh opened the debate in a letter of December 1750: 'I own I do not approve of great learning in women. I believe it rarely turns out to their advantage' (*Correspondence*: 6.52). Richardson replied (again according to Barbauld's arrangement of the letters), quoting Lady Bradshaigh without attribution in his first sentence and modulating into his own view in the second:

> DEAR MADAM,
> You do not approve of great learning in women. Learning in women may be either rightly or wrongly placed, according to the uses made of it by them.
>
> (*Correspondence*: 6.57–8)

Lady Bradshaigh was unpersuadable, however: 'I will not approve of learning in women. You, even you, shall not persuade me to it' (*Correspondence*: 6.70). Richardson's reply quotes this and Lady Bradshaigh's earlier letters with varying degrees of attribution:

> Your Ladyship will not 'approve of learning in women'. I cannot help it. But do not you think, Madam, that the woman, who additionally to the advantages she has from nature, 'has been taught to read and converse with ease and propriety'; who can read, spell, and speak English; may not be as justly feared by half the pretty fellows of this age, as if she could read and understand Latin? I do not allow, that, because a man is superficial, a woman must be so too, for fear she should meet with a husband to whom she may have a superior understanding. Do not you remember whose these words are? 'What pity it is that true genius and merit should be veiled under the cloud of inactivity and modesty'. – 'Strange! (adds this favourite of mine) that people will lap up their talents, and hide them.'
> In your Ladyship's, of January 6, you say, 'I hate to hear Latin out of a woman's mouth. . . .' But . . . [a]re there not pedantic men?
>
> (*Correspondence*: 6.78–9; cf. *Letters*: 177)

In the first sentence cited above, Richardson repeats Lady Bradshaigh's words with quotation marks but without conventional tag or inquit: his 'will not "approve . . ."' is what I called, in 1986, a 'double-voiced' verb since Richardson both quotes it from Lady

Bradshaigh's sentence and uses it at the tag or inquit of *his* sentence (note too that he repeats, without shifting, the 'will' that was emphatic in her first-person sentence). Since this sentence, were it *without* quotation marks, would be indistinguishable from FID, we might call it 'FID with quotation marks', which, like FID with italics, identifies which words are quoted but does not identify *whose* words they are. Because of its double-voiced verb, this whole first sentence of Richardson's back-shifts a whole sentence of Lady Bradshaigh's (because of her rank, shifting her 'I' to 'Your Ladyship' in this sentence is more correct than the familiar 'you' of Richardson's earlier 'You do not approve of great learning in women'). Richardson's second sentence does not quote but is, as Bakhtin phrases it, 'oriented toward' Lady Bradshaigh's 'You, even you, shall not persuade me' (Bakhtin 1981: 279). And the last sentence in the first paragraph cited is words-and-phrases FID both with and *without* quotation marks. For example, Richardson quotes with quotation marks (though slightly inaccurately) from Lady Bradshaigh's 'No farther would I have them to advance, than to what would enable them to write and converse with ease and propriety, and make themselves useful in every stage of life' (*Correspondence*: 6.52–3). But later in the same passage Lady Bradshaigh laments that it was earlier 'thought unnecessary for a woman to read, to spell, or speak English' and mentions the 'advantage' that women have 'by nature' over men (*Correspondence*: 6.54): this Richardson repeats without quotation marks.

The first sentence of Richardson's second paragraph paraphrases without attribution part of Lady Bradshaigh's earlier argument, conflating her 'superior' and 'better understanding' (*Correspondence*: 6.53) into his 'superior understanding'. Its third and fourth sentences quote, presumably, an earlier letter from Richardson's 'favourite' correspondent (I have not been able to identify it). Note, however, that in quoting Lady Bradshaigh's own former words against her, Richardson expects her to identify them as her own without more than the hints in his second and fourth sentences. This seems worthy of commenting on as a lesser degree of attribution since, in his next paragraph, Richardson identifies by date even the very recent letter he quotes (see *Correspondence*: 6.53). This variety of forms of quotation and degrees of attribution demonstrates, in other words, that Richardson remembered, and expected his correspondents to remember, the course of their epistolary debates nearly as much as his fictional characters do. (For example, though Richardson presumably copied Lady Bradshaigh's praise of 'true genius and merit' directly from her earlier letter, he had to remember that such a passage existed before he could find it among his 'Volumes of Epistolary Correspondencies'.)

When Richardson reminds Lady Bradshaigh of (in his view) her apparently more admirable earlier views on 'true genius and merit', he implies too that, though dishonourable language should be rejected, admirable language like hers should be remembered and appropriated even without attribution. That is, like 'true genius and merit', admirable language should not 'hide'. Moral sentiments are – or should be – common property, in Richardson's view, just as private letters should be shared when they open 'Windows' into 'Hearts' whose moral beauties can be viewed with 'Advantage' (*Letters*: 315–16, quoted on p. 131, above). I have argued that Richardson himself wanted – and FID in his letters and fiction suggests this – to *invite* this kind of appropriation, appropriation without attribution. If characters in eighteenth-century fiction who quote and discuss each others' discourse become models for – if not mirrors of – how contemporary readers could – or did – quote and discuss their own conversations and reading, then FID also models in fiction how readers, satirically or admiringly, can – and do – reject or appropriate social and literary discourse. The claim by Ann Banfield (1982), for example, that such double-voicedness is impossible, and that FID is impossible outside literature, thus opposes not only common sense and the evidence, for example, of Richardson's private letters, but also a central concern of eighteenth-century didactic fiction. Such a model of narrative verges on suggesting that readers cannot evaluate and appropriate what they read.

FID may thus be central to fictional narrative after all, but in a precisely opposite way. Instead of marking literature off from everyday language as a separate, irreconcilable discourse, FID's double voice shows how the language of real life and fiction can merge, how literature may indeed – as Richardson intended – 'go to [the] heart[s]' and inform the thoughts of its readers. FID as used by *Grandison*'s characters testifies to the attention one character pays to another: how flattering to Richardson's heroes and heroines that their words have gone to their friends' hearts and are so well remembered and correctly quoted. If Richardson succeeded – as he seems to have with Jane Austen and many generations of readers – in making *Grandison* so well attended, remembered, and quoted, small wonder that its influence on the eighteenth- and nineteenth-century novel – including its contribution to FID's subsequent widespread use – is greater than its current readership reflects. But FID in *Grandison* does more than show how the language of real life and fiction can merge, or how the language of one author of fiction can influence the language of subsequent authors. FID in *Grandison* suggests that FID may be central to more than fictional narrative: as Bakhtin's theory suggests, its double-voicedness serves as a model for how we assimilate or reject one another's real-life discourse as well as literary discourse. If we now believe that human subjects are created by the discourse of their culture, eighteenth-century writers like Richardson believed that human subjects can and should participate *consciously* in their own creation through the kind of discourse they choose to appropriate. FID shows how that participation might occur.

Editor's preface

Norman Macleod's essay shows, with exemplary attention to the detail of linguistic interpretation, how sentences about Stephen Blackpool at the close of a chapter from *Hard Times* contradict the sentimental closure they, on first reading, appear to supply. In this way one narratorial voice – bland, reconciliatory – is recognized on fuller acquaintance to be an illusion that cannot mask the unignorable contrasting message, of the good Christian Stephen's revulsion and alienation from his wife. Macleod's second example of sophisticated narratorial strategy concerns the faltering incremental process of recognition (in the fullest sense of that term) of Joe Gargery as his guardian angel and healing spirit, by a fever-ridden Pip in *Great Expectations*. Finally the essay isolates the textual means by which the eponymous narrator of *David Copperfield* adopts, at the very outset of the book, the vantage point of the reader in relation to his own yet-to-be-unfolded life-story. The implication is that the book is written so that David can make sense of his life *to himself*, and secondarily so that he can make sense of it to us, the work's 'second' readers. A strength of the essay is its combination of elements of systemic linguistic description (as in chapter 3, by Francis and Kramer-Dahl) with eclectic use of insights on grammar and semantics from other contemporary linguistic traditions.

In all three discoursal 'moments' explored, the reader encounters a passage and a narrated situation which we expect to be transparent, even formulaic – preset or preconditioned by generic expectations about (in the first scene) marital reconciliation, or (in the third) uncomplicated self-disclosure. But in actuality each passage turns out to be artfully removed from the formulaic, more complex, more arresting, more suggestive of unreconciled contradictions, uncertainties, oppositions, than the experiencing reader might have first thought possible: can the good Christian, Stephen, really view his wife with such murderous loathing as this closer reading suggests? – one wouldn't at first have dreamt it.

In all three cases, real but neglected grammatical effects, among the most difficult even for native speakers to isolate and describe, are demonstrated to be at work. For many years now it has been commonplace to assert that any native speaker has full command of that native language. There are ways in which this must be correct, but one consequence of such thinking has been great resistance to subtle grammatical discriminations (particularly when asserted of specific texts, rather than on some abstract theoretical plane) unless those discriminations can be readily verified by the person in the street. (In which case, clearly, the discrimination is not so terribly subtle.) Essays such as Macleod's are, as it were, unfashionably discriminative in their interest in the communicative effects of even the slightest grammatical changes – an interest which is as vital as it is unfashionable, for without it no major advances in our understanding of the details of text production and processing are possible.

6 Lexicogrammar and the reader

Three examples from Dickens

Norman Macleod

In this chapter I want to discuss three intriguing examples of the language of Charles Dickens, about each of which the same interrelated set of claims can be made. First of all, these examples – one each from *Hard Times* (1854), *Great Expectations* (1860–1), and *David Copperfield* (1849–50) – involve the reader in being very keenly conscious of his or her experience while reading. All three involve the reader in becoming aware of having to make some kind of readjustment of understanding while reading, with this recognition being centrally significant for how the reader finally understands (and appreciates) the piece involved. The reader's unsettled experience (whether it consists of being disconcerted progressively, or of being kept in a prolonged state of uncertainty, or of being forced drastically to readjust or cancel expectations) becomes a principal means of recognizing meanings and effects associated with the text. Finally, and very significantly, the reader's accommodating experience can be shown, in all three cases, to be involved with – in a very clear sense, to be about – the processing of subtle lexicogrammatical arrangements.

My overall purpose in the analyses that follow is to show that, from the point of view of stylistics, a reader's engagement need not be a passive one with a text that is static and determinately singular; but that this engagement is not either one that is free from what the text has to offer. The central claim is for the relevance of the reader's processing of text, the particular illustration provided by these Dickensian examples being of cases whose complete appreciation depends on one's becoming aware of one's processing role as one engages in it.

I

The first example comes from *Hard Times*, Book the First, Chapter Ten, in a closing scene which shows Stephen Blackpool, returning home late at night just after parting from Rachael outside, to find that his estranged, drunken, and pitiful wife has returned. They exchange hostile words, his wife demands that Stephen give her his bed for the night, and Stephen yields, moving away from the bed as she approaches. There then comes the following chapter-closing paragraph (where, to begin with, our interest will be taken up with the final two sentences):

> As she staggered to it, he avoided her with a shudder, and passed – his face still hidden – to the opposite end of the room. She threw herself upon the bed heavily, and soon was snoring hard. He sunk into a chair, and moved but once all that night. It was to throw a covering over her; as if his hands were not enough to hide her, even in the darkness.[1]

A very curious feature of the last two sentences of this very brief extract is that, even in that very limited compass, at almost every stage we encounter a conflict between what the text goes on to say and what we think the text has just fundamentally conveyed, so that at every point at which we reach a 'completed' stage or discursive 'move' we find that we have to alter – fundamentally and diametrically – the 'picture' of what the text has said, and on which we assumed we could rely as we set out to read and 'take in' the later stage that we have just been negotiating. At every stance-taking stage of the above brief sequence of discourse 'moves' – that is, between the separately punctuated clauses of the first sentence of the pair, then between the two sentences, then at the semi-colon which firmly separates the two halves of the second sentence, after that at the comma which separates the final phrase from all that has preceded, and finally at the end of the sentence – at every one of these points, our interpretative certainty (based on what we have so far taken in) is countermanded by a need fundamentally to revise and reinterpret (based on what we have now latterly taken in). Each successive statement, and the sense and implications conveyed by each of them, is shown in a new light by what is revealed in the immediately following statement. Natural implications or entailments accompanying what is asserted by a particular statement are cancelled or contradicted by what is asserted in the next expression. Overall, accompanying what appear to be the main, informative meanings conveyed at the most overt textual surface, there is, as well, something of a sub-text existing as an opposed set of meanings conveyed by less prominent or covert connections between the superficially straightforward remarks.

We can begin by considering the second clause of the first sentence – *[he] moved but once all that night* (we will advisedly leave the opening clause *He sunk into a chair* for consideration in the light of our discussion of the rest of the sentence: suffice it to say here that typically that opening clause will be read as indicating or suggesting that Stephen is overcome, overwhelmed, by profound tiredness, leading to his being instantly asleep – all this constituting an interpretative presumption that affects our predisposed understanding of *[he] moved but once all that night*).

Syntactically, in *[he] moved but once all that night*, the verb *moved* occurs intransitively with a subject *he* referring to a human (and therefore sentient and intelligent) being. In such a construction, we may be uncertain about what exactly is being said. What is being described may be one or another type of involvement – either an action or an event – depending on how we see the entity (here, a human being) that is named by the subject being involved in the process described by the verb (the discussions of transitivity here, and relational processes below, draw on the systemic-functional grammar presented in Halliday 1985). The whole description may be one where the subject of the verb relates to the process mentioned by the verb only as the affected participant *or* alternatively as a participant that fulfils both the roles of the entity that causes and the entity that is affected by that process. (In a transitive structure, as we shall see, these roles would be differently associated with the separate syntactic functions of subject and object: where a structure is intransitive, as here, both roles may be – but need not be – associated with the subject: in English, whenever only one role is associated with the subject of an intransitive clause, that role is always the one of affected participant, not the causal participant). An instance of an intransitive use of *moved* where the human subject is both causer and affected would be a sentence like

John moved in order to avoid the approaching car,

or

The bull charged and just at the last moment – deftly and nonchalantly – John moved out of the way,

or one like

John moved, smartly and just enough and without wasting a second, and easily got out of the way of the on-rushing truck.

In such sentences, *moved* is equivalent in sense to 'he moved himself', but is not equivalent syntactically to *moved* in the form *he moved himself*. A reflexive expression is transitive syntactically, and in the cases above *moved* (which has no reflexive, or other kind of, object) is intransitive. The meaning of the references to John moving in the constructed instances above is of 'John bestirring himself', equating with the idea that, in the intransitive construct *John moved*, *John* is both causer and affected in relation to the process of moving. In such usages, *move* describes an action that is brought about by a specifiable and intelligent causer and that is centred on that same entity: the entity affected is the entity causing.

But the verb *move* can also describe a virtually self-engendered event, where the subject of the verb, again intransitive, relates to the process described by the verb as a participant only in the role of the entity affected by the process. This is the basic sense (except in fairy stories, science-fiction stories, or fantasies of animation, and the like) of a sentence like *The stone moved*. But this kind of event-descriptive, syntactically intransitive use of *moved* can also be found where the subject refers to a human (and/or sentient or intelligent) being. In such a form, *He moved* or *John moved*, what we have is a description of reflex or instinctive or unmotivated action, for which no specifiable causer can be identified. This sense of *moved*, where the general meaning of the verb is 'be affected by movement', is the one found in

John moved restlessly in his sleep,

or in

Lying there, sick as a dog, John moved every time the boat rolled,

or in

John moved, slightly, just once, only a twitch, but that was enough to show the doctors he was alive.

In these cases, *John moved* can be glossed (a little unsatisfactorily) as equivalent to 'Moving happened to John'.

It is surely in the latter sense that we at first take *moved* in the conjoined clause that completes the penultimate sentence of the extract from *Hard Times* – *and* [sc. *he*] *moved but once all that night*. Our reading of the whole sentence takes in the sense of its two constituent clauses separately and in sequence, the reading of the first affecting how we set about reading the second. *He sunk into a chair*, descriptive of behaviour evincing extreme tiredness and betokening imminent sleep, leaves us with a picture of an exhausted

Stephen falling instantly asleep, and that leads us to read *and moved but once all that night* as reporting that his sleep was so deep and total that it was marked by the usual instinctive and jactitatory movement only once during the night. At the end of the first sentence, we have a clear view of Stephen, utterly tired, instantly and deeply asleep, lying virtually motionless – sleeping 'like a log'.

But this reading, this consoling view of Stephen, is countermanded – indeed, cancelled – by the first clause of the following sentence. Previously lulled into acceptance of a particular, seemingly certain, reading, we are now – unlike Stephen – shaken rudely awake by what we read: *It was to throw a covering over her*. There are various ambiguities or uncertainties here, as we shall see, but at this stage – very much prompted by the topicalizing cleft-structure *It was to throw a covering over her* – we are strongly drawn to see this new sentence as explaining an earlier action by now specifying or supplying the purpose behind that earlier action. The best way to construe *It was to throw a covering over her* is as the significant remnant of the contextually reduced cleft sentence *It was to throw a covering over her* [sc. *that he moved*], and as explaining or clarifying the previously unstated reason for his having moved. But as well as clearing up the reason for his movement, *It was to throw a covering over her* clarifies something else that was, before this, not recognized as being uncertain – the nature of his movement. *It was to throw a covering over her* clarifies his earlier movement by specifying a purpose he had in mind in moving – a new factor which forces us to regard his earlier movement (in *and moved but once all that night*) as something he did and not something that happened to him, that is, as an action not an event, and as a purposeful and intentional action at that.

The contextualizing framework that we have previously constructed needs to be radically altered, changing our interpretation of the earlier *he moved* from what we securely took it to mean (*he [affected] moved [instinctively]*) to the previously unconsidered alternative (*he [causer and affected] moved [intentionally]*). We now read the passage with an even more positive and consoling sense of Stephen, reading what we are told about him as a description of considerate, even vestigially loving, action, where Stephen gets up to cover and protect his wife.

We read on: and again what we move to, approached with a seemingly settled conception of how the text has so far developed, turns out to be something of which the meaning is quite contrary to our expectations, and the assimilation to the framework by which we proceed demands that we also reconstruct already-established fundamental elements of that framework. As we move from the clause

It was to throw a covering over her, which we have already taken as unambiguously indicating that Stephen has wished to protect his wife and has done something positive towards that end, we come to the next clause, *as if his hands were not enough to hide her*. This clause is a clause of comparison which – being introduced by the subordinator *as if* – establishes the comparison that it expresses on the basis of an assumption that we have already understood the particular factor in the preceding statement which this comparison connects up with – that she is already sufficiently hidden from him without his having *to throw a covering over her*, and that his motive in moving *to throw a covering over her* was not a generous and loving one of protection but, instead, something much less noble.

This shift of interpretation is made apparent – indeed, is compelled – only when we move on from the clause *It was to throw a covering over her* (certain that it indicates a protective act on Stephen's part) and try to relate that settled interpretation to the following comparative clause, *as if his hands were not enough to hide her*. But the earlier settled meaning and the strongest implication of this later clause cannot be correlated. The later clause assumes that an earlier purpose of concealment rather than protection is to be associated with the interpretation of *It was to throw a covering over her*, forcing us to realize that this clause not only can mean something different from what we took it to mean but also that this newly introduced meaning is the only one the clause can possibly have in this particular sequence. We arrive at a picture – stark, not consoling – of Stephen, throwing something over his wife to hide her from his sight, then sitting melodramatically averting his sight behind his upraised hands. We no longer can have it, as seemed to be indicated earlier, that Stephen is overwhelmingly asleep, nor even that – being awake – he moves protectively to place a covering over his wife. Now our understanding is quite the opposite from what we initially thought. Stephen is not asleep, nor positive and conciliatory, but starkly awake, vigilantly repelled in his wife's presence.

Even the very last phrase of the closing sentence alters the perspective of understanding we have developed from our reading of everything that has preceded. The qualifying and amplifying tag, *even in the darkness*, now countermands what has been implied in the preceding clause *as if his hands were not enough to hide her* – namely, that Stephen hides his wife from his own sight because he feels a physical sense of revulsion or disgust at her appearance. The tag *even in the darkness* seems to exclude the possibility that Stephen can see his wife, and moves our sense of his revulsion from a physical to a moral level. Important in the structure of *even in the darkness* is the adverb *even*. *Even* is one of those words (*especially* is another) which serve to connect part of an utterance – the part made prominent by the use of the *even* – to some other part of an utterance the meaning of which provides a background against which the prominent or focused-on part of the utterance is asserted and made explicit. Asserting something is normally concerned with making explicit something that is not obvious, given, or taken as read, or that has not already been made explicit or been conveyed by an earlier assertion. An adverb like *even* makes emphatically explicit something that is asserted in connection with something expressed earlier, by indicating that what *even* makes prominent is surprisingly and additionally part of what needs to be said. *Even* assimilates what has gone before to a new standard of explicitness and accuracy, telling us that what has gone before, while true, was not fully explicit, and is also true – is *especially* and particularly true – with the explicit additional detail made prominent after *even*.

The additional tag *even in the darkness* tells us that Stephen's covering of his eyes with his hands could not be an action indicating physical revulsion or simply intended to keep his wife from his sight. We have to take that action of Stephen's as a sign of moral rejection: it is some deeper horror than just the sight of her that Stephen expresses with his upraised hands. Once again, our view of Stephen has to be altered: we see him now awake, horrified, his stance melodramatically expressing moral revulsion.

At every interpretative stage in this brief sequence impressions conveyed firmly at one stage have had to be revised at the very next stage. The one stage I have not at all considered yet – the opening clause of the first sentence, *He sunk into a chair* – also fits with this pattern. I have postponed consideration of this opening stage until now since this clause involves a series of revealing revisions made by Dickens whose significance becomes clearest once we see them in terms of the general quality I have argued for in the rest of the sequence. It has been necessary to look at the whole of the rest of this sequence to establish a clear picture of that quality before considering the opening clause.

The now-accepted form of the clause, *He sunk into a chair*, was not the only form considered by Dickens. *He sunk into a chair* was the last form essayed by Dickens in the text of *Hard Times* published as a serial in Dickens's own weekly magazine, *Household Words*, between April and August 1854. But before that, Dickens had considered two slight, but nevertheless significant, variants. His original manuscript form was *He sunk over a chair*, which became *He sunk in a chair* on surviving corrected proofs, this latter presumably being altered again, at some additional stage of proof correction, to appear as the serial (and now textually standard) form *He sunk into a chair*. Dickens's revisions, and the search for accuracy behind them, are very particular, each time replacing one preposition with another, *over* giving way to *in* and that yielding to *into*. Either Dickens is being very pernickety, wastefully engaging in costly changes, or there is some artistic and/or expressive purpose which is not being fulfilled to his perfect satisfaction. It may be some kind of pedantry, to do with what was most idiomatic or most normal. In present-day English (where we standardly have *sank* rather than *sunk* as the past tense form of the vocalic verb *sink*), all three expressions – *sank over*, *sank in*, *sank into* – are possible in the frame *He [verb] [prep] a chair*: the only distinction seems to be that *sank into* is the most frequently encountered of the three. But there may be a deeper, and more interesting, linguistic reason for Dickens's second, and third, thoughts here.

There is an important semantic difference between Dickens's first two rejected efforts and the apparently final, and acceptable, third form. The prepositions *in* and *over* express an idea of location; and in some way additionally indicate disposition at that location – so that *in* locates a thing in relation to another in which it is included or confined, and *over* expresses a body's location in relation to something above or across which it is placed. But *into*, as well as expressing location and locative disposition, also indicates direction: neither *in* nor *over* makes a directional element explicit.

The presence of a directional, as well as a locative, element in the semantics of *into* means that a preceding verb can be seen as describing a process as directed and deliberate. This means, in turn, that – accompanied by a human subject *He* – a verb phrase like *sunk into a chair* (where the central verb – *sink* – has a basic motional meaning of downward change of location) will have available an agentive or purposive sense, and an alternative sense of accidental occurrence. In other words, in *He sunk into a chair*, where the nominal *a chair* identifies the participant range (identifying the circumstantial range or scope of the process specified by the verb *sink into*), the subject nominal *He* may either be the affected participant solely, or may be both causer and affected: *sunk into* is thus a verb like *move*. The alternative verb and preposition choices Dickens considered here lack this ambivalence, showing that a good deal depends on the preposition finally settled on.

When Dickens says of Stephen *He sunk into a chair*, he uses an expression capable of being interpreted as describing a process in which the subject of the verb is involved only as an affected participant or one where the subject is identified as both causer and affected in the process described. This ambiguity means that the clause *He sunk into a chair* can have a sense fitting with either interpretation of the following conjoined clause *and moved but once all that night*. *[He] moved but once all that night* can also be read in one of two ways, as we recall: taking the subject of the verb only as the affected participant or as both the causer and affected. Taking the whole sequence *He sunk into a chair and moved but once all that night*, and putting together congruent interpretations of both its clauses, we are led to two diametrically opposed presentations: one (perhaps more obvious, and the one we first take in – superficially – before going on to read further) where Stephen is overcome by tiredness, and just drops, being overcome by total and utterly undisturbed sleep; and another reading (brought to the fore as we read further, and allowed for by semantic–syntactic aspects of both clauses) where Stephen melodramatically acts out the overcome victim he seems to be, but does not really sleep, and indeed at one stage gets up to throw a covering over his wife, apparently protectively, but that too is to be countermanded as we read on.

I have devoted some considerable space to my analysis of this brief but intriguing illustration from Dickens's text. An important question, hovering around all the above discussion, which needs to be considered is the question of the function, in terms of stylistic or other effects, such linguistic arrangements have. This final matter needs to be considered, not only to round out all of our argument above, but indeed, as the main point deriving from all that has been argued for so far. Without being associated with some literary or communicative function, the various linguistic arrangements noted above could be dismissed as distractions – 'noisy' linguistic features, perhaps arising from inattentive formulation, but having nothing designedly to do with whatever uncontroversial content the language *does* convey.

It is worth noting how markedly melodramatic is the language of the paragraph from *Hard Times*. Indeed, the first two or three sentences read like melodramatic stage directions, simply assimilated to the past tense and recast as narrative. This melodramatic language registers the demeanour and behaviour of the characters in terms of simplified gestures expressing crude emotional reactions. Everything is presented starkly: the wife's shambolic and drunken state, and Stephen's horrified revulsion, are both described in the language of hackneyed, overdone mime – creating a mechanical, gestural realism, and making the characters ciphers in a tawdry, suspenseful *vignette*. But additionally, in the closing two sentences (the end of the chapter, and a suitable location for a melodramatic 'happy ending'), the extract becomes more complicated. At first, in keeping with what has gone before, we read the sentence *He sunk into a chair, and moved but once all that night* as simplistically of a piece with the conventions of the scene so far unfolded. Only (we inevitably take it) when the sound of his wife's snoring tells Stephen that she is harmlessly asleep does he give way to deep tiredness and despair, dropping down where he stands and soon being so deeply asleep that he hardly moves. That reading is then utterly upset by the next clause: rather than being asleep Stephen is starkly awake – even at one stage moves to protect his wife. But that, too, is then not the case: what he is doing is hiding her, not simply to get her out of his sight, but even (it at last seems) to get her out of his mind, so complete is his moral revulsion.

The prose now incorporates two diametrically opposed impulses – one which insistently presents the uncompromising reality of Stephen's position, as he spends the dark night in wakeful hatred; and one which offers a sentimental note of human reconciliation, not a 'happy ending' perhaps, but one which answers to pressures and expectations of convention and any reader's human wishes. The first of these insists on the truth of Stephen's alienation, a truth that exceeds any melodramatic convention, and makes its insistence against the tug of a false, but sentimentally satisfying, literary closure. By raising only to diminish our readerly sense of a consoling ending, the narrative of *Hard Times* doubly emphasizes its own sense of an appropriate uncompromising conclusion. Fundamental to this effect are the two competing voicings that come together appropriately in the single syntactic sequence of the quoted paragraph – appropriately, since *Hard Times* is a fiction whose narrative is characterized by qualities of intersubjectivity and multi- or poly-vocality. In this instance, hard-nosed narrative realism drowns and silences the voicing of the reader's easier and more sentimental resolution.

II

The next example involves a short paragraph from *Great Expectations*, which comes at the point (in Chapter 57) where Pip, recovering from delirium and fever, slowly realizes that now he is not hallucinating or imagining things, and that it *is* trusty, reliable, faithful Joe Gargery that he sees sitting by his bedside. The preceding paragraph, describing Pip's nightmare of delirium as he undergoes (and begins to recover from) the standard Dickensian ordeal by fever, has concluded with Pip's making out that people seemed to be there tending him while he was ill, and further that these people – no matter how maniacally transformed by Pip's fevered perception – showed a tendency sooner or later to settle down into the likeness of Joe. There then follows immediately this brief paragraph of further narrative (sentences have been numbered for later convenient reference):

> (1) After I had turned the worst point of my illness, I began to notice that while all its other features changed, this one consistent feature did not change. (2) Whoever came about me, still settled down into Joe. (3) I opened my eyes in the night, and I saw in the great chair at the bedside, Joe. (4) I opened my eyes in the day, and sitting on the window-seat, smoking his pipe in the shaded open window, still I saw Joe. (5) I asked for cooling drink, and the dear hand that gave it me was Joe's. (6) I sank back on my pillow after drinking, and the face that looked so hopefully and tenderly on me was the face of Joe.[2]

This passage has already been commented on in interesting terms by Garrett Stewart (although I had formed my own view of it before reading his discussion). Stewart (1975: 400) observes that after Pip's feverish confrontation with a series of nearly unidentifiable selves and hallucinated assailants, the prose turns serenely to a gradual recognition of Joe. For Stewart, central to this 'gradual recognition' is the rhetorically most prominent feature of the paragraph – that, of its six sentences, the closing five sentences all close down unwaveringly on the word 'Joe', an observation Stewart goes on to develop:

> Five times repeated this profound noun – which almost seems to have a linguistic value of its own as a homely unit of native diction – provides all the held focus toward which the other words themselves and the impressions they set down have wavered, narrowed, and telescoped. Over and over the scene resolves, syntactically as well as optically, into the image of Joe, the one certain identity reclaimed from the mania of Pip's fever.
>
> (Stewart 1975: 400)

Stewart's attention is given to the prominently repeated noun *Joe*, a rhetorical feature of the paragraph that can neither be missed nor ignored. But that noun has not only a uniform substantial function (by being repeatedly – five times over – the final word of a sequence of sentences): it also has a variable formal role, shown by the fact that *Joe*, in its five occurrences, occupies, each time, a different syntactic position in the structure of the sentences of which it is a part. Thus, the noun *Joe* is variously, one after the other, part of the indirect object as the complement of a preposition (*into Joe* – sentence (2)); the right-dislocated direct object of the verb *see* (*I saw . . . Joe* – (3)); again the object of *see* but this time positioned immediately after the governing verb, and now with an emphasizing and insistent adverb (*still I saw Joe* – (4)); the dependent possessive modifier of a head noun, *hand*, deleted under lexical identity with an earlier occurrence (*the dear hand . . . was Joe's* – (5)); and finally the head noun of a prepositional phrase embedded as qualifier within a larger noun phrase whose structure – involving post-head elements – does not this time permit deletion of the lexically repeated head noun (*the face that . . . was the face of Joe* – (6)).

The lexicogrammatical variety of the sentential relationships involving the noun *Joe* is as interesting as the rhetorical uniformity of its repeated, sentence-end placings. Alongside the material fact of the repeated position of the word *Joe* there must also be taken into account the formal variety of syntactic relations it enters into: so that it becomes necessary to pay attention to *Joe* not only 'vertically', as it were, as it turns up, from one sentence to the next, in final position, but also 'horizontally', in terms of how it relates to the structure of each sentence of which it is a part. Attending to *Joe* in this bifocal way is necessary if we are fully to appreciate the effects achieved by Dickens in this paragraph, since the rhetorical and grammatical roles of *Joe* are the complementary means by which Dickens involves the reader in sharing Pip's dawning awareness of the real bedside presence of Joe Gargery. The whole complex arrangement of this crucial paragraph serves to involve the reader in a state of uncertainty that reaches only a very late clarification, over the question of whether Joe was there or not, with each stage involving the inescapable but tantalizingly unconfirmed observation of Joe being there and with each succeeding stage marking a greater, emergent clarity in the growing but incomplete assurance that Joe was there. The reader's experience in this paragraph is not simply one of, as Stewart puts it (1975: 401), 'Over and over the scene resolv[ing], syntactically as well as optically, into the image of Joe, the one certain identity reclaimed from the mania of Pip's fever.' This is to give too much attention to the rhetorical emphasis upon *Joe* at the end of each sentence, as well as confusing rhetorical contrivance with syntactic structure. It is not Pip's experience that he is, all the time, certain that Joe is there, and that, periodically, hallucination clarifies into momentary but secure optical certainty. Instead, the whole burden of Pip's experience (and the experience shared by the reader) is of a consistent or continuous uncertainty over whether what he sees is what is to be seen, and over whether what he recurrently and periodically makes out – 'the likeness of Joe' as he puts it at the end of the earlier paragraph – is or is not Joe. This is the 'one consistent feature [that] did not change' – that he kept seeing Joe but could not ever be sure that it was Joe, from one instance to the next. The paragraph proceeds with a step-by-step increase in the likely certainty that Joe is there, but does not confirm this until near the very end. Reading the superficial rhetoric alone, then, Joe's definite presence is recurrently established: but attending both to the syntactic relations of *Joe*, as well as to its rhetorical positioning, all that is allowed is the strong and always strengthening possibility that Joe is there, without that being confirmed until near the very end.

There are various lexicogrammatical means by which Dickens shapes the reader's continuing (but lessening) uncertainty, and final acceptance, that Joe is indeed there. Sentence (2), whose very thesis is that people either became or were Joe, makes its point by doing without any clarifying factive (*I realized that . . .*) or non-factive (*I imagined that . . .*) cognitive frame. Without a cognitive or perceptual main clause, there is no security as to which participant, Identified (*Whoever came about me*) or Identifying (*Joe*), carries the role of Token and which the role of Value. As the sentence *the best students are the greatest worriers* is ambiguous as to which of the two qualities specified of the same group is being assumed and which asserted, so Pip's sentence, *Whoever came about me still settled down into Joe*, giving a name and a characterization to the same individual, remains ambiguous as to whether it is the individual as characterized, or the individual identified by name, that provides the certain point of reference to which the sentence's report of transformation – clarifying or deluding? – is attached. There is a Token-to-Value reading – 'Whoever (at all) came turned into "Joe"', and a Value-to-Token reading – 'Whoever (unrecognized) came turned out to be Joe', and they continually overlap, neither permanently to the fore.

Pip's succeeding sentences, except the last one, maintain this duality, keeping the reader guessing over whether Joe is there or not. Sentences (3) and (4) offer essentially the same clause *I saw Joe*, differently structured in terms of circumstantial accompaniments but each time conjoined to a preceding clause, descriptive of the preparatory action *I opened my eyes*. With various accompaniments, sentences (3) and (4) each effectively says *I opened my eyes and I saw Joe*. ((4) simply says it more emphatically than (3), and more certainly, giving a contiguous unity to subject, verb, and object, prefaced with the insistent adverb *still*.) The question is why, then, does the reader not straightforwardly take the second clause without hesitation as a true report of Joe's actual visibility? The key is in the verb phrase of the second clause *I saw Joe*, and in its simple, unmodalized character. Verbs of perception that are not accompanied by a modal seem to permit a possible interpretation whereby the reported perception may arise without an empirical correlate, whereas modalized forms seem not to prompt this additional ambivalence and to be involved simply in reporting a perception that arises from a real external stimulus. *I hear music* is somehow more subjective than *I can hear music*. Depending on the setting, and the predisposition it suggests, modalized and non-modalized forms are variably suitable:

Whenever I open that window, I can hear shouting from next door. (The simple *I hear shouting* is also possible with the same sense.)

But then compare:

Whenever I drink Laphroaig, I hear Old Pollóchan telling his stories again. (The modal form would not here suit the intended fanciful meaning.)

I saw Joe allows an ambivalence that *I could see Joe* would not have promoted. Furthermore, this is additionally supported by the co-ordinative link established between the preparatory and perceptual acts of *I opened my eyes . . . and I saw Joe*, and by the temporally separated reiteration of that report (*in the night*, and then *in the day*). A single, subordinating summary (*Whenever I opened my eyes, I saw Joe*) would have reduced the effect of ambivalence allowed by the two occurrences of the non-modalized *saw*. The effective reiteration of *I opened my eyes . . . and I saw Joe* gives and takes away – insisting on what it claims, but allowing what it claims to be seen ambivalently.

Sentences (5) and (6) differ crucially from what has gone before, since the evidence of Joe's presence is no longer tantalizingly and simply visual, but seems to become tangibly physical as well. Pip's request for a drink (5) leads to his drinking (6) and in between – *the dear hand that gave it me was Joe's* – an actual drink seems to be provided. 'Seems' is advisable, since for all the pressure of that physical detail and of the implication of a real object exchanged between real people, sentence (5) remarkably continues to maintain at least a degree of the ambivalence of meaning that has prevailed beforehand. Even taking due account of what (5) does say, there continues to cling still the possibility that Pip was deluded – and that the proffered hand and drinking vessel were still cruelly unreal. Only with sentence (6), and then suddenly and emphatically, does the reality of Joe's presence seem to be established. It is not that (6) completes a process of clarification begun in (5). For all that their contents are related (indeed, that the same complex content – of asking for, being given, and taking drink – is distributed between (5) and (6)), these two sentences are quite different in effect, in meaning, and – in one crucial respect – formally, so that in these terms (5) is more akin to the sentences that precede it than to the sentence following it. Indeed, the movement between (5) and (6) represents a decisive and dramatic break from the ambivalence of the whole of the rest of the paragraph and the clear meaning – and the literal sense of a real Joe – finally and singly established in (6).

The difference between (5) and (6) rests, again, on significant lexicogrammatical subtlety. It has been observed on several occasions that the repetition of lexical and/or grammatical (= proformal) material within a sentence can involve making that sentence differ in meaning from a counterpart where potentially repeatable material has been optionally deleted as identical with the earlier occurrence. Thus, sentences like

John is taller than Wilt 'the Stilt' Chamberlain

and

John is richer than Rockefeller

have been observed to differ in meaning – since they involve only fanciful or figurative comparison for emphatic effect – from more explicit counterparts such as

John is taller than Wilt 'the Stilt' is (tall)

and

John is richer than Rockefeller was (rich)

which more clearly indicate a true comparison involving actual measurement or assessment (see also Morgan 1975). Greater explicitness, even involving lexical (or other) repetition, seems to prompt a sense of greater literalness. This is certainly the case with the following pair:

Whichever book I picked up turned out to be Joe's.
Whichever book I picked up turned out to be Joe's book.

Suppose that I have gone round to see my friend Joe, intending to retrieve from him various books of mine that I claim he has borrowed from me and failed to return, and further suppose that afterwards, back from confronting Joe, I explain to you what happened. Imagine also that there are two possible outcomes to the encounter with Joe, both leaving me bookless but for different reasons: one where the books on Joe's shelves that I claim are mine all turn out to have old signatures of his on the fly-leaf, to be embossed with the labels of bookshops I have never heard of, and to carry all sorts of other indications leading to my friendly but disconcerted recognition that the books do truly belong to Joe; and another situation where I frustratedly claim to recognize my books, even though they bear no signs of anyone's ownership, but cannot convince an intransigently counter-claiming Joe, who (until I leave, angry and empty-handed) goes on insisting that the books I want to have all belong to him. Whichever of these frustrations eventuates for me, imagine that, later that evening, I tell you – either in tones of nonplussed resignation or ironically sneering exasperation – of my encounter with Joe, and that I choose succinctly to express the essence of that unsatisfactory stand-off either by saying *Whichever book I picked up turned out to be Joe's*, or by saying – not simply for the sake of insistence, but also as a way of stating a different view of things – *Whichever book I picked up turned out to be Joe's book*. Which of these two forms will fit better with the circumstances of the first situation outlined above, and which with those of the second?

The answer seems to me to be very clear. While the form *not* involving repetition could fit both situations (with a very slight possibility of it being more suitable to the second), the form which involves repetition of *book* seems very much better suited to reporting the first situation, and to be suited hardly – if at all – to the second. It is noteworthy that the conclusion of Pip's sentence (5) . . . *and the dear hand that gave it me was Joe's* has a form, whatever the contextual pressures, that accords with the reader still seeing it as uncertain that Joe is there. Only with the closing sentence (6), and its significantly different, *repetitive*, form, . . . *and the face that looked so hopefully and tenderly upon me was the face of Joe*, does the reader's sense of ambivalence finally disappear, giving way to the excited and heart-warming realization that what was sentimentally true was also actually true – that Joe Gargery was there. Even though Pip may have difficulty admitting it, we always knew Joe would be there, and now at last it says so unequivocally.

There is a final point, relating to the forms of (5) and (6). The whole quality of the paragraph – and especially the effectiveness of its climax – would have been spoilt if Dickens, in writing the closing sentences, had made different choices from those he did make. Change the endings of sentences (5) and (6), from (5) . . . *Joe's* to . . . *Joe's hand*, and from (6) . . . *the face of Joe* to . . . *Joe's*, and the whole quality of the original goes, showing that the difference between elliptical (5) and repetitive (6) may be centrally significant to the effects that are registered by the reader.

III

The third example involves the opening paragraph of Chapter I of *David Copperfield*:

I am Born

Whether I shall turn out to be the hero of my own life, or whether that station will be held by anyone else, these pages must show. To begin my life with the beginning of my life, I record that I was born (as I have been informed and believe) on a Friday, at twelve o'clock at night. It was remarked that the clock began to strike, and I began to cry, simultaneously.[3]

The preliminaries of *David Copperfield* foreshadow the cancellation of the normal bookish regularities, first in the bracketed addendum of the title identifying this 'Personal History' of the author as one 'Which He never meant to be Published on any Account', and then in the merging of the actual and the textual in the opening chapter title – 'I am Born'. This unique present-tense form of *be born* (vestigially an incidental chapter summary – 'In which I am born' – rather than a straightforward title) is more in keeping with a reader's, rather than a writer's, sense of the opening incident of the book. But in all sorts of ways this chapter opening sees Copperfield's life as something read about rather than lived, all the time directing the reader to see the readerly processing of the narrator's material as no different from the processing of that material by the narrating David.

The opening sentence announces and introduces the story that is to follow from a perspective which senses its written completion, and from a vantage point which is more that of a reader taking up a book that is about to be read than of a writer inscribing the first sentence of a book (concerning his own life) that is otherwise yet to be written: *Whether I shall turn out to be the hero of my own life, or whether that station will be held by anybody else, these pages must show*. This thematically marked sentence, with the adversative conjunction of subordinate interrogative clauses topicalized, belongs at the end of a paragraph, the end of a chapter, or the end of a book, not – as in *David Copperfield* – at the start of all three. Its structure-determined normal function is to summarize and keep in balance alternatives that have at least been broached, and that are at least implicitly knowable, from the reader's vantage point at the position where such a sentence occurs. An example of a more standard occurrence of such a sentence structure is found in the following paragraph (the second in the book) from Philip Roth, *When She Was Good*:

> One of Willard's strongest boyhood recollections is of the time a full-blooded Chippewa squaw came to their cabin with a root for his sister to chew when Ginny was incandescent with scarlet fever. Willard was seven and Ginny was one and the squaw, as Willard tells it today, was over a hundred. The delirious little girl did not die of the disease, though Willard was later to understand his father to believe it would have been better if she had. In only a few years they were to discover that poor little Ginny could not learn to add two and two, or to recite in their order the days of the week. Whether this was a consequence of the fever or she had been born that way, nobody was ever to know.
>
> (1968: 3–4)

But brusquely marking the start of *David Copperfield*, and insisting on – not drawing out – the dilemma it states, the sentence disconcerts the reader, until there comes the realization that it is with a *reader's* perspective that David relates to the narrative he now initiates, his own life (and his role in it) not separate from – indeed, only to be understood within – the literary confines of the experience of reading the book he is setting out to write. David talks of *these pages* as if the book of his life was already imaginatively written and ready to be read (and as it *actually* already is for the real-world reader). In an interesting and corresponding reversal, at the start of his last chapter, where he takes 'A Last Retrospect', David clearly relates to his material as a person who is finishing writing it down, talking of 'my written story' and – with a sense of manuscript rather than book – of 'these leaves'; 'And now my written story ends. I look back, once more – for the last time – before I close these leaves.'[4]

The sense of a coalition of the perspectives of writer and reader, fact and account, life and story, continues. David straightaway announces *To begin my life with the beginning of my life*, a correlation that wholly equalizes story and experience. The non-finite nominalized forms of the infinitival *To begin my life* and the gerundive *the beginning of my life* do not make explicit, as would do clausal forms such as *I began my life* and *my life began*, whether *my life* holds an object or subject relation to the verb *begin*. Both nominal forms necessarily place the potential verbal element before the dependent substantive forms, and that neutralizes and makes covert the direct *(S) VO* and *SV* opposition between transitive *(I) begin my life* and intransitive *My life began* normally allowed by the syntactically dualistic verb *begin*. This cancellation – effectively an obliteration of the distinction between the initiation of an undertaking (such as beginning a life story) and the start of one's experience (as in a life beginning) – is complemented by the fact that the twice-occurring noun phrase *my life* is ambiguous between the senses of life as a story in a book and life as one's lived and temporal experience. The complementary pairs of ambivalences make any priority discernible in *To begin my life with the beginning of my life*, as between the senses of one's life starting and one starting on one's life story, seem only accidental.

David, narrating, has only the same privileges as his reader. Reading something, and thereby being informed of and coming to believe what is said, is the normal experience of a reader newly engaging with a piece of writing (the author of that writing being someone already knowledgeable from experience and capable of informing from foreknowledge). But such distinctions seem cancelled, and to be verging on the reverse, at the start of *David Copperfield*: David records the onset of his life as something known with the perspective that a reader would bring to the facts he proffers, as suggested by the aside *as I have been informed and believe*: and the real reader has to readjust – and thus become aware of – his usual expectations through the experience of reading this subtle and unusual opening. As Mark Kinkead-Weekes has perceptively remarked:

> the voice that begins *David Copperfield* is that of an 'author' who will only learn how to read and evaluate his life by the process of voicing his story. From the start, also, the voice is oddly both inside itself and aware of itself from the outside, announcing a personal life, but with a very public tone. *So the process of discovery, which the reader will share, must also involve an adjustment of private and public perspective.* The original readers who bought the novel in monthly instalments hardly needed to be reminded to read it as an unresolved process in time; but it is only when we think that way, that the implication of those changing nicknames dawns: – Davy, Daisy, Doady, and only then David. For each points to a

phase of reading: a *different* relation of author and hero, of inner and outer, and of author and reader. The changing voice requires different kinds of listening.

(Kinkead-Weekes 1980: 169, italics added)

IV

Contexts are not monolithic; neither are they stable. A context can be altered by the very expression it contextualizes, just as much as the interpretation of an expression can depend on its context. Indeed, appropriate reading is as much a matter of seeing the context that the lexicogrammar of an expression calls forth, as it is a matter of seeing this lexicogrammar in terms of some determinate and pre-existent context.

NOTES

1 *Hard Times* (The Norton Critical Edition), edited by George Ford and Sylvere Monod, New York, 1960: 52. The apparatus supplied in this splendid edition (specifically at p. 250) is the source of information about revisions used later in the discussion of the quoted extract.
2 *Great Expectations* (Penguin English Library), edited by Angus Calder, Harmondsworth, 1965: 472.
3 *David Copperfield* (The Clarendon Dickens), edited by Nina Burgis, Oxford, 1981: 1.
4 ibid., 748.

Part III

Positioning styles: framing women in language

Editor's preface

'Power and mutuality in *Middlemarch*' has interesting connections with both the McHale and the Mills essays (chapters 1 and 8): like the former, it emphasizes the importance of frames and framing in our interpretations of people and texts; like the latter, it invokes the Althusserian notion that texts invariably attempt a kind of 'positioning' (another kind of framing, in effect) of the reading-subject.

Hastert and Weber explore the epistemic and deontic aspects of 'powerful framings' – the fractured and fracturing patriarchal ideology that speaks through Casaubon and seeks to define and dominate Dorothea, Dorothea's sense of self, their joint relationship, Dorothea's view of Will Ladislaw – and, potentially, everything else. Samples of dialogue between Casaubon and Dorothea are used to show how Casaubon exercises power via both direct and indirect strategies: direct strategies include coercive yes–no questions and pervasively negative commentary; indirect ones include verbal distancing and exclusion. All serve to deny or prevent mutuality.

Indeed what are seen as separating the major characters here are quite different allegiances to ideas of power vs mutuality, and the clash of a patriarchal frame of femininity, and a feminist frame of masculinity. The masculine world and frame are epistemically empowered; relationally and inherently, the feminine world is treated from this perspective as epistemically lacking and dependent, and indeed as 'naturally' supposed to remain so. With masculine epistemic empowerment come ownership rights and responsibilities – particularly to define and maintain the world and behaviour of objectivized women. This Hastert and Weber call 'a deontic world of duty and principle'; it is one which attempts to articulate (or simply make assumptions about) what it is that women should be and do. An interesting final section of the chapter suggests that the verbal expression of feminine power contrasts sharply with the negative orientation of masculine power: 'Feminine power consists in the verbal imposition of positive expectations.' In Dorothea's case such an orientation of 'optimistic impositiveness' is in wretched conflict with the negative self-image that Casaubon reflects back to her.

An invaluable aspect of Hastert and Weber's discussion is their appeal to linguistically well-founded diagnostic instruments. For instance, they apply the scale of transitivity/agency postulated by Hopper and Thompson (1980) as a means of characterizing and comparing the degree of agency and effectiveness implicit in different canonical types of syntactic structure (cf. Hasan's scale of dynamism, using systemic linguistic categories: Hasan 1985). Roughly speaking, the Hopper and Thompson model predicts the syntactic characteristics of clauses which are most highly transitive (a distinct process extending from an agentive individual to a directly affected individual), or transitive to lesser degrees. By such means Hastert and Weber display the principle of 'operationalizability' which always underlies stylistics: in the course of articulating their contextualized reading of a text, stylisticians seek out accounts of linguistic form, of the lexicogrammar of texts in general, which may serve as useful diagnostic instruments in uncovering patterns, tendencies, textual omissions, or silences or foregroundings (in short, style).

7 Power and mutuality in *Middlemarch*[1]

Marie Paule Hastert and Jean Jacques Weber

In this chapter we hope to contribute to a semiotics of dialogue, as adumbrated in Toolan (1985, 1988, and 1989), which proceeds 'from the assumption that verbal interaction is by its very nature a negotiation of positions (ideological, social, emotional)' (Toolan 1988: 249); and more specifically to contribute to an understanding of how the main protagonists of George Eliot's *Middlemarch* negotiate their ideological positions on a scale ranging from *power* at one end to *mutuality* at the other. In our attempt to grasp these notions, we found ourselves drawing eclectically upon a number of critical strands. First, our approach has been strongly influenced by the 'critical linguistics' movement of Fowler, Kress *et al.*, which uses Halliday's theory of language as social semiotic in order to understand the problematic relationship of texts to social knowledge and beliefs. This highly exciting and extremely productive development within linguistics has also spurred a new contextualized approach in stylistics.[2] Starting as it does from the impossibility of separating text and context, it has highlighted the absurdity of any purely formalist stylistics which ignores the ideological substructure of language. Its aim is to uncover textually realized 'ideologies' or systems of knowledge and beliefs, with the ultimate educational goal of 'equipping readers for demystificatory readings of ideology-laden texts' (Fowler 1987: 485).

In a similar vein, Elaine Showalter (1979: 25) has defined Anglo-American feminist criticism as a

> historically grounded inquiry which probes the ideological assumptions of literary phenomena. Its subjects include the images and stereotypes of women in literature, the omissions and misconceptions about women in criticism, and the fissures in male-constructed literary history.

The present essay works towards a convergence between the obviously related aims of critical linguistics and feminist literary criticism, with critical linguistics helping feminism to sharpen its analytic tools and feminism providing critical linguistics with a thorough analysis of the historical determinants of one specific area of ideological conflict. As such, it builds upon related attempts to bring these two traditions together by Deirdre Burton (1982) and Terry Threadgold (1986 and forthcoming).

The first encouraging results of such a synthesis of feminism and critical linguistics into a new and powerful 'contextualized stylistics' have already been achieved in the analysis of 'power'. An increasing number of researchers are studying the ways in which discourse, and in particular sexist discourse, functions to construct, or to maintain, asymmetrical power relationships in society (see Kedar 1987 and Wodak 1988 for two recent and representative collections of papers). From a more pedagogical point of view, Fowler (1985: 61–75), who defines 'power' as the 'ability of people and institutions to control the behaviour and material lives of others', also provides an extremely useful check-list of items, or categories of structure, that seem to figure prominently in the linguistic practice of power. His argument is that systematic syntactic or lexical choices can throw a certain slant upon the presentation of 'reality', and hence be indicative of ideology. Similarly, in this paper, we shall argue that relations of power are reflected in the choices made (by George Eliot) from within the transitivity component of the grammar – though the transitivity model which we use in our analysis is Hopper and Thompson's rather than Halliday's.

Finally our approach relies crucially on the notion of 'frame', which has been developed in artificial intelligence as an important unit in information processing. When we interpret an utterance, we draw upon our background assumptions, our knowledge of the world, in order to infer its meaning. Frames are clusters, 'families' of such background assumptions. In literature, these assumptions arise out of the creative interplay of text and reader: in other words, we analyse what we assume the characters assume about each other in their interpretation or misinterpretation of events happening within the fictional world of the novel.[3] In particular, we focus on two of these second-order frames: the two sexes' views of each other. We shall refer to these ideological constructs as, respectively, the frame of femininity and the frame of masculinity. They can be analytically expanded into sets of contextually inferred propositions: for example, the patriarchal frame of femininity would stipulate that women are different from men, that women are inferior to men, etc. It thus implies a *dichotomous* view of the world, which clashes ontologically with what we shall call the *inclusive* world-view of many George Eliot heroines.

THE WORLD OF MASCULINE POWER

We shall start with a number of claims about the dichotomous structure of George Eliot's fictional world, which we hope will be largely uncontroversial:

1 The masculine world is an epistemic world of knowledge which is kept *inaccessible* to the feminine world.
2 The inaccessibility of masculine knowledge (witness e.g. the failure of Dorothea's quest for such knowledge) puts the masculine world in a position of *power vis-à-vis* the feminine world.
3 The masculine world uses its power to establish or consolidate a *deontic* world of duty and principles, which it coercively imposes upon the feminine world.
4 The masculine world thus denies the essential subjectivity of women, by reducing it to an *objective* image or 'frame', which is projected by the masculine world and to which the feminine world is expected to conform.

The tendency towards objectification is illustrated by Casaubon's narrow image of Dorothea. He fails to see the depth of her nature and merely looks for the stereotyped cliché of what a woman is considered to be according to conventional, generalized, and patriarchal conceptions. The tragedy of Dorothea's life consists in her acceptance of this mirror-image, without realizing (until it is too late) that the mirror is narrow, and its reflections distorted or, at best, incomplete. However, not all of George Eliot's heroines suffer from these mirror-images: in *Daniel Deronda*, for instance, the male-projected images of admiration strengthen Gwendolen Harleth's self-confidence and give her an illusion of power – which is, however, quickly undermined not only by Grandcourt but also by Deronda, whose critical appraisal of her behaviour helps to bring out her deep-seated sense of insecurity.

Thus, a frame of femininity is explicitly constructed in the text; an epistemic structure which describes the typical or expected behaviour, character, etc. of women; a conceptual model which is imposed from outside and to which women are expected to conform. There is a clear limit between what belongs to the frame and what doesn't: Lydgate sees Rosamond as an embodiment of 'perfect womanhood', an 'accomplished creature . . . who was instructed to the true womanly limit and not a hair's-breadth beyond – docile, therefore, and ready to carry out behests which came from beyond that limit' (387).[4] Casaubon, too, harps on the limit which Dorothea ought not to transgress:

> What I now wish you to understand is, that I accept no revision, still less dictation *within that range of affairs which I have deliberated upon as distinctly and properly mine.*
>
> (410)

All unexpected behaviour, all frame-breaking femininity is seen as mysterious, threatening, and subversive. For example, when Dorothea urges Casaubon to 'begin to write the book which will make [his] vast knowledge useful to the world', she expresses her own need to be of some use 'in a most unaccountable, darkly-feminine manner'. These words, the narrator tells us, 'were among the most cutting and irritating to him that she could have been impelled to use'. To Casaubon, Dorothea 'seemed to present herself as a spy watching everything with a malign power of inference' (232–3).

In order to suppress the threatening aspect of woman's self, in order to force her back into the predetermined mould or frame, Casaubon – just like Grandcourt in *Daniel Deronda* and Tom Tulliver in *The Mill on the Floss* – misuses his masculine power in a destructive way. But first it is necessary to understand the nature of a fulfilling relationship before we can appreciate the extent to which a relationship can be perverted through the destructive misuse of masculine power. In George Eliot's fictional world, a fulfilling relationship between a man and a woman seems to presuppose mental androgyny: ideally each partner should accept or embrace the element of the opposite sex in his/her own self as something natural and normal. Thus the men who find fulfilment are all androgynous creatures in this sense: typical examples are Daniel Deronda and, in *Middlemarch*, Will Ladislaw. And just as Will has a number of feminine attributes, so Dorothea, too, has – or yearns to have – some masculine attributes (such as desire for knowledge). Each has achieved some sort of inner balance between masculine and feminine principles, and this in turn allows them to achieve an outer balance in their relationship. The linguistic representation of balance, of mutuality is *transitivity*: Dorothea and Will talk to each other, they affect each other, and they actually talk about how one affects or is affected by the other. Their relationship is characterized by the presence in their speech of transitive constructions of the type: *I – V – you* and *you – V –*

me. We shall refer to the presence of both types of constructions as two-way transitivity, and as two-way high-transitivity if, moreover, the following three parameters based on Hopper and Thompson (1980: 252) are fulfilled:[5]

1 The subject must be high in potency.
2 The object must be highly individuated.
 (This is another way of saying that for high-transitivity both subject and object are ideally human beings, which is ensured by our formulating them as 'I' and 'you', where 'you' refers exclusively to the partner – all examples with other referents being ignored below.)
3 The verb must be in the realis mode.
 (If the verb is in the irrealis mode, as in: 'I will/may/didn't/ . . . kick you', we have low-transitivity, since, as Hopper and Thompson (1980: 252) put it, 'an action which either did not occur, or which is presented as occurring in a non-real (contingent) world, is obviously less effective than one whose occurrence is actually asserted as corresponding directly with a real event'.)

Thus a relationship of 'mutual knowledge and affection' (230) between two individuals is also a relationship of two-way high-transitivity. Here, for instance, are the lexicogrammatical patterns of high-transitivity between Dorothea and Will in two crucial scenes, the first in Rome (252–6) and the second in Lowick (398–402):

Dorothea affects/is affected by Will:

 Indeed you mistake me. (252)
 I like you very much. (255)
 What very kind things you say to me. (256)
 I shall remember how well you wish me. (256)
 I quite hoped we should be friends when I first saw you. (256)
 It seems strange to me how many things I said to you. (398)
 You correct me. (399)

Will affects/is affected by Dorothea:

 You questioned me about the matter of fact, not of feeling. (254)
 I quite agree with you. (255)
 But now I am telling you what is not new to you. (401)
 You teach me better. (402)

These examples reflect the balance which Dorothea and Will achieve in their relationship, and which is the precondition for a fulfilling relationship. In particular, they show Will being affected by Dorothea in a way Casaubon never is!

Casaubon, on the other hand, perverts his relationship with Dorothea through a destructive misuse of masculine power. He uses both institutional power (the codicil to his will) and linguistic power in an attempt to control the threatening 'otherness' of Dorothea. There are in fact two different verbal strategies of power, and Casaubon avails himself of both. The first strategy, *the direct or manifest use of power*, consists in turning the two-way transitivity into one-way transitivity. It is an attempt to have total control over the other, a *denial of mutuality*. Grandcourt tries to subjugate Gwendolen in this way, mostly through his use of certain restrictive modals (e.g. 'You will understand that you are not to compromise yourself' (503); 'But you will please to observe that you are not to go near that house again' (654)), while Casaubon's favourite technique of linguistic coercion is a two-step one of question and negation. In the first step, he uses a coercive yes–no question such as:

> Did he [Will Ladislaw] mention the precise order of occupation to which he would addict himself?
>
> (257)

which reduces a complex issue (the future course of Will's life) to a simple binary one: did he follow my instructions or not? Then, in the second step, Casaubon accumulates a number of negatives in order to inhibit any further response:

> 'The young man, I confess, is *not* otherwise an object of interest to me, *nor* need we, I think, discuss his future course, which it is *not* ours to determine beyond the limits which I have sufficiently indicated.'
> Dorothea did not mention Will again.
>
> (258)

Casaubon uses the same technique in the scene of Dorothea's proposal of a fixed settlement for Will. The aggressive yes–no question, imputing selfish motives to Will and to Dorothea a secret collusion with Will at Casaubon's expense ('Mr Ladislaw has probably been speaking to you on this subject?' (409)), is followed by a longer speech in which Casaubon reasserts the limit by means of a five-fold repetition of the negative (one negative per sentence, plus other inherently negative lexical items such as 'forfeiture', 'criticism' and 'still less', repeated twice):

Dorothea, my love, this is *not* the first occasion, but it were well
that it should be the last, on which you have assumed a judgement
on subjects beyond your scope. Into the question how far conduct,
especially in the matter of alliances, constitutes a forfeiture of
family claims, I do *not* now enter. Suffice it, that you are *not* here
qualified to discriminate. What I now wish you to understand is,
that I accept *no* revision, still less dictation within that range of
affairs which I have deliberated upon as distinctly and properly
mine. It is *not* for you to interfere between me and Mr Ladislaw,
and still less to encourage communications from him to you which
constitute a criticism on my procedure.

(410)

This is the voice of power, where relational processes take precedence
over mental and material process clauses, where the dynamic world
of interhuman processes is reified into a static world of immutable
precepts and interdicts, which weigh like a heavy burden upon the
individual.

And so, it is no wonder that Will, in his letter, describes Casaubon
as having a restrictive, negative influence upon other people's lives:

A benefactor's veto might impose such a negation on a man's life
that the consequent blank might be more cruel than the benefaction
was generous.

(410–11)

Will thus rejects Casaubon's attempt to tilt the balance of power in
his favour; and Dorothea, too, though made weaker by her pity, can
resist such attempts to some extent:

You showed me the rows of notebooks – you have often spoken of
them – you have often said that they wanted digesting. . . . *I only
begged you* to let me be of some good to you.

(233–4)

You speak to me as if I were something you had to contend against.

(316)

These rare examples of high-transitivity in Dorothea's speech to
Casaubon are the only moments when she can actually get through
to him, but only in a negative way, by protesting against the male-
imposed limit in outbreaks of open fighting between herself and her
husband.

Casaubon, however, in order to preclude any such scenes, also uses a second, more frightening strategy: the indirect, latent use of power. Right from the beginning, when he proposes to Dorothea in writing (66–7), he only sees her as supplying his own needs; he keeps his relationship with her on the frame-level, by abstracting away from Dorothea as a real individual with her own vital needs. As a result, their relationship acquires an air of unreality, what the narrator calls 'the dream-like strangeness of her bridal life' (224). Casaubon keeps Dorothea at a distance, and so she cannot get through to him. This is a strategy that Tom Tulliver uses, too, in *The Mill on the Floss*, when he withdraws his love in order to punish Maggie. With Casaubon, however, it is more diffuse, and permeates the whole of his married life. It may be less of a deliberate strategy and more of an inadequacy of self; nevertheless it is also an insidious and therefore extremely effective way of exercising power. For here Dorothea cannot even resist; she is excluded by definition as it were. Though she is not aware of any definite reason for her frustration (224–6), it has a no less debilitating effect on her.

Casaubon achieves this effect by refraining from any kind of direct contact with Dorothea: their relationship is marked by a lack of physical, mental, and verbal contact. He skilfully alternates between studied taciturnity and linguistic indirection. If he doesn't actually retreat into silence, he uses low-transitivity with verbs in the irrealis mode functioning as markers of both social and ontological distance. Here is the complete list of *I – V – you* and *you – V – me* constructions in Casaubon's speech to Dorothea:

I – V – you:

> let me introduce to you my cousin. (104)
> I could put you both (= Dorothea and another lady) . . . (113)
> I shall be able to indicate to you . . . (517)
> I ask you to obey mine. (519)

you – V – me:

> I wish you to favour me . . . (100)
> you may rely upon me . . . (233)
> if you will read me a few pages of Lowth. (409)
> Were you waiting for me? (465)
> You will oblige me . . . (517)
> You would oblige me . . . (518)
> you will let me know . . . (518)
> You can now, I hope, give me an answer. (522)

We can see that there is a marked absence of high-transitivity in Casaubon's speech to Dorothea – which clearly differentiates Casaubon's *fear of mutuality* from Will's *desire for mutuality*. There is only one exception which occurs at the very end, the day before his death:

> But you would use your own judgement: *I ask you* to obey mine; you refuse.

(519)

where the asking is realis, though the obeying is not. This is Casaubon's desperate attempt to bind Dorothea even beyond his death, his ultimate moment of reassertion of the limit; it is also the only example of a transitive *I – V (realis) – you* construction in Casaubon's speech to Dorothea. And there is no example of *you – V (realis) – me*. The most he shows himself to be affected by a physical action of Dorothea's is *Were you waiting for me?*, which is the only non-mental process (though a rather forceless one) in the *you – V – me* category. It is also, interestingly, the only moment of tenderness between Dorothea and Casaubon during the whole of their married life.

At this stage it might be helpful to try and pull together the various strands discussed above by analysing the power struggle underlying one particular interaction in greater detail. We have chosen the honeymoon scene, briefly referred to above, where Dorothea expresses her ardent desire to help Casaubon in his work:

> 'Yes,' said Mr Casaubon with that peculiar pitch of voice which makes the word half a negative. 'I have been led farther than I had foreseen, and various subjects for annotation have presented themselves which, though I have no direct need of them, I could not pretermit. The task, notwithstanding the assistance of my amanuensis, has been a somewhat laborious one, but your society has happily prevented me from that too continuous prosecution of thought beyond the hours of study which has been the snare of my solitary life.'

(231)

At first sight, Casaubon's 'your society has happily prevented me' seems to be a transitive construction of the type *you – V (realis) – me* and thus to constitute a counterexample to the claim made above. But in fact, this utterance does not qualify for high-transitivity, since it fails on Hopper and Thompson's first parameter, which specifies that the subject must be high in potency. Here, however, the subject is not *you*, but *your society*, and the latter is clearly low in potency. Hence,

Casaubon's utterance is no counterexample to, but a corroboration of, the above claim. Indeed, the abstract noun phrase *your society* blurs the distinction between individual and frame, thus revealing again that Casaubon does not see Dorothea as a real individual, but only in terms of the default-value of his patriarchal frame ('a little moon . . . to adorn the remaining quadrant of his course' (121)).

> 'Doubtless, my dear,' said Mr Casaubon with a slight bow. 'The notes I have here made will want sifting, and you can, if you please, extract them under my direction.'
>
> 'And all your notes,' said Dorothea, whose heart had already burned within her on this subject so that now she could not help speaking with her tongue. 'All those rows of volumes – will you not now do what you used to speak of? – will you not make up your mind what part of them you will use, and begin to write the book which will make your vast knowledge useful to the world? I will write to your dictation, or I will copy and extract what you tell me: I can be of no other use.'
>
> (232)

Dorothea's expectations, buttressed by the chiastic pattern of first- and second-person pronouns in Casaubon's utterance, lead her to interpret the latter as an offer of mutuality, however limited ('under my direction'). This gives her the confidence to invoke mutual knowledge ('what you used to speak of') and to advise her husband. At the same time she also expresses her own overwhelming wish to help, which makes her end 'with a slight sob and eyes full of tears'. She feels frustrated because she cannot help much; she regrets that she cannot fully live up to what she saw as her husband's offer of mutuality.

However, Casaubon is totally unable to comprehend the full strength of Dorothea's desire to help. His frame of woman is deficient, he has a narrow image of Dorothea – as a result of which he misinterprets or distorts the speech-act value of Dorothea's utterance. He sees the illocutionary force of Dorothea's speech act not as advising, but as challenging and reproaching. He draws an inference which was unintended by Dorothea: she is frustrated because he (Casaubon) does not do enough!

Thus, any behaviour of Dorothea's which transcends the narrow bounds of Casaubon's frame is seen by him as subversive of masculine authority. For him, the conversation has become a negotiation of blame: Dorothea has claimed a false status for herself, to which she must be denied access. This explains the almost irrational violence of

Casaubon's reaction, in which he identifies Dorothea with the hostile external world of scornful 'chatterers' and 'ignorant onlookers'.

Dorothea is shocked at the baseness of such accusations:

> 'My judgement *was* a very superficial one – such as I am capable of forming,' she answered, with a prompt resentment, that needed no rehearsal. 'You showed me the rows of notebooks – you have often spoken of them – you have often said that they wanted digesting. But I never heard you speak of the writing that is to be published. Those were very simple facts, and my judgement went no farther. I only begged you to let me be of some good to you.'
>
> (233–4)

She tries to clear up the misunderstanding, to make explicit the illocutionary force of her previous intervention ('I only begged you . . .') – but in vain. Her behaviour is frame-breaking behaviour; therefore, Casaubon cannot even begin to fathom the depth of her feelings. The conflict is located at the presuppositional level: presuppositions are not shared, hence no real communication is possible. Such a presuppositional conflict, or frame-conflict, is particularly hard to solve, unless the participants are willing and able to revise their frames – which would mean Casaubon accepting Dorothea as a real individual with her own needs, interests, and goals. But this Casaubon is obviously not prepared to do, and so his reaction is the usual retreat into hostile silence. Thus it is no wonder that Dorothea, continuously running into this wall of silence, takes refuge (like so many other George Eliot heroines) in the world of the boudoir, the world of female subjectivity, where frame-breaking femininity can be freely released. But solipsistic entrapment within female subjectivity can be destructive, too (e.g. 'In such a crisis as this, some women begin to hate' (464)), unless the women are redeemed by altruistic values of love or tenderness:

> But in Dorothea's mind there was a current into which all thought and feeling were apt sooner or later to flow – the reaching forward of the whole consciousness towards the fullest truth, the least partial good. There was clearly something better than anger and despondency.
>
> (235)

Before we turn to the analysis of feminine power, it is necessary to clarify one final point, namely that a frame-conflict may be a sufficient, but by no means a necessary condition for a breakdown of mutuality. For example, another unsuccessful couple in *Middlemarch*, Rosamond and Lydgate, share the same traditional frame of woman as an ornament. Lydgate sees Rosamond as 'that perfect piece of womanhood who would reverence her husband's mind after the fashion of an accomplished mermaid, using her comb and looking-glass and singing her song for the relaxation of his adored wisdom alone' (628). And Rosamond, 'the flower of Mrs Lemon's school' (123), bases her whole attitude on the premise that for a woman to be an ornament, she has to be provided by her husband with all that she needs:

> There was nothing financial, still less sordid, in her previsions: she cared about what were considered refinements, and not about the money that was to pay for them.
>
> (146)
>
> In fact, she never thought of money except as something necessary which other people would always provide.
>
> (301)

There is no frame-conflict here, and yet there are misunderstandings galore, as Robert Kiely (1975: 120) for instance has shown: 'From the beginning, he and Rosamond have regarded each other as types, capable of being dominated but not understood.' In fact, Rosamond uses the same masculine strategy of indirect power that Casaubon uses:

> Her pretty, good-tempered air of unconsciousness was a studied negation by which she satisfied her inward opposition to him without compromise of propriety.
>
> (692)

And her deliberate *withdrawal of mutuality* also has a debilitating effect upon its victim: Lydgate eventually sees her as 'his basil plant', who 'had flourished wonderfully on a murdered man's brains' (893). We can conclude that the real obstacle to communication, to mutuality is not an incompatibility of frames, but the inability of people to break through the restrictive patriarchal frames, to get through to the real individual hidden behind.

THE NATURE OF FEMININE POWER

We have just seen that the masculine strategies of power can also be used by women. Rosamond is one woman who uses them quite successfully; others are Mrs Transome in *Felix Holt*, the Princess Halm-Eberstein in *Daniel Deronda* and, in an abortive attempt, Gwendolen Harleth. However, the result is as destructive as in the reverse situation, when men use these strategies against women; and all these women are highly disapproved of by the author. But this leaves us with a question about women like Dorothea who do not use such strategies. Have they no power at all? Is there no specifically feminine power?

In order to answer these questions, it may be useful to follow the same heuristic as above, where the analysis of the patriarchal frame of femininity helped us to understand the mechanisms of masculine power. Similarly, here, an analysis of women's 'frame of masculinity' might provide us with an insight into the nature of feminine power. But is there really a frame of masculinity? Certainly, it is not constructed as explicitly in the text as the frame of femininity. And yet its existence can hardly be denied: after all, it should be obvious that, when Dorothea encounters a man, she judges him not on the basis of a cultural or social *tabula rasa* in her mind, but on the basis of a prior frame-structure of expectations. It is this cognitive structure which allows her to draw inferences from what Casaubon says, and to integrate new information into the existing frame, through such strategies as gap-filling:

> Dorothea's faith supplied all that Mr Casaubon's words seemed to leave unsaid.
>
> (73–4)

> She filled up all blanks with unmanifested perfections.
>
> (100)

and attribution of causality:

> – 'He talks very little', said Celia.
> – 'There is no one for him to talk to.'
>
> (43)

> Again, the matter-of-course statement and tone of dismissal with which he treated what to her wwere the most stirring thoughts, was easily accounted for as belonging to the sense of haste and preoccupation in which she herself shared during their engagement.
>
> (228)

These quotations throw light upon an essential difference between feminine and masculine power: feminine power is positive, as opposed to masculine power, which as we have seen is essentially negative.

Feminine power consists in the verbal imposition of positive expectations:

> But that simplicity of hers, holding up an ideal for others in her believing conception of them, was one of the great powers of her womanhood.
>
> (829)

Dorothea's ideal image of the man she cares about is a much more complex structure of expectations than Casaubon's frame of femininity: it substitutes for the men's dichotomous view of the sexes an inclusive view, where women embrace the masculine element within themselves and men the feminine element within themselves, which would allow each to understand the other's vital needs and to respond to them in a constructive, mutually fulfilling way. This inclusive view in fact amounts to a deconstruction of the patriarchal frame, a breaking down of all limits, of all boundary control. Only Will lives up to such expectations of mental androgyny and mutuality (at least to some extent), as seen for example in his balanced statement of two-way transitivity:

> Even if *you loved me* as well as *I love you* . . .
>
> (868)

Casaubon, on the other hand, can only recoil in fear, an elemental fear of both personal and social chaos, and he desperately tries to hold on to the old-established 'certainties'. Thus we find Dorothea – in a grammatical structure highly reminiscent of Will's – trying to rationalize the fact that Casaubon sadly falls short of her expectations:

> How can I have a husband who is so much above me without knowing that *he needs me* less than *I need him*?
>
> (114)

Dorothea's awareness of her ignorance and her ardent feelings of inferiority in relation to Casaubon ('a husband who is so much above me') make her see herself in a negative light ('he needs me less than I need him'). On the other hand, however, her blind faith in the importance of 'masculine knowledge', combined with her belief in her own ability to gain such knowledge and fulfil her ideal aspirations, are elements of a positive image of self. This conflict between her positive and negative self-images lead her into a suppression of high-transitivity, a suppression of her expectations of mutuality, and an erroneous belief in the impossibility for her to achieve full mutuality with Casaubon:

'He thinks with me,' said Dorothea to herself, 'or rather, he thinks a whole world of which my thought is but a poor two-penny mirror.'

(47)

The balanced structure, 'He thinks with me', reflects her positive belief in her intellectual power on a level with Casaubon's. This thought, however, is quickly corrected as a lapsus, to reflect her conscious self-image of inferiority. The correction suggests that in the 'pool' of her consciousness Dorothea's belief in her potential is a strong current which she consciously suppresses, perhaps out of respect for Casaubon, and later for fear of causing another attack and possibly his death. The conscious devaluation of her self-image is of course also part of her Puritan idealism in which self-mortification plays an important role.

By now our analysis of the Dorothea–Casaubon relationship has turned the tables on the view of George Eliot's fictional world which we assumed at the beginning of the paper: we have moved from an asymmetrical world of masculine power and feminine impotence to an asymmetrical world of feminine power and masculine impotence, with the continued absence of the logos, Casaubon's *Key to All Mythologies*, as the symbol of the latter. It is women who impose expectations of symmetry, of mutuality, and men who resent the women's imposition of these expectations, because they are felt as threats to the established patriarchal system, because they force the men into an awareness of their own inadequacies. Hence, many men – as their last defence – resort to the destructive strategies of masculine power, often forcing the women to take refuge in the equally destructive world of female subjectivity. The result is solipsistic entrapment in their sex roles, just the opposite of the women's original wish for reconciliation in mental androgyny.

Finally, we note that the power struggle fought out by the characters on the diegetic level of the plot is reflected on the extradiegetic level of the narrator. Like Casaubon, the narrator 'George Eliot' uses both a direct strategy of power over her material (killing off a character) and an indirect one (reducing a character to virtual silence). In her hands the direct strategy becomes an instrument of feminist revenge, as can be seen in the way punishment is meted out when her characters are caught in the cycle of destruction: it is the patriarchal character who suffers most from the unleashed destructiveness, whereas Dorothea comes out largely unscathed with the promise of a better life ahead of her.[6] But the indirect strategy also reveals a deep-rooted fear of mutuality in 'George Eliot': indeed, at the very moment of her liberation, Dorothea fades into the background; she is almost reduced to the ignominious status of a minor character in the unfolding plot; and at the end, she is only granted the rather dubious fate of becoming Will's right arm. Thus, 'George Eliot's' powerful portrait of a woman struggling against insuperable odds yields contradictory glimpses of a real woman hidden behind, Mary Ann Evans, who – like her heroine – must have had high expectations of mutuality, but at the same time suffered from a conflict of positive and negative self-images, which for many years had led her into a suppression of these expectations, and an erroneous belief in the impossibility for her as a woman to achieve full mutuality with men.

NOTES

1   We should like to thank Sara Mills for her most helpful comments on an earlier version of this paper.
2   For some of the latest developments in critical linguistics and stylistics, see Birch (1989), Birch and O'Toole (1988), Fowler (1986 and 1987), Kress (1985), Kress and Hodge (1988).
3   For a similar definition of 'frame' in terms of structures of expectations, see Tannen (1979). On the usefulness of the concept in literary criticism, see Weber (1982).
4   Page references are to the Penguin editions of George Eliot's novels. All italics and words within brackets are ours.
5   All in all, high-transitivity is defined by ten parameters in Hopper and Thompson (1980: 252): 1. two or more participants, Agent and Object 2. action 3. telic aspect 4. punctuality 5. volitionality 6. affirmation 7. realis mode 8. Agent high in potency 9. Object totally affected 10. Object highly individuated.
6   See, e.g., Gilbert and Gubar (1979) and Lundberg (1986). In this final paragraph, we follow Lundberg in her use of quotes to refer to 'George Eliot', the (androgynous) narrator of *Middlemarch*.

Editor's preface

Sara Mills begins 'Knowing your place' by considering how we should model and represent the contextualizedness which, we are claiming throughout this collection, conditions the nature of the stylistic analysis undertaken and achieved. She argues that context is a cover term for the entire area of human activities, of production and reception, entailed in the creation of literary text. These activities of exchange inevitably involve conflict and negotiation, as the different interests of different parties jostle for validation. Hence for Mills the individual reader is neither wholly free to interpret at whim, nor wholly constrained: dominant readings there certainly are, and these are an important element of the context of all particular instances of literary production and reception (see also the idea of the dominant discourse types and conventions, in Fairclough, 1989; it is not irrelevant that the notion of the dominant is one of the most important elements in Russian Formalist and Prague School poetics), but there are always occasions of resistance and 'active' reading.

What is entailed in resistant reading is now elaborated by Mills. If, following Althusser, we say texts 'situate' readers by hailing them (interpellating) in distinct ways, nevertheless that act of situating/defining/characterizing only properly goes through or takes effect if the reader complies with and acknowledges those hailings. But readers can resist, ignore, and detach themselves from the position a text may be seeming to wish to put them in. Mills is most interested in (non-Althusserian) indirect interpellations (unnoticed but covertly effective hailings), and their positioning of the reader.

Like other texts in this collection, the one considered here (John Fuller's poem 'Valentine') may be profitably scrutinized within a Hallidayan systemic framework. For instance, Mills notes some of the patterning involved in the poem's alternations between statements beginning with the declaration 'I like' and those beginning 'I'd like' – in both of which there are undertones of menace and power. In systemic grammatical terms we may add that *I like* and *I'd like* are both clearly subjective, thematizing the speaker as 'point of departure' for these messages. But then contrasts emerge: in *I like* the speaker is the Senser, reporting a mental process of reaction/affect, to some action or event (i.e. a material process) which in some way displays the object (*sic*) of attention or affection, the woman. The *I like*s are evaluative tags to (typically) habitual or ongoing events (events in the realis mode: see chapter 7 by Hastert and Weber) – hence not a proper narrative, and particularly not a narrative within which the speaker is an integral participant. By contrast the *I'd like*s are evaluative of a narrative (in Labov's sense), being comparators; in Hallidayan terms they express the speaker's modality (here, inclination) towards the event or situation described, but the tense confirms that this scattered narrative (in which the speaker would indeed be powerful participant) is irrealis, a wish or fantasy rather than a predictable outcome.

As one of the more politicized essays in this collection, the essay has a special value (perhaps especially for male readers including myself) due to the counter-pulls of argumentation that it provokes – themselves, very possibly, the mediated reflexes of patriarchal thinking. In short, this reader finds it hard to be as critical of the Fuller poem as Mills so eloquently is. Much perhaps hinges on a practice and a genre (even, a language game): the practice of valentine-giving, and its heteroglossic carnivalistic aspects, and the genre of valentine messages. Quite what is involved in the practice and the genre is itself open to discussion. Mills writes of the 'voyeuristic admiring' involved in the sending of cards/messages by men to women. But there is also a voyeurism the other way, too: it is the male (at least, his voice and discourse) that is revealed, on display, in a valentine card. Even if the card specifies the various loved or desired characteristics of the woman, the recipient is afforded the opportunity of viewing this man-shaped portrait of herself. (And if this is so, what, we may wonder, is the particular consequence of our being the readers of this poem/valentine? Are we not thereby positioned as similarly powerful voyeurs, with similar ratificatory privileges?) Senders of valentines, in a bizarrely traditionalist way, are supplicants or suitors, making representations. And – here too is a major contrast with more typical representations of women by men – the canonical situation of sending the card privately to the woman concerned allows that recipient a rather privileged power of ratification of the text: the conventional subtext of valentines seems often to be something like 'Make of this (and do with me) what you will'.

A defence of the poem's seeming indefensible positionings (of male reader (as speaker) and female reader (as addressee)) may lie in considering the extent to which, taking a text-type saturated with controversial gender-categorizations, the speaker intends his words to be understood ironically. This would mean that much of the poem was double-accented or dialogical, in Bakhtin's sense: written, and to be read, with an 'intonation' or slant which is in addition to, and at odds with, the accent of menace and domination that is so blatant. Reading these lines dialogically and as ironic is to see them as mentions of utterances masquerading as uses (cf. the discussion of use vs. mention in the preliminaries to Neumann's essay, p. 112).

On all these matters, finally, it is for you, the now multiply-positioned reader, to judge.

8 Knowing your place: a Marxist feminist stylistic analysis

Sara Mills

INTRODUCTION

In this essay I would like to attempt to define a Marxist feminist contextualized stylistics. For this purpose I shall be drawing on the distinctly unfashionable work of Louis Althusser, a Marxist literary theorist, together with feminist stylistic and literary theory (Althusser 1984; see also Burton 1982 and Threadgold 1988a, 1988b). It may be argued that the combination of Marxism, feminism, and stylistics is indeed a heady brew, but it is a necessary combination in order to overcome some of the problems encountered both in traditional stylistic analysis and in Marxist analysis. These theoretical positions can be combined to produce an analysis which is theoretically rigorous and which at the same time enables the reader to engage with a text.

THE READER AND ADDRESS IN CONTEXTUALIZED STYLISTICS

Contextualized stylistics is a radically new departure for stylistics – a move away from text immanent criticism to a more theoretical concern with the factors outside the text that may determine or interact with the elements which appear in the text. This may sound like a rediscovery of traditional literary criticism's concern with socio-historical context, but a concern with context can be handled in a more interesting theoretical way than has been the case with literary critics. An emphasis on lexical items and the way they interact with their context can help the reader to avoid some of the over-generalized cause–effect relations posited by traditional literary critics.

I wish to present a particular reading of the terms 'context' and 'contextualized' which may not accord with traditional literary models, nor for that matter with the other essays within this book. Most definitions of context centre on the historical and social background in which the text is produced. For example, stylistic analysis has so far shown itself to be largely uninterested in the world outside the text except for the role of the author who plays a determining role in the production and explanation of the linguistic devices which are discovered in the text. As Montgomery states:

> Stylistics has traditionally been concerned preeminently with the differences between or within texts, and those differences have commonly been explored in terms of the formal parameters of lexico-grammar.

(1988)

It is only now with the advent of discourse stylistics that there seems to be a move in the direction of the analysis of context (see Carter and Simpson 1988; and Coupland 1988). However, I would argue that even discourse stylistics is saddled with a very traditional model of context (see Figure 8.1). Within this model of text, the author is in control of the material s/he produces, that is, there are patterns and effects within the text which the author decides upon and which it is the job of the stylistician to detect. However, there are obvious problems with such a model: first, the writer is clearly not in complete control of her/his material. As many literary theorists such as Culler (1975), Barthes (1977) and Bloom (1977) have shown, there is a range of literary conventions which structure the possibilities of expression at a given time. Authorial choice is made within a limited set of parameters. A second problem with the model is that it is based on the notion of hindsight; it would be impossible to prove that the writer had intended the patterns and effects which the reader succeeded in tracing. Fish (1980) has argued that, in fact, these patternings are largely a result of a literary process which the reader puts into effect when reading texts which have been labelled 'literary'. A third problem with the model is that context does not include the role of the reader, which obviously has a greater role to play in the process of interpretation than this model will allow. However, rather than adopting a Fish approach, which would give the reader the position of the creator of the text, usurping that of the author and thus remaining within the same model, I propose the following model of the text which would avoid some of these problems and broaden our definition of context (see Figure 8.2).

One advantage of this model is that textual production and reception are considered to be part of context, and not simply the context of production, which as I have mentioned is the way in

Context

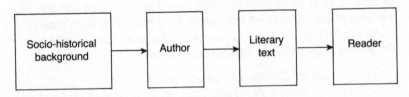

Figure 8.1 The model of context in traditional discourse stylistics

which the term is conventionally used. A second advantage is that the reader's role is given more prominence: it is clear that the reader is addressed by the text, and that s/he is affected by and can make an effect on the interpretation of the text. S/he is an active participant, negotiating with the meanings which are being foisted onto her/him, and resisting or questioning some of those meanings. This is in direct contrast to the passive recipient of the text of Figure 8.1.

I should make it clear at this point that I am not proposing a model of text which is 'open' in Umberto Eco's usage (1979); that is, the text can mean anything and it is up to readers to impose their meanings upon the text. I propose that the reader is positioned by the text in a range of ways which can be accepted or resisted. If there were no

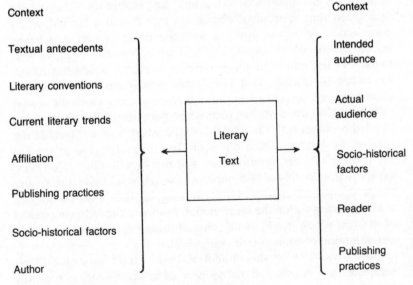

Figure 8.2 A revised model of context in discourse

dominant reading/s, then there would be no consensus whatsoever as to what texts meant. Although it must be stated that there is a wide range of readings which a text can have, nevertheless the possibilities for dominant readings are certainly not endless. Later in this essay, I will define in more detail the constituents of a dominant reading.

This model takes into account the interactional nature of the relation between texts and their context. Thus, texts are determined by a wide range of pressures on their processes of production and reception, and also have an effect on their audience and on the processes of production of further texts. It will be clear that with a more complex model such as this, it is more difficult to make the straightforward statements beloved of stylisticians, such as, a particular formal pattern leads us to interpret the poem in a particular way. Instead, more modest statements can be made about, for example, the way that the text might be addressing the reader and the limits of resisting that address. It is the way that the reader is addressed by the text which is the focus of this essay. The positioning of the reader has been considered by feminist theorists such as Fetterley (1981), Williamson (1978), Marshment *et al.* (1988), Betterton (1987), and – in feminist film theory – by Kuhn (1982) and Mulvey (1981). However, positioning is simply asserted by these theorists; there is little attempt to trace formal features in the text which might serve as markers, to the reader, of this positioning.

THE POSITIONING OF THE READER

It is surprising that in literary studies there has been so little work which considers the positioning of the reader at any length. There have been theories of reader-response and reception theories (e.g. Suleiman and Crosman 1981), but they have been primarily concerned with examining a consensus of interpretation through the notion of the implied or ideal reader. Even those critics who do consider reader positioning pay little attention to the formal features in the text which signal the dominant reading to the reader. In order to formulate a mode of analysis which considers formal features and the way they relate to context and reader address, I would like to consider the work of Louis Althusser on interpellation and obviousness and then go on to discuss the work of critics who have been concerned with the notion of positioning of the reader.

Louis Althusser's work on ideological state apparatuses (1984: 1–60) is an interesting combination of Marxist theory and psycho-analysis, and has received a great deal of attention. The basis of his argument is that ideological state apparatuses are those elements whose indirect effect is to reproduce the conditions of production within a society. In order for a capitalist society to continue to function, workers must be made to recognize their position within that society and accept those roles. This happens through two main mechanisms: the repressive state apparatuses, consisting of the police, the army, and the state, which achieve this aim through force or violence; and the ideological state apparatuses, consisting of the educational system, the media, and so on, which achieve this aim through a constant barrage of images and information which map out the role of the subject. The effects of repressive state apparatuses have been well documented and it is on the ideological state apparatuses that Althusser concentrates. He describes the way in which individuals are called into a position of subjecthood – when you recognize your role/s in society, you become a subject in both senses of the word: you are a subject in that you are an individual psyche, and you are also subject to the state and authority. In this way, you are forced to mis/recognize the imaginary (i.e. ideological) conditions of your relation to the means of production. Althusser states that interpellation or hailing is one of the mechanisms whereby this is achieved; he gives the much-cited and maligned example of a police officer in the street calling 'Hey you'. In the process of turning round, the individual has recognized not only her/himself as an individual who may be guilty of something, but also as a subject in relation to a position of authority. Thus, interpellation constructs the subject into a role or position in the very act of hailing it.

Althusser's model has been rightly criticized for being too simplistic an account of the way that interpellation works, because the construction of subjecthood is obviously a much more complicated process than the simple responding to a name or call. With his model of hailing there is a one-to-one fit between the calling and the recognition. However, as Durant has pointed out, when interpellated by a text, the reader can adopt either the position of the supposed speaker or the role of the supposed addressee, or can be positioned as an overhearer of the interaction (Durant 1989). Furthermore, there are clearly other elements in the text which position the reader, but which are more indirect than this model suggests. There is an unending series of hailings, both direct and indirect, to which the reader responds or does not respond. Thus, although certain texts attempt to address themselves to the reader, she may be critical of them and may decide not to take them at face value. However, even the hailings which are not intended for the reader, or which are intended for her and not received, nevertheless do have an effect on the reader and it is this effect of indirect interpellation which I will attempt to describe in this essay. Despite these problems with the theory of interpellation, rather than rejecting the theory wholesale, it seems more useful to try to work on the theory itself, modifying it slightly so that it will more adequately describe the way that subjects are constituted by texts.

A second point of interest from Althusser's ideological state apparatuses article is the notion of common sense or 'obviousness' which, along with interpellation, is a strong element in the positioning of the reader. In each text, there are elements which are posed as self-evidently true and Althusser asserts that these are the most truly ideological:

> It is indeed a peculiarity of ideology that it imposes (without appearing to do so, since these are 'obviousnesses') obviousnesses as obviousnesses, which we cannot *fail to recognize* and before which we have the inevitable and natural reaction of crying out (aloud or in the 'still, small voice of conscience'): 'That's obvious! That's right! That's true!'

> (1984: 46)

Each text contains an ideological message which we accept (or reject) as given or obvious, and it is in this way that the reader is positioned by what I would like to class as the dominant reading. This is a seemingly coherent message which the text carries, and which the reader is supposed to find as 'obviously' what the text is about. Althusser's notion of obviousness has remarkable similarity to Roland Barthes' (1975) 'cultural code' which I discuss later in the description of dominant readings.

I would now like to consider the ways in which critics, such as Williams, Montgomery, and Durant have treated the idea of address to the reader, or reader positioning. Although these critics are concerned with issues of language, few of them are concerned with issues of gender or politics. It is possible to trace an undercurrent of Althusserian interpellation, but in general this work has not taken on board the political elements of Althusser. Instead, interpellation has been simply used as a term to mean 'hailing', without considering the effects this might have on the subject hailed, as Althusser does. Nor are they concerned with the ways in which the reader is positioned apart from the obvious forms of direct address, that is, when the reader is actually called upon by the narrator, for example, by the use of the pronoun 'you'. Despite these problems, the work of these critics does suggest ways in which the analysis of formal elements may help in the description of reader positioning.

Raymond Williams attempts in his article on monologue and soliloquy (1983) to analyse the ways in which the reader is addressed, either in a direct, semi-direct, or indirect way. Unlike literary theory and stylistics, drama analysis and film theory have considered the way the text addresses the audience to be crucial. Williams tries to map out the linguistic elements in Shakespearian texts which can distinguish between these three kinds of address. However, his work does not seem, in this instance, to be anything other than descriptive, and he does not discuss the effect of these types of address on the audience.

Martin Montgomery's work on DJ talk (1986, 1988) is useful in that it is one of the few examples of an attempt to deal with reader-address using linguistics. Montgomery concentrates on the analysis of direct address to the reader in the form principally of deixis (this/that/I/you, etc.) vocatives (you/Bob Sproat), and selectors (all of you in Edinburgh). He shows the way in which an audience is addressed by a text as 'you' or as a subsection of that 'you', and he notes:

> The audience is not uniformly implicated all in the same way the whole of the time . . . while the use of selectors has the effect of singling out sometimes quite specific addressees, the talk is always available for others than those directly named as addressees.
>
> (Montgomery 1988: 13)

He draws attention to the fact that there are various sections of the audience who will be overhearing elements of the talk by DJs at various times. He compares this to the case of lyric poetry where he shows that, unlike this direct address, 'the addressee of dramatic lyric poetry is almost always someone other than the actual reader of the text' (1988: 14). He also notes that in DJ talk, 'as listeners we are made constantly aware of other (invisible) elements in the audience of which we form a part'(ibid.). This is particularly interesting for the purposes of this essay, as I hope to show that gender is a crucial element for determining whether readers consider that they are being directly addressed or whether in fact they are in the position of overhearing.

Montgomery goes on to state that the same forms of direct address may be used in lyric and romantic poetry and yet, because of the changes in publishing conventions, these forms of address are interpreted in different ways. This is interesting in this context because I shall be arguing that the same forms in the same poem can in fact be interpreted in different ways according to the gender of the reader and the affiliations of that reader. Montgomery's work is interesting because of his attention to the linguistic elements which constitute direct address. However, I would like to argue that the reader is addressed in a much more complex and indirect way. A further element which needs to be integrated into the analysis is that of gender.

Alan Durant draws on Montgomery's work on address, but uses it for the analysis of pop music lyrics (Durant 1989). He distinguishes between the various positions which a listener can adopt when listening to a pop song: for him, there is the position of the singer or the singer's persona, the role of the addressee, or the role of someone who is overhearing this interaction. For Durant, the reader chooses which position to adopt. While this is clearly an advance in that it maps out several alternative positions for the reader if applied to literary texts, the notion of a willed positioning by the reader eliminates any of the ideological positioning described by Althusser. In Althusser's work, the reader is, in the main, unaware of the processes at work in the interpellation; in fact it is the very obviousness of the messages received which prevents the positioned reader becoming aware of his/her ideological nature. Thus, although Durant's work on the varying positions available to the reader seems interesting, within the context of this essay it is not necessary to agree with the notion of reader choice. There are clearly texts which suggest to you what your position is: for example it is unlikely (but not impossible) that a female listener will sing along out loud with the Rolling Stones song 'I can't get no satisfaction' and thus position herself in the role of the singer. It is necessary therefore to draw elements from Durant's work on variable positions of the reader, but to add to this both an analysis of the way roles are foisted onto listeners/readers and also an analysis of the gendering of that reading/listening process.

As I have noted, none of these critics considers gender as a factor in the positioning of the reader, and all of them have tended to use Althusser's terminology without reference to the political framework of the original work. I will attempt to reinscribe that political edge and argue for a gendered reading process.

INDIRECT ADDRESS AND DOMINANT READING

One of the major problems with Althusser's concept of interpellation, as I have noted above, is the notion of the *direct* addressing of the subject, and this problem is reinforced by the work of Montgomery and Durant. It is clear that the reader is also addressed in an *indirect* way. Unless readers analyse texts for the way that they are being positioned, this type of address goes largely unnoticed, because it is more difficult to locate. There are, however, several markers of indirect address which I will now describe; I will then go on to discuss the way that indirect address helps to constitute a dominant reading. I will concentrate on two markers of indirect address: mediation, and the cultural code, or obviousness. Colin McCabe's work on realism (1981) is useful for a discussion of mediation, because he notes that in realist texts there is a hierarchy of discourses or voices within the text. The discourse which occupies the position of truth in this hierarchy is also the one with which the reader aligns herself. He states that in realist texts this dominant voice mediates all of the other voices within the text, that is, the dominant voice gives instructions to the reader about the position she should take on other information or characters within the text. The reader is led to align herself with the voice which is not mediated, that is, the voice or discourse which is not judged by another discourse. In novels, it is clear that there are sub-plots which we are encouraged to view through the dominant discourse, for example, the reader is led to the position where she questions the truth-value of one of the character's statements, because she has been given a negative description of this character by the narrator, or by another character. This mediation of characters can be traced in texts by analysis of the different voices within the text and can lead the reader to the dominant reading.

A second factor which constitutes indirect address is Barthes' notion of the 'cultural code' referred to above. The cultural code consists of a range of statements at which the reader will nod her head sagely or which she will simply accept as self-evidently 'true' within that culture. Barthes suggests that we can detect these elements of the cultural code since these statements can be prefaced by 'we all know that' or 'it is evident that'. Thus, texts contain a substantial amount of information to which we agree indirectly, and which, in that process, constitutes a role for us as readers. These two factors of indirect address lead to the reader being able to discern the dominant reading which the text offers.

The notion of a dominant reading has been much debated in literary theory. Much post-structuralist work has argued that dominant readings do not exist, or are more unstable than has been suggested. However, even the strongest reading of the 'playful' text, i.e. a deconstructive one, does implicitly rely on the notion of a dominant reading, which is then proved to be unstable by deconstructive analysis. Yet it would seem that most readers can recognize the 'obvious' role/s, positions, and interpretations which the text maps out for them. This dominant reading is not the writer's intention (which is unrecoverable), but a position (or positions) which the text offers or proffers to the reader within a particular historical moment, because of the range of ideological positions available which make that text understandable. This reading will be one which is reinforced by various ideologies circulating within the culture of the time; thus, for example, a text which constructs feminity in a particular way will be made understandable because it is reinforced by a range of other texts and discourses on feminity. Without these other discourses, the text would be difficult to understand or may be incomprehensible. The link between indirect address and dominant readings is therefore that unmediated, seemingly obvious information – ideological information reinforced by other discourses – is one of the factors in the constitution of a dominant reading.

Judith Williamson (1978) has discussed these ideas of dominant readings to some extent in her work on advertisements. She has analysed the ways in which advertisements address the reader, and the way in which the reader is in fact a key element in the making sense of seeming incoherent texts. She gives the example of juxtapositions in advertisements, such as Catherine Deneuve's picture which is fronted by a picture of a bottle of Chanel perfume. The reader makes a cognitive leap to make sense of these juxtaposed images by adopting the message of the advertisement: i.e. that if you want to be as beautiful, rich, and famous as Deneuve, you should use Chanel perfume. It is an interesting form of advertisement, because it does not seem to address the reader directly (there is no text which 'hails' the reader as 'you'), and yet indirectly it is positioning the reader into a discourse of upward aspiration through consumerism. In making that cognitive leap to make sense of the advertisement, Williamson asserts, the reader has in fact made herself into a subject, i.e. a consuming subject. The notion that texts are necessarily incomplete and incoherent and require the reader to resolve that incoherence is suggestive, and it is one which I will be drawing on later in the essay.

To sum up, I would argue that address is, in the main, partial and indirect rather than the successful and complete hailing which Althusser described, and for this reason it is possible to track it down when it is unsuccessful and to construct positions for reading, other than the dominant one. Because texts are always overdetermined, there are always other elements intermingled with the dominant reading. It is these elements which lead to a different oppositional reading, which I would now like to consider.

GENDER AND READER POSITION

I have argued that gender is one of the factors that many critics have omitted in their discussion of address and positioning. Judith Fetterley considers the importance of gender in reading: she has described the way that most texts in American literature appear to address a general audience, while in fact they are addressing the reader as a male:

> One of the main things that keeps the design of our literature unavailable to the consciousness of the woman reader, and hence impalpable, is the very posture of the apolitical, the pretense that literature speaks universal truths through forms from which all the merely personal, the purely subjective, has been burned away or at least transformed through the medium of art into the representative.
>
> (Fetterley 1981: xi)

Her work is primarily a content-analysis, that is she examines various depictions of female characters which it is difficult for females to read easily unless they adopt the position of a male reader. She states: 'To read the canon of what is currently considered classic American literature is perforce to identify as male' (1981: xii). She suggests, and Elaine Showalter's work in this area would seem to reinforce her point, that it is standard reading practice for women students at university studying literature to position themselves as males in order to make sense of the text (Showalter 1971). Both Showalter and Fetterley have rather a simplistic model of the relation between literary texts and reality, for they each consider that literary texts reflect reality and this runs the risk of flawing their argument about address (further treatment of these issues is in Mills, forthcoming). Another problem with both Showalter's and Fetterley's work is that they simply assert that texts address the reader as male on the basis of content analysis and do not provide any language analysis to prove their assertions. It is clear from an analysis of texts which are written by males that there are a large number of elements which can be focused upon which signal to the reader that this is a man-to-man dialogue and it is on these elements that I hope to focus in my analysis below.

However, despite these problems of theoretical position, there are interesting elements in Fetterley's work, for example, when she says:

While women obviously cannot rewrite literary works so that they become ours by virtue of reflecting our reality, we can accurately name the reality that they do reflect and so change literary criticism from a closed conversation to an active dialogue.

(Fetterley, 1981: xxiii)

By describing the position that these texts are addressing and constructing, we can then go on to challenge literary criticism's avoidance of gender issues in the analysis of address, and we can also map out a position for ourselves as female readers in the process of doing so. It is this notion of a 'resisting reader', which is a space from which female readers can read against the grain, that I find most suggestive for this essay. Thus, although texts may address us as males, we as female readers can construct a space of reading which resists the dominant reading.

It is possible, drawing on the work of other theorists, to use Fetterley's basic position and to try and discover elements which can justify her assertions. For example, Deborah Cameron (1985) has shown that by the use of generic pronouns such as 'he' to refer to both male and female, texts signal to the reader what gender the dominant reading position is. She goes on to show that generic nouns are also used to similar effect. She gives the example of a newspaper article which uses the generic noun 'neighbour' to mean male neighbour, which has to be modified to 'neighbour's wife' if a female neighbour is referred to. She notes that when texts use generics in this gender-specific way, there is a clear signal to readers that the position which the text is offering them is male. Female readers are less likely to feel that the text is addressed to them if generics are used in this way.

A further example of textual markers of indirect address is the work of Robert Scholes on an Ernest Hemingway short story ('Decoding papa', in Scholes 1982). He shows that although the focalization in the text appears at first glance to be equally distributed between the two characters, a man and a woman, on analysis it is clear that this seemingly neutral narration is focalized on the male. He demonstrates this by rewriting the text from the male and from the female point of view, using the pronoun 'I'. In several parts of the text it is impossible to do this with the female voice and it is therefore clear that the focalization in this text, as in many others, is gendered; this has an effect on the way that the reader processes the text and the position which the reader can take up.

However, it must be stated that, despite all of these elements within the text which lead readers to be positioned as male, it is clear that all women do not read in the same way; women are not a coherent group and are subject to other affiliations such as class and race. One major distinction within women readers which should be made are those who are male-affiliated and those who are female-affiliated. These categories are ones which may be in play at various stages within a text, and in different texts; they do not necessarily constitute a permanent reading position (see also the critique of polarization in Morris 1989). The term 'female affiliation' was coined by Sandra Gilbert and Susan Gubar (1988) to describe the problem which women writers face when they decide to write: whether to align themselves with a male or a female tradition. The same question poses itself for the female reader, although not necessarily in a conscious way: whether to take up the position allotted to the male reader of the text, or whether to attempt to resist that position and formulate another position from which to read, as Judith Fetterley has described. Female affiliation is a frame of reference and usually occurs with feminist consciousness-raising; it is a framework of reading adopted in order to resist reading as a male. Therefore, it should be clear that it is a position which is taken up, and not something which is inherent in all females. There are of course texts which position you as female, and there has been a certain amount of feminist work on this area, for example, see Marshment *et al.* (1988). These theorists are concerned to analyse those texts which overtly signal that they are addressed to a female audience. Although this is beyond the scope of my essay it might be interesting to examine the way in which certain texts which position the reader as female are read by males and male-affiliated women. The one problem with these texts is that unless they position the reader within a dominant ideological position, they are difficult to make sense of; thus feminist texts such as *The Color Purple* are frequently misunderstood by male readers as a male-hating diatribe. In some cases, this is the only frame of reference which ideology offers for males reading feminist or female-addressed texts.

To summarize the position which I have attempted to formulate: address to the reader or interpellation is more complex than conventionally described, and I have therefore found it necessary to integrate into this framework the notion of indirect address and its relation to the production of a dominant reading. Furthermore, I have also argued that gender is an important element in the construction of the reader's position. I would like to move now to an analysis of a poem to see how this Marxist feminist stylistics can describe the positioning of the reader.

ANALYSIS

I have chosen a poem by John Fuller entitled 'Valentine' because, when taught on a summer school by a male colleague, the poem aroused a great deal of discussion. The students seemed to be almost completely polarized: the female students felt anger, but most of the male students found the poem amusing. Subsequent readers have, by and large, repeated this response. This seemed to me to be due at least in part to the way that the reader's position is mapped out as male, with little room for a female reader to manoeuvre.

Valentine
John Fuller

The things about you I appreciate
May seem indelicate:
I'd like to find you in the shower
And chase the soap for half an hour
I'd like to have you in my power
And see your eyes dilate
I'd like to have your back to scour
And other parts to lubricate.
Sometimes I feel it is my fate
To chase you screaming up a tower
or make you cower
By asking you to differentiate
Nietzsche from Schopenhauer.
I'd like successfully to guess your weight
And win you at a fete.
I'd like to offer you a flower.

I like the water upon your shoulders
Falling like water upon boulders.
I like the shoulders, too; they are essential.
Your collar-bones have great potential
(I'd like all your particulars in folders
Marked *Confidential*).

I like your cheeks, I like your nose
I like the way your lips disclose
The neat arrangement of your teeth
(Half above and half beneath)
In rows.

I like your eyes, I like their fringes.
the way they focus on me gives me twinges.
Your upper arms drive me berserk.
I like the way your elbows work,
On hinges.

I like your wrists, I like your glands,
I like the fingers on your hands.
I'd like to teach them how to count,
And certain things we might exchange
Something familiar for something strange.
I'd like to give you just the right amount
And get some change.

I like it when you tilt your cheek up.
I like the way you nod and hold a teacup.
I like your legs when you unwind them.
Even in trousers I don't mind them.
I like each softly-molded kneecap.
I like the little crease behind them.
I'd always know, without a recap,
Where to find them.

I like the sculpture of your ears.
I like the way your profile disappears
Whenever you decide to turn and face me.
I'd like to cross two hemispheres
And have you chase me.
I'd like to smuggle you across frontiers
Or sail with you at night into Tangiers.
I'd like you to embrace me.

I'd like to see you ironing your skirt
And cancelling other dates.
I'd like to button up your shirt.
I like the way your chest inflates.
I'd like to soothe you when you're hurt
Or frightened senseless by invert-
ebrates.

I'd like you even if you were malign
And had a yen for sudden homicide.
I'd let you put insecticide

Into my wine.
I'd even like you if you were the Bride
of Frankenstein
Or something ghoulish out of Mamoulian's
Jekyll and Hyde
I'd even like you as my Julian
Of Norwich or Cathleen ni Houlihan.
How melodramatic
If you were something muttering in attics
Like Mrs Rochester or a student of Boolean
Mathematics.

You are the end of self-abuse.
You are the eternal feminine.
I'd like to find a good excuse
To call on you and find you in.
I'd like to put my hand beneath your chin,
And see you grin.
I'd like to taste your Charlotte Russe,
I'd like to feel my lips upon your skin,
I'd like to make you reproduce.

I'd like you in my confidence.
I'd like to be your second look.
I'd like to let you try the French defence.
And mate you with my rook.
I'd like to be your preference
And hence
I'd like to be around when you unhook.
I'd like to be your only audience,
The final name in your appointment book,
Your future tense.

The poem consists largely of direct address marked by deixis (I, you);
this discourse occupies a dominant position because it is unmediated
by any other voice. There are four positions which can be adopted
according to gender and affiliation. The male reader is offered a
position which I would argue is the dominant reading of this poem;
the reader's position is elided with that of the speaking 'I'. That is
not to say that the reader and the 'I' become the same, but the
reader can adopt that 'I' position without thinking. It would be less
likely for a male reader to read the text from the addressed position
of the female because of indirect address as I show later. The female

reader has three positions: (1) to read the text as if it is addressed to her, the dominant reading for the text, which constitutes her within the dominant male view of femininity; (2) to affiliate as a malee, that is to read it as if the text positions her as the speaker. This is a curious position because she can make sense of the poem as a male-affiliated female, and yet there are several points at which she has to read as an overhearing reader. In both cases the female reader laughs at the jokes and is interpellated into a position where certain ideological knowledges about the nature of men and women have to be accepted as true. (3) A third position for the female reader is one of resistance, and is what I will term female affiliated. This is a position outside the dominant readings which are offered by the text.

First, let us consider the dominant reading position: the one that we as readers are encouraged to adopt and to view as natural. This reading, I would argue, is directed to a male reader. It is evident that the poem is directed from a male 'I' to a female 'you'. There are many textual antecedents for this type of love poem, and there are several clues in the text to show that the love-object is female (although there are not as many as you would think). The element which signals the reader as male is the humour which often accompanies poems which make reifying statements about females; there is a long tradition of disguising sexism with humour, so that when challenged, the humour of the text can be cited as a means of deflecting the charges (see, e.g., the dismissals of sexism in Jonson's 'That Women are but Men's Shadows', on the grounds of the poem's prevailing wit and elegance, in Gibbons 1979).

As I noted earlier (p. 191), Judith Williamson suggests that it is in trying to 'make sense' of the text that the reader's position is constructed. In this poem humour is a central factor in interpellation. The text is humorous in that readers can only make sense of most of the statements if they see that these are exaggerated, and therefore not to be taken at face value: for example, 'I'd like successfully to guess your weight/ And win you at a fete.' Together with the bathetic rhyme, this sentence can only be interpreted, within a dominant reading, as humorous: other examples are: 'I'd let you put insecticide/ Into my wine.' There is also humour in the clash of collocation which can only be resolved if the reader interprets the text as humorous; for example, 'I'd like to make you reproduce.' In general usage, 'reproduce' is a fairly technical, medical term which is not appropriate in casual or intimate conversation; thus the combination of 'I'd like' and 'reproduce' causes a clash of expectations, which can only be resolved by being interpreted as humorous. Furthermore, there are

other elements in the text which can be made sense of only if
interpreted as humorous, because in a love-poem they would normally
be seen as trivial and not fitting in with the literary conventions of
love poetry; for example, 'I'd like to see you ironing your skirt'
alongside more conventionally romantic claims such as 'I'd like to
smuggle you across frontiers/ Or sail with you at night into Tangiers.'
Humour is also the means by which the text manages to co-opt
the reader into aligning with the position of the male 'I' or the
female 'you'; in the act of laughing you have positioned yourself
in the signifying gap, as Williamson puts it, and thus made yourself
into a male or female subject, both of whom would agree with
certain ideological statements about women, as I show later in more
detail.

There are other elements of humour such as the *doubles entendres*,
a specifically sexual form of humour, where the joke rests on the
ability of the reader to see that the sentence has two meanings, one
of which is sexual; for example, '(I'd like all your particulars in folders/
Marked *Confidential*)'; 'I'd like to let you try the French defence. And
mate you with my rook. and 'And certain things we might exchange/
Something familiar for something strange./I'd like to give you just
the right amount/ And get some change.' The first two examples
are fairly straightforward *doubles entendres*, where 'particulars' takes
on a secondary meaning of sexual characteristics, and in the second,
'French' stands as an indicator of sexuality. 'Mate' is being used as
a truly double-meaning word, and 'rook' therefore takes on a sexual
meaning. In the third example, because of the presence of other
doubles entendres in the text, and because it is not possible to interpret
the phrase in any other way, it seems to take on a sexual meaning. It
is in the nature of *doubles entendres* that once they are encountered
in a text, anything which is not immediately understandable can be
reduced to sexual innuendo.

The rhyme scheme and the metre also reinforce this notion of a
funny-clever poem; because of the conventions of twentieth-century
poetry, it would be extremely unlikely for a serious, contemporary
poem to have a rhyme scheme on the model of the first stanza:
aa/bb/ba/ba/ab/ba/ab/aa/b. Variations on this heavily patterned rhyme
scheme occur in all of the stanzas, and because the reader is aware of
the rarity of this type of rhyme in serious poetry and because s/he
knows that it occurs in limericks and children's verse, the reader
is led to classify the poem as humorous. Many of the rhymes are
also of the type which serious poets would shy away from: for
example, appreciate/delicate/lubricate/differentiate/weight/fete; and

unwind them/ mind them/ behind them. 'Appreciate' and 'delicate' are only sight rhymes and the rhyme falls very clumsily on the others, therefore we must assume that a dominant reading would construe these as humorous. Added to this is the fact that there are also elements of chiasmus in the rhymes which makes them appear even more humorous: for example, dates/inflates/ invert-/ebrates, where the last word is split between two lines, for no better reason than humour.

Because of the clumsy rhymes, it has the feel of a schoolboy poem, or even a commercial valentine card with its pedestrian rhymes and plodding metre; therefore the poem seems to retain a certain innocence within this dominant reading. For a male reader it is a very modern love poem in that it falls neither in the tradition of excessive emotion, nor is it totally cynical about love, but mixes excessive emotion with everyday, down-to-earth details. A dominant reading would see strong emotion handled in a funny way so that it can be admitted to without losing face. Because it is written as a valentine, the reader in the dominant reading can align himself with the 'I' position and imagine himself sending the poem to someone he loves.

In terms of indirect address, the poem fits in with a long tradition of extolling the virtues of the loved one, by representing each of her most beautiful parts in turn. Frequently the body parts are likened to parts of nature: doves, sunbeams, flowers, clouds, and so on, and thus objectified. The effect is to reify the woman's body but also to make it safe, since in the main, the elements chosen for comparison are soft, passive and non-threatening. In this poem, the parts of the woman's body are lovingly described, both the ones conventionally described in love poetry: eyes, cheeks, nose, lips, profile, but also more unconventional ones (hence the modern feel to the poem): upper arms, elbows, collar-bones, and even glands. This type of description is seen to be 'normal' within love poetry, and in order to make sense of this listing of body parts, the reader has to draw on elements of the cultural code whereby 'we all know' that female bodies should be described in this way. It is possible to find elements of this type of body part listing in many discourses circulating images of femininity or femaleness, for example, in pornography and advertising (see Betterton 1987). The strangeness of this type of description can be clearly seen if the text is rewritten from a female speaker to a male addressee; there are few textual precedents for women speakers extolling the virtues of a male addressee's body and there are no discourses which would reinforce this type of reading. Therefore the text would appear odd or incomprehensible.

The male reader is also encouraged to align himself with the 'I' figure, because it is in a position of power, a seemingly 'obvious' position given the discourses which circulate through society ratifying the 'naturalness' of male dominance. In each of the statements it is this male 'I' who possesses knowledge: he asks her to 'differentiate Nietzsche from Schopenhauer' which presumes that he knows the difference himself; further references to Julian of Norwich, Cathleen ni Houlihan, Mrs Rochester and Boolean mathematics suggest a position of wide knowledge, which the speaker positions as un-mediated common knowledge. The 'I' position is also in a position of strength from which it is seen as 'natural' that as part of romantic love he should terrify the female, for example, he feels it is his 'fate' to chase her 'screaming up a tower'. Rather than it being his choice, the action is described as being 'fate', i.e. within what is ideologically ratified. This position of knowledge and strength is one which has traditionally been granted to the male, and is one which other discourses ratify and reinforce that this is a 'naturally' male position. Thus by reading himself as the 'I' the male reader gratifyingly reassures himself of his subject position and his normality.

For the female reader within the dominant reading, the only viable position available is that of the objectified female addressee. This is a position which, because of the ideological discourses of romantic love and femininity, is very comfortable for many females: being the object of excessive male emotion is structured as a goal for women and a sign of 'normality' (see Modleski 1982). Women's magazines strive to encourage women readers to examine each body part and improve it by buying cosmetics: hair, cheeks, lips, etc., and the reward for this labour is for a male to be intoxicated with the body part. Thus, this poem, in its cataloguing of the body parts, speaks directly to the narcissism encouraged by the ideology of femininity. Each part is described as perfect, even the ones which women's magazines do not normally encourage labour on: 'I like the way your elbows work,/ On hinges', and the speaker remarks on 'the sculpture of your ears'.

Rosemary Betterton's collection of essays *Looking On* (1987) also discusses this quality of representation of femininity and how it is received by female readers, as does Laura Mulvey in her concept of 'to-be-looked-at-ness' (Mulvey 1981). Valentine cards are part of this view of femininity: they are generally sent by men to women to demonstrate their romantic love, and they are sometimes sent by secret anonymous admirers. This secret voyeuristic admiring is something which the ideology of femininity encourages. As John Berger has noted (1976), women are encouraged to behave as if they have a constant viewer, as if they are always under inspection even at their most private moments. This can be seen in the poem in lines like 'I like it when you tilt your cheek up./I like the way you nod and hold a teacup.'

The female reader in this dominant reading partakes of the humour, realizing that in this way the addresser is able to express excessive emotion, and is able to articulate the excessive admiration which is required by femininity: for example, 'Your upper arms drive me berserk.' The speaker expresses excessive emotion, but within an ironic, humorous framework. The poem also contains elements of chivalry which females within a dominant reading are supposed to appreciate: 'I'd like to offer you a flower.' The poem seems to construct the 'I' as a version of the New Man, the mythical beast beloved of journalism: someone who is caring (I like you, I like you), strong (I'd like to have you in my power), aware of his faults ('Even in trousers I don't mind them' – he is aware that he shouldn't be thinking this), and above all, humorous. The final lines of the poem show the reader that the addresser is serious in his intentions; this can be interpreted as showing that the addresser is not simply infatuated with the woman's body, but is prepared to marry her; he will be the final name in her appointment book, and will be with her in her 'future tense'. Thus the poem is a mixture of elements which position a female reader in the role of the 'you' the adored female, and since she draws on discourses of femininity to make sense of the poem, successfully interpellate her into a position of feminine subjecthood.

A female or male reader can also read the poem as 'overhearers' rather than directly aligning themselves with addresser or addressee. Nevertheless I would still argue that even in this slightly distanced form of reading, the ideological messages of indirect address have to be agreed to in order to understand the poem. Thus even here the reader will be interpellated by the poem.

As is well documented, feminists do not have a sense of humour. A female-affiliated resisting reading of this poem would refuse the subject positions proffered by the dominant reading. Refusing the discourses of femininity and the seductions of sex-object status, and refusing to make sense of the poem by being lured by the humour, this reader produces a quite different interpretation and stresses different elements within the text. This resisting reader is prepared to read the poem critically as a series of incoherent statements which can only be made sense of through drawing on ideological discourses of femininity. In this reading, some elements of the text will indeed be left as incoherent, as inexplicable: the aim will be to analyse the way the text proffers a dominant reading, as we have done in the previous sections, and then to produce an alternative reading position. The resisting reader decides consciously to mis-read the poem: to read the poem against the grain of the dominant reading.

Instead of a simple valentine card, this poem can be seen to be portraying a set of strategies akin to those of the protagonist in John Fowles's book *The Collector*. In this novel, the collector of butterflies turns his attention to women; he captures one and keeps her prisoner in his cellar. In Fuller's poem, the collector stalks the victim and catalogues the body parts of his prey, the ones that he has been able to see as he has watched her from a distance. He does not know the woman at all and has never talked to her, that is why 'The things about you I appreciate/ May seem indelicate'; sexual fantasies may seem predatory and manipulative if indulged in fetishistically in this way without knowing the woman. The speaker mentions 'You are the end of self-abuse' which clearly signals that self-abuse has been the order of the day. In this sense, it is a typical valentine: a card from an admiring male to a woman who is unaware of his attentions.

When read from this position we notice the difference between the 'I'd like' clauses and the 'I like' clauses: the 'I like' clauses are mainly concerned with parts of the body which could be seen by an unknown observer (cheeks, eyes, nose, wrists, fingers, etc.), whereas the 'I'd like' clauses seem to be concerned with sexual activities the observer would like to perform with his unknowing victim ('I'd like to find you in the shower'; 'I'd like to be around when you unhook'). The parallels with pornography and other practices of fetishism are evident: the fragmentation of the woman's body parts, and the dwelling on them, particularly her sexual characteristics, in order to stimulate the male. The speaker is not interested in the simple cataloguing of the woman's body parts as in conventional love poetry, but in seeing each of them as sexual: 'I'd like to . . . see your eyes dilate/ I'd like to have your back to scour/ And other parts to lubricate.' In addition, as I have already noted, each of the 'I'd like' clauses is also concerned with power through force or violence; this sadism is of a sexual nature: he'd like to 'make you cower' or to 'scour your back'. The normal collocation here would be 'to scrub' someone's back; but instead 'scour' has been used, which is a much more violent term. In a similar fashion, the line '(I'd like all your particulars in folders/ Marked *Confidential*)' begins to take on a more sinister tone when read in conjunction with the other lines which catalogue the woman's body parts.

The reader can tell that the clauses are of a hypothetical nature and that the speaker does not know the woman because of statements like 'I'd like to see you ironing your skirt/ And cancelling other dates/ I'd like to button up your shirt' and also 'I'd like to be around when you unhook./ I'd like to be your only audience' which we can presume are statements about events which have never taken place. The next sentence shows us what he has actually seen: 'I like the way your chest inflates.' However, he states: 'I'd like to be your second look', and presumably the woman has not given him a second look nor is she 'in my confidence'. The observer has studied each part of the woman carefully, 'I'd always know, without a recap/ Where to find them.' The idea of the woman being at a distance and unaware of her observer is reinforced by such statements as: 'I like the way your profile disappears/ Whenever you decide to turn and face me.'

Read from this position, the reader can see the rather contradictory elements contained in the ideology of romantic love: violence, power, chivalry, attraction, murder, pain, madness. These elements can only be read as coherent if they are positioned within a discourse of romantic love, and if the reader indirectly assents to them as 'obvious'. Indeed, 'you are the eternal feminine' works in a similar way: any contradictory elements could be placed under the heading of 'feminine' and thereby made to appear to be consistent or coherent since it is a construct. For example, in this poem, within femininity is classified: madness, murder, physical attractiveness, and religious mysticism. It is clear that what the observer wants is a Woman, a combination of all of the elements of sexual attractiveness, and he is prepared to put up with any of the problematic elements of femininity, such as madness, or murderous intent, so that he can put an 'end to self-abuse'. Any woman would do. In line with the 'collector' reading, it is possible to read the final lines of the poem in a rather chilling way: the only meeting the woman will have with the speaker will in fact be her last.

Thus, the female-affiliated reader cannot take up either of the positions or roles offered by the poem as the dominant reading; that does not mean to say that she is unaffected by them, but that she is more concerned to describe, analyse, and resist the effects of the poem. By drawing on a description of direct and indirect address, and also attempting to make apparent the incoherences which the reader has to try to resolve in reading the poem, the reader can arrive at a description of the dominant reading. Once that has been located, this dominant reading can be criticized and the reader can move on to developing a position of resistance to those meanings. It is this notion of resistance to the dominant meanings of a text which, if it has hitherto rarely been found in stylistic analysis, can be seen as a starting point for the necessary description of the different interpretations of a text.

Editor's preface

Using descriptive categories from systemic grammar, Kate Clark's chapter characterizes the ways in which cases of sexual violence perpetrated by men on women were and are reported in the British tabloid newspaper, *The Sun*. One may begin by noting that in an area which is so extensively gendered in its detailed treatment, it is a predictable irony that many of the standard sociological descriptive phrases are gender-neutral – 'sexual violence', 'spouse abuse' 'marital abuse' make no acknowledgement of the overwhelming tendency for the violence to be by men on women.

Most immediately evident, from the headlines and key opening paragraphs of these reports, is a tendency to attenuate or obscure the criminal culpability of the male perpetrator of these acts, and a concomitant tendency to project the attacked woman as, by the normative standards of *Sun* readers, being in their very nature and conditions ('pretty young blonde divorcee', etc.) a provocation and, more specifically, a sexual one. That the provocation is sexual is an important intermediate step in *The Sun*'s ideologically motivated representation of matters: to reassert that rape is primarily a 'problem' of sexuality (and not an act of power, domination, and cruelty) facilitates the further step that responsibility and blame are not all on one side but may involve 'both parties'. By contrast with violence, sexuality is a subject that our society continues to be ambivalent about: its proper forms, its implications, whether state or societal interests should constrain its expressions in any way.

One of the things Clark's paper shows very visibly is how, in its reporting of violent crime, *The Sun* attempts to 'sexualize' the crimes if at all possible: where violence is done by one person to another, the fact that the perpetrator is male and the victim female is treated as highly salient. Having thus gendered the crime, the next step is to insinuate that the responsibility lies not solely –

and perhaps not even chiefly – with the individual, but that it is also due to sexual drives, perversions, and obsessions beyond the individual's control. Since sexuality and its malcontents are societal preoccupations (this is certainly so for the reader of *The Sun* who, in reading that newspaper, is co-opted into a gossip-ridden community of part-voyeurs, part-censors), *The Sun*'s readers are afforded the further titillation of feeling part of a collective implicated in the brutality that has erupted.

Here, too, one might remark on the problematic nature of the compound 'sexual violence', which may tend to naturalize the assumption that there is a kind of violence which is to do with sex and sexuality and which should be understood in that relation (cf. 'mental violence', 'family violence'). If a corrected understanding of rape is to enter the common ground (e.g. the pages of *The Sun*) this compound may need to be supplanted. The point about the category 'family violence' is that such violence does occur in the determining context of the family and all the pressures that the family entails; in the case of rape, one might wish to argue, the determining context is not sexuality and sexual drive in any strictly analogous way, though these factors are contributory. The pressure to effect such re-namings and re-conceptualizings should always be noticeable in such areas (perhaps particularly gender and ethnicity) of contest and change, where dominant mores and assumptions are under challenge. In this area, for instance, there are – at least in the United States – other motivated shifts in naming practices going on: a 'repeat sexual offender' is now beginning to be named by some as a 'sexual predator', and a 'rape victim' is now preferably termed a 'rape survivor'.

9 The linguistics of blame

Representations of women in *The Sun*'s reporting of crimes of sexual violence

Kate Clark

In our society men commit acts of violence on women every day. All women's lives are affected by this: by actual violence or by the fear of it. For this reason, the messages that a popular newspaper engenders in its reporting of such crimes are critical. In this study of reports by *The Sun* newspaper (a tabloid daily with the largest circulation of all the British dailies) of male violence against women and girls, I am interested in who is blamed for an attack and how language is used to convey that blame.

Language forms a useful method of examining ideology. Sometimes *The Sun*'s point of view is manifested very blatantly (consider, for example, a report entitled 'VICTIM MUST TAKE THE BLAME', of January 1982). Often, however, language is used to convey blame subtly, with the motivating value system only subliminally present, so that an analysis of that language is not just an end in itself, but a way of decodifying and laying bare the patterns of blame.

These patterns found in *The Sun* will be familiar to anyone who has looked at how sexual violence is usually treated in contemporary British society. The attacker is not always held responsible for his actions, even though the attacks reported tend to be of the most brutal kind; the victim or another person (always a woman, incidentally) may be blamed. Of interest is the way in which language is used to manipulate this blame. What will probably not be familiar is a study of the language used to portray women in the media. Almost always, studies in this area have looked at 'images' of women (an overdue corrective is Cameron and Frazer's *Loved to Death* (1989), which includes some analysis of the language and reporting of sex-murders). And yet a stylistics-orientated analysis has definite advantages over an 'image'-based approach. It examines language in the study of a language-based medium and its framework allows a systematic and subtle analysis of the text. It also offers a theoretical basis for the study of language and ideology. The theory that people encode their world-view into language using its 'ideological function' (Halliday 1970: 143) legitimizes a linguistic investigation with the aim of exploring this world-view.

All news items are processed through minds. They must always be subjective, therefore, conditioned by the ideology of the language user. And, as Trew has said: 'All perception involves theory or ideology and there are no raw, uninterpreted, theory-free facts' (in Fowler *et al.* 1979: 95). *The Sun*'s bias often seems to be more than an unconscious subjectivity, arising from its particular world-view. For example, in one of the reports discussed in this article, the paper clearly takes a radically different stance not only from other newspapers, but also from the source, a legal ruling. This sort of reinterpretation suggests a more conscious bias, amounting to manipulation.

In this study, copies of *The Sun* from 10 November 1986 to 3 January 1987 were examined (copies of other newspapers were consulted for comparative and consultative purposes). This yielded fifty-three reports from *The Sun*, dealing with thirty-six cases, of male/female violence. All types of violence were included, as it was found that *The Sun*'s treatment was the same for all attacks, whether sexual (e.g. indecent assault, rape) or not (e.g. murder, assault, hit-and-run). The gender of the participants was the overriding factor in the nature of the reporting, and one to which I shall return later.

Two frameworks were used, naming analysis and transitivity analysis. Both work by showing the range of forms through which something can be expressed. The actual forms used in a report are chosen from this range. By comparing the selected form with the available options, the probable effects and the possible motivations can be deduced. Before showing how *The Sun* uses transitivity and naming to construct blame, I shall give an outline of these two frameworks.

NAMING ANALYSIS

Naming is a powerful ideological tool. It is also an accurate pointer to the ideology of the namer. Different names for an object represent different ways of perceiving it. An example from another area of violence illustrates this: how do you refer to a person who seeks political aims using aggression? Is s/he a terrorist, guerrilla, freedom-fighter, rebel, or resistance fighter? Different connotations of legitimacy and approval are carried by these labels. The naming of the participants in a case of assault works in a similar way.

The attacker

The Sun has two naming choices for an attacker: whether to regard him as sub-human or not. It may name him as a *fiend*, *beast*, *monster*, *maniac*, or *ripper*, using verbs which further suggest his non-humanness:

MONSTER CAGED (29/11/86, p. 22)
DOUBLE MURDER MANIAC PROWLS CITY OF TERROR (26/12/86, p. 1)

or it may keep solely to terms which treat him in terms of social normality, i.e., name, address, age, or occupation. Apart from those men who are arrested, on trial, or have been found 'not guilty', where the laws of libel or contempt of court prevent the use of 'fiend' naming, *The Sun* has a free choice. The emotive hyperbole of a term like 'fiend' indicates how utterly alien, terrible, and scandalous the newspaper finds the attacker and his actions. An absence of these names implies that *The Sun* does not find an attacker or his actions particularly shocking. A last naming option, occasionally used, is to name an attacker sympathetically. This is done, as will be seen later, by building apparent excuses into an attacker's name.

The victim

The naming of the victim (and this applies to any other woman involved) takes the form of a selection of personal details. She is identified by such information as her name, address, age, appearance, occupation, marital status, and whether she is a mother or not. Few victims have all details given. There are some legal restrictions: for example, it is illegal in Britain to publish the names and addresses of rape victims. Otherwise, *The Sun* again has a free choice on how to name, and its selection of details varies from report to report.

Almost always details are given not so as to individualize the victim but to label her. Such labels include *wife*, *unmarried*, *mum*, *mother of two*, and *vice-girl*. It should be stressed that these role-assignments are somewhat at the newspaper's discretion. Thus a woman who has blonde hair, four children and is divorced could be labelled as either 'mother of four' or 'blonde divorcee'. What is not arbitrary is the correlation between the naming of attackers and victims: only certain victim roles are linked to 'fiend' attackers.

Of the thirty-one reports where it was possible to name the attacker as 'fiend' (i.e. his identity was unknown or he had been found guilty in court), *The Sun* chose to refer to the attackers as *fiend, monster, beast,* or similar in thirteen reports. In these reports the victims were given the following names:

    wife (2)
    bride
    housewife
    mother (3)
    young woman
    girl, schoolgirl, girl guide (3)
    daughter
    blonde
    prostitute
    woman/victim (no role)
    individualized (no role)

There were also a few reports which, although not using the hyperbolic fiend terms, did convey blame of the attacker with such terms as *thug, gang,* and *kidnapper.* Victims in these reports were named in the following way:

    mother and children
    girl (in fact, a young woman)
    old woman

The labels for victims in those reports where the attacker was named sympathetically or in terms of normality are noticeably different. Apart from those attackers who were related to their victims (where completely different rules apply) and one short report where sexual murders were treated jokingly because they took place in Australia (too far away from the parochial *Sun* for it to get worried), victims of 'non-fiend' attackers were given the following names:

    blonde
    unmarried mum
    Lolita (in *Sun* language, a sexually active under-age girl)
    blonde divorcee/mum
    woman/victim (no role)

Similar labels are given to those women other than the victim who are sometimes held responsible for an attack, e.g. 'Blonde' and 'Blonde Divorcee'. These names seem to relate to a supposed sexual availability: 'fiends' attack 'unavailable' females (wives, mothers, and girls) while 'non-fiends' attack 'available' females (unmarried mothers, blondes, and sexually active girls). (The 'blonde' (16/12/86) and the 'prostitute' (11/11/86, p. 1) who were attacked by 'fiends' and the 'girl' who was attacked by a 'non-fiend' are anomalies to this general rule and will be looked at in more detail in due course.)

TRANSITIVITY

Blame or lack of responsibility, absence, emphasis or prominence of a participant can all be encoded into a report by *The Sun* through its choice of transitivity (on this model of transitivity analysis see Halliday 1985). Transitivity is concerned with language at the level of clauses. These are potentially made up of three components:

1 The Process – material, mental, verbal, or relational.
2 The Participants in the process.
3 The Circumstances of the process.

The elements in this theory most relevant to the reports studied are material processes and participants. Material processes involve 'doing'. There are two possible roles for participants: the Agent who 'does' the process and the Goal who is affected by the process. The Agent role is obligatory (i.e. always inherent in the process), but the Goal is only optional:

[Query]
HUBBY (Agent) KICKED (process) NO-SEX WIFE (Goal) OUT
(4/12/86, p. 3)
RAPED GIRL (Agent) WEEPS (process) (no Goal)
(13/12/86, p. 1)

In clauses where both Agent and Goal are inherent, the Agent may be emphasized by the choice of active voice or the Goal may be put into focus as the grammatical subject by choice of passive voice, with optional agent-deletion:

Hubby kicked No-sex wife out of bed. (active voice)
No-sex wife kicked out of bed by Hubby. (passive, with agent)
No-sex wife kicked out of bed. (passive, agent deleted)

In the violent acts reported by *The Sun*, the attacker affects the victim. In transitivity terms, he acts as Agent in a material process on the victim as Goal. If an attack is reported in this way, the attacker is shown acting intentionally upon the victim and the responsibility for the attack is (usually) seen to be his. There are several linguistic strategies used by *The Sun* to ensure that the attacker is not shown in his role as Agent affecting the victim as Goal. In these ways, blame for the attack can be withheld from the attacker and transferred to the victim or to someone else. This will be seen in the following analyses of the reports.

THE REPORTS

By itself, one clause or sentence is not very significant because a piece of writing is usually varied. Where a pattern emerges or one form is used insistently, the selection becomes more meaningful. Headlines are an exception. They can stand investigation by themselves because newspapers use them to encapsulate the view of the whole report. The headline below demonstrates how language can be used to focus blame upon an attacker. Not only is he shown as Agent acting upon the victim as Goal, but his naming as 'fiend' (and later also as 'sex-fiend', 'beast', and 'rapist'), and the naming of his victim in the report as a married woman, clearly point to his culpability:

FIEND RAPES WOMAN IN A BIG MAC BAR

(27/11/86, p. 23)

The Sun has several strategies for not blaming an attacker. One of the most common is to lessen the awareness of a man's guilt by making him invisible. Sometimes, this non-blaming will be masked by blaming someone else. Both these devices are used in this report (headline and opening sentence reproduced here) of 20/12/86, p. 7:

GIRL 7 MURDERED WHILE MUM DRANK AT THE PUB
Little Nicola Spencer was strangled in her bedsit home – while her Mum was out drinking and playing pool in local pubs.

Both these sentences have two clauses, one details the murder, the other describes what the victim's mother, Christine Spencer, was doing at the time of the murder. The 'murder' clauses are passive and the murderer is made invisible by deletion. This minimizes the reader's awareness of his guilt: compare 'Girl 7 murdered' with 'Man Murdered Girl, 7'. This structure – a 'drinking mother' clause linked to 'a murder-less murder' clause – is used in four out of the five sentences. The insistent repetition joins the child's death and the mother's absence so directly and so forcibly that a causal relationship is formed. The implication is that Nicola Spencer died because Christine Spencer was out. The naming of Nicola and her mother underscores the mother's supposed responsibility. Nicola's names all refer to her small size and age, which is usual for child victims. However, whereas in all other similar reports the connotations of innocence and vulnerability given by this naming emphasize the cruelty of a 'fiend' attacker, here, with the murderer invisible, the naming of the child implies that the mother is heartless. Christine Spencer is put further beyond the pale by her own naming, as 'blonde divorcee' (in *The Sun*'s coding she is an 'unrespectable woman').

Blaming the mother of the victim is a judgement passed by the newspaper. A radically different perception of the crime could have been given by choosing other structures, within the newspaper's normal range. In the example below, blame and attention are focused on the now visible murderer, who is seen to act intentionally, on the victim. Christine Spencer is no longer callous but suffering.

FIEND STRANGLES ONLY CHILD, 7 [headline]
Divorced Mum Grieves Alone [sub-heading]

In a report of 11/11/86, pp. 1, 4, and 5, the interpretation of a case where the attacker is again not held responsible is even more clearly a consciously chosen one. *The Sun* diverges in its judgement of the case, not only from other newspapers but from its source – a legal ruling. In court, the attacker, John Steed, was sentenced to four life-sentences for raping three women and killing a fourth. The killing was accepted as manslaughter, on the grounds of diminished responsibility (Steed was taking drugs at the time). Otherwise, the court saw him as responsible and blameworthy. Throughout its interpretation of the case, *The Sun* casts Steed in a passive role. Rather than affecting his victims, he is himself shown being acted upon, at times a victim himself. Simultaneously, the women involved in his life are shown as the real criminals. In this seventy-eight sentence report, the *Sun* chose to devote 63 per cent of the space to the defence lawyer's summing-up while only 4 per cent is used actually detailing the attacks. The paper's views are apparent in its encoding of events in the Page One headline:

SHARON'S DEADLY SILENCE [headline]
Lover Shielded M4 Sex Fiend [subheading]

The crimes are not mentioned here. Neither are the victims. Both are implicated in the term, 'sex fiend', but this is not an emphatic or conspicuous reference. They are certainly not the focus of the headline. Instead, the theme (Halliday 1970: 160–2) and the person shown acting refer not to Steed but to his girlfriend, Sharon Bovil. The attacker is relegated to the sub-heading, to an inactive role and furthermore to a role where Bovil acts upon him, as Goal. This makes it seem as though *the* central event of the case was one in which Bovil was active, Steed was acted upon and the victims were not involved. Bovil is blamed for Steed's crimes, by the newspaper, because she failed to inform the police about them. Whether this is a fair assessment of her actions, let alone a fair assessment of Steed's attacks will be looked at later. For now, it suffices to notice that, already, a shift of blame has taken place. Just as the word 'deadly' has been taken away from the actual killer, so, in a wider sense, Steed's deadliness has been transferred, by *The Sun*, to Bovil.

At the same time, Bovil is presented as an 'unrespectable' woman: she is 'blonde', 'beautiful', and 'petite' (cf. non-sexual synonym – 'small'). Steed is named with some fiend references, but rather than indicate his guilt, these are used to point to Bovil's responsibility. He is named as evil only in relation to her. Some possessives are used, indicating their relationship and her supposed control over him:

> Blonde, Sharon Bovil . . . M4 rapist John Steed
>
> (sentence 1)
>
> Bovil, 21 . . . her psychopath boyfriend
>
> (sentence 2)

Elsewhere, his naming ameliorates markedly to non-fiend references, for example, when the attacks are being described. These take up only three sentences, which in a seventy-eight sentence report is unusually short. They are not in a prominent position, but are a continuation of the Page One report which has Bovil as its theme (the numbers in parentheses refer to the sentence number of the original text):

> Two of Steed's rape victims – aged 20 and 19 – had a screwdriver held at their throats as they were forced to submit (21)(a). His third victim, a 39 year old mother of three was attacked at gunpoint after Steed forced her car off the M4 (22). Two days later, he gunned down call-girl, Jacqueline Murray, 23, after picking her up in London's Park Lane (23).

In both descriptions of the rapes (21 and 22) the perception of Steed as rapist is reduced by making the sentences passive and deleting him as Agent. This perception is further reduced by using the euphemism 'attacked' to mask the terrible details of abduction, repeated rape, and death threats (not mentioned at all in this newspaper).

The description of the manslaughter makes a startling contrast. This is an exceptional sentence; it is the only one where Steed is shown acting intentionally and therefore blameworthily against a victim. The sentence is active and the nature of the attack is specified and forcibly described. This anomaly may be explained as being due to Jacqueline Murray being named as a 'call-girl' and 'prostitute', killed only after being 'picked up'. In a report where the attacker's guilt is assessed at an absolute minimum, it is only the 'unrespectable' woman who the attacker can be shown as intentionally killing.

After Steed's responsibility for his actions is minimized on page one, the part of the report on pages four and five forms a further exhortation to excuse him. As a defence lawyer, quoted in sentence 27, says with coerciveness: '. . . we must search for the causes.' Again, Steed is put into a passive role. He is seen as a victim, as being created by his past.

PSYCHO SAW MUM RAPED

Boyhood horror 'scared M4 sex fiend for life'

Sex killer John Steed was set on the path to evil by seeing his mother raped when he was a little boy, it was claimed yesterday (24). The M4 monster's lawyer Mr Robert Flack told the Old Bailey that young Steed had walked into his mother's bedroom when she was being raped by his father (25). 'He saw her struggles and heard her screams and suffered the first trauma to his mind' said Mr Flack (26). He added: 'On the face of it, the horror of this case precludes sympathy with the defendant, but we must search for the causes' (27). 'The tragedy that caused four women to cross the path of John Steed has left one of them dead and three with horrendous memories that can never be erased' (28). Mr Flack then outlined 23 year old Steed's grim childhood that led to him becoming a woman-hating, sex-mad, psychopathic killer (29).

The rape of his mother is given as the central cause of Steed's deviance and of his later crimes. Interestingly, it is the rape of the mother and not the father's act of raping which is shown as the cause. In the headline, the father-rapist is unrealized and the rape process passivized. With no explicit agency given, the rape becomes a quality of the woman rather than an act upon her. The mother and her 'raped-ness' are Steed's 'boyhood horror', not the father's attack. Only once is the father actualized, in sentence 25. Even here, the mother is still the focus because the sentence is passive. As in the Page One part of the report, Steed only appears as a 'fiend' in relation to the woman who is being blamed:

Psycho . . . Mum
Boyhood horror . . . M4 sex fiend
sex-killer, John Steed . . . his mother
young Steed . . . his father
four women . . . John Steed

grim childhood . . . woman-hating, sex-mad, psychopathic killer

Sentence 28 in the extract exemplifies the extent to which blaming an attacker can be withheld, using linguistic manipulation. It is a general summing up of the attacks, quoted directly from the defence lawyer. In this interpretation of events, the agent which 'caused' the women's movements and 'left' them dead or raped is not the actual attacker, Steed, but 'tragedy'. The use of this word implies that the attacks were an unavoidable misfortune, something which no-one – and certainly not Steed – was responsible for. Steed actually performs no act in this sentence. Indeed, he is the Goal, affected by the actions of the victims when they 'cross' his 'path'. In this way, the defence lawyer (and *The Sun*, which chooses to quote him verbatim) suggests that the women were in some measure responsible for the attacks on them.

Girlfriend, mother, victims: at every stage it is the women who are blamed, while the actual attackers, the men – both Steed and his father – are released from the responsibility for their crimes. This is a chosen stance. Within its own ideology of blame *The Sun* could have indicated the 'genuineness' of the victims, by using a different naming strategy. Only the manslaughter victim is cast in the usually given role, which indicates the blame or non-blame of the attacker and, as mentioned before, as a 'vice-girl' this role, if anything, obscures rather than acknowledges the evident guilt of her attacker. Information is so lacking about the first two victims – only their ages are given – that it is difficult even to picture them. Although the third victim is named once as 'mother of three', no mention is made of her being pregnant when she was abducted and repeatedly raped.

Other interpretations are possible. The court saw Steed as guilty enough to receive four life sentences. Other papers followed this line. While all except for the *Daily Mirror* focus not on the victims, but on Bovil and the father's rape of the mother, they do not, for example, find Bovil blameworthy. Other papers interpreted Bovil's actions not as intentional or voluntary, but motivated by fear of Steed, for example:

SECRET TERROR OF M4 RAPIST'S GIRLFRIEND

(*Daily Telegraph*)

SHARON'S SECRET
Terror of Girlfriend

(*Daily Mirror*)

Most quote the policeman in charge of the investigation:

'She was no different from his other victims. She herself was in stark terror of him.'

The coverage of the rape by Steed's father of his mother points to one last area of male/female violence which I would like to consider, that of husband/wife attacks. So far, all the reports I have examined have been of attacks on women by strangers. In the Steed report the husband-rapist was not blamed. This is not an uncommon way of perceiving such attacks, as the following headline indicates:

HUBBY KICKED NO-SEX WIFE OUT OF BED

(4/12/86, p. 3)

In terms of transitivity, this headline is identical to the 'Big Mac' heading, but the attacker here is not viewed with the same abhorrence as the rapist then was. Here it is the naming which is the conveyor of blame. The attacker in this case was so violent that his wife had to obtain a divorce. Yet, he is named as 'Hubby', a term not of censure, but a diminutive name of affection – an odd choice in this context. The naming of the victim is similarly odd. There is a tension between 'no-sex' and 'wife'. Rather like 'lady doctor' or 'male nurse', the use of 'no-sex' implies a deviation from the norm. The implication is that a 'normal' wife would have sex with her husband. This feeling is reinforced by her second naming: 'his pretty blonde wife' perceives the woman in terms of her sexual attractiveness and her husband's possession of her ('his . . . wife'). Given this naming, it seems understandable that he became 'sex-mad' (sentence 1) and 'kicked her out of bed'. As in the following report, sex is perceived as a wife's duty and a husband's right. Failure to service a husband's sexual needs is seen as a justification for violence, either against his wife or against another woman. In the case below, 'the other woman' was a 16-year-old girl:

SEX-STARVED SQUADDIE STRANGLED BLONDE, 16
Love ban by teenage wife

(29/11/86, p. 11)

The pattern of blame and language is similar: the naming of the victim by her hair colour fails to individualize her in any way which could draw sympathy towards her. Instead, it portrays her in terms of her sexual attractiveness, as something which any man, especially one named as 'sex-starved', could not help responding to. Indeed, this sympathetic naming of the attacker, in combination with the paper making a reference to his wife not wishing to have sex with him, implies that the person to blame for the murder was the murderer's wife.

Women are often held responsible, by the newspaper, for the actions of their husbands or boyfriends, although the link is never explicitly made, just assumed to be true (why should sexual frustration lead to a tendency towards homicide?). For women who are attacked by their own partners, this is especially true. There is a clear division between 'stranger-attackers' and 'husband-attackers' in *The Sun*'s world-view. Although the attacks by husbands can be as serious and as bloody as the fiendish stranger-attackers, they are almost never named as fiends. The divergence between the gravity of the attacks and the non-blaming of the husband-attackers, as judged by their naming in the headlines and first sentences, can be seen below:

VIOLENT HUBBY
Violent husband, Bob Sleightholme
The victim was beaten over a period of twelve years by her husband, before he almost killed her.

(21/11/86, p. 13)

CRAZED WIFE-KILLER
A tormented husband
The husband almost decapitated his wife with a knife.

(28/11/86, p. 13)

DOCTOR DEATH
Wife-killer
An evil doctor
The man murdered his first wife and attempted to murder his second.

(19/12/86, p. 16)

DEBT-RIDDEN DAD
Tormented Kevin Banks
A woman was murdered by her husband, who then killed himself.

(19/12/86, p. 11)

HUSBAND
Spurned husband, Derek Ord
A man shot his wife and her mother dead.

(27/12/86, p. 1)

For all the reports, after the first sentence, the naming of the husband consisted of references to his status as husband or father, and his job, appearance, or age, i.e. in terms of social normality. Only in one of the reports (19/12/86, p. 16) is an attacker ever referred to in fiendish terms. Even then, he is mainly referred to with non-fiendish names (two fiendish and nine non-fiendish). Significantly, all the other men who murdered their wives are seen as themselves suffering: they are 'debt-ridden', 'tormented', 'crazed', or 'spurned'. This is the key note, not the suffering they themselves have caused, but their own plight. These men are named sympathetically, with excuses built into the naming. They are seen as suffering so much they became 'crazed' or 'tormented' and then committed murder. This makes it seem that they were not responsible for their actions – a man who is mad cannot be blamed. It also raises the question of why they were suffering. Kevin Banks was under financial pressure and killed both his wife and himself, but Derek Ord and the 'crazed wife-killer' of 28/11/86 were both suffering because their wives had left them and, in the latter case, because she had also taken a new lover. In other words, the wives are shown to cause the suffering which supposedly lead to their husbands killing them. This cause is particularly highlighted in the Ord case by the use of the emotive adjective, 'spurned', meaning to 'reject with disdain . . . treat with contempt . . . repel with one's foot' (*OED*).

This lack of fiends, monsters, and beasts in the ranks of the husbands must be due to husband-attackers being an anomaly in *The Sun*'s ideology. A fiend is outside human society and a man who attacks a stranger can be viewed as abnormal and alien. A husband is always and unarguably within society. It is a position ratified by society in the marriage institution. As such it is difficult for a husband to be seen as a fiend. Therefore, these violent men are normalized and humanized by 'suffering' naming. This keeps the ideology intact, although it does mean that the women victims must take the blame. They bear the burden of reconciling anomaly to ideology. The tension between the theory and actuality is revealed in the Sleightholme headline. On one level the man is seen as 'violent', on another he is affectionately seen as 'hubby'. These two concepts are incompatible and contradictory. The forcing together of them into a single name shows the tension these husband-attackers create in the ideology.

POSSIBLE MOTIVATIONS

This chapter has attempted to demonstrate that *The Sun* does manipulate blame. It has also shown some of the ways in which this is linguistically achieved. It has not yet tackled the question of why the newspaper should want to do this. There can only be conjecture as to *The Sun*'s motivations, but clearly, the linguistic analysis points to the world-view through which the events are mediated and encoded. Two possible reasons are implied by the manipulations of language.

The Sun's interest in attacks involving male violence against women and girls may be part of its general concern with sex. This might seem far-fetched because not all the crimes are sexually violent. However, in its encoding of blame, the type of attack (whether sexual or not) had no effect on the blaming pattern. The significant factor was not the type of crime, but the gender of the participants. Murder, assault, even hit-and-run victims were cast in roles of sexual availability or unavailability and their attackers were named as fiends or not. This indicates that the reporting of male/female attacks could well be conditioned by an interest in sex. If this is so, these reports would tie in with other facets of this fascination: with the sexual mores of the 'stars' (and there is a clear crossover here – MOWER HIT ME FOR SAYING NO TO SEX (16/12/86, p. 15), MURDER QUIZ FOR ESTHER'S IN-LAW (10/12/86, pp. 1, 4), WIFE BEATER, SHILTON IN CELLS (4/12/86, p. 1), with offers of sexy lingerie, with advice on 'your love-life', and with *The Sun's* 'Page Three Girl' – the soft-porn photographs of models which daily appear in this paper). In the last instance, there is a definite merger of interest.

In the Steed report, the photographs clearly show a Page Three influence. Two pictures of Bovil, the attacker's girlfriend, dominate. The second one, covering most of pages four and five, shows Bovil full length with a low-cut black leather dress pushed up her thighs in an eminently 'rapeable', Page Three posture. Like the Page Three Girls she is viewed here and in the text as a sexual 'bad girl'.

The concurrence of interest is no more clearly shown than when the newspaper's favourite 'model' is involved with a rapist, albeit indirectly. The report – SAM FOX AND THE RAPIST (16/12/86, p. 1) – tells how a man, Raymond Genas, was arrested after his victim noticed a photograph of Genas, with Samantha Fox, in the car in which he raped her. (Genas and Fox met only once on a brief and impromptu occasion when Fox let the photograph be taken as a favour to her fan.) Most of the front page is taken up by a huge reproduction of this photo, an image of the brutal rapist with his arms around the soft-porn star. This titillating proximity is the theme of the report, completely eclipsing the victim's suffering. In the headline, it is not the victim or the process of rape which is given priority, but the supposed relationship between Fox and Genas. The real interest in the case also emerges in the naming; Genas is only portrayed as a fiend in sentences relating to Fox. With the victim, apart from one racist reference, he is named simply as 'Genas':

An evil rapist . . . Sam Fox
The Beast . . . Beauty
Hulking, 17 stone, Raymond Genas . . . the Page Three Beauty

Genas . . . the terrified blonde (a reference to the victim)
Genas, 23 . . . the girl
The Black Giant . . . his victim

A general interest in sex seems to be a strong motivation for *The Sun*'s way of reporting events of male/female violence. Certainly, the neo-Gothic naming of men as beasts, fiends, and monsters helps to sensationalize the attacks and maybe helps to sell papers. Perhaps, also, labelling victims, as opposed to individualizing them, lends itself to a voyeuristic rather than a sympathetic reading of events.

A possible alternative to fiend naming would be a more neutral style. It could be argued that fiend naming is preferable to this because it, at least, conveys some of the horror of the events and the culpability of the attackers. It is dubious whether this sort of naming does in fact carry much blame towards the attackers (as will be argued below). It also seems doubtful whether it actually conveys much horror. Rather, it seems to trivialize. When victims are portrayed as roles, rather than as individuals, it is difficult fully to imagine and sympathize with their experiences. It is also hard to believe the outrage apparently intended by the hyperbolic fiend naming when it is withheld from 'non-genuine' victims and used in the same routine way with all attackers of 'genuine' victims, no matter how serious the attack was; according to these values a sex-murderer can be and is (22/12/86, p. 23) treated in the same way as a male motorist who accidentally hit female pedestrians with his car (NB they were 'respectable' victims, 'a mother strolling with her baby'). Both attackers are perceived to be fiends.

Perhaps most importantly, it is highly unlikely that fiend naming or *The Sun*'s general choice of language, does anything to change the present conditions which produce men who commit violence against women. But 'Sex as a good sell' can only be a partial reason for *The Sun*'s style of reporting events: it explains the general interest but not the intricate patterns of blame and language. A more detailed examination of the newspaper's conditioning world-view supplies the rest of the probable motivation for *The Sun*'s choice of language. Several pieces of linguistic evidence indicate this world-view, the central one being the naming patterns of the victims and attackers. *The Sun*'s ideology is based on the premise that fiend attackers are distinguishable from non-fiends and 'genuine' victims from 'non genuine' ones. Furthermore, these distinctions are based not on what is done, but on who it is done against, as defined by the paper, of course. Any attack is fiendish when committed against a female who is named as 'respectable', i.e. sexually 'unavailable' and as a stranger to her attacker (and also when another woman is not held responsible for the attack). It is not seen as fiendish when committed against a woman who the attacker is married to or against a woman who is named as 'unrespectable'.

The naming of the victims clearly reflects a patriarchal viewpoint because women are categorized in terms of possible sexual encounters with men, rather than as autonomous individuals. It is also getting close to a 'property' view of male violence. 'Availability' could be rephrased as 'unattachment to a man'. So, for example, attacks on other men's wives are treated with abhorrence, while those on a man's own wife are seen as 'legitimate' or understandable.

The distinction between fiends and non-fiends is also a patriarchal myth. It assumes that violent, anti-female attitudes are abnormally rare and that strangers are the men to be feared. Actually attitudes and attacks by men known to their victims are extremely common. Just how ordinary the inclination to rape is, for example, can be seen by looking at the attitudes of male undergraduates, usually seen as 'normal' (i.e. intelligent, mainly white, and middle-class) men. A survey in America found that of 341 male students, 87 had made at least one attempt at:

> coital access with a rejecting female during the course of which physical coercion is utilized to the degree that offended responses are elicited from the females.
>
> (Kirkpatrick, quoted in Toner 1977: 83)

Russel (1982: 133) also quotes 'several recent studies' of male college students undertaken to find out if there was 'some likelihood they would rape a woman if they could get away with it'. Results ranged from 35 per cent to 51 per cent positive.

Actual acts of violence by men on women are also very common and the men from whom women are most at risk are not strangers but those they know and those they live with. The 'Rape Counselling and Research Project' found that 'over 50% of women have had some prior contact with the man who raped them' (1979: 7). This is undoubtedly an underestimate because their sample included only those reported to the police, which would exclude marital rape, which at the time was legal in Britain. Russel found, in a statistically impeccable study, that one in seven wives are or have been raped by their husbands and that married women are six times more likely to be raped by their husbands than by strangers (1982: 1, 67). She also discovered that 21 per cent of wives had been 'subjected to physical abuse by a husband'. Eighty per cent of sex crimes committed against children are by attackers well known to them and 50 per cent are by the father (Laneless, quoted in Ward 1984: 82). The largest category of murders is of spouses or co-habitees (24 per cent) and of these more than 80 per cent of the victims are female (Home Office figures for 1979, quoted in NCCL 1983: 12). If it is thought that an attack from someone who the victim knows is less devastating, less 'fiendish', this also is false: violence from someone known will probably be endured over a longer period of time, access to the victim is usually unlimited, and the after-effects are harder to recover from because a trust has been violated and the victim is less likely to confide in others and, if she does, is less likely to be believed (Ward 1984: 82–7; D. Martin 1976: 63).

Given that the idea of a 'fiend' attacker is so very false, there must be strong reasons for *The Sun* to use it. It does mean that in every permutation of blame the men always win. This is obvious where the attacker is not held responsible, but is less so if he is apparently blamed. Fiend naming suggests that the attacker is so evil and so alien that he is utterly outside human kind and society. This is in effect an excuse for his crime because a fiend or a monster or a beast cannot be held responsible for its actions. By implying that these men are extra-societal, this naming also excuses our society which produces them. By creating a false dichotomy between fiends and non-fiends, *The Sun* blurs the wider continuum of male violence against females. The intense hyperbole of fiend naming focuses a self-righteous fury on stranger-attacks, which are actually a very small area of male/female violence. By obscuring the whole range of aggressive acts, it becomes impossible even to ask the vitally important question of why, in our society, so many men commit acts of violence against women and girls. Under its veneer of moral indignation against fiends, therefore, *The Sun* helps to maintain the status quo.

Editor's preface

Rukmini Bhaya Nair answers a series of marriage advertisements, placed in Indian, British, and American journals. Her answer incorporates gynocriticism, grammatical analysis, and reflections on marginalized genres. Patterns of noun phrases, main verbs, and lexical collocation are some of the textual features dwelt upon. One of the noun phrases which inevitably invites scrutiny is the putative genre label, marriage advertisements. That label is now widely superseded in the western press, by other related and not-so-related terms: heartsearch, person-to-person, personal column, to name only three. Such variant labels may disguise an underlying commonality of purpose, but this cannot be simply assumed; some of the advertisers in western magazines seem to seek companionship rather than a sexual partner, or a sexual partner but not a long-term relationship: the genre is undergoing change.

In examining the matrimonial advertisement column, Nair is looking at what she calls 'a linguistic nexus', a cultural place and pressure-point where studies of gender, genre, and grammar meet. All three framing-discourses rely on a principle of productivity, applied to whatever are identified as the 'primary features' (of a genre, or gender, or language). That is, all three postulate core units and rules for the combination and transformation, underlying situated instances or displays of their subject-matter. In the present instance, then, what might be the primary features, and generative rules, of matrimonial advertisements? And how do these differ from one newspaper to the next, from India to Britain to America? Thus begins Nair's study, which proceeds to question all manner of theoretical assumptions not only in the above three parent-discourses, but also in two further frameworks: postmodernism and feminism. For these and other discourses have been increasingly challenged by a resistance to their reductive idealizations, and their marginalizing of context-dependency.

In fact marginalization (of non-western texts, genres, languages) is the uppermost theme in Nair's essay. Personal relationship advertisements, themselves, have in the past been treated as marginal, though this seems to have changed since the 1970s, and not only in western countries, where new interactions of 'information-age technology', social and geographical mobility, and commodification might be expected to promote the genre. Equally marginalized, one might argue, is the individuality of each and all those participating in the personal-ad language-game. As Nair puts it, 'prototypes of the desirable female and acceptable male emerge, separate and certainly unequal, from both Indian and "western" representations'. Furthermore, in the Indian advertisements, the potential bride and groom are also embedded, if not marginalized, within powerful familial frames: there is more alliance than dalliance in these communications, in which one family seeks out a compatible other, with a view to mutually satisfactory union.

Particularly suggestive are Nair's remarks on the marriage advertisements placed on behalf of 'Green Card holders' – typically, talented and successful Indian men normally resident in a western country. These advertisements she characterizes as 'texts of crisis'; certainly, in terms of numerous criteria – cultural and ethnic identity, national affiliation, social and moral values, assumptions about the place of the individual relative to family and society, and about gender and sexuality – these texts are a significant window onto an ongoing redefinition of received categorizations. Many of the issues can be conceptualized as reinscriptions of the politics of 'place' and 'space' (on which see Gupta and Ferguson forthcoming); metaphors of location and locating are pervasive in discourses about identity. The essay concludes with a firm insistence that while text-linguistic structural analysis is indeed, as poststructuralism argues, insufficient, it is nevertheless *necessary*; it is equally necessary, in Nair's view, that the linguistic analysis be integrated with an uncovering of social ideology, and consequences of whatever kind.

10 Gender, genre, and generative grammar

Deconstructing the matrimonial column

Rukmini Bhaya Nair

I

Any *-ism*, from antinomianism to zoroastrianism, typically encodes a central thesis, which can be given a strong and simple formulation. Poststructuralism, however, is unusual among *-isms* because it initially appears to lack a core set of statements; indeed, its temporal prefix *post* makes its status as an *-ism* heavily dependent on its dominant predecessor, namely, structuralism. Many have claimed that this is an essential weakness in conceptualizing the poststructuralist position (Barth 1980, Kostelanetz 1982, and the aptly named Newman 1984). Its intellectual role in historical terms is one that might be assigned to a footnote; it (merely) constitutes a critical commentary on the great structuralist enterprise which spanned the middle decades of the twentieth century. Recent arguments by critics such as McHale (1987), however, challenge this marginal view of the postmodernist phase.[1] McHale suggests that there has been a marked philosophical shift in the transition from a structuralist perspective, which embodied a poetics dominated by *epistemological* issues to a poststructuralist perspective, which incorporates a poetics dominated by *ontological* issues.

This chapter examines McHale's contention that the *ism* in poststructuralism is vastly more significant than the *post* by focusing on a linguistic nexus – between studies of *gender* as they have been interpreted within feminist and postfeminist debates, studies of *genre* as these are analysed in contemporary literary theory and studies of *grammar* as these are represented by the Chomskyan and subsequently the postgenerative paradigms. As is apparent from their common etymological origin, or in this case literally *genesis*, the nouns 'gender' and 'genre' as well as the adjective 'generative', applied to recursive grammars of the Chomskyan type, have a shared prehistory.

These concepts overlap in so far as they all relate to a) productiveness b) primary features.

By 'productiveness' is meant the creative competence which Chomsky and others maintain enables human beings to produce an infinite number of sentences and/or texts based on a finite number of learned and/or innate structures. In mainstream linguistics of, broadly speaking, the structuralist persuasion, there appears to be widespread agreement that humans uniquely use linguistic rules of deletion, movement, etc. to *transform* relations between underlying conceptual entities like subjects, objects, and actions into myriad overt verbal forms. Within social anthropology and literary theory it is also recognized that whole genres, including the folktale (Propp 1968, Greimas 1973), the myth (Lévi-Strauss 1968), and the Gothic/Harlequin romance (Modleski 1982), have been analysed using an apparatus that consists of limited epistemic categories and rules of combination which allow numerous permutations and disallow others.

By 'primary features' are meant those semantic or social characteristics that define sets such as the feminine, the self, the other, the transitive, the fictive, and so on. Grammatical entities, genders, and genres, in their diverse manifestations, may all be analysed in terms of characteristic features that are typically associated with them. This reductionism inherent in the methodology of structuralism is both the source of an attractive universalist ideology and of a growing discomfort with an exclusivism that disregards or rejects untidy evidence that will not fit into preconceived slots.

The ontological obsession of poststructuralism with heterocosms seems, at least partially, a manifestation of a strongly felt reaction against the perceived reductionist mode of structuralism. This becomes obvious as soon as we interrogate the stylistic preferences of postmodernist writers (Celan, Borges, Rushdie) and, even more profoundly, the critical practices of current literary theory and social psychology (Lacan, Derrida, Kristeva). Postmodernist criticism has rapidly developed a vocabulary that constantly emphasizes the contradictions, slippages, discontinuities, gaps, randomness, excessive inclusion, breaks, ruptures, and multiple diegetics in any textual rendering. The world of the postmodernist text seems to consist of several quasi-worlds; magical worlds that are imbued with a sense of the everyday and historical worlds that are overwhelmed by atemporal ones. We are forced into a position of uncertainty about the status and locus of the self. The questions posed by the postmodernist text, or a poststructuralist reading of any text, whatever its period, are not the epistemic 'who am I?' 'what is this world?,' but rather the ontological 'which of my selves is this?' 'which of my worlds?' Herein lies the crux of that argument of McHale's mentioned earlier. Defamiliarization in the poststructuralist mode is achieved through cognitive indeterminacy; and the structuralist certainty that a few fundamental categories, staples of human consciousness, can account for our multitudinous apprehensions, thereby stands impugned.

Within linguistics, too, the consolidation of subdisciplines such as sociolinguistics, pragmatics, and ethnomethodology, which stress the importance of context and use in determining linguistic meaning, poses some problems for the universalist Chomskyan model where syntactic competence is accorded preeminence. It is the utterance, bounded by speaker-to-hearer reciprocal relationships, and emphatically not the sentence, bounded by abstract-to-surface unidirectional relations, that motivates enquiry in these areas of linguistic investigation. However, there is still place, as I shall show in the subsequent sections on the fragment of discourse known as a 'matrimonial advertisement', for a view of language that sees studies of sentence and utterance as complementary rather than opposed, and poststructuralism as an energetic synthesis rather than the antithesis of structuralism.

Although the late twentieth-century backlash against structuralism has continuously gathered momentum, it can often be equated with a mood, and not so much a methodology or an intellectual position. For, the extent to which poststructuralism still relies on pre-existing structural analyses in order to effect its own programme of deconstruction remains considerable. Gayatri Chakravorti Spivak, explicating Derrida, for example, has described the text as a device to keep (linguistic) chaos at bay (1987: 45–6). The nature of such a device, when contrasted as it explicitly is with 'chaos', cannot *but* be structural. The arbitrary, formal, and recognizable patterning that occurs recurrently when human beings articulate sentences and texts is precisely what structuralists from every discipline have contended gives language its awesome power as a 'device' for ordering and systematizing an otherwise inchoate world. If the underlying patterns of sentences and texts are clearly analysed and exposed, using the machinery of structuralism, it is indeed possible, and desirable, to critique the results of such an analysis, as well as the tools which produced such limited results. But if we do not accept the presuppositions of a structural analysis, its premise that there are basic categories like subjects vs. objects, masculine vs. feminine, etc. expressed in the verbal, pronominal, and/or lexical systems of the world's languages, it becomes significantly more difficult to insist that these categories have been misinterpreted and misrepresented. How, then, do we proceed with the postmodernist project of deconstructing such systems?

Derrida proposes an apparently quite radical answer that Todd summarizes, and subsequently joins issue with:

> In Derrida's formulation the sexes are not opposed and their traditional opposition is [to be] denaturalized, made unfamiliar, so that they may be rendered equivalent. The questions to ask then are precisely *not* those of feminist criticism, caught firmly in the old-fashioned metaphysics – how women may become subjects in their own right, for example, . . . how they might write outside the patterns of patriarchal culture – since such questions are asked entirely within the phallogocentric world that should be opposed; feminism in this view becomes nothing but the operation of women who aspire to be like men.
>
> 'Woman' is then what is not feminist and the question becomes one of style not content. The feminine or 'the name of woman' is a kind of pre-logical destabilizing of texts, a writing which subverts logic and the traditional history of binary metaphysics. The texts Derrida chooses on the whole are by men and in [his analysis of] them . . . the body image with which women have been saddled in traditional culture begins a strange disintegration into 'labyrinths of female voices, hymens, veils, vaginas, *tocseins*, traces and texts. And it is from within these labyrinths that Derrida pulls on the female thread, 'unravelling the fabric of Western thought'. It is all very complicated, metaphoric, excited and exciting but, like Lacan's formulation, it can be 'deconstructed' into some pretty traditional, predictable, and libertine notions. . . . Women have not only become 'woman', but they have (re)acquired associations with the curious, the perverse and the tactless.
>
> (1988: 126–7)

Other feminists have, unlike Todd, been much less hostile to Derrida's approach, concluding, as Showalter (1985) does, that 'there has been a critical consolidation in the 1980s . . . because poststructuralists, feminists, and Afro-American critics share the same enemies: the right-wing champions of a nostalgic humanism'.[3] In fact, Todd herself partially subscribes to this position when she writes, in response to Showalter,

> I would like to add to this that the new theoretical methods – poststructuralism, deconstruction, and psychoanalysis – should

make an absolute difference (if one can still use this word in an unreconstructed way) to feminist criticism. Their emphasis on language is one that feminist criticism needed and still needs, and their insistence on problematizing all 'truth' is a salutary example.

(1988: 128–9)

It has been necessary to describe these cross-currents of recent western thought in some detail in order strategically to situate the somewhat unusual, and mostly Indian, material that we are about to analyse. Since gender, genre, and grammar intersect in especial ways in culturally specific varieties of the 'matrimonial column', these texts should provide a site in which it becomes possible to test feminist/poststructuralist claims about 'genre as a system of historical and literary expectations and assumptions' (Todd 1988: 99). Since there are both overt and covert ideologies associated with particular literary forms, the method of analysing gender and genre in tandem, could also, according to Todd, be applied to 'the study of popular culture so that genres that have been despised as popular or feminine can be illuminated and the uncanonized can be connected with the canonized in startling ways to break down the 'aristocracy of discourse' (1988: 99–100). It is this claim about *hierarchies of discourse*, which also applies to the marginal value and critical space assigned to non-western texts, genres, and languages in 'world-wide' debates on poststructuralist methodologies, which will be of genuine concern to the following analysis of the 'matrimonial'.

II

This section considers the newspaper/magazine as a composite genre that disintegrates into a number of subgenres, of which the matrimonial advertisement is simply one non-obligatory part. Among popular forms of written discourse, the daily newspapers offer, in microcosm, one of the most interesting examples of the ways in which very different written forms may be juxtaposed without incoherence. In a newspaper, classified advertisements may coexist peacefully[2] with sports items and headlines of world crisis with weather reports; and much the same latitude exists in a magazine. Increasingly, the numerous marriage and dating advertisements that appear in newspapers/journals in societies as otherwise different as India and the United Kingdom and United States offer evidence that new conduits for social interaction are being formed.[3] If, as recent feminist criticism emphasizes, many traditional forms of patriarchy are in the process of a radical, but nevertheless often imperceptible, reconstitution taking place in postcolonial as well as postindustrial societies, then the matrimonial columns of newspapers provide useful evidence of this far from negligible change.[4]

From the linguistic point of view, moreover, this apparently peripheral genre not only displays a characteristic content relating to social stereotypes in different societies, it also shows distinctive features of lexis, syntax, and discourse organization which set it starkly in contrast with other classified advertisements. A study of this subvariety of written language is of theoretical interest both because it has considerable human and social implications and because in form and style it is quite amenable to strictly linguistic analysis.

A number of recent sociolinguistic studies which attempt to demonstrate the reciprocal effects of language and culture on each other have gender as their focus (Cameron 1985, Schielflin and Ochs 1987). Cultural discriminations on the basis of sex are shown to be encoded in the forms of language that a community uses. Many of the world's languages are like English in that they possess pronominal or other grammatical systems that are sensitive to the cultural salience of sex. Such grammaticalization of sex in terms of gender is an indication both of cultural conceptualization and attitude. As Wilkinson has picturesquely put it:

> even obvious concepts like 'man' and 'woman' are human creations in the sense that we choose to think of their sex as their most noticeable feature. If we lived in a society of giraffe-like people, where height was the main thing that mattered (if you couldn't reach your food from tall trees, you would be in difficulties) we might instead have 'talls' and 'shorts' as the basic classification.
>
> (1971: 82)

Investigations into child language acquisition have tended to support the position that children in a variety of linguistic communities do not instinctively single out differences of sex as worthy of particular notice since they continue to confuse gender pronominals such as 'he', 'she', 'him', and 'her' until a comparatively late stage in their language development.[5] Left to their own devices, they might indeed, as Wilkinson suggests, categorize human beings as large or small, adult or child, but the language that they are in the process of acquiring powerfully influences their perceptions of relevance. Although there are languages like Bengali that do not mark gender grammatically via verbal endings, pronouns, and honorifics, sexual differences are none the less guaranteed salience in these languages through lexicalization (*dada, didi, ma, baba, budo, budi, bhai, ban*) as well as through discourse strategies.

Sexual differences are socially institutionalized and linguistically realized. In an overwhelming majority of cultures, women's social roles are assigned to render them 'separate but unequal'. Women dress differently, act and interact differently, and, as a simple corollary, often speak differently from men. Lakoff (1975), in a controversial and now classic paper, isolated a number of features of women's speech that seem to reinforce, in the American cultural context, perceptions of women as relatively powerless. Other researchers have since shown that 'the semantic derogation of women'[6] is accomplished not only *by* women through their own style of speech but is also achieved through language *about* women in a whole range of discourse contexts reinforcing patriarchy. This paper extends the scope of these studies to a hitherto neglected corpus of texts.

Matchmaking advertisements are a comparatively recent discourse type designed to provide a solution to a much older social problem. In India, the mobile, literate, numerically very large, and economically and culturally quite confident, middle classes are no longer adequately served by the more traditional means of uniting the sexes.[7] Thus leading and highly respectable Indian newspapers like *The Statesman* and *The Times*, themselves metaphors of the patriarchal, in terms of their dominance and of their association with the elite colonial tongue – English – cater to the newly created social needs of their readership by prolifically publishing column upon column of matchmaking material. Sriniwas (1981) and Kishwar (1984) have argued, in a vastly more serious but connected context, that the practices and vocabulary of dowry perniciously percolated from economically and historically advantaged communities to others less fortunate.[8] Similarly, the advertising routine, a colonial heritage, has now been taken over from the English language papers into the regional Indian papers.[9] It is not too far-fetched, in such a context, to argue that the *homogenization of cultural preferences* in post-Independence India finds one channel in the language of the ubiquitous matrimonial advertisement. Marriage and dating advertisements in the personal columns of elite American and British journals such as the *New York Review of Books* and the *New Statesman and Society* also share several of the structural features of the Indian advertisement, although multiple differences do emerge upon a close reading. Taken together, the data from these Indian, American, and British papers demonstrate the embedding of social ideologies and cultural presuppositions in particular forms of discourse. Prototypes of the desirable female and acceptable male emerge, separate and certainly unequal, from both Indian and 'western' representations. In this limited arena, it becomes possible to focus sharply on gender roles as they are created in relation to the social institutions of dating, marriage, and family, which, except in unusual circumstances, necessarily involve both sexes. The advantages of examining match-making advertisements in two very different cultures may be summed up as follows:

1 They constitute a well-structured, identifiable, but new discourse type, of a brevity which makes detailed *grammatical* analysis feasible, while concurrently being situated at the intersection of two well-established discourse types, namely, journalese and advertising.
2 They provide a test-case for the elusive Whorfian hypothesis, which in its weak formulation, states that the language(s) we use may influence and perpetuate, but not determine our conceptions of the world, in this case, especially *gender and patriarchy*.[10]
3 They are an ideal locus for demonstrating how poststructuralist heterological, ahistorical readings of *genres* may be integrated with structuralist homological, historical explanations.

In a ponderously alliterative, but perhaps forgivable phrase, the grammar of the genre simultaneously generates its genderlects and its potential for gynocriticism.

III

This section concerns itself with the actual analysis and presentation of data. The raw data here consist of 100 matrimonial advertisements from *The Times of India* (henceforth *TI*), 100 advertisements from the *Hindustan Times* (henceforth *HT*), and 50 advertisements each from the *New York Review of Books* and the *New Statesman and Society* (henceforth *NYR* and *NSS*). Although the main emphasis in this paper is on qualitative analysis, simple quantitative counts are used as supportive evidence wherever appropriate.

The methodology[11] involves an analysis of sentential structures, including the grammatical processes of passivization, deletion, and topicalization. Noun phrases and main verbs are considered in especial detail. Lexis, and in particular the collocational range of certain lexical items, are examined separately, and here quantitative analysis plays a limited part. The framework adopted for stylistic discussion is broadly Hallidayan, but owes some debt to studies of language and power by Fowler, Trew, O'Barr, Kraemarae *et al.*

I begin by reproducing six typical matrimonials from the Indian papers *TI* and *HT* and four personal advertisements from the American and British journals *NYR* and *NSS*. As far as possible, an effort has been made to preserve the original format of the advertisements.

1 CORRESPONDENCE INVITED FROM doctors, engineers, business executives, for charming M.Sc. Sikh Arora girl, height 155 cms., match based in Bombay preferred. Reply Box XX.

(TI)

2 ALLIANCE INVITED FROM DECENTLY employed persons around 35 for a Kousika vadama bride, 29, Swati, 160 cms., matriculate, medium complexion and domestically well-trained, Dosha Jathagam. Also for her brother 36 Avittam, matriculate, 170 cms., bank officer and well settled. Mutual also can be considered. Reply with horoscope Box XX.

(TI)

3 WE WOULD LIKE TO PROPOSE TO AN educated Sindhi girl, a Sindhi boy arriving shortly from USA on a month's vacation. Apply Box XX.

(TI)

4 REALLY beautiful, slim, educated, homely girl, from top business industrial family for extremely handsome Brahmin, Graduate, Textile Engineer, Gold Medallist, 23 years, 172 cms., Executive in country's leading textile concern, no bars, only son of Senior Class-I Engineer, highly connected status family. Box XX.

(HT)

5 SUITABLE match, preferably Engineer, for 23/155 fair, slim, beautiful, non-working Engineer girl. Dowryless marriage. Write Box XX.

(HT)

6 WANTED a very fair (Gori) sharp-featured, well educated, homely, non-Mittal, tall girl, from a decent highly connected family for a 178 cms., Rajasthani groom, Management Graduate, income in six figures, belonging to worldwide connected trading house. Kindly write to GPO Box XX with complete details including place, date and time of birth. Advertisement for wider choice only.

(HT)

7   BAY AREA MAN OF LETTERS: articulate and analytical, essentially serious and emotionally stable, romantic but cynical: tall, fit, handsome & financially secure; variously described as adventuresome, habitual, lyrical, aloof, wilful, a hedonist, a dandy, a mischief-maker, DESIRES distinctive, gentle, slim, unpretentious, amusing woman 28–43. This opportunity is almost too good to be true. Almost. Write w/photo: Dear Sir Box XX.

(*NYR*)

8   INTELLIGENT, PRETTY SWF, 34, trim, brunette with warm, friendly smile seeks SWM, 30–40, inquisitive, mature, with gentle sense of humor for quiet dinners, rainy Saturdays at the movies, Sunday afternoons in Soho dancing, theater and forays beyond NYC. Are you looking for romance and a serious relationship? Write and tell me about yourself. Box XX.

(*NYR*)

9   STYLISH MAN, financially independent, mid-forties, slim, medium height, brown hair, varied interests (not too interesting), seeks lady with plenty of flexible time to share long lunches, leisurely afternoons, evenings, holidays, but especially sincere friendship. If you are under 40, slim, attractive, fun loving, independent, please write. Ideally London area. Box XX.

(*NSS*)

10 ADVENTUROUS PROFESSIONAL WOMAN, 36. Interests include green issues, travel, cycling. Would like to meet similar man. View to committed relationship. Photo and telephone number appreciated and returned with mine. Gloucestershire. Please write to Box XX.

(*NSS*)

Halliday's theory of language is, in his own words,

> one which attempts to explain linguistic structure, and linguistic phenomena, by reference to the notion that language . . . is required to serve certain universal types of demand. The demands we make on language, as speakers and writers, listeners and readers, are infinitely many and varied. They can be derived ultimately, from *a small number of very general headings*; but what these headings are will depend on what questions we are asking.
>
> (Halliday 1981: 326)

The phrase that I have italicized indicates very clearly Halliday's commitment to the structuralist mode. However, he also leaves it to us to raise the relevant questions, which in this case are questions about the ideology of gender.

First, we may ask how the syntax of the matrimonial advertisements influences our constructions of gender. Here we find two crucial, and very basic, differences in the syntactic patterning of the Indian versus the 'western' advertisements. The Indian ones consist of a passive structure with agent deletion as well as auxiliary deletion; the western ones, by contrast, have an active structure, with the agent as the subject noun phrase. Moreover, the Indian matrimonials typically have an overt clausal structure, whereas the western ones have a sentential structure. This is easy to visualize as the Indian and Western rubrics show.

Table 10.1 A simple grammar of the Indian matrimonial advertisement

Decent suitable matrimonial	proposal/ match/ alliance	Is invited/ solicited/ wanted/ sought, etc.	For/from x description M/[F]	From/for y description	by z F/[M]
		—(semantic realizations) —			
NP→ADJ+N (optional)		V(cop.) VP→V (deleted) (opt.)	PP→ prep+NP (obligatory)	PP→ (prep)+NP (oblig.)	PP→ (prep+NP) (deleted)
		—(syntactic forms) —			

Thus the briefest Indian advertisement, comprising all and only the obligatory elements, would have the syntactic from PP+NP or for X, Y, where X and Y stand for mutually exclusive descriptions of the two genders. Such a format, with its exclusion of the agentive BY prepositional phrase (*who* is it that wants/solicits, etc. X for Y?), together with the choice of a highly formal lexis ('matrimonial alliance solicited') reinforces our impression of distance between the two negotiating parties. As the structure of advertisement 3, above, shows, in the rare instances where an active sentence structure is used, the agent is a plural 'we' ('we would like to propose to an educated Sindhi girl, a Sindhi boy'). His family, not the boy himself, does the proposing. Thus the mysterious agents of the deleted BY clause turn out to be a multiple set. We will return to this point, but before we proceed, we must consider the contrasting syntactic rubric for the western advertisement, in Table 10.2.

It is obvious that the western advertisement is much more direct than

Table 10.2 A simple grammar of the western matrimonial advertisement

Description X M/[F]	Seeks/ desires/ wants/ needs	Description Y F/[M]	+S [question clause imperative exclamation greeting, etc.]
(semantic realizations)			
Complex NP with several pre- and post-modifications (obligatory)	VP (oblig.)	Complex NP with several pre- and post-modifications (obligatory)	Sentence or clause (optional)
(syntactic forms)			

the Indian, consisting as it does of active sentences, far fewer optional elements, no systematic deletions and a less formal, highly emotive lexis. Advertisement 7 is a good example of the use of such affective lexis; the numerous NP modifications as well as the use of verbs such as 'desires', 'seeks', etc. instead of 'solicits' 'invites', etc. strengthen our perception of an attempt at direct contact between individual parties. Often, the additional sentence at the end seems designed to initiate a conversation, voiced rather than merely scripted, between the advertiser and an unknown but potentially exciting partner ('Are you looking for romance and a serious relationship? Write and tell me about yourself'). The active agent of these advertisements is a grammatically singular person, unlike the plural protagonists in the Indian advertisements.

In terms of a grammatically familiar system of rewrite rules and tree diagrams, but making use of Hallidayan terminology, the underlying structure of *both* Indian and western advertisements could be set out as shown in Table 10.3. If the marriage advertisement is considered as a self-contained discourse unit, the structural trees which contrastively characterize the Indian and western matrimonial advertisements can be derived from the above phrase structure rules as in Figure 10.1. As the simple, if laboured, analytic exercise in Figure 10.1 illustrates, both Indian and western matrimonial advertisements have basic features in common. Yet, the complex grammatical structures of the Indian advertisements repeatedly offer far greater scope for circumlocution; in contrast, the relatively limited structural options exercised in the western advertisement seem to reflect a high cultural value attached to addressing potential partners as directly as possible, almost as if they are physically present.

Several commentators have remarked on the differences between

Table 10.3 A generalized grammar of matrimonial advertisements

Structural description	Syntactic/lexical realization		
Marriage advertisement→ Description X	→ NP	(PP)	
Description Y	→ NP	(PP)	
(Description A)	→ NP		
(Description B)	→ NP	(PP)	
(question, imperative, greeting, exclamation) → S/clause			
Description X, Y, (A), (B) → Item X, Y, (A), (B) → head noun			
(Descriptors X, Y, (A), (B) → Pre- and post-modifiers, i.e. adjectives and rel. clauses			
Item X, Y, → Connectors → verb, preposition			
Sex → male, female, bisexual			
Caste, social group → Brahmin, Sikh, Jew, Bay Area Man, etc.			
Profession → engineer, nurse, man of letters, etc.			
Descriptors X, Y, → Age → 18 to 70 approx.			
Looks, Male → tall, fair handsome, etc.			
Female → fair, beautiful, slim, tall			
Attributes, Male → earning four-figure salary, own business, green card holder, settled abroad, etc.			
Female → domestically well-trained, charming, earning, with a warm, friendly smile, etc.			
Character, Male → respectable, sober cynical, debonair, etc.			
Female (family and status) → homely, loving, etc., highly connected family, aristocratic, educated, etc.			
Profession, Male → engineer, doctor, academic, lawyer, etc.			
(Item B) → parents, we, etc.			
(Descriptors B) → well-connected, Bengali, Kayastha, etc.			
(Item A) → match, alliance, etc.			
(Descriptor A) → suitable, decent, etc.			

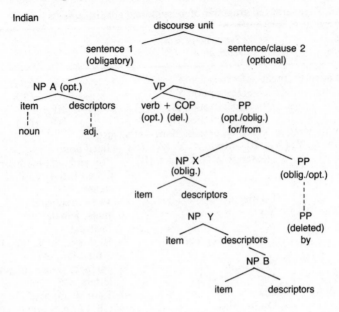

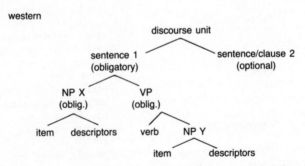

Figure 10.1 Tree diagrams for the Indian and western matrimonial advertisements

the non-individualistic patterns of Indian thought, exhibited also in its social paradigms, and the highly individualistic projections of western consciousness.[12] A series of points drawn from this restricted and, as Todd would have it, non-canonical corpus are serially presented below as possible evidence for such putative Whorfian doctrines.

1   The use of the cover term 'Matrimonial' itself reveals an ideology reifying marriage, apparently common to both cultures, but it is a theme literally interpreted in India while the western advertisements allow a greater latitude for non-conventional readings of the dominant

ideology. In India it would be unthinkable to advertise for a girlfriend, or for a relationship with a married person, or to mention homosexual inclinations. In the west, such desires are often explicitly stated in columns headed 'Personal', rather than 'Matrimonial'. The notion of marriage itself thus seems much more homogeneous, 'non-individualistic' in the former society than in the latter, especially when it is noted that the *NSS* column actually calls itself 'Heartsearch', stressing the importance of an ideal, particular partner.

2 The adjectival modifications in the Indian advertisements are obviously based on parental/familial assessments as the continual references to caste and family status indicate. The sense of personal distance, of the individual personality seen at second remove, through others' eyes, is emphasized. Fulsome though the praise is for the advertising party in an Indian column, an impression of modest decorum is retained through the overarching presence of the family, which lends its weight to any assessment of the individual's merits and desires. Western advertisements, on the contrary, rely on self assessment, although in rare cases (e.g. advertisement 7) the opinion of others is referred to, but even here the primary voice is that of the advertiser himself. The self is presented as its own best knower, directly involved in its dealings with others. Intermediaries in the shape of controlling families are never the powerful presence in western marriage advertisements that they are in the Indian.

3 Indeed, it may be argued that the semantics of the Indian advertisement essentially consists of a quadrilateral relationship between two sets of families and their children, as the vocabulary used in these advertisements shows. The importance of the family, revealed earlier in an analysis of the syntax of multiple agency, is further brought out by references to (a) sons, daughters, sisters, brothers, brides, grooms, girls, boys (b) alliances, matches, proposals, and (c) castes, subcastes and *gotras*, regional groups, horoscopes and star positions. It is interesting to note that even men and women in their late thirties and forties can be defined as 'boys' and 'girls' and even 'virgins' as in the following advertisements.

11 WANTED SUITABLE ALLIANCE FOR Tamil Iyer graduate handsome boy 38 drawing 1800 per month, & etc.

(*TI*)

12 WANTED for well-educated man, aged 44 years, decently settled, independent business, homely girl of good . . . background, dowry no bar, & etc.

(*HT*)

13   UNIVERSITY Lecturer, 42, virgin, Ph.D., 163 cms., slim attractive, girl, seeks Delhi based bachelor match, & etc.

(*HT*)

By dint of such description, the dependence of individuals, and especially women, on the protective, as well as binding and limiting circle of family relationships, is made apparent. True, their essential innocence, their 'virginity', their right to be a 'bride' or 'groom' stands ideologically preserved notwithstanding advanced years, but their helplessness as solitary beings is equally emphasized. Semantically, in Hallidayan terms, the obligatory parts of an Indian advertisement seem to be Affected/Medium and Beneficiary (cf. the title of the old film 'Seven Brides for Seven Brothers'). Moreover, the Indian descriptors mostly consist of given features (160 cms., Brahmin, convent educated, etc.), whereas western descriptors are more achieved, features for which personal credit can be claimed (mature, intelligent, adventurous, etc.), which also supports the explanation of the primary advertising parties in the two cultures differing according to some basic Affected versus Agent categories.

These lexical features in (a) to (c) above reflect the concern in Indian society, by and large, with the compatibility of large units of which the individual forms only a circumscribed part. When families merge, making a triangle out of a quadrilateral (see Figure 10.2), it is they who remain at the apex, moderating the strands between individuals. In contrast, the semantic relationship between the parties in a western advertisement may be represented as a *bilateral relationship* where a dialogue is established between two singular voices who emphasize the details of their personal preferences and character which individuate them from other members of their larger social group. Although it may be that persons in the western world are no less influenced by their families and environment than in India, we find embedded in a minor, non-canonical but prolific form of discourse like the matrimonial column striking differences in the *projection* of this influence. The encompassing family, so pervasive in the Indian advertisement, is quite factored out in the western mode of representation (see Figure 10.2). The stark singularity of western reciprocal relations, already remarked on, conveys the impression that the main protagonists in these advertisements are literally *sui generis* while Indian agents, to coin a phrase, are *alteri/omnis generis*.

4 As the almost mandatory use of the noun 'alliance' and verbs like 'invite' and 'solicit' show, the stress in the Indian situation is also on formal relations while in the western ethos affective relationship, expressed by verbs like 'desire' and 'seek', prevails. In this context, it might be said that a recurrent pattern in the western column is the classic literary motif of *the quest* (Heartsearch) for a romantic partner; the Indian theme, on the contrary, is that of *the request*, the solicitation. Indian advertisers ask for a 'suitable match'; Western advertisers for a 'perfect mate'. This is related to the point raised earlier while discussing syntax, that the western advertisements aim at starting up a conversation while the Indian advertisements attempt to begin a negotiation, which may include discussions of dowry, horoscope predictions, and so on.

5 The common denominators in both sets of advertisements that must be specified are sex and age; in addition, height is almost always mentioned. However, there is not a single advertisement in this sample of over 300 which confines itself to this minimalist description. And it is at this point that manifestations in the two cultures radically diverge. In the Indian advertisements, the modifications relating to personal characteristics are severely restricted or underspecified; in the western ones, they are expanded prolifically or overspecified. An example of this difference can be read into the willingness of western suitors to mention negative personal attributes, such as proneness to anger, impatience, cynicism, mischief-making,[13] but such latitude is never allowed in the Indian context, where, as argued earlier, it is the family which assesses the advertiser's character. By leaving it to others to outline one's profile, the Indian advertiser gains credit for

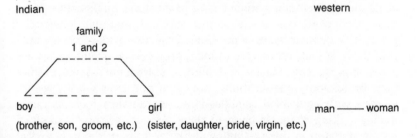

Figure 10.2 Familial relations in Indian and western matrimonials

being at once flawless and modest, but loses in terms of self-definition and self-determination.

6 The profiles of the desirable middle-class Indian male and female emerge quite readily from these advertisements and there appears to be a much higher degree of consensus about criteria of assessment. The most frequent modifiers, together with percentages of their occurrence in my sample, are given in Table 10.4. It emerges from the tally in this table that certain norms may be predictable in a patriarchal society. First, looks and respectability are more desirable in a female than a male; second, males are required to be authoritatively older than their female partners; and, third, family groups play an overwhelmingly decisive role, one which could aptly be described as 'paternal', in settling a 'matrimonial alliance'.

Table 10.4 Indian criteria of marital desirability

Indian man	Indian woman
– age about 32 (on average)	– age about 25 (on average)
– handsome, tall, fair 47%	– beautiful, fair, pretty, tall, charming, slim 67%
– family group 86%	– family group 91%
– financial status (4–6 figures) 65%	– financial status 39%
– profession, education, businessman, officer 70%	– profession, education 86%
– respectable, decent, ambitious 12%	– homely, sober, respectable 44%

Initially, it appears surprising that significantly more women (86 per cent) specify their educational and/or professional qualifications than men (70 per cent); conversely, more men (65 per cent) than women (39 per cent) state their financial positions. From this evidence, a possible hypothesis is that, in the case of men, professional qualifications are not so important once financial stability is assured; but women, despite their professional qualifications, are often not as financially secure as men with equivalent qualifications, nor do they have as many money-making channels open to them. Hence, a close reading of simple statistics in these columns uncovers some of the paradoxical assumptions of a legally democratic but culturally paternalistic society. It may be true that women, and especially the middle-class women who advertise in the *TI* and *HT*, are permitted equal access to education and entry into the professions but this does not generally mean either that they are financially independent or that they can freely decide to pursue a career after marriage. The high 86 per cent of women who state their educational degrees are merely expressing their *potential* for further professional attainments, as well as their suitability as partners for similarly or better qualified men. Unlike Indian men, full control over their careers is not necessarily vested in Indian women and this seems clearly reflected in the unwillingness, and perhaps inability, of Indian women to declare their financial status, while concurrently stating their, mostly unrealized, financial possibilities.

7   To move from quantitative to qualitative analysis, it cannot fail to strike any reader familiar with popular Indian cinema and fiction that the above prescriptions for ideal partners gleaned from matrimonial columns are wholly reminiscent of familiar images of romantic heroes and heroines. Women, especially, are described within the classical but also very current 'Sati-Savitri' (devoted wife) frame of reference, which encompasses one of the most influential feminine ideals in the culture.[14] Analysis of this marginal form of discourse teaches us that creative literary portrayals may converge unobtrusively but powerfully with pragmatic newspaper advertisements in the service of a widespread social ideology.

Much of the vocabulary in an Indian matrimonial column is highly specialized and distinguishes the genre as an independent discourse type, designed to perpetuate a particular format for gender descriptions. I give below a brief list of such typical lexis.

(a) alliance	marriage by family arrangement
(b) caste no bar	will marry outside caste group
(c) convent educated	can speak English
(d) earning 4–6 figures	a respectable rupee income
(e) girl only consideration	no dowry will be demanded; (significantly, this phrase does not occur in the form 'boy only consideration' since the flow of dowry is unidirectional in this society)
(f) homely	skilled at housework, homebound (only describes females)
(g) horoscope/star position	indicates compatibility
(h) medico	not yet a fully fledged doctor
(i) medium/wheatish	refers to colour of skin
(j) mutual	brother and sister pair to marry sister and brother pair
(k) status family	shows social standing

(l) with(out) encumbrances   (no) children (hence the Indian
                                reader knows this phrase only
                                occurs when the advertiser is
                                divorced or widowed)

Here, we return briefly to the way in which lexis in Indian advertisements is often read literally, so that the same word may connote quite
different qualities from those implied by its use in western columns.
Two instances will suffice. The word 'white' in Britain and America,
standardly reduced to acronyms such as WJM (white Jewish male) or
WASF (white Anglo-Saxon female), describes the racial and social
group to which the advertiser belongs; in India, the frequent use of
the same word refers specifically to the actual colouring or complexion
of the advertiser, as in the following examples:

14   GREEN CARD HOLDER, U.S. EDUCATED Gujerati Jain
     engineer, Smart; handsome, *white-complexioned*, age 25 ht. 165
     cms., from well-to-do rich family, invites matrimonial correspon-
     dence from good-looking, tall girl from cultured and respectable
     family . . . & etc.

                                                              (*TI*)
15   PARENTS INVITE MATRIMONIAL CORRESPONDENCE
     from well educated Sindhi gentlemen for their daughter 22,
     height 155 cms. shortly completing bachelor's degree in accounts,
     gainfully employed permanent resident in the USA, earning 12000
     dollars annually, modest, slim, charming, very good character,
     white complexioned and homely . . . & etc.

                                                              (*TI*)

Similarly, the use of the word 'homely' in the Indian advertisements
(see 15, above) does not signify, as it does in the west, drabness and
a lack of glamour but rather, respectability, dedication to building a
home life and skill at household tasks. Even when, as in advertisement
5, the advertiser is someone fully qualified to earn her own living,
being an engineer, considerable concession is made to the ideal of
a home-maker when she is explicitly described as 'non-working'.[15]
Hardly ever does the western advertisement mention talent at
household tasks. Naturally, this difference can be explicated in
terms of the very different social conditions which characterize the
middle classes in India and the west, but it remains the case that
verbal representations, and therefore perceptions, of the desirable
female are focused in a highly dissimilar way in the two cultures.

8 A survey of the western personal columns fails to yield the clear-cut consensual profiles that characterize 'suitable' Indian 'matches', although good looks and height appear to be as prized. Among the most ubiquitous adjectives in the western context are the words 'interesting' and 'attractive', which occur in 68 per cent of these advertisements but hardly ever in the Indian columns, the former especially being completely absent. 'A sense of humour' is also a phrase that recurs in western advertisements, but is conspicuous by its total absence as a requirement of any sort in Indian advertisements. Indeed the space accorded to the advertisement itself can offer the western advertiser an arena for a display of humour, as when the writer of advertisement 7 protests that his offer 'is almost too good to be true. Almost.' Such frivolity is simply not permissible in an Indian column where the dignity of family and community is at stake.

In general, the profile of a desirable partner is much more fragmented and therefore more difficult to extricate from western matrimonial columns, since tastes as particular as 'Soho dancing' and 'rainy Saturdays at the movies' (advertisement 8) are permitted expression. Of course, it could very plausibly be argued that these seemingly individual demands have as a basis a fairly commonplace ideology of romantic involvement, detectable in western popular fiction, theatre, and film. But then again, what differentiates the western mode from the Indian is not that romantic aspirations are disallowed within Indian culture (see point 7 above), but that these are subservient in representational terms to the motif of family respectability in this particular form of discourse.

9 Advertising in matrimonial columns seems to bring in its wake a certain inevitable defensiveness, for two main reasons. First, matrimonial advertisements often appear cheek by jowl with other 'Classified Ads' such as 'Property to let', 'Motor vehicles' and even, in our sample, 'Astrology' advertisements. Such incongruous juxtaposition underscores the uncomfortable resemblance of males and females to commodities, nicely packaged, and then left to their fate, to be buffeted about by market forces. There is, doubtless, a latent insinuation here that human beings have as little dignified control over their destinies as a car or truck and are equally driven by social pressures. Second, it is also tacitly understood that other, more usual channels of social intercourse have not proved successful in acquiring a partner for the advertiser. One implication of this putative lack of success is, common-sensically, that the advertiser is not without flaws. If such implicatures are granted, it becomes easier to explain the defensive designing of matrimonial advertisements, which finds overt expression in Indian columns in the addition of optional clauses such as 'Advertisement for wider choice only' (advertisement 6) and also in the constant preoccupation with respectability, family responsibility, and status (see advertisements 2, 3, 4, 6, 12, 13, and 15).

10   A possible locus of ideological conflict in this connection, to be identified in the contemporary Indian advertisement, is the perennial presence of the non-resident Indian. Indian advertisers who live or earn abroad but feel constrained to marry someone from within their 'own' culture face a classical immigrant's dilemma. They are, generally, most attractive in economic terms, since standards of prosperity in, say, Britain, America, or the Middle East, obviously compare very favourably with those in India; but they are also regarded with considerable suspicion because their immersion in another culture may have weaned them away from 'Indian' norms of respectability. Additionally, they are in India only for a short period, usually three to four weeks (see advertisement 3, for example), during which time the marriage negotiations and the marriage itself must be completed. Often, this lack of time is cited as a compelling reason for advertising in a newspaper. A sense of urgency thus informs most advertisements by 'Green Card holders', making it appropriate to describe their texts as '*texts of crisis*', moments in the Indian matrimonial columns when economic aspirations may conflict with social suspicions and the comfort of the familiar be offset by the romance of the rich and strange. Ideologically, the onus is on the non-residents to prove that they still inhabit their own culture, despite geographical distance. An important way to defend their respectability is to let their parents speak for them and emphasize their modesty, sobriety, and, in the case of women, 'homeliness', as in advertisement 15; another way, as in advertisement 14, is to insist on 'matrimonial correspondence' only with those whose families who are 'cultured and respectable', thereby obliquely establishing one's own unquestionable credentials.

On rare occasions, a non-resident partially reveals his allegiance to the values of the 'other' society in which he truly finds himself at home, and here the cultural crisis can be observed in an intense form.

18   AUSTRALIAN BORN HINDU BRAHMAN man, middle aged, well settled, self employed, idealistic and phylosophic [*sic*] invites matrimonial correspondence from strikingly attractive Indian or Anglo Indian ladies 28–35. A good command of English is

necessary and a warm-hearted personality coupled with a high intelligence would be appreciated. Must be willing to settle in Australia. Apply Box XX

(*TI*)

A 'resident' Indian would never specify that he was both a Hindu and a Brahmin, since the latter entails the former; nor would he fail to mention a more particular kin group, since this procedure confers authenticity on a claim of brahminhood. Moreover, even those in India who declare caste and creed no bar would probably exclude 'Anglo Indian ladies' unless they themselves happened to be Anglo Indian. Indeed, the use of the lexical item 'lady' is highly unusual in Indian advertisements, as is the phrase 'strikingly attractive'. A 'warm-hearted personality coupled with a high degree of intelligence' focuses on the sort of personality traits often at a premium in western cultures but rarely, it appears from the evidence of these advertisements, demanded in the Indian context. The advertiser's description of himself as 'idealistic and philosophic' also reinforces the argument advanced earlier that an emphasis on individual character is required in western self representations. Each of these features, in addition to the absence of any reference to familial moorings, sets this advertiser apart from the majority of others in Indian columns. Yet, the fact that he is constrained to mention his high caste and his Hindu origin shows how necessary it is to establish a cultural connection, in order to avoid the direct clash of two sets of cultural values and secure a defence against ideological crisis.

In western advertisements, it is initially difficult to detect a similar defensiveness about respectability and cultural anchoring. However, we may trace tell-tale phrases in all the four western advertisements chosen as samples (7–10 above) that could betray a parallel concern. The jaunty male in advertisement 7, for example, describes himself as essentially serious and emotionally stable as well as financially secure; in advertisement 8, the female advertiser claims she is 'mature' and in search of a 'serious relationship'; in advertisement 9, the 'adventurous professional woman' wants 'a committed relationship'; in advertisement 10, the 'stylish, financially independent man' makes a point of his 'varied interests' not being 'too interesting', too *outré*, and stresses 'especially sincere friendship'.

Seriousness of purpose, emotional stability, honesty, sincerity, and maturity emerge as a cluster of qualities which also serve as a defence against any imputation that the person advertising lacks in personal respectability, just because s/he has resorted to a matrimonial column. In sum, I argue that establishing respectability is an important goal in western, as in Indian, columns, although it is differently achieved through declarations of individual merit and not defined in terms of family or caste status.

Most canonical texts, the aristocratic literary texts of a culture, centre on some crisis that threatens characters in the text, and also readers, in so far as they identify with characters and interpret events in the text. Now, in this plebeian but ideologically permeated form of discourse, too, we may read the modalities of crisis, if we are motivated by the poststructuralist concern with *uncovering ideologies*. To this recurrent point about the interconections between the literary and non-literary we return in the final section of this chapter. The points made in the foregoing analysis about the ideological perspectives inherent in the syntax, lexis, and format of a non-literary genre are briefly related, in a concluding section, to some of the broader issues discussed earlier.

IV

Poststructuralism as a critical school attempts to demonstrate that a lattice of productive rules and primary features, such as the phrase structure rules and typical lexical items which we showed in section III generated and constituted the discourse of the marriage advertisement, simply cannot explain how language becomes laden with ideology. Therefore, it is more important to explore the consequences, presuppositions, and implications of grammatical constructions than simply to postulate skeletal rules of grammar that perfectly describe a discourse. Uncovering social ideologies must follow the discovering of linguistic structures, but it should be clarified that the 'follow' in this statement is as crucial as the 'must', in my view. Differently from, but not entirely unlike, McHale, I argue here that the tools of structuralism should be skilfully used in the service of poststructuralist concerns rather than discarded completely; only thus might the *-ism* in poststructuralism balance and contend with the *post*. It is with this intent that I followed the Hallidayan structural analysis with a series of points that sought to bring an interpretative dimension to the discussion. Despite this, of course, there remains the usual problem with any such detailed attention to a limited genre, that, in the end, it only confirms what we pragmatically 'already know'. To this objection, I can only reply that analysis is a different sort of enterprise from assertion and yields a different sort of harvest.

Analysis of Indian and western advertisements shows that grammatically similar tree-structures can come to fruition in very different ways. India and 'the west', like men and women, turn out to be linguistically attested cultural, and not merely physical, entities. Each has its prototypical flora and fauna, each its unmapped territories. Or, in the phraseology of poststructuralism, each set of matrimonial columns has its characteristic pattern of cracks; there are gaps in the western text where family connections are eradicated, there are lacunae in the Indian text where individual personality traits are erased. These differences lend support to the Sapir–Whorf hypothesis of linguistically influenced relativistic differences between the world-views of distinct cultures. In Sapir's words:

> It is quite an illusion to imagine that one adjusts to reality without the use of language and that language is merely an incidental means of solving specific problems of communication and reflection. The fact of the matter is that 'the real world' is to a large extent unconsciously built up on the language habits of the group. . . . We see and hear very largely as we do because the language habits of our community predispose certain choices of interpretation.
>
> (1921: 162)

To draw a literary analogy, the western advertisements seem to be Beckettian texts, where individuals are revealed in isolation; while the Indian matrimonials appear to be Brechtian texts, with all of society milling around. Which brings us somewhat circuitously to the vexed question of the relationship between 'high' literary forms and 'low' non-literary discourses like the marriage advertisement. It is generally assumed that critical methodologies are best applied to literary texts because great writing amply repays analytic effort in a manner that texts of the sort studied in this chapter do not. This philosophy has the not altogether happy consequence that many affinities between canonical and non-canonical literature, between critics as academic and as social beings, are ignored. By fixing on an invisible form like the matrimonial, it may be possible to render visible some of those prejudices and preconceptions of gender that inhere in our finest literary masterpieces. Popular opinion may be formed as powerfully through such media as through contact with works of imagination. If literary critics, especially those of the poststructuralist persuasion who wish to encourage a healthy diversity of texts and opinion, do not pay attention to other vibrant discourses, they may be open to the same charge of narrowness of vision that they once levelled against the structuralists.

The very brevity, the telegraphic language of the marriage advertisement forces upon the form a need to excise redundant information, and a concomitant explicitness. As we have seen, the relations between unequal pairs such as men and women, western and Indian, canonical and non-canonical texts, structuralism and poststructuralism, are therefore comparatively easy to discuss in the context of this discourse. I have tried to show how representations of gender are grammaticalized in a particular genre by deliberately attending to the subaltern member of each of these pairs. Todd (1988: 129) regards the problematizing of apparently incontrovertible 'truths' as one of the tasks which current literary, linguistic, feminist, and philosophical theories must address. It is, I hope, the spirit of this enterprise that the present essay endorses.

NOTES

1   The meta-labels 'postmodern' and 'poststructuralist' are not, of course, synonymous, but it could be argued that they are, to a considerable extent, co-extensive. For the limited purposes of this exposition, it will not be necessary strictly to demarcate these terms.

2   M. Toolan (personal communication) objects, understandably, to the ambiguity of the clause 'may coexist peacefully'. He asks, 'Is this a "may" of possibility or permission? And how do we know we're witnessing peaceful coexistence rather than dialogism and contradiction, in which the murder report "violates" the Court circular page?' The point is taken, maybe!

3   However, in an article in the *Spectator*, 1984, Dhiren Bhagat argues that the matrimonial column is not a new form but one prevalent in eighteenth- and nineteenth-century newspapers in Britain. He cites a British Museum collection entitled *Matrimonial Advertisements 1746 –1862* 'which has hundreds of such samples', drawn from the *Gazetteer*, the *Gloucestershire Chronicle*, the *Public Advertiser*, etc. Three such advertisements are quoted below, though not in full:

> A Young Gentleman, a Native of North Britain, (but with very little of the Brogue), of a genteel Profession, tall in Stature, finely shaped and well proportioned, has a delicate Head of Hair, white Hand, a large Calf, strong Back, broad Shoulders. (1760)

> MATRIMONY – A Gentleman of RANK, a Protestant, and possessing an unencumbered income of 1,000 l. per annum is desirous of a union with an accomplished Young Lady of a suitable age, and whose station in society and connections are least on par with his own. (1839)

> (A Woman Wanted)
> With manners quite gentle, bewitching and bland
> Mozart and Rossini she must understand.
> Her eyes must be blue, – her complexion fair

Her form be well moulded, and dark brown her hair;
Her eyelashes long, her teeth very white,
And her lips invite kisses from morning to night. (1830)

The social emphasis on looks and status is apparent from these advertisements, but the romantic 'literary' quality of the last example now requires a different, brisker idiom in 'western' culture for reasons this article partially attempts to analyse.

4 See, for example Sangari and Vaid's introduction to *Recasting Women* (1989) for a fuller discussion of this point, with particular reference to the context of colonialism.

5 Susan Carey (1982) in her article 'Semantic development: the state of the art', in Wanner and Gleitman (eds), details work from several sources (Baron and Kaiser 1975, Karmiloff-Smith 1979, Levy 1980), which seems to show that 'even in languages where gender is marked syntactically, it might be expected to be marked late onto the semantic distinction between male and female'.

6 This phrase was coined by West and Zimmerman in their work on American women's style(s) of speech, which reinforced a perception of them as more feeble, intellectually as well as socially, than their male peers.

7 Such traditional means included, for example, the *ghatak*, or matchmaker (literal etymology, 'one who makes [things] happen'), who was able to carry news of suitable matches within more homogeneous communities. In the modern Indian urban context, ironically, the impersonal newspapers assume some of the informative functions of this earlier, highly personalized figure. And like him, they command a fee for their services, although in terms of accountability, credibility, and scope of service, it could be argued that the *ghatak*'s role, in a society where word of mouth took precedence over sparse, written communication, was far more substantive/substantial.

8 Sriniwas (1981), an anthropologist, produces evidence to show that in South India, the Brahminical practice of dowry, confined to that caste, was only later imitatively incorporated by the other, lower castes. Kishwar (1984), a feminist, has extensively documented the victimization of women on account of dowry in North India. Her work also demonstrates that it is among the upper and middle urban classes, of the sort who might arrange marriages through the alienated medium of newspaper advertisements, that 'dowry-deaths' are most common.

9 Meenakshi Mukherjee (personal communication) questions my claim that marriage advertisements have worked their way through the English language newspapers into the regional ones. She writes: 'Is there any ground to substantiate this? In my childhood, I never saw them in English newspapers, only in Bangla.' Citing Bhagat's research into early British marriage advertisements is relevant here (see n. 3), but the matter needs more investigation, since the tracing of cultural influences may be complex here, appearing, disappearing, and appearing again.

10 In its strong formulation, the Sapir–Whorf hypothesis is virtually unfalsifiable, and therefore unsuited to an analysis of this sort, which examines the 'same' discourse type across cultures, thus assuming some degree of

comparability.

11   For another, very different, analysis of the grammar of the Indian matrimonial column, see the article by R. R. Mehrohtra noted in the Bibliography.

12   Contributors to *Daedalus* (Fall 1989) provide a range of examples which seek to differentiate Indian and western modes of thinking and being.

13   Although Meenakshi Mukherjee points out (personal communication) that none of these attributes is truly negative, especially as self-description by the western male.

14   The 'Sati-Savitri' combine glorifies the wife who sacrifices her life for her husband. Sati burns herself to death on the funeral pyre of her husband, while Savitri, in legend, rescues her beloved husband by challenging Yama (Death) himself. The close interconnection of marriage and sacrifice unto death is evident here. We could also note that Sati is an anagram of Sita, phonetically suggestive of the most cherished portrait of Hindu wife/womanhood in the epic *Ramayana*, so significant in the cultural life of the subcontinent.

15   There is some evidence, in the economic context of urban India, where two incomes are often necessary to maintain a middle-class home, that this preference for including 'non-working' as an approbatory adjective is changing. However, as M. Toolan notes (personal communication), in western advertisements, reference to homemaking skills 'is part of a larger fictionalisation or fantasy (some at least of the Western advertisers are misfits or human disaster areas). The Indian advertisements, by contrast, stick to the realm of *facts*, and are, presumably, *honest*.' Mukherjee too feels that this is a major point of difference between the two.

> The formal transactional aspect of the Indian advertisements refers to presumably permanent arrangements, hence the emphasis on hard incontrovertible 'facts' (height, educational qualifications etc.), while the Western ones often imply casual, impermanent relations – hence whimsicality is possible, and also demands for unquantifiable, elusive traits of character like a 'sense of humour'.
>
> (personal communication)

Part IV

Styles of incongruity: the pragmatics of oddness and daftness

Editor's preface

Geoffrey Leech takes up the Russian Formalist and Prague School notion of 'foregrounding' (see especially Mukarovsky 1978) and seeks to extend this to, or operationalize it in, the relations between pieces of language and their fictional or real-world contexts. Foregrounding – as do irony, metaphor, and other important resources of verbal communication, such as indirect speech acts – depends in part on a *perceptible mismatch* between the standard or normative application of a linguistic utterance, and the context of situation which is assumed to hold on a particular occasion of use of that utterance. (The terms 'match' and 'mismatch' I have adopted should be used with caution here: alternative terms include 'fit', 'congruity', 'appropriacy', and 'relevance'. The match we expect between language and context is not a like-to-like match of the kind involved in hanging adjacent strips of patterned wallpaper, but rather the kind of congruity involved in recognizing that the face of a hammer matches the head of a nail, or that the teeth of a saw match the plank of wood we want to cut.)

Shaw's *You Never Can Tell* is a comedy of manners, of hidden rather than mistaken identities, and of shifting social accommodations. In showing all this from a linguistic perspective, no means are as useful as pragmatic principles of co-operative interaction as discussed by Grice (1975), Leech (1983), Brown and Levinson (1987), and others. In this essay, Leech is particularly interested in the way that 'the recurrent comic dilemma of truth and information (how do we uphold both the Maxim of Quality and the Maxim of Quantity?) interacts with the dilemma of how to uphold both the CP and the PP' (p. 268).

For the larger part of the play, characters' attempts to resolve the dilemma (in so far as they seem even to be aware of it) are idiosyncratic, eccentric, and laughable. And in highlighting the interactive eccentricity of each of the major characters – each of them displays a somewhat idiosyncratic assessment of just how attentive they should be to the menu of conversational maxims (of co-operation and politeness) that underpin all talk – Leech demonstrates how these maxims are evidently attended to variably, rather than categorically. Amusingly, two of the characters who end the play betrothed are assisted to that resolution by the antithetical nature of their interactive eccentricities: Valentine's marked preference for even quite shocking truth-telling – quality-maxim observation – sits particularly well with Gloria's revealed aversion to compliments and flattery (approbation maxim). In this way two incongruities turn out to be mutually congruent, and opposites of a kind become attracted. In fact, a pairing-up of all eight main characters can be proposed, along these lines of 'repulsion vs. attraction' to particular norms of polite and co-operative dialogue. If all this seems overly schematic and static, it has to be added that the movement of the play itself (which is to say, the consequences – in large part – of the characters' adherence to their various eccentric models of appropriate talk, as that is revealed throughout the play's action) brings several of the characters to varieties of come-uppance: rejection, penalty, or other cost to Self.

There should be productive applications of this contrastive descriptive method, which focuses on characters' distinctivenesses of attention to maxims of politeness and co-operation, in both character study and genre study. In the latter domain, increasingly explored by systemic linguists, we might predict that, allowing for the influence of a multitude of other dimensions of contrast, there will be differences of both kind and degree in the breach vs. attendance of these various maxims by central characters in, say, a Shakespearian tragedy, by contrast with the kinds and degrees of breach we find in Shaw's social-realist moral comedy, and that these differences are an important constituent of the genre difference that holds between two such plays.

11 Pragmatic principles in Shaw's *You Never Can Tell*

Geoffrey Leech

INTRODUCTION

The notion of poetic *foregrounding*, as a touchstone of literary effect through the use of language, has been inherited from the Russian Formalists via the Prague School structuralists (see van Peer 1986: 1–24). With such a background, it is not obvious that this concept can be revealingly applied to the study of literary discourse in relation to its context – whether we are concerned with the fictional or real-world context of a work of literature.

I shall argue in this chapter, however, that foregrounding – significant literary 'deviation' against the background of a non-literary norm – is just as applicable to the pragmatic study of language in context as to other, more formal, aspects of language. Consider those well-known classical devices of literary expression, the apostrophe (*Death be not proud*) and the rhetorical question (*Was marriage ever out of fashion?*). In spite of their hackneyed literariness over the centuries, they still clearly gain their effect through a mismatch between language and context: in the former case, the abnormality of addressing an inappropriate addressee; in the latter case, that of asking a question where no informative reply can be forthcoming.

But my plan now is for a more extended examination of contextual incongruity in literature, with reference to George Bernard Shaw's comedy *You Never Can Tell* (1898). In this, I hope to show how the concept of foregrounding has a broader application than has been generally appreciated. We think of its application most centrally to poetry (where abnormalities in the use of language are most obvious), and less centrally to prose style (see, for example, Leech and Short 1981: 48–50, 138–46). Its application to drama has on the whole been neglected, except where dramatic language is seen to have its own counterpart of poetic deviation, in the discoursal incongruities and inarticulacies of the theatre of the absurd. (Of relevance here are the stylistic studies on Pinter and Ionesco respectively in Short 1989 and Simpson 1989.)

You Never Can Tell, on the other hand, is more fittingly described as a comedy of manners: almost all its major characters are associated with comic exaggerations of conversational behaviour. To reveal the richness and significance of this behaviour, I will have recourse to a theory of pragmatics which seems to be well-equipped for this purpose: viz. the Gricean model based on the Co-operative Principle (Grice 1975), augmented by the Principle of Politeness as presented in Leech (1983: 104–51).[1]

THE PLOT OF SHAW'S *YOU NEVER CAN TELL*

First, it will be necessary to sketch the plot of the play, and to introduce its main characters.

In this, one of Shaw's earliest and most popular comedies, Valentine, a young dentist, has just set up in practice at a seaside resort. Here he meets the Clandon family, consisting of Mrs Clandon, a strong supporter of women's rights, and her three children, Gloria, Dolly, and Philip. [The latter two are 17-year-old twins.]

Mrs Clandon has long since left a dictatorial husband, and has brought up her children in Madeira under a name other than that of their father. However, when Valentine arrives for lunch, Mrs Clandon discovers to her dismay that his landlord, Mr Crampton, is her former husband. Dolly and Philip appeal to William, a tactful waiter, who gently informs Mr Crampton that he is dining with his family after 18 years of separation. Valentine, in love with Gloria, proposes marriage. Mr M'Comas, Mrs Clandon's solicitor, calls on Mr Crampton, who is resentful of his family's casual attitude. He believes that they and Valentine are plotting to annoy him, and demands the custody of the younger children. M'Comas engages the services of Bohun, a famous barrister, and arranges for a conference with Crampton that evening.

The hotel is giving a fancy-dress ball, and Bohun arrives in costume. It turns out that he is the son of William, who has discovered that his son's successful career hampers him as a waiter, and so spells his name 'Boon'. Bohun straightens out Crampton's difficulties with his family, and Valentine's engagement to Gloria is accepted. All ends happily.

(Summary from Haydn and Fuller 1978: 810–11)

PRAGMATIC PRINCIPLES AND PRAGMATIC DEVIATION

To characterize deviations from 'normal' conversational behaviour, we have first to characterize 'norms'. The constituent maxims of Grice's CP (= Co-operative Principle), and the constituent maxims of the PP (= Politeness Principle) provide a relevant framework: Grice's Maxims of Quantity (informativeness), Quality (truthfulness), Relation (relevance), and Manner (clarity, etc.) are well-known (see pp. 286–9 of Simpson's essay in this volume for useful explication). Less familiar are the Maxims of the PP (Leech 1983: 131–42):

1 The TACT Maxim:
   (a) minimize the cost to *others*;
   (b) maximize the benefit to *others*.
2 The GENEROSITY Maxim:
   (a) minimize the benefit to *self*;
   (b) maximize the cost to *self*.
3 The APPROBATION (or Flattery) Maxim:
   (a) minimize dispraise of *others*;
   (b) maximize praise of *others*.
4 The MODESTY Maxim:
   (a) minimize praise of *self*;
   (b) maximize dispraise of *self*.
5 The AGREEMENT Maxim:
   (a) minimize disagreement between *self* and *others*;
   (b) maximize agreement between *self* and *others*.
6 The SYMPATHY Maxim:
   (a) minimize antipathy between *self* and *others*;
   (b) maximize sympathy between *self* and *others*.

A number of points should be made about these maxims: like the maxims of the CP, they are (a) associated with pragmatic scales or gradients, (b) capable of being infringed, viz. governed by a *ceteris paribus* condition, (c) capable of conflicting with one another, and with the maxims of the CP. These maxims, like those of the CP, are purely descriptive: postulated for the purpose of explaining observed behaviour (e.g. accounting for communicative indirectness, asymmetries of speaker-reference vs. addressee-reference, pragmatic 'paradoxes', gradations of linguistic politeness, pragmatic unacceptability). It should also be explained that in the wording of the maxims, 'maximize benefit to *others*', etc. I describe a linguistic, rather than social imperative, which should be more carefully worded: 'maximize the expression of beliefs implying benefit to *others*.'

I assume, as part of this principle-constrained theory of pragmatics, that humans carry around with them a conception of what is a norm (in part societal, in part personal) of co-operative or polite behaviour for a given conversational situation. These norms are variable according to who the speakers are; what the social relations between them are; what the situational background in terms of what kind of activity they are engaged in is; what goods or services are being transacted; what the background presumptions regarding the rights and obligations of individuals are, and the relative weightiness of various rights and obligations, goods and services. I also assume that manifest deviations from such norms are recognizable, even though such deviant linguistic behaviour might be totally normal in a different situation.

(UN)CO-OPERATIVE AND (IM)POLITE BEHAVIOUR IN THE PLAY

Some of these maxims, and some rather obvious violations of them, can be illustrated from the play itself. First, the Maxim of Quality (truthfulness). At the beginning of the play, the twins (Dolly and Philip) are being treated by the novice dentist, Valentine. At this stage, we do not yet know their names:

(1)   DENTIST. . . . Why didn't you let me give you gas?
       YOUNG LADY. Because you said it would be five shillings extra.
       DENTIST. [*shocked*] Oh, dont say that. It makes me feel as if I
          had hurt you for the sake of five shillings.
       YOUNG LADY. [*with cool insolence*] Well, so you have.
                                                              (I, 212)[2]

Dolly's last, blunt remark is typical of her, in that she speaks the truth (Maxim of Quality) at the expense of politeness (Maxim of Approbation). Where the CP and the PP conflict (e.g. where to speak the truth would cause offence), human beings tend to take refuge in craven compromise. We tell 'white lies', or we tone down the assertion of any truthful utterance that might hurt or challenge the interlocutor (e.g. when asked by our dinner hosts if we enjoyed the meal, few of us would say no, even if that would be true). Dolly suffers from none of these niceties. She and her brother have been brought up by their 'advanced' mother abroad, far away from the evils, but also the civilities, of English society.

Similarly, Dolly believes in the Maxim of Quantity (informativeness) at all costs: she does not believe in withholding her own 'private' information from others, or in allowing others to withhold *their* information from her. So she fires a series of personal questions at the dentist:[3]

(2) THE YOUNG LADY. . . . your rooms. Are they expensive?
     DENTIST. Yes . . .

(I, 212)

(3) THE YOUNG LADY. . . . . I suppose you havent been here long?
     DENTIST. Six weeks. Is there anything else youd like to know?
     THE YOUNG LADY. [*the hint quite lost on her*] Any family?

(ibid.)

Here is another respect in which politeness and co-operativeness conflict. Individuals' 'ownership' of information is analogous to their ownership of property. It is not normally acceptable (in western society) to ask other people to give you the details of their private lives, any more than it is acceptable to ask them to give you their private possessions. But for Dolly, the Maxim of Quantity is clearly supreme: or rather, she defines the Maxim ('make your contribution as informative as is required') for her own purposes, rather than for others'. She demands personal information from a stranger, blindly unaware of the power of the Tact Maxim to conceal information in British society (and more particularly in late Victorian upper-middle-class society).

The Maxim of Quantity, however, can also be violated. This is shown later on in the opening scene of the play, when Valentine (the dentist) expresses himself tautologically:

(4) VALENTINE. . . . But – and now will you excuse my frankness?
     [*They nod*]. Thank you. Well, in a seaside resort theres one thing you must have before anyone can afford to be seen going about with you; and thats a father, alive or dead.

(I, 217–18)

Naturally, everyone has a father – alive or dead – so Valentine's statement is necessarily, hence vacuously, true. Such a tautology overtly transgresses the Maxim of Quantity, because tautologies convey no information. But, of course, one interprets Valentine's remark, like many tautologies, as implicitly informative: it implies that the supremely middle-class, supremely respectable society into which the twins have strayed is one in which appearances matter. 'Having a father' means having a respectable background. The twins lack such a requisite: their mother (Mrs Clandon) refuses even to mention the husband she abandoned, because of his gross and tyrannical behaviour, many years ago.

Another ironical tautology is uttered by the male twin, Philip, when Mrs Clandon joins her children in the dentist's surgery:

(5) PHILIP. . . . Now my knowledge of human nature leads me to believe that we had a father, and that you probably know who he was.

MRS CLANDON. [*her agitation rising*] Stop, Phil. Your father is nothing to you, nor to me. [*Vehemently*] That is enough.

GLORIA. [*advancing*] Mother: we have a right to know.

(I, 224)

Mrs Clandon's reply to her son is significant, again, in terms of the CP: in spite of her 'liberated' views on every other topic, she exercises an embargo on information about her estranged husband. She justifies her violation of the Quantity Maxim by an apparent violation of the Quality Maxim: it is obviously untrue that a father is 'nothing': but by this hyperbolic literal untruth, Mrs Clandon implies that no information worth the name is being withheld. In adding 'That is enough', she also appears to proclaim her particularly restrictive application of the Quantity Maxim, clearly at odds with that of the children. Thus her implication is not accepted by her elder daughter, Gloria – a comely, somewhat priggish paragon of female independence – who at this point claims the children's right to freedom of information on this matter of personal importance.

Here, we have an inversion of the situation in examples (2) and (3) – where one character denied to another the right to withhold information personal to the latter. Here, one character claims from another the right to obtain information personal to the latter (and in fact to both). The Maxim of Quantity, we discover, is intimately bound up with the rights and obligations of individuals in relation to such informational 'property'.

The third maxim of the CP, Grice's Maxim of Relation (relevance) is, like the others, most noticeable when it is manifestly violated. In the following exchange, Dolly and her sister are doing their best to make polite conversation to a middle-aged man, Mr Crampton, who is Valentine's uncouth and unaccommodating landlord:

(6) DOLLY. [*suddenly, to keep things going*] How old are you, Mr Crampton?

GLORIA. [*hastily*] I am afraid we must be going, Mr Valentine.

(I, 231)

I called this an 'exchange', but actually Gloria's remark has no overt connection with that of Dolly. In other words, Gloria appears to break the Maxim of Relation. Grice's argument in favour of the Maxim of Relation, however, is that we *infer* relevance where none appears on the surface; thus we infer, from Gloria's interruption of the conversation, that she is trying to combat the embarrassment of her sister's tactless question. As often happens, a superficial violation of the CP is explicable as an attempt to mitigate impoliteness (i.e. to observe the PP).

However, Gloria's ploy fails, and after the interruption Mr Crampton answers Dolly's question, only to be thrown by a further instance of her rudeness (breaking the Maxim of Approbation in favour of the Maxim of Quality):

(7) CRAMPTON. . . . So you want to know my age, do you? I'm fifty-seven.
    DOLLY. [*with conviction*] You look it.

(I, 231)

The positive side of the PP is amply demonstrated by the benignly ingratiating behaviour of the waiter William, who is a paragon of politeness in every sense. At the beginning of Act II, he is talking to Mrs Clandon's old friend and solicitor, Mr M'Comas, who has arrived at her hotel from London to see her (I quote Shaw's detailed description of William on his first entry, to give the flavour of his character, which has a key role in the play):

(8) WAITER. Quite sure, sir. She expects you at a quarter to one, sir. [*The gentleman, soothed by the waiter's voice, looks at him with a lazy smile. It is a quiet voice, with a gentle melody in it that gives sympathetic interest to his most commonplace remark: and he speaks with the sweetest propriety, neither dropping his aitches nor misplacing them, nor committing any other vulgarism. He looks at his watch as he continues*] Not that as yet sir? 12.43, sir. Only two minutes to wait, sir. Nice morning, sir!
    GENTLEMAN. Yes: very fresh after London.
    WAITER. Yes, sir: so all our visitors say, sir. Very nice family, Mrs Clandon's sir.

(II, 238)

The last sentence, praising Mrs Clandon's family for no particular reason other than phatic communion, is an example of the

Approbation Maxim. The preceding remark *Only two minutes to wait, sir* illustrates the Tact Maxim – minimizing the cost of waiting for his interlocutor. The Agreement Maxim appears in the *Yes* and *Yes, sir* of both men, and in William's 'phatic' remark *Nice day, sir.* (Phatic communion is essentially a way of seeking ground for agreement on matters on which disagreement is virtually impossible.) There is, further, a hint of the Modesty Maxim in the waiter's addition: *so all our visitors say, sir.* Since Mr M'Comas has made a complimentary remark about the seaside resort where the waiter works, the waiter is obliged by modesty to attribute his agreement to the opinions of others. A further sign of politeness in the waiter's behaviour is his excessive use of respectful vocatives – here, *sir*.[4]

It is noteworthy that William's behaviour, in vocatives as in other respects, is the opposite of that of the twins, who scandalize their mother by their overfamiliar use, in addressing Mr M'Comas, of his first name *Finch*. William's behaviour is the comical extremity of *over*politeness, whereas that of Dolly and Philip is the extremity of *under*politeness (not to be confused with *im*politeness, since the twins appear to cause offence in all innocence of the norms required). These are, therefore, two contrasting examples of exaggerated conversational behaviour – and it is significant that William and the twins are on the best of terms throughout the play, since William's departure from the norm in one direction compensates for the twins' departure in the other.

In this case, and in the play more generally, it is important to note that the conversational singularities of different characters are related to one another in a system of similarities and contrasts. This will be elucidated in due course (pp. 269–74), and summarized in table form. But first, some observations on the general significance in *You Never Can Tell* of the Maxims of Quality and Quantity.

QUALITY AND QUANTITY: RIGHTS AND OBLIGATIONS

A recurrent problem for the play's characters is how to deal with unpleasant truths. For example, when Dolly and Philip demand to know who their father is, Mrs Clandon passes the buck to M'Comas, who has the unpleasant duty of informing them that their father is none other than the objectionable Fergus Crampton:

(9) MRS CLANDON. [*earnestly, even a little peremptorily*] Dolly: Mr M'Comas has something more serious than that to tell you . . .

MR M'COMAS. [*nervously*] . . . I was hardly prepared – er –

DOLLY. [*suspiciously*] Oh, we dont want anything prepared.

PHILIP. [*exhorting him*] Tell us the truth.

DOLLY. [*emphatically*] Bald headed.

M'COMAS. [*nettled*] I hope you intend to take what I have to say seriously.

(II, 243)

The twins (believers, as we have seen, in freedom of information) see nothing problematic about telling the truth outright; their elders, on the other hand, appear to regard this attitude as frivolous: truth, when unpalatable, should be told indirectly, if at all.

Ironically, when the truth is out, M'Comas is blamed for his role as breaker of bad news:

(10) PHILIP. Mr M'Comas: your conduct is heartless. Here you find a family enjoying the unspeakable peace and freedom of being orphans. We have never seen the face of a relative: never known a claim except the claim of freely chosen friendship. And now you wish to thrust into the most intimate relationship with us a man whom we dont know –

DOLLY. [*vehemently*] An a w f u l old man. [*Reproachfully*] And you began as if you had quite a nice father for us!

M'COMAS. . . . what right have you to choose your own father?

(II, 242)

M'Comas's reply to this unjust accusation is a rhetorical question which confronts them with another recurrent theme of the play, interrelated with that of information and truth: the theme of rights and responsibilities. In effect, he is saying that, although the twins may have a right to information, they have no right to change truth into falsehood.

When Mr Crampton is about to join the party, another awkward question of truth-telling arises: who is to tell him that these unspeakably unmannered children, Dolly and Philip, are his own offspring?

(11) GLORIA. Which of us is to tell him the truth? . . .

MRS CLANDON. Finch, you must tell him.

DOLLY. Oh, Finch is no good at telling things. Look at the mess he made at telling us.

(II, 245)

(Dolly, like Philip, shows herself to be a more modern equivalent of the king who executes the messenger bringing ill tidings.) Finally, a solution is found:

> (12)　PHILIP.　. . . Mr M'Comas: this communication should be made, should it not, by a man of infinite tact?
> M'COMAS. It will require tact, certainly.
>
> > (II, 246)

The obvious candidate is the waiter:

> (13)　PHILIP. William: you remember my request to you to regard me as your son?
> WAITER. [*with respectful indulgence*] Yes, sir. Anything y o u please, sir.
> PHILIP. William: at the very outset of your career as my father, a rival has appeared on the scene.
> WILLIAM. Your real father, sir? . . .
>
> > (ibid.)

William finds the ideal way of telling Mr Crampton the bad news, by treating it as a joke. Talking of Philip, he says:

> (14)　WAITER. [*smoothly melodious*] Yes, sir. Great flow of spirits, sir. A vein of pleasantry, as you might say sir. . . . The young gentleman's latest is that youre his father, sir.
> CRAMPTON. What!
> WAITER. Only his joke, sir, his favourite joke. Yesterday *I* was to be his father. . . .
>
> > (II, 248)

In this way, he exploits the previous joke (a licensed suspension of the Maxim of Quality) about his own paternity of the twins, and conveys the truth without causing offence, by appearing to tell an innocuous falsehood. Manifestly, William is an ingenious communicator: skilled in upholding the PP without sacrificing the CP.

The recurrent comic dilemma of truth and information (how do we uphold both the Maxim of Quality and the Maxim of Quantity?) interacts with the dilemma of how to uphold both the CP and the PP. This, in turn, raises the problem of how to reconcile rights with responsibilities. Whereas the twins assert their right to *know*, Mrs Clandon asserts her right to withhold *private* knowledge. Mr Crampton asserts his right to consideration as a (long-lost) parent, and the twins assert their right to choose their own parent. The assertion of a right frequently imposes a responsibility on others. So Mrs Clandon reluctantly accepts the responsibility to make sure her children know the truth. Mr Crampton (later in the play) asserts his right to parental respect, although he has assumed none of the responsibilities of parenthood. In the last act the twins beguile him into the discovery that to be truly considered a father, one has to grant one's children the right to be themselves.

PRAGMATIC ABNORMALITIES OF CHARACTER

Like William and the twins (see (3) above), the other characters exhibit deviant conversational behaviour with respect to the CP and the PP. Let us consider first Mr Crampton, whose 'deviation' appears to be a cynical distrust of others' words: in terms of pragmatic principles, he rejects the CP in interpreting the utterances of others, taking to extremes the well-motivated assumption that the PP must make the CP unreliable. Hence he repeatedly reads impolite meanings into other people's words, obsessively seeking causes for grievance under the polite or innocent surface of what is said. Thus, after meeting her husband for the first time in eighteen years, Mrs Clandon finds that breaking the ice can lead to immersion in cold water:

(15) MRS CLANDON. . . . . Fergus: you are greatly changed.
   CRAMPTON. [*grimly*] I daresay. A man does change in eighteen years.
   MRS CLANDON. [*troubled*] I – I did not mean that. I hope your health is good.

(II, 251)

In a similar fashion, Crampton succeeds in offending M'Comas, who is doing his limited best to keep the conversation alive at the lunch table:

(16) M'COMAS. We are getting on very nicely after all.
   DOLLY. [*critically*] After all! After all what, Finch?
   CRAMPTON. [*sarcastically*] He means that you are getting on very nicely in spite of the presence of your father. Do I take your point rightly, Mr M'Comas?
   M'COMAS. [*disconcerted*] No, no. I only said 'after all' to round off the sentence. I – er – er – er
   WAITER. [*tactfully*] Turbot, sir?

(II, 253)

William, again, shows his supreme tact by intervening just where the conversation is grinding to a disastrous halt. But Crampton has more pretexts for displeasure: on the sensitive matter of vocatives (see note 4), he quarrels with the twins for addressing him as 'Mr' – as a stranger (which, of course, he is):

(17) CRAMPTON . . . M i s t e r Crampton! What right have they to talk to me like that? I'm their father: . . . have I no rights, no claims? . . . [*Frantically*] My own children! M i s t e r Crampton! My –

VALENTINE. Come, come! theyre only children. She called you father.

CRAMPTON. Yes: 'goodbye, father'. Goodbye! Oh yes: s h e got at my feelings: with a stab!

(II, 259)

As this extract shows, Crampton perversely finds further fault when it is pointed out that his elder daughter Gloria did call him 'father'. Still on the subject of names, he takes umbrage once again on discovering that the daughter he named 'Sophronia' was renamed 'Gloria' by her mother. (The right of parents to name their children is one which few people, even today, would challenge.)

(18) GLORIA. Then my mother gave me a new name.

CRAMPTON. [*angrily*] She had no right to do it!

(II, 264)

Here once more, we note a key connection between impoliteness and the upholding of one's own rights at the expense of those of others.[5] Where normal behaviour is to look for implied *polite* meanings in what others say, his conversational pathology consists in finding *offensive* meanings where none was presumably intended.

We turn now to the pragmatic peculiarity of Gloria herself, which is her refusal to accept the patronage, or compliments, of others:

(19) VALENTINE. [*Pretending to forget himself*] How could that man [i.e. Crampton] have so beautiful a daughter!

GLORIA. . . . That seems to be an attempt at what is called a pretty speech. Let me say at once, Mr Valentine, that pretty speeches make very sickly conversation. . . .

(II, 267)

The duel of love between Gloria and Valentine depends on a double irony: Valentine, the philanderer, finds himself in love, so that his flattery of Gloria is sincere in spite of himself. On the other hand, Gloria, who has been taught by her mother to be immune to such male blandishments, rejects his flattery, only to be utterly taken in by his cunningly insincere insults:

(20) VALENTINE. . . . Youre a prig: a feminine prig: thats what you are. [*Rising*] Now I suppose youve done with me for ever . . .

GLORIA. [*with elaborate calm, sitting up like a High-school-mistress posing to be photographed*] That shews how very little you understand my real character. I am not in the least offended.

(II, 269)

Flattery and insult are defined conversationally in terms of the Maxim of Approbation. To insult is to violate the maxim; to flatter is to obey the maxim, perhaps to the extent of violating the Maxim of Quality. Gloria's response – to reject a compliment and accept an insult – is an inversion of normal conversational practice. She has acquired (under her mother's influence) a strong commitment to a woman's right to independence, especially from the opposite sex. Hence, while a man's praise is suspect, a man's dispraise may reasonably be respected as genuine.

Her mother, Mrs Clandon, an author of books on modern parenthood, prides herself on granting independence to her children, whose privacy she respects by never asking them questions. Thus, back in Act I, she reproaches Philip for questioning her on the matter of the twins' paternity, and rebukes Dolly for her habit of asking personal questions, even of the stranger Valentine:

(21) MRS CLANDON. . . . Phil: I never ask you about your private concerns. You are not going to question me, are you?

(I, 224)

(22) DOLLY. [*eagerly*] Oh, tell us. How long has he given you to pay?

MRS CLANDON. [*distracted by her child's manners*] Dolly, Dolly, Dolly, d e a r! You m u s t not ask questions.

DOLLY. [*demurely*] So sorry. Youll tell us, wont you, Mr Valentine?

(I, 227)

Mrs Clandon's vehemence in these matters reflects her strong conviction that *personal* information is not free, but belongs to the individual. However, that conviction is comically overruled when she finds her own curiosity and concern about Gloria's involvement with Valentine getting the better of her desire not to interfere:

(23) MRS CLANDON. . . . My dear?
    GLORIA. . . . Yes.
    MRS CLANDON. You know I never ask questions.
    GLORIA. . . . I know, I know.

                                                              (III, 273)

Mrs Clandon's broad hint that she would like information without
breaking her non-questioning rule is ignored by her daughter, who
takes her remark 'You know I never ask questions' at its face value.
This is an ironic inversion of the situation in (22) above, where Dolly
apologizes for asking questions, but then elicits the information from
Valentine none the less!

Valentine, in his turn, has a strange pragmatic eccentricity for a
practised philanderer: an embarrassing predilection for telling the
truth (observing Maxim of Quality):

(24) GLORIA. . . . Is it true? Did you ever say that before? Did you
    ever feel that before? for another woman?
    VALENTINE. [*bluntly*] Yes.

                                                              (III, 282)

In spite of such unpromising exchanges, the love match between
Gloria and the impecunious Valentine prospers. Yet, even pressure
from the family solicitor fails to deter Valentine from disarmingly and
outrageously telling the truth:

(25) M'COMAS. . . . Miss Clandon: it is my duty to tell you that
    your father has also persuaded himself that Mr Valentine
    wishes to marry you –
    VALENTINE. [*interposing adroitly*] I do.
    M'COMAS. [*huffily*] In that case, sir, you must not be surprised
    to find yourself regarded by the young lady's father as a
    fortune hunter.
    VALENTINE. So I am. Do you expect my wife to live on what I
    earn?

                                                              (III, p. 286)

(Note that Valentine not only tells a 'bare-faced truth', but also does
so cleverly, in a way that reinterprets fortune hunting as a generous
act, for the benefit of *others* rather than *self*.)

Improbable as the match between Gloria and Valentine is, there is a
good pragmatic reason behind it: Valentine's eccentricity (for a lover)
of being a slave of the Maxim of Quality helps him to win Gloria's
heart because it is the antithesis of her own eccentricity – a marked

aversion to compliments, even when sincere.

The last two characters to be considered are the two lawyers – the solicitor M'Comas and the barrister Bohun. M'Comas is the least appealing character, in many ways a stock Shavian Aunt Sally.[6] In spite of his earlier reputation for advanced ideas, he is an ageing mouthpiece for conventional Victorian values. If he has an eccentricity, it is the eccentricity of his type: a tendency to take offence (thus frustrating the function of the PP) at the unconventionalities (especially an unconventional devotion to the Maxim of Quality) of younger characters. This characteristic of M'Comas has been sufficiently illustrated in (9), (10), and (25) above.

The particularly infuriating eccentricity of Bohun is his habit of assuming control over the conversation, and denying conversational rights to others. This kind of conversational impoliteness may be appreciated by observing that turn-taking in conversation is a matter of exercising and granting rights to the 'conversational floor'.[7] To interrupt others, to usurp their conversational ground, is a kind of rudeness akin to taking something that belongs to another person. Hence, in the real world, claiming the floor, particularly by interruption, is often accompanied by apologies, hedges, and indirect requests: 'If I may put in a word here – . . .', 'Could I just say . . .', etc. Bohun, however, assuming the bullying, railroading manner of a stage advocate even in private conversation, dominates the floor, and has no compunction about refusing conversational rights to others:

(26) BOHUN. . . . In this family, it appears the husband's name is Crampton: the wife's, Clandon. Thus we have on the very threshold of the case an element of confusion.

VALENTINE. . . . But it's perfectly simple –

BOHUN. [*annihilating him with a vocal thunderbolt*] It is. Mrs Crampton has adopted another name. That is the obvious explanation which you feared I could not find out for myself. You mistrust my intelligence, Mr Valentine. – [*stopping him as he is about to protest*] no: I don't want you to answer that: I want you to think over it when you feel your next impulse to interrupt me.

(IV, 300)

His tactics are similarly domineering in persuading Mr Crampton that he would not benefit from claiming custody of the twins:

(27) BOHUN. . . . Now, Mr Crampton, . . . You think youd like to have your two youngest children to live with you.

Well, you wouldn't – [*Crampton tries to protest*] no you wouldnt: you think you would; but I know better than you . . .

(IV, 305–6)

Conversely, when Mrs Clandon, representing more normal conversational behaviour, apologizes for interrupting Bohun, Bohun brushes her apology aside, refusing to give the customary 'minimizing' response such as *Not at all*:

(28)   MRS CLANDON. I am afraid we interrupted you, Mr Bohun.
       BOHUN. [*calmly*] You did.

(IV, 303)

A further aspect of Bohun's pragmatic eccentricity is his tendency to make assertions about matters which are private or internal to other characters, or else are already known to them (cf. Labov and Fanshel (1977) on A events and A/B events). For example, in (26) above he prohibits Valentine's intervention on a matter about which Valentine, not he, is informed, and insists instead on making the statement 'Mrs Crampton has adopted another name' himself. In (27) he suppresses Crampton's attempt to interrupt his own predictions of Crampton's present and future states of mind. This extreme form of conversational arrogance falls foul of the CP both by informing people of what they may be expected to know already (Maxim of Quantity) and by making claims about others' personal lives apparently without adequate evidence (Maxim of Quality). Bohun's behaviour, in this respect, invites contrast with that of Mrs Clandon, who (as we noted earlier, pp. 266–9) asserts her right to withhold personal information from the people (her children) most entitled to know it.

A SYSTEM OF PRAGMATIC CONTRASTS

The following table is a summary of the pragmatic deviances of the various characters as they have been noted above. This table suggests certain ways in which the characters naturally form pairs, in terms of their deviation from pragmatic norms. The relations may be either of repulsion or attraction, helping to explain why the plot of *You Never Can Tell*, as expressed through dialogue, is one of repulsion and attraction between different conversational 'styles' and the characters associated with them.

However, the table oversimplifies, particularly in suggesting a

The Twins:	overrating CP (Quality, Quantity) and correspondingly undervaluing the PP
William:	overrating PP (without sacrificing CP)
Valentine:	overrating Quality (willing to sacrifice PP)
Gloria:	underrating PP (unwilling to sacrifice CP?)
Mrs Clandon:	overrating children's right to independence and underrating Quantity
Mr Crampton:	underrating children's right to independence, overrating PP, and underrating CP in others' language
M'Comas:	taking offence (negative infringement of PP) especially at others' overrating of CP
Bohun:	giving offence (positive infringement of PP) and misconstrual of CP

stereotyping of character, whereas in the play itself there is character development, as the participants in the comedy learn through experience the mistakes associated with their particular pragmatic abnormalities.

Each character, except the irrepressible twins (and to a lesser extent M'Comas) finds that the eccentricity leads to discomfiture: each meets his or her 'come-uppance' before the end of the play. Bohun, the most stereotyped character of all, meets his severest come-uppance when Dolly quells him in the way he has quelled other conversational participants:

(29) DOLLY. [*striking in as Bohun, frowning formidably, collects himself for a fresh grapple with the case*] Youre going to bully us, Mr Bohun.
    BOHUN. I –
    DOLLY. [*interrupting him*] Oh yes, you are: you think youre not; but you are. I know by your eyebrows.

(IV, 306)

Correspondingly, William's discomfiture is acute when he is asked to sit down and behave as if he were an equal, rather than as an inferior, caring for the rest of the company:

(30) WAITER. [*earnestly*] Oh, if you please, maam, I really must draw the line at sitting down. I couldn't let myself be seen doing such a thing, maam: thank you, I am sure, all the same. [*He looks round from face to face wretchedly, with an expression that would melt a heart of stone*].

(IV, 299)

Mrs Clandon and Crampton, as we have seen, are both mortified by their children's uncontrollable ability to set at nought their own ideas of 'polite' or 'correct' behaviour. Gloria and Valentine, on the other hand, are mortified by the experience of being in love with one another – their betrothal (at the end of the play) signalling their complete surrender to the fate of being under the control of the opposite sex: a bitter pill indeed for Gloria who has seen herself as the paragon of 'independent womanhood', and for Valentine 'the Duellist of Sex'.

'YOU NEVER CAN TELL'

The title of the play is a catch phrase used by William, the waiter, as a panacea for all future ills. In Act II, he uses the phrase to soothe the disconsolate Crampton, whose daughter appears likely to marry the penniless Valentine:

(31) WAITER. [*philosophically*] Well, sir, you never can tell. Thats a principle of life with me, sir, if youll excuse my having such a thing, sir. [*Delicately sinking the philosopher in the waiter for a moment*] Perhaps you havent noticed that you hadnt touched that seltzer and Irish, sir, when the party broke up. [*He takes the tumbler and sets it before Crampton*] Yes, sir, you never can tell. There was my son, sir! Who ever thought that he would rise to wear a silk gown, sir? And yet, today, sir, nothing less than fifty guineas. What a lesson sir!

(II, 261)

This apparently empty phrase sounds the consolatory note of the waiter's character: this paragon of politeness, submerging his own desires and interests in those of other characters, resolves the enmities and tensions exhibited through the conversational deformations of other characters. His 'overpoliteness', counteracting the 'underpoliteness' of other characters, finds a favourable resolution of all difficulties in the vague sentiment that the future is unpredictable, and things may well turn out better than you feared. So, at last, under William's administrations, Crampton and Mrs Clandon are mollified; the children are reconciled with their father, and Gloria and Valentine bury their antipathies in a marriage which, nevertheless, promises to be less than blissful. The play ends with William's last words of comfort to Valentine:

> (32) VALENTINE. [*collapsing on the ottoman and staring at the waiter*]
> I might as well be a married man already.
> WAITER. [. . . *with ineffable benignity*] Cheer up, sir, cheer
> up. Every man is frightened of marriage when it comes
> to the point; but it often turns out very comfortable, very
> enjoyable and happy indeed, sir – from time to time. *I*
> never was master in my own house, sir: my wife was like
> your young lady. . . . But if I had my life to live twice over,
> I'd do it again: I'd do it again, I assure you. You never can
> tell, sir: you never can tell.
>
> (IV, 316)

NOTES

1 An alternative pragmatic framework for analysing politeness in terms of 'face needs' is that of Brown and Levinson (1987), which has been applied to the analysis of drama by Simpson (1989).

2 Quotations and their page references are taken from Shaw, G. B. (1898), *Plays Pleasant*, Harmondsworth: Penguin Edition (1946). Ellipses indicate where I have omitted words from the original text. The singularities of Shaw's spelling have been retained.

3 Examples of characters' conversational behaviour shown in this text are illustrative of a tendency which I regard as to some extent typical. A more thorough analysis than has been undertaken here would contain a quantitative survey of pragmatic features as observed in the speech of different characters throughout the play.

4 Positions on the scale of Politeness (and of a closely related scale of respect/deference) are often signalled by the use of vocatives and other forms of personal reference (see Ervin-Tripp 1972, Quirk *et al.* 1985: 773–5). In *You Never Can Tell*, deviation in the use of vocatives is at various points a clear manifestation of pragmatic foregrounding. William's excessive use of vocatives as markers of respect is noted not only in (8) above, but in the following exchange, in which his *maam* contrasts with Mrs Clandon's familiar use of the first name *William*:

> MRS CLANDON. We shall have two more gentlemen at lunch, *William*.
> WAITER. Right, *maam*. Thank you, *maam*.
>
> (II, 239)

Note also how Dolly's outrageous addressing of M'Comas by his first name, *Finch*, is gently reproved by her mother's substitution of the more respectful form *Mr M'Commas*:

> DOLLY. [*to Mrs Clandon*] Has Finch had a drink?
> MRS CLANDON. [*remonstrating*] Dearest: Mr M'Comas will lunch with us.
>
> (II, 242)

Mrs Clandon's use of *dearest* above also brings to mind the power of familiar vocatives (in Mrs Clandon's case somewhat overused) to indicate loving family relationships. In this connection, we have seen Mr Crampton's sense of insult, in (17), when his own daughter addresses him with respectful distance as *Mr Crampton*. In the last act, the reconciliation between Crampton and his children is correspondingly indicated by the familiar vocatives *Dad* (used by Philip to his father) and *my boy* (used by Crampton to Philip):

> CRAMPTON. [. . . *with an attempt at genial fatherliness*]
>   Come along, my boy. Come along. [*He goes*]
> PHILIP. [*Cheerily, following him*] Coming, dad, coming.
>
> (IV, 309)

In contrast, William continues to use the deferential *sir* to his own son Bohun, pointedly refusing to claim familiarity with someone so much above him in social station.

5   On the relevance to politeness of rights and responsibilities, see Thomas (1983).
6   M'Comas bears a close similarity, in this respect, to the ageing 'advanced thinker' Roebuck Ramsden in *Man and Superman*.
7   On turn-taking and its relevance to politeness, see Sacks, Schegloff and Jefferson (1974) and Leech (1983: 139–42).

Editor's preface

In 'The pragmatics of nonsense' Paul Simpson examines the linguistic pragmatic roots of unintentional humour of the Colemanballs variety. With Brian McHale's chapter, we began with the provocative role that postmodernism plays in attempting a cognitive mapping of the new or counter sense that is motivated non-sense. Here we close with the gaffes and incongruities that sometimes enliven the sober, sensible commentaries of the British TV sports reporter David Coleman and others of his ilk. This is common or garden nonsense: daft remarks which the reader/listener can relate back to the (usually pedestrian) sensible discourse one supposes the speaker was aiming at. In other words, Colemanballs material can often be tracked back to some more pragmatically coherent formulation, and the humour lies in the observable gulf between the intention and the performance. So 'trackable' is the coherent variant, and so noticeable the contrast between the intended and the achieved, that these solecisms are comprehensible – are perhaps funnier – when removed from their original context, and placed in the new one of the pages of *Private Eye*: a satirical British weekly dedicated to the exposure and ridicule of, especially, those who in the magazine's opinion are unjustifiably high and mighty.

Simpson finds that Colemanballs gaffes are most commonly flout-ings of either the Quantity or Quality Maxim for co-operative talk. That is, the erring speaker – accidentally, we assume – noticeably departs from (a) making sufficiently informative remarks on the topic under way, or (b) supplying information that is likely to be true, in view of the facts already known. Commonest sources of Colemanballs-ups are then vacuous tautologies (a Quantity-Maxim flout) and contradictions (a Quality-Maxim flout).

Simpson isolates a tendency he calls the 'literalness condition' – an interpreter's strategy of withholding participation in the CP, in deriving the implicatures speakers may intend their utterances, when interpreted non-literally, to convey. (We may note that this literalness condition particularly afflicts academics in the humanities, poring over exam scripts for student 'howlers'.) As the term 'literal' suggests, it is an interpretative slant or preference towards the written language and its freer standing characteristics, and is typically most at work on spoken language (as in the Colemanballs examples), which is then transcribed into the cold print of writing, for display and ridicule (Simpson's 'Recontextualization Strategy'). The twin procedures of (a) taking a remark literally and (b) recontextualizing it as writing have the effect of highlighting the pompous foolishness, as dysfunctional tautologies, even of remarks that in their original context may have some informative point, or some contextual significance. The connection with exam 'howlers' can be sustained here, since students' writing under the duress of exam conditions often shifts away from, for instance, the norms of the reflective written essay, and towards the oral style, or a transcript of an oral answer, with little planning or monitoring time intervening between mental formulation and the actual writing out.

One is tempted to add that a further important contextual factor in the recycling of Colemanballs oddities may be the typical evaluation of TV sports commentators – especially the more widely paraded ones whose judgements and personalities are felt to intrude to a large degree in the broadcast – on the part of typical *Private Eye* readers. This evaluation includes elements of envy and contempt, since real-time sports commentaries sometimes appear to be something any alert sports fan could do. For the intelligent sports viewer, large extents of the play-by-play commentary may be strictly superfluous, a relaying of what is known or obvious already. (This is not to deny that, even where of limited informational value, such commentaries can contribute to atmosphere, engagement with the event, and information about off-camera matters.) And so it may be the case that this encompassing context of reception of sports commentaries, as constantly teetering on the brink of informational redundancy, conditions and sharpens our delight in those moments where the speaker slips and falls in. In short, the sociocultural context within which Colemanballs is located is one of reader hostility towards TV commentators, and concomitant resistance to placid conformity with the co-operative principle. Simpson's example discourse type may be representative of a host of other interactive situations marked by hostility, alienation, or resistance, where, similarly, recontextualizing literalness in evaluating overt tautologies and contradictions may be common practice.

12 The pragmatics of nonsense
Towards a stylistics of *Private Eye*'s Colemanballs

Paul Simpson

INTRODUCTION

In the satirical magazine *Private Eye* there appears regularly a selection of linguistic blunders made by television and radio presenters. This selection is headed, in bold print, by the title Colemanballs; so named because the eponymous David Coleman, a BBC sports commentator, is a perennial offender in this area and is responsible for more of these *faux pas* than any other presenter. The tokens which comprise Colemanballs are collected by, presumably, *Private Eye* readers who are rewarded, on publication of their contribution, by a small payment from the magazine. So popular has Colemanballs become in the United Kingdom that three collections have been published, and these volumes are frequently on display in newsagents, bookshops, airport terminals, railway stations, and such like. This essay will simply draw on a range of techniques in linguistic pragmatics in order to explain how Colemanballs humour is created. It will attempt to highlight the regular patterns of error and provide some framework for assessing the natural categories into which many of the examples fall. Such an analysis will, of necessity, be qualitative rather than quantative, drawing on over fifty tokens from the three Colemanballs collections.

The interface between pragmatics and humour is still relatively underexplored. Furthermore, and with the possible exception of Nash (1985: 149–51), the unintentional humour that characterizes the Colemanballs genre has received little attention within stylistics. For instance, in a study of oxymoron, Hughes cites three tokens from Colemanballs as examples of 'verbal tautology', although his analysis is, by his own admission, highly informal (Hughes 1984: 27). By contrast, a number of studies of humour which have drawn on linguistic models have tended to examine only *intentional* humour, that is to say, the humour consciously produced by 'humor manu-facturers and deliverers' (Raskin 1988: 1). This is especially true of those studies which use pragmatic models. (See, for instance, Raskin 1985 and Marino 1988). Given this focus of attention it is not surprising that Colemanballs discourse does not slot neatly into the categories of humour proposed by humorologists. For instance, of the five functions of humour proposed by Ziv only two are potentially applicable to the Colemanballs corpus. These are:

1 The *intellectual* function . . . based on absurdities, word play, and nonsense. Here the pleasure of humour resides in the temporary freedom from the strict rules and rationality.
2 The *aggressive* function . . . directed towards a 'victim'. The victim who is made fun of, ridiculed, disparaged can be an individual, a group, or an institution. Humour in this case allows nonvictims a feeling of superiority.

(1988: 225, italics added)

The second of these is particularly interesting given the type of language that will be examined shortly. Indeed, there is an echo in Ziv's formulation of Thomas Hobbes's explanation of the cause of laughter, which is worth recalling here:

sudden glory is the passion which maketh those *grimaces* called LAUGHTER; and is caused either by some sudden act of their own, that pleaseth them; or by the apprehension of some deformed thing in another, by comparison whereof they suddenly applaud themselves. And it is incident most to them, that are conscious of the fewest abilities in themselves; who are forced to keep themselves in their own favour, by observing the imperfections of other men. And therefore much laughter at the defects of others is a sign of pusillanimity.

(Hobbes [1651] 1962: 93)

A salutary reminder of what Hughes (1984: 27) describes as the 'cruel intent' of the *Private Eye* magazine.

This study also breaks with traditional stylistics in that it is not primarily concerned with the analysis of literary texts. Unlike the studies of, say, Pratt (1977), and Short (1989) which draw on pragmatic models in order to examine specifically literary communication, the following analysis will apply those models to a highly unusual type of discourse. It is unlikely that such an application was ever envisaged by the pragmaticians who developed the models, and one concomitant of this may be that the following study will provide a useful testing ground for some aspects of pragmatic theory.

Finally, to a problem which pervades any systematic study of funny language. The tokens selected from the Colemanballs corpus should certainly provide some amusement for the reader of this essay, even bearing in mind the sobering remarks of Hobbes. However, the same is unlikely to be true (one would hope) of the analysis which will be conducted on these tokens. As Raskin points out (1988: 3), this represents a central dilemma in humorology: hoping to derive amusement from an academic study of humour is somewhat akin to hoping to enjoy gastronomically the recipe for a delicious dish!

PSYCHOLINGUISTIC EVIDENCE

Since the investigation which follows is broadly concerned with the analysis of linguistic errors, an appropriate point of entry might be provided by some of the findings of psycholinguistic research on slips of the tongue. (For two important collections, see Fromkin 1973 and 1980). The aims of such psycholinguistic research are generally incompatible with those of the present study in that the speech error data are used, among other things, to provide insights into cognitive processing and to provide a basis for explanations of the hierarchically-ordered planning stages of speech production. Nevertheless, the potential for humour in speech errors has not gone unnoticed:

> That speech errors so often produce unintended but meaningful utterances makes them strong candidates for humor.
>
> (Fromkin 1971: 39)

The psycholinguistic evidence points to the existence of a number of speech error prototypes, among which phonological errors are particularly common. Of those phonological errors, three patterns involving segmental substitution predominate. These are, following Fromkin (1971: 30–1):

1 *Anticipations*

A(ctual) U(tterance)	T(arget) U(tterance)
alsho share	also share
sub observation	such observation
reek long race	week long race

In each of the examples in the AU column, a sound has been substituted in anticipation of a sound which occurs later in the

utterance; in other words, the interfering segment follows the substituted segment. Anticipations are arguably the most common type
of phonological error. (See Van den Broecke and Goldstein 1980: 48.)

2 *Perseverances* (or *perseveratory substitutions*)

AU	TU
John gave the goy	John gave the boy
irrepraceable	irreplaceable
Chomsky and Challe	Chomsky and Halle

In contrast to anticipations, the interfering segment in perseverances precedes the affected segment.

3 *Methatheses* (or *classic spoonerisms*)

AU	TU
teep a cape	keep a tape
with this wing I do red	with this ring I do wed
I'll die yes lung	I'll die less young
in the fast pew weeks	in the past few weeks

This type of error might be viewed as a combination of anticipation
and perseverance errors in that two segments are reversed. Furthermore, the items derived from such metatheses are normally 'lexically
real' (Baars 1980: 315). That is to say, a metathesis of the type which
converts 'barn door' into 'darn bore' is more likely to occur than the
conversion of 'dart board' into 'bart doard'. This tendency is unlikely
to have provided any comfort for the eponymous Rev. Spooner,
among whose hapless linguistic errors is reputed to have been the
following:

> You have hissed all my mystery lectures. I saw you fight a liar in
> the back quad. In fact, you have tasted a whole worm.
>
> (reported in Fromkin 1971: 30)

Despite the frequency of occurrence of these three types of speech
error in naturally occuring conversation, I can isolate only one token
from the Colemanballs corpus which might be considered an instance
of phonological substitution:

> (1)　Steve Ovett, Sebastian Coe, Steve Cram – the vanguard of our
> cream.
>
> (Ron Pickering; *C3*: 2)[1]

On the face of it, this example is a perseveratory substitution, with the
interfering velar and continuant cluster (the /kr/ in 'Cram' generating
a blunder on the TU word 'team'. This results in the AU word

'cream' (/kri:m/). Such a description squares with general predictions about perseverances in that, for instance, the distance between the interfering segment and the affected segment is no more than seven syllables and the result is a phonologically permissible string in the given language. However, this is by no means a complete or exclusive explanation. The selection of 'cream', which is compatible semantically with the sense 'best of our team', might suggest that paradigmatic substitution of a lexical item has occurred. As Fromkin (1971: 46) points out, speakers match semantic features of lexical items with their phonological specifications in the planning stages of an utterance by bringing them into a linguistic 'buffer storage compartment'. From this storage compartment final selections are made. An error in the final selection may result in the substitution of a phonologically similar word, a word with semantic features in common with the TU item, or, as in the case of example (1), both. In fact the substitution of items which display phonological similarity, but semantic incompatibility, accounts for a few other tokens in Colemanballs, as can be seen from the following:

(2) I needed a break from the programme in order to regurgitate myself.

(TU: 'rejuvenate')   (Fred Feast; *C3*: 50)

(3) Steve Davis has a tough consignment in front of him.

(TU: 'assignment')   (Ted Lowe; *C2*: 84)

(4) That pot puts the game beyond reproach.

(TU: 'reach')   (Ted Lowe; *C2*: 84)

(5) Again Mariner and Butcher are trying to work the oracle on the near post.

(TU: 'miracle')   (Martin Tyler; *C2*: 41)

(6) Henry Rono . . . the man with those tremendous, asbestos lungs.

(TU: ?)   (Ron Pickering; *C1*: 10)

Closely aligned to errors of the type displayed by examples (2–6) is the substitution of a strong collocate of a particular lexical item:

(7) Also in the news, the case of Rudolph Hess, the guy who's in Spandau Ballet . . .

(Simon Bates; *C3*: 72)

Here, the high degree of collocational restriction on 'Spandau' leaves the disc jockey with only two possibilities: 'Spandau prison' or, the name of a popular British rock band, 'Spandau Ballet'. The Colemanballs cartoonist is quick to exploit the unfortunate consequences of the erroneous final selection as this token is headed by a picture of a group of slick young musicians fronted by an ageing Nazi goosestepping across the stage.

Examples (1) to (7) represent the few tokens which are amenable to explication within psycholinguistic terms. Whether this is because commentators and presenters are less prone to this type of performance error or whether viewers and listeners are generally more sympathetic to these kinds of slips is difficult to say. What is clear, however, is that the bulk of psycholinguistic work on speech errors fails to account for – or at least is not concerned with – the *interactive* consequences of such errors. As a result, existing psycholinguistic models will have little to say about the majority of the Colemanballs tokens which are, as I will argue later, very much a product of the communicative context in which they occur. In this regard, these tokens might be viewed more strictly as *communicative* rather than *speech* errors, and subsequent analysis of such tokens will need to account for their discoursal and pragmatic properties. One of the models available for such analysis will be reviewed in the following section.

MAXIMS AND IMPLICATURE

It now seems generally accepted among linguists that H. P. Grice's theory of conversational implicature has become a central concept within pragmatics. (See Levinson (1983: ch. 3) for a full review.) And as this theory will underpin much of the analysis that follows, a brief account of the major tenets of Grice's model is necessary at this stage.

Grice (1975: 45) notes that conversations normally exhibit some degree of coherence and continuity, which suggests that speakers are obeying some general principle of co-operation. This Co-operative Principle (CP) Grice defines as a basic shared assumption among interactants that speakers should make their conversational contributions such as are required by the accepted purpose or direction of the talk in which they are engaged. Speakers, will, according to Grice, observe the CP by adhering to four sets of highly normative conversational maxims. These are:

1 Maxims of QUANTITY
  (a) 'Make your contribution as informative as is required (for the current purposes of the exchange).'
  (b) 'Do not make your contribution more informative than is required.'
2 Maxims of QUALITY
  Supermaxim: 'Try to make your contribution one that is true.'
  Maxims: (a) 'Do not say what you believe to be false.'
              (b) 'Do not say that for which you lack adequate evidence.'
3 Maxim of RELATION
  (a) 'Be relevant.'
4 Maxims of MANNER
  Supermaxim: 'Be perspicuous.'
  Maxims: (a) 'Avoid obscurity of expression.'
              (b) 'Avoid ambiguity.'
              (c) 'Be brief (avoid unnecessary prolixity).'
              (d) 'Be orderly.'

If speakers choose to follow the maxims faithfully, they will be speaking in a maximally efficient, rational, and co-operative way. However, the most significant aspect of Grice's theory concerns instances where speakers knowingly depart from rational efficiency by ostentatiously flouting one or more of the maxims. Consider, for instance, speaker B's response in the following exchange:

A: Did John go to the party last night?
B: Yes, and don't let anyone tell you anything different!

Here, B flouts the maxim of quantity by providing more information than would be conventionally required as a response to A's question. In effect, B is thus able to imply a meaning beyond the literal reference of the words used. This type of 'non-natural' meaning Grice labels as a conversational implicature. Flouting the Maxim of Quantity through underinformativeness may also yield conversational implicatures. Imagine that the following example constitutes a reference written on behalf of a candidate who has applied for a post in philosophy:

Dear Sir, Mr. X's command of English is excellent, and his attendance at tutorials has been regular.

(Grice 1975: 52)

Clearly, the lack of information about Mr X's specific abilities *implicates* that the referee thinks that the candidate is unsuitable for the job; although the referee will not have committed himself to any *overt* criticism in this reference. Of course, the successful uptake of the implicature will depend on the addressee assuming that the CP, although superficially jeopardized, is still being observed at some deeper level: for the CP to have been genuinely abandoned in this example, the referee would simply not have written anything at all.

More extreme examples of quantity implicatures occur in the form of patent tautologies. The following three examples (from Levinson 1983: 111) are, in strictly logical terms, *necessary truths*; that is to say, they are true in virtue of the laws of logic and none of the three makes any new assertion:

(a)   War is war. $(\forall x\ (W\ (x) \rightarrow W(x))^2$
(b)   Either John will come or he won't. $(p \vee \sim p)$
(c)   If he does it, he does it. $(p \rightarrow p)$

Nevertheless, such examples need not be devoid of any communicative significance. Example (1), for instance, may implicate something like 'disasters always happen in war, and there's no point in being angry about it', while (b) may implicate that John's arrival or otherwise is entirely a matter for him, so there's nothing either the speaker or the addressee can do about it. Example (c) might implicate something like 'it's none of our business' or 'it's out of our hands'. Therefore, (a–c) are meaningful at the level of what is implicated; recourse to truth-conditions alone is not enough to ensure that addressees will derive satisfactory meanings from these sentences in a particular context of utterance.

Conversational implicatures may be generated by flouting any of the other three maxims. As we have now established the basic pattern of implicature, brief illustrations of each type should suffice at this stage. In the following exchange, the Maxim of Relevance has been flouted:

A: Mrs X is an awful windbag.
B: Lovely weather we're having for February.

The nature of what B's response implicates will obviously depend on the context of interaction. If A's remark is made at a genteel social gathering, then B may be implicating that A has committed a social gaffe; if, on the other hand, A makes the remark unaware that Mrs X happens to be within earshot, B may be implicating that a timely change of topic is needed.

In the following example, B's response blatantly fails to fulfil the Maxim of Quality.

A: You failed your exam.
B: Terrific!

Clearly, B is stating that which is manifestly untrue, thereby implicating that the genuine sentiment is in fact the opposite of what is actually expressed.

And finally, as an illustration of how speakers flout the Maxim of Manner, Grice provides the following example:

Miss X. produced a series of sounds that corresponded closely with the score of 'Home Sweet Home'.

(1975: 55)

Here, the reviewer of Miss X's performance, by failing to be succinct, implicates that Miss X's version of 'Home Sweet Home' is seriously flawed in some way.

It is perhaps not surprising that such a superficially neat theory of conversational interaction should be undermined by a number of significant theoretical problems. For instance, Grice himself contends that all four sets of maxims are arguably overridden by the single supermaxim 'Be polite', although this contention is not developed in any way. Furthermore, it should be clear from the foregoing account, that some of the maxims tend to overlap: the Manner submaxim 'Be brief' conceivably encroaches on the Quantity Maxim, while the 'Avoid obscurity' submaxim is closely related to the Quality Maxim. Part of the reason for this kind of theoretical 'leakage' may be due to the generally unrigorous nature of Grice's explanations – described by Gazdar, for instance, as 'self-consciously informal' (1979: 7). This informality has led to extensive reshaping of Grice's main proposals within formal pragmatic models, a number of which are developed in the following works: Wilson (1975); Gazdar (1979); Leech (1983); Levinson (1983); Sperber and Wilson (1986). Where appropriate, reference will be made to this more rigorous work in the subsequent analyses.

The pragmatic analysis of selected tokens from the Colemanballs corpus will be structured as follows. In the next section, attention will be focused on those tokens which in some way flout the Maxims of Quantity, while in the penultimate section, tokens which attempt to flout the Maxims of Quality will be examined. For reasons touched on above, potential manner implicatures will be subsumed under the discussion of quality implicatures. This leaves the Maxim of

Relevance. As the criterion of relevance has to do with the structure of dyadic discourse, and the bulk of the Colemanballs corpus is essentially one-party talk, then a survey of violations of the relevance maxim will yield little of interest for the present study. This is not to suggest that presenters, in their attempts to maintain ongoing talk, do not string together totally unrelated remarks. The following bizarre sequence should illustrate this:

(8)   Oh and that's a brilliant shot. The odd thing is his mum's not very keen on snooker.

(Ted Lowe; *C2*: 82)

Especially unfortunate is the following sequence, where the DJ links a news item to the record he is about to play:

(9)   This was the year we lost Sir Ralph Richardson, and gained THIS from Kajagoogoo.

(Simon Bates; *C3*: 75; original emphasis)

It is unlikely, however, that in either case any implicature is intended through deliberate violation of the Maxim of Relevance.

QUANTITY IMPLICATURES

(10) The loss of a life is – well – the loss of a life, and that's something you can't take away.

(Secretary, British Olympic Team; *C1*: 7)

Despite the fact that, within the terms of the Gricean model, this token is a paradigmatic example of a flout on the Maxim of Quantity, it – and many like it – still find their way into Colemanballs. In fact, it realizes a logical structure similar to that of the tautological example (a) discussed on p. 288. In this respect it may be paraphrased as the following argument:

(10′)For any entity (x), if (x) is the loss of a life, then (x) is the loss of a life

and symbolized as: $\forall x \ (L(x) \rightarrow L(x))$.

Clearly, (10) is a necessary truth which, in principle, should have no communicative import. But it is precisely this type of utterance that, by flouting the Maxim of Quantity in this way, can generate implicatures – the implicature in this instance being something along the lines 'The seriousness of the loss of a life should not be underestimated'. Why then are tokens like (10), which are well-formed at least in terms of pragmatic inferencing, considered good candidates for humour by the Colemanballs collector? Part of the answer to this, I would contend, is provided by two interrelated processes. The first of these I shall refer to as the Literalness Condition and define as an interpretative strategy whereby addressees read the meaning of an utterance in purely semantic terms. In this way, the viewer/listener withholds participation in the CP so that when presenters jeopardize the CP by ostentatiously flouting one or more maxims, their utterances are interpreted literally and are accessed through reference to truth-conditions alone. Any potential implicatures are thereby suspended. The LC is supplemented by a second process, a Recontextualization Strategy (RS), whereby what is originally unscripted *spoken* discourse is transcribed into the *written* discourse that comprises the Coleman-balls column. That the spoken and written modes of language are radically different systems is widely recognized in linguistics, and transcription of the former into the latter often has an estranging or defamiliarizing effect (Stubbs 1983: 20). And one crucial aspect of many conversational implicatures is that they are strongly context-bound. To show just how effective the combination of the LC and the RS are in making intended implicatures evaporate, consider the following two examples:

(11) Lillian's great strength is her strength.

(David Coleman; *C1*: 6)

(12) And our next race is the next race.

(David Coleman; *C1*: 5)

The thorough decontextualization created by the RS, together with the LC's restriction on the uptake of implicatures, leave both utterances dangerously exposed.

Disjunctive tautologies of the sort exemplified by (b) on p. 288 are also common in the Colemanballs corpus; and are equally prone to the effects of the LC and RS:

(13) Hurricane Higgins can either win or lose this final match tomorrow.

(Archie McPherson; *C1*: 83)

(14) Alderman knows that he is either going to get a wicket – or he isn't.

(Steve Brenkley; *C3*: 10)

Again, the humorous potential of these tokens is dependent on the blockage of intended implicatures. As any pragmatic inferencing is thus suspended, there remains only the underlying (tautological) disjunctive form: $(p \vee \sim p)$.

Expressions which contain other natural language connectives may also create problems for presenters who risk flouting the Quantity Maxim. Some conditionals, for instance, are either liable to tautology in a way which parallels example (c) on p. 288, or liable to be invalidated through the addition of extra premises. Consider the following as instances of the former type:

(15) I think if you've got a safe pair of hands, you've got a safe pair of hands.

(Tom Graveney; *C2*: 18)

(16) And he can't afford to be beaten because, if he is, he'll be beaten.

(Tony Gubba; *C1*: 3)

Grice (1975: 56) notes that many types of implicature are *particularized*; that is to say, they require a specific context in order to be successfully interpreted. In these examples, however, the RS separates context from form, leaving both utterances susceptible to a literal reading.

The second type of conditional is represented by the following:

(17) If she gets the jitters now, then she isn't the great champion that she is.

(Max Robertson; *C3*: 89)

The first two premises ('If she gets the jitters now' and 'then she isn't the great champion') constitute the antecedent and consequent of a well-formed conditional $(J \rightarrow \sim C)$. But the addition of the extra premise, which asserts that she *is* a great champion in any case, invalidates the conditional. Nevertheless, it's not difficult to trace the intended implicature of (17) – not difficult, that is, should one be predisposed to do so in the first place.

The remaining set of quantity implicatures adds an extra dimension to the discussion in that it demonstrates to some extent how error data may actually provide empirical support for an aspect of current pragmatic theory. One of the important developments of Grice's model involves the notion of scalar implicatures. (See Gazdar 1979: 55; for further elaboration see Levinson 1983: 132.) However, in order to reach a definition of scalar implicatures one must first invoke the idea of a quantitative scale. Quantitative scales are simply sets of contrastive expressions of the same grammatical category which may be ordered in terms of semantic strength or general informativeness. Here are three such scales.

<all, most, many, some, few . . . >
<ten, nine, eight, seven, six . . . >
<must, should, may . . . >

(Gazdar 1979: 56)

Now, a speaker who selects a particular term from a scale will implicate that any leftwards term does *not* obtain. Thus, in uttering

John scored eight points,

a speaker conversationally implicates that John *did not* score nine points or ten points and so on. It is important to stress that such scalar implicatures are pragmatic inferences and not logical consequences. In fact, this utterance will be logically entailed if John *has* scored nine points, as will be other statements which draw on rightwards terms (e.g. 'John has scored seven points', 'John has scored six points'). But if a speaker is assumed to be co-operating, and is in a position to state that a stronger term on the scale holds, then it will be taken that the speaker *should* state the stronger term.

In the light of this framework, the following tokens from Coleman-balls might be considered pragmatically ill-formed:

(18) Nick Holmes also got two today, as Southampton won 3–0 at Leeds. Nick Holmes got the other.

(Tony Gubba, *C1*: 34)

(19) And Meade had a hat-trick. He scored two goals.

(Richard Whitmore; *C2*: 21)

(20) Fifty-two thousand people here at Maine Road tonight, but my goodness me, it seems like fifty thousand.

(Bryon Butler; *C3*: 16)

Levinson notes (1983: 136) that it is a characteristic of scalar implicatures that they commit speakers to relatively strong assumptions and beliefs, so that the speaker of (18) for instance, will be implicating in the first sentence that he *knows* that Holmes did not score more than two goals. The second sentence of (18) creates the problem, leaving the addressee wondering why a stronger, leftwards term was not selected from the scale in the first place. Token (19) is comparably defective, although superficially the pattern is reversed. Here the stronger term is selected first ('hat-trick') consequently rendering mention of any weaker item gratuitous. The problem with (20), by contrast, is the leftwards term is selected first and is then followed by a comparative form which, in the context, would predict that an item which lies further *left*, rather than further *right*, on the scale should be selected. In the given context ('my goodness me') it also falls foul of an expectation of *contrastive* numbering. If Butler had said 'it seems like 55,000' that would be acceptable in scalar terms but still discoursally odd. What is needed is a contrast (so that even 'but it seems like only 15,000 are here, the crowd is so quiet', though counter to scalar expectations, would be fine). These rather infelicitous attempts to generate scalar implicatures would tend to lend empirical support to the argument that the quantitative scale possesses considerable predictive power. Listeners are quick to identify tokens which this aspect of pragmatic theory would predict as deviant in some way.

It should be clear from the preceding discussion that the humorous impact of intended implicatures is as much a product of hearers' processing strategies as the luckless presenters' linguistic *faux pas*. Indeed, some intended implicatures, such as those in tokens (10), (13), and (14–17), are still relatively easily accessed even after thorough decontextualization. Others, such as (11), (12), and (18–20), are not so easily interpreted and it is difficult to envisage what kind of pragmatic inferencing would have been required of the addressee in the original context. Part of the explanation for the relative opacity of the second category may lie simply in the mechanics of broadcasting; tokens such as (18) and (19), for instance, may result from confusion created when producers send conflicting information through earpieces to presenters who are involved in ongoing talk. Any resulting communicative blunders, however, are in no way granted immunity by the Colemanballs collector.

In the following section, I shall examine further the unfortunate consequences which occur when presenters take calculated risks by placing the CP in jeopardy. The category of Quality implicatures will provide the framework for discussion and particular attention will be focused on contradictory statements, idiomatic expressions, and metaphors.

QUALITY IMPLICATURES

Broadly speaking, speakers flout the Maxim of Quality by saying something which is manifestly false in context. According to Grice, such quality implicatures will incorporate all sorts of traditional rhetorical devices, such as irony, metaphor, meiosis (understatement), and hyperbole. Thus, a metaphorical remark like 'you are the cream in my coffee', which is a categorial falsity, will leave the addressee with the task of inferencing which non-literal aspects of meaning the speaker intends to convey. Comparable inferencing strategies will be required to unravel hyperboles, such as 'I've told you a million times already', and understatements such as 'He was a little intoxicated' (when said of someone who has just smashed up all the furniture). If, however, addressees reject the underlying assumption of co-operation and refuse to undertake the interactive work required by flouts of the quality maxim, then the resulting utterance will naturally be read as false – often absurdly so. And, as I shall attempt to demonstrate, this has important implications for Colemanballs discourse.

Consider the following tokens, where a soccer commentator flouts the Maxim of Quality by uttering a semantic contradiction:

(21) Lawrenson slipped the ball through to Williams, and he beat Shilton from 35 yards . . . and you don't beat Shilton from 35 yards.

(Peter Jones; *C1*: 40)

In this example, two contradictory assertions are made: 'he beat Shilton' and 'you don't beat Shilton'. As one of these assertions must be false, then the whole argument must be false. None the less, a generalized implicature along the lines of 'Beating Shilton from 35 yards is an exceptional feat' is still derivable from this quality flout. A comparable point might be made about the following token:

(22) saved by Bailey, son of Roy Bailey, once the Ipswich goal-keeper. He's no longer being called the son of Roy Bailey.

(Peter Jones; *C1*: 42)

Again, despite the semantically anomalous nature of this remark, a generalized implicature like 'the younger Bailey is no longer overshadowed by the accomplishments of his father' may still be read from it – even given the effects of the RS. However, the LC ensures that such an implicature is blocked. It is worth adding that (22) is accompanied by a cartoon depicting a soccer spectator shouting 'Bastard!' at a disconsolate-looking goalkeeper.

Not all quality flouts which take the form of contradictions are generalized; that is to say, there are a number of contradictory tokens which, without the original context of utterance, leave potential implicatures opaque.

(23) We estimate, and this isn't an estimation, that Greta Waitz is 80 seconds behind.

(David Coleman; *C3*: 5)

(24) It's not one of Bruno's fastest wins . . . but it's one of them.

(Harry Carpenter; *C3*: 7)

(25) No fighter comes into the ring hoping to win – he goes in hoping to win.

(Henry Cooper; *C2*: 5)

(26) Well Ibrox is filling up slowly, but rapidly.

(James Sanderson; *C2*: 31)

It is difficult indeed to imagine what communicative import such nonsense would have had in its original context of utterance.

Metaphorical expressions constitute another important type of violation of the Quality Maxim. In addition to its centrality in literary works, metaphor accounts for a large proportion of ordinary language use. Given this, it is perhaps not surprising that since Grice's initial observations some attention has been given to the study of metaphor within linguistic pragmatics. (For some useful developments in this area, see Levinson 1983: 147–62 and Sperber and Wilson 1986: 231–7). Irrespective of how conventionalized it is, a metaphor, in semantic terms, expresses a categorial falsity. The amount of communicative risk that this poses for presenters is therefore considerable – even a minor infelicity is liable to provoke a literal interpretation. In the Colemanballs data utterances containing metaphors tend to misfire in two ways. In the first instance, they may produce metaphorical *blends*:

(27) and Peter Booth, who stands to break a personal milestone in this match . . .

(Peter Walker; *C1*: 19)

(28) For a player to ask for a transfer has opened everybody's eyebrows.

(Bobby Robson; *C1*: 25)

(29) He's been burning the midnight oil at both ends.

(Sid Waddell; *C2*: 20)

(30) In the Scottish Cup you only get one crack at the cherry against Rangers or Celtic.

(Tom Ferrie; *C3*: 16)

It seems in each of these examples that two conventional idioms are intermeshed in a way comparable to lexical blends. In her discussion of lexical blends as performance errors, Fromkin (1971: 46; and see also pp. 283–5 above) notes that since speakers are often confronted with a number of appropriate lexical entries for a particular TU, they may erroneously blend two items in the AU. (Two of the examples she provides are 'maistly', for 'mostly'/'mainly' and 'swindged' for 'switched'/'changed'). A comparable process – albeit at a higher linguistic level – seems to operate in tokens (27) to (30). As more than one metaphorical expression would be appropriate for each of the TUs, the error results when a blend of two expressions is produced in the AU. Incidentally, the two 'competing plans' in each token are:

(27′) break a . . . record
      pass a . . . milestone
(28′) opened . . . eyes
      raised . . . eyebrows
(29′) burning the candle at both ends
      burning the midnight oil
(30′) one crack of the whip
      one bite at the cherry

The second major category of infelicitous metaphorical expressions seems to be what are traditionally termed mixed metaphors. Consider the following:

(31) I have other irons in the fire, but I'm keeping them close to my chest.

                      (John Bond; *C1*: 29)

(32) A lot of people think the hard noses of Fleet Street don't have a soft centre, but they do you know.

            (Gerald Williams; *C3*: 58)

(33) Zivojinovic seems to be able to pull the big bullet out of the top drawer.

             (Mike Ingham; *C3*: 89)

(34) He and his colleagues, are like hungry hounds galloping after a red herring.

           (William Shelton; *C3*: 68)

One explanation for the oddity of these examples may be that presenters, in their efforts to maintain ongoing vivid commentary, tend to 'overflout' the Quality maxim by compounding two or more fairly conventional metaphors. Unlike the metaphorical blends realized by tokens (27–30), which appear to be primarily errors in linguistic performance, the mixed metaphors of (31–4) are the products of a basic miscalculation of the degree to which the CP may be jeopardized. The resulting tokens are therefore liable to a literal reading – which explains why many of the mixed-metaphor-type tokens are accompanied by cartoons depicting the strange consequences of the expression. Token (34), for instance, is headed by a picture of a group of submerged fox-hounds swimming after a puzzled fish). Alternately, the resulting token may simply be obscure, suggesting that the speaker has arguably unintentionally violated the Manner maxims. The following example is especially opaque:

> (35) He has had to put his finger in the dyke in order to prevent any fall-out from this having a boomerang effect.
>
> (Hearst Newspapers Reporter; *C2*: 64)

As was the case with the Quantity implicatures discussed previously, in many of the intended Quality implicatures covered in this section it is still possible to 'see what the speaker is getting at'. This is in spite of the effects created by the RS. However, the LC ensures that even the slightest linguistic infelicity is punished, whether this be a risk-laden contradictory statement, an unintentional blend of two idioms or an overenthusiastic mixture of two or more conventional metaphors.

EXTENDING THE ANALYSIS

In this brief section, I shall suggest some ways in which the pragmatic analysis undertaken in the two preceding sections might be usefully extended. The features of discourse that will be examined shortly are intended to supplement the broader Gricean study, and hopefully, some additional insights into the nature of the Colemanballs corpus may be gained.

One aspect of the Colemanballs discourse not touched upon so far concerns the type of metalinguistic activity in which presenters are engaged. Such metalinguistic activity (broadly 'language about language') takes the form of either discourse deixis or modality. Levinson (1983: 85) defines the former as the use of expressions within some utterance to refer to some portion of the discourse that contains that utterance. Speakers thus explicitly locate their utterances within an overall discourse framework by signalling how the current utterance relates to preceding and subsequent discourse. Moving straight to the Colemanballs collection, a number of tokens may be isolated where attempts to use deictic markers in this way misfire:

> (36) only one word for that – magic darts!
>
> (Tony Green; *C1*: 24)
>
> (37) At 7 . . . Eamonn will approach another surprised personality with his famous three words – 'This Is Your Life'.
>
> (Kathy Secker; *C1*: 63)

(38) This week's mailbag topic is 'Is Christianity Eyewash?' – which is quite a statement.

(Andy Peebles; *C1*: 68)

The prospective metacommentary in (36) ('only one word for that') and (37) ('his famous three words') inaccurately describes the parts of the utterance to which it relates. Token (38) is similar, in that the deictic marker 'quite a statement' retrospectively misclassifies a question. Comparable metalinguistic activity is often directed towards the nature of the speech acts presenters are in the process of performing. In the following token, for instance, an explicit denial of the speech act of *apologizing* is immediately followed by what, on any reckoning, would count as an apology:

(39) I make no apologies for their absence; I'm sorry they're not here.

(Murray Walker; *C1*: 53)

Similarly, in (40) the explicit performative verb 'promise' is followed by a reflexive denial of the performative function:

(40) I promise results, not promises.

(John Bond; *C1*: 27)

And finally, consider how, in the following token, discourse deictic markers are conflated with a temporal deictic marker ('previous'), producing a very peculiar remark indeed:

(41) I don't want to make any previous statement on that.

(George Schultz; *C2*: 71)

In spoken American English *previous* often means 'premature' (i.e. it is Schultz-speak for deictic deferral: 'now is not the time'). But the absurdity stands, for British English readers unaware of this.

Modality constitutes the second important metadiscoursal function. Like discourse deictics, modal expressions are non-propositional in that they lie outside the major information carrying components of the utterance. Modality, however, is the realization of the ways in which speakers convey attitudes to and judgements on the nature of the propositions they utter. In contrast to discourse deixis therefore, modal expressions comment on the content rather than structure of an utterance. Here are some examples of modalized utterances from the Colemanballs corpus:

(42) And Harvey Smith is on the phone now and I think that means he's on the phone.

(Raymond Brookes-Ward; *C1*: 49)

(43) John Bond has brought in a young left sided midfield player who, I guess, will play on the left side of midfield.

(Jimmy Armfield; *C2*: 42)

(44) and their manager, Terry Neil, isn't here today, which suggests he is elsewhere.

(Brian Moore; *C1*: 28)

The peculiarity of (42) derives from the explicit qualification, in the form of 'I think that means', of what is originally unmodalized information. An explanation for why such weak commitment should follow stronger commitment is not easy; one reason may be that it simply reflects the presenter's preoccupation with maintaining ongoing talk at all costs. The other two tokens are comparably odd in that unwarranted tentativeness is conveyed by the modal expressions 'I guess' and 'suggests' respectively.

At this stage, it might be worth considering how the present discussion can be integrated with the earlier discussion of maxim flouting. A small group of modalized expressions in the Colemanballs corpus are also attempts to flout one or more of the maxims. The following two examples, for instance, both contain modal disjuncts. However, they also flout the Quantity Maxim by providing more information than would be reasonably required in the context.

(45) And now to hole eight which is, in fact, the eighth hole.

(Peter Alliss; *C3*: 41)

(46) After 12 frames, they stand all square. The next frame, believe it or not, is the 13th.

(David Vine; *C3*: 81)

There is a suggestion here that these presenters, through their use of the modal disjuncts 'in fact' and 'believe it or not', are actually parodying the very obviousness of the information they are conveying. One of the consequences of the RS is that valuable prosodic clues are stripped from the original spoken utterance and in these examples such prosodic information would be crucial in any search for the intended meaning. As it is, we are left with remarks which seem curiously over-informative in the context, and any intended irony – or even humour – on the part of the presenters has been lost.

One final comment on the type of modalized utterances that appear in Colemanballs is necessary. This concerns the large group of tokens which contain the style disjunct 'literally'. In current English usage there appear to be two ways in which this adverb may be used. The first is when it signals that the content of an utterance is literally true; so that, in this sense, a remark like 'John was literally killed' would only be considered valid on the condition that John is actually dead. The second type of usage conveys rhetorical emphasis, rather than literal truth – a good example of which is the famous opening of Joyce's short story *The Dead*:

> Lily, the caretaker's daughter, was literally run off her feet. Hardly had she brought one gentleman into the pantry . . . than the wheezy hall-door bell clanged again and she had to scamper along the bare hallway to let in another guest.[3]

It is unlikely, given subsequent development of the text, that Lily was *actually* run off her feet.

The contrast between these two interpretations of 'literally' accounts for a number of Colemanballs tokens. Using the adverb for rhetorical emphasis is potentially hazardous given the predisposition of the literal-minded and, it must be said, fairly linguistically prescriptive Colemanballs collector. Here are some examples:

(47) And Alex has literally come back from the dead!

(Ted Lowe; *C1*: 86)

(48) Tavare has literally dropped anchor.

(Trevor Bailey; *C1*: 18)

(49) The audience are literally electrified and glued to their seats.

(Ted Lowe; *C1*: 87)

(50) Anybody buying the record can be assured that the pound they pay will literally go into someone's mouth.

(Bob Geldof; *C3*: 73)

The potential for the cartoonist here should be noted: each of these tokens is accompanied by a depiction of the bizarre consequences of what a literal interpretation of the token would yield. Indeed, nowhere are the constraints of the LC more manifest than when an audience chooses to take 'literally' literally.

CONCLUDING REMARKS

Hopefully, the foregoing analyses will have gone some way towards explaining how Colemanballs-type humour is developed. As a rule, the humorous potential of tokens does not reside in phonological, morphological, or syntactic structure, nor is it a property of lexical or sentence semantics. Rather, I have argued, the 'deviant' nature of the tokens is largely a product of the type of pragmatic inferencing

required of addressees. In this respect, the humour is actively constructed by the recipient of the message. Specific emphasis is to be
placed on the role of the LC and RS in this process; both conditions
function to strip away the layer of pragmatic inferencing required for
the uptake of many utterances. This generalized decontextualization
reduces utterances to raw sentences which are often semantically
unacceptable or patently absurd on a literal reading.

This is not to say that the 'pragmatics of nonsense' proposed here
will handle all the tokens in the Colemanballs corpus. There are
a number of examples which are only readily explained through
reference to cognitive or encyclopedic schemata. According to
Sperber and Wilson (1986: 86), a particular concept will be stored
in memory as an encyclopedic *entry*. This they define as a set of
information about the extension and denotation of that concept.
Thus, the encyclopedic entry for the concept *cat* would contain a
set of assumptions about cats, while an encyclopedic entry for the
concept *argue* will contain a set of assumptions about arguing. In the
light of this cognitive framework, consider the following token:

(51) Here we are in the Holy Land of Israel – a Mecca for
tourists.

(David Vine; *C1*: 7)

Here the humorous reading will be derived from assumptions about
the relationship between Islam and Judaism, along with assumptions
about the denotational range of the item 'Mecca' (i.e. that it
can refer generally to a place sought by a number of people).
Comparable cognitive inferencing will be required to derive humorous
interpretations of the following remarks:

(52) Ah yes, Mohammed – that's one of the most common
Christian names in the world.

(Kid Jensen; *C1*: 63)
(53) Agatha Christie is such a well-known name, her books sell all
over the world – and other places as well.

(Michael Grade; *C1*: 67)

Unfortunately, further discussion of the potential of cognitive models
– such as that of Sperber and Wilson – is beyond the scope of this
essay.

In any study of pragmatic meaning, the role of context is crucial.
With regard to Colemanballs discourse, it was noted that collectors,
and subsequently readers, tend not to access implicatures when
presenters flout maxims. The point to be made here however is

that comparable maxim flouting in other contexts may have entirely different interactive consequences. One context with which a useful comparison might be made is that of literary communication. Take, as a brief illustration, the following short extracts from Samuel Beckett's *Molloy* where the fictional narrator flouts the Maxim of Quality in some way:

> he had come from afar, from the other end of the island even, and was approaching the town for the first time or returning to it after a long absence. A little dog followed him, *a pomeranian I think, but I don't think so.*[4]

> Empty your pockets, I said. He began to empty them. It must not be forgotten that all this time I was lying down. He did not know *I was ill*. Besides *I was not ill*.[5]

> I pushed and pulled in vain, the wheels would not turn. It was as though *the brakes* were jammed, and heaven knows they were not, for my bicycle had *no brakes*.[6]

In the first extract a straightforward semantic contradiction is made which has much in common with those exhibited by tokens (21–6) (see pp. 295–6 above). Similarly, in the second extract, there is explicit denial of what has been logically presupposed, while in the third the existential presupposition 'my bicycle has brakes' is denied. All three contradictions may therefore be regarded, in strictly semantic terms, as non-informative. Nevertheless, all three may still yield meaning at the level of what is implicated – assuming that is, that readers of the text should be predisposed to undertake some inferencing work. Indeed, some literary critics have used such 'anti-language' as a basis for explaining what they see as major thematic elements in Beckett's fiction. Kenner, for instance, suggests that this type of language leads to a 'dilapidation of structure' (1973: 98), whilst Moorjani argues that it creates a 'schizo-structure' and a 'disarticulation of fictional discourse' (1982: 41). The assumption that maxim flouting is motivated for specifically literary purposes seems to trigger complex inferencing strategies on the part of the reader. Clearly, the same cannot be said of such tokens as (21–6) which, despite their semantic similarity to the Beckett examples, are not privileged with the same interactive co-operation. In short, it is very much a question of how one decides to treat nonsense. Humorous readings have to be constructed just as critical readings have to be constructed and neither type of reading is derived solely from the linguistic properties of the text itself.

Finally, what are the implications of this study for the luckless Colemanballs presenter? Well, one route to comparative linguistic safety would be available to them if they chose to adhere faithfully to the four sets of conversational maxims. Rather than jeopardizing the CP by flouting maxims, they could speak in a literal, rational, and optimally efficient way. This proposal is clearly unreasonable. The discourse which would result from such a strategy would be quite bizarre, simply in that it would be out of keeping with the bulk of ordinary language usage. The dilemma is one from which presenters are, unfortunately, unlikely to escape.

There is, however, at least one instance of a happy outcome for a presenter who discovered that he had unwittingly contributed to Colemanballs, a brief comment on which will provide a fitting endnote to our discussion. The following utterance, perpetrated by snooker commentator Ted Lowe, is perhaps the best-known of all the Colemanball's tokens:

> (54) Griffiths is snookered on the brown, which, for those of you watching in black and white, is the ball directly behind the pink.

> (Ted Lowe; *C1*: 88)

The notoriety which this gaffe achieved was enough to assure the presenter of a lucrative advertising contract with the major cheese producers of England and Wales. The resulting advertisement, shown regularly on British TV, presents a sumptious spread of assorted cheeses over which Mr Lowe's commentary runs:

> and for those of you watching in black and white, the blue cheshire is the one between the red and the white.

Either the worm has literally turned – or it hasn't!

NOTES

1 The system of reference for Colemanballs tokens is as follows:

> *C1 Colemanballs* (1982), ed. Barry Fantoni, London: Private Eye/ André Deutsch.
> *C2 Colemanballs 2* (1984), ed. Barry Fantoni, London: Private Eye/André Deutsch.
> *C3 Colemanballs 3* (1986), ed. Barry Fantoni, London: Private Eye/André Deutsch.

2 For clear and concise introductions to basic logical symbolization, see Pospesel (1974) and (1976).

3 From James Joyce (1977), *The Dubliners*, London: Granada, p. 160. Collection first published in 1914.

4 From Samuel Beckett, *The Beckett Trilogy: Molloy. Malone Dies. The Unnamable*, London: Picador, 1979, p. 13 (emphasis added here and *passim*).
5 ibid., p. 130.
6 ibid., p. 44.

Bibliography

Allerton, D. J., Carney, E., and Holdcroft, D. (eds) (1979) *Function and Context in Linguistic Analysis: A Festschrift for William Haas*, Cambridge, Cambridge University Press.

Althusser, L. (1984) *Essays on Ideology*, London: Verso.

Ashbery, J. (1979) *As We Know*, New York: Viking.

Austen, J. (1965) *The Novels of Jane Austen*, ed. R. W. Chapman, London: Oxford University Press.

Austen Leigh, J. (1906) *A Memoir of Jane Austen*, London: Macmillan.

Baars, B. J. (1980) 'On eliciting predictable speech errors in the laboratory', in V. Fromkin (ed.), *Errors in Linguistic Performance: Slips of the Tongue, Ear, Pen, and Hand*, New York: Academic Press, 307–18.

Bakhtin, M. M. [V. N. Volosinov] (1973) *Marxism and the Philosophy of Language*, trans. L. Matejka and I. Titunik, New York: Seminar.

——(1981) 'Discourse in the novel', in *The Dialogic Imagination*, trans. C. Emerson and M. Holquist, Austin: University of Texas Press, 259–422.

——(1984) *Problems of Dostoevsky's Poetics*, ed. and trans. C. Emerson, Minneapolis: University of Minnesota Press.

Baldwin, T. W. (1944) *William Shakspere's Small Latine & Lesse Greeke*, vol. 1, Urbana: University of Illinois Press.

Banfield, A. (1982) *Unspeakable Sentences*, Boston: Routledge & Kegan Paul.

Barth, J. (1980) 'The history of replenishment', *Atlantic Monthly*, June.

Barthes, R. (1973) *Mythologies*, trans. A. Lavers, London: Paladin.

——(1975) *S/Z*, London: Cape.

——(1977) *Image-Music-Text*, trans. S. Heath, London: Fontana.

Bartlett, L. (1986) 'What is "language poetry"?', *Critical Inquiry*, 12 (Summer): 741–52.

Bazerman, C. (1988) *Shaping Written Knowledge*, Madison: University of Wisconsin Press.

Berger, J. (1976) *Ways of Seeing*, Harmondsworth: Penguin.

Bernstein, C. (1986) *Content's Dream: Essays 1975–1984*, Los Angeles: Sun and Moon Press.

——(1987) *Artifice of Absorption*, Philadelphia: Singing Horse Press/Paper Air.

——and Andrews, B. (eds) (1984) *The L=A=N=G=U=A=G=E Book*, Carbondale: Southern Illinois University Press.

Betterton, R. (ed.) (1987) *Looking On*, London: Pandora.

Birch, D. (1989) '"Working effects with words" – whose words?: stylistics and reader intertextuality', in R. Carter and P. Simpson (eds), *Language, Literature and Discourse*, London: Unwin Hyman, 259–77.

——and O'Toole, M. (eds) (1988) *Functions of Style*, London: Pinter.

Bloom, Harold (1975) *The Anxiety of Influence*, Oxford: Oxford University Press.

Brown, P. and Levinson S. (1978) 'Universals in language usage: politeness phenomena', in E. Goody (ed.), *Questions and Politeness: Strategies in Social Interaction*, Cambridge: Cambridge University Press, 56–311.

——(1987) *Politeness: Some Universals in Language Usage*, 2nd edn, Cambridge: Cambridge University Press.

Bruffee, K. (1984) 'Collaborative learning and the "conversation of mankind"', *College English*, 46: 635–52.

Burke, K. (1950) *A Rhetoric of Motives*, Englewood Cliffs, NJ: Prentice Hall.

Burton, D. (1982) 'Through glass darkly: through dark glasses', in R. Carter (ed.), *Language and Literature: An Introductory Reader in Stylistics*, London: Allen & Unwin, 195–214.

Cameron, Deborah (1985) *Feminism and Linguistic Theory*, London: Macmillan.

——and Frazer, E. (1989) *Loved to Death*, London: Macmillan.

Carroll, P. (1968) 'If only he had left from the Finland Station', in *The Poem In Its Skin*, Chicago: Follett.

Carter, R. and Simpson, P. (eds) (1989) *Language, Literature and Discourse: An Introduction to Discourse Stylistics*, London: Unwin Hyman.

Chatman, S. (1978) *Story and Discourse*, Ithaca, NY: Cornell University Press.

Chomsky, N. (1982) *Some Concepts and Consequences of the Theory of Government and Binding*, Cambridge, MA: MIT Press.

Codrescu, A. (ed.) (1987) *Up Late: American Poetry Since 1970*, New York: Four Walls Eight Windows.

Cohen, K. (1980) Ashbery's dismantling of bourgeois discourse, in D. Lehman (ed.), *Beyond Amazement: New Essays on John Ashbery*, Ithaca, NY: Cornell University Press, 128–49.

Comprone, J. (1988) 'Reading Oliver Sacks in a writing-across-the-curriculum course', *Journal of Advanced Composition*, 8: 158–66.

Coulomb, G. G. and Williams, J. M. (1985) 'Perceiving structure in professional prose', in L. Odell and D. Goswami (eds), *Writing in Nonacademic Settings*, New York: Guilford Press, 85–128.

Coupland, N. (ed.) (1988) *Styles of Discourse*, Beckenham: Croom Helm.

Culler, J. (1975) *Structuralist Poetics*, London: Routledge & Kegan Paul/ Ithaca, NY: Cornell University Press.

——(1981) *The Pursuit of Signs*, Ithaca, NY: Cornell University Press.

Daedalus (1989) special issue on 'Another India' (Fall) 118:4.

Derrick, T. J. (1982) 'Critical Introduction' to *Arte of Rhetorique* by Thomas Wilson (1553), New York: Garland.

Derrida, J. (1976) *Of Grammatology*, trans. G. C. Spivak, Baltimore: Johns Hopkins University Press.

Dillon, G. (1981) *Constructing Texts: Elements of a Theory of Composition and Style*, Bloomington: Indiana University Press.

Durant, A. (1989) 'The position of the listener in popular music lyrics', unpublished seminar paper, John Logie Baird Centre, University of Strathclyde.

Eco, U. (1979) *The Role of the Reader*, Bloomington: Indiana University Press.

Empson, W. (1947) *Seven Types of Ambiguity*, 2nd edn, New York: New Directions.

Erasmus, D. (1978) *Literary and Educational Writings 2: De Copia/De Ratione Studii*, ed. Craig R. Thompson, Toronto: University of Toronto Press.

Ervin-Tripp, S. (1972) 'Sociolinguistic rules of address', in J. B. Pride and J. Holmes (eds), *Sociolinguistics*, Harmondsworth: Penguin, 225–40.

Fahnestock, J. (1986) 'Accommodating science: the rhetorical life of scientific facts', *Written Communication*, 3: 275–96.

Fairclough, N. (1998) *Language and Power*, London: Longman.

Fetterley, J. (1981) *The Resisting Reader*, Bloomington: Indiana University Press.

Fillmore, C. (1971) 'Some problems for case grammar', *Georgetown University Round Table on Languages and Linguistics*, vol. 24, Washington, DC: Georgetown University Press.

——(1977) 'Topics in lexical semantics', in R. Cole (ed.), *Current Issues in Linguistic Theory*, New York: Holt, Rinehart & Winston.

Fish, S. (1980) *Is There a Text in this Class?*, Cambridge, MA: Harvard University Press.

Forrest-Thomson, V. (1971) 'Irrationality and artifice: a problem in recent poetics', *British Journal of Aesthetics*, 11 (2): 123–33.

——(1972) 'Levels in poetic convention', *Journal of European Studies*, 2: 35–51.

——(1973) 'Necessary artifice: form and theory in the poetry of *Tel Quel*', *Language and Style*, 4 (1): 3–26.

——(1978) *Poetic Artifice: A Theory of Twentieth-Century Poetry*, Manchester: Manchester University Press.

Foucault, Michel (1988) *The History of Sexuality*, trans. P. Hurley, New York: Vintage Books.

Fowler, R. (1985) 'Power', in T. Van Dijk (ed.), *Handbook of Discourse Analysis*, vol. 4, London: Academic Press, 61–82.

——(1986) *Linguistic Criticism*, Oxford: Oxford University Press.

——(1987) 'Notes on critical linguistics', in R. Steele and T. Threadgold, (eds), *Language Topics*, vol. 2, Amsterdam: Benjamins, 481–92.

——, Hodge, R., Kress, G. and Trew, T. (1979) *Language and Control*, London: Routledge & Kegan Paul.

Fowles, John (1979) *The Collector*, London: Cape.

Fries, Peter (1983) 'On the status of theme in English: arguments from discourse', in J. Petofi and E. Sozer (eds), *Micro and Macro Connexity of Texts*, Hamburg: Buske Verlag.

——, (1991) 'Towards a discussion of the flow of information in written text', in W. Mann and S. Thompson (eds), *Discourse Analysis: Diverse Analyses of a Fundraising Letter*, Amsterdam: Benjamins.

Fromkin, V. (1971) 'The non-anomalous nature of anomalous utterances', *Language*, 47: 27–52.

——(ed.) (1973) *Speech Errors as Linguistic Evidence*, The Hague: Mouton.

——(ed.) (1980) *Errors in Linguistic Performance: Slips of the Tongue, Ear, Pen, and Hand*, New York: Academic Press.

Gazdar, G. (1979) *Pragmatics: Implicature, Presupposition and Logical Form*, New York: Academic Press.

Geertz, C. (1983) *Local Knowledge: Further Essays in Interpretive Anthropology*, New York: Basic Books.

Gibbons, T. (1979) *Literature and Awareness*, London: Edward Arnold.

Gilbert, N. and Mulkay, M. (1984) *Opening Pandora's Box*, Cambridge: Cambridge University Press.

Gilbert, S. and Gubar, S. (1979) *The Madwoman in the Attic*, New Haven, CN: Yale University Press.

——(1988) *The War of the Words*, New Haven, CN: Yale University Press.

Greimas, A. G. (1966) *Semantique Structurale*, Paris: Larousse.

Grice, P. (1975) 'Logic and conversation', in P. Cole and J. Morgan, (eds), *Syntax and Semantics*, vol. 3: *Speech Acts*, New York: Academic Press, 41–58.

Guha, R. (ed) (1988) *Selected Subaltern Studies*, New Delhi: Oxford University Press.

Gupta, A. and Ferguson, J. (eds) (forthcoming) *Beyond 'Culture': Space, Identity, and the Politics of Difference*.

Gusfield, J. (1981) *The Culture of Public Problems: Drinking-Driving and the Social Order*, Chicago: University of Chicago Press.

Halliday, M. A. K. (1970) 'Language structure and language function', in J. Lyons (ed.), *New Horizons in Linguistics*, Harmondsworth: Penguin, 140–65.

——(1979) 'Modes of meaning and modes of expression: types of grammatical structure, and their determination by different semantic functions', in D. J. Allerton, E. Carney and D. Holdcroft (eds), *Function and Context in Linguistic Analysis: A Festschrift for William Haas*, Cambridge: Cambridge University Press, 56–79.

——(1981) 'Language function and literary style: an enquiry into the language of William Golding', in D. C. Freeman (ed.), *Essays in Modern Stylistics*, London and New York: Methuen.

——(1985) *An Introduction to Functional Grammar*, London: Edward Arnold.

——(1988) 'Poetry as scientific discourse: the nuclear sections of Tennyson's "In Memoriam"', in D. Birch and M. O'Toole (eds), *Functions of Style*, London, Pinter, 31–44.

Harari, J. (ed.) (1979) *Textual Strategies: Perspectives in Post-Structuralist Criticism*, Ithaca, NY: Cornell University Press.

Hartley, G. (1989) *Textual Politics and the Language Poets*, Bloomington: Indiana University Press.

Harvey, G. ([1577] 1945) *Gabriel Harvey's Ciceronianus*, ed. H. S. Wilson, trans. C. A. Forbes, University of Nebraska Studies in the Humanities 4, Lincoln: University of Nebraska Press.

Hasan, R. (1985) *Linguistics, Language, and Verbal Art*, Deakin: Deakin University Press.

——, (1988) 'The analysis of one poem: theoretical issues in practice', in D. Birch and M. O'Toole (eds), *Functions of Style*, London: Pinter, 45–73.

Haydn, H. and Fuller, E. (compilers) (1978) *Thesaurus of Book Digests*, New York: Avenel Books.

Hickey, L. (ed.) (1989) *The Pragmatics of Style*, London: Routledge.

Hobbes, T. ([1651] 1962) *Leviathan*, London: Fontana.

Hopper, P. and Thompson, S. (1980) 'Transitivity in grammar and discourse', *Language*, 56: 251–99.

Hoskyns, J. ([1599] 1935) *Directions for Speech and Style*, ed. H. H. Hudson, Princeton: Princeton University Press.

Hrushovski [Harshav], B. (1979) 'The structure of semiotic objects: a three-dimensional model', *Poetics Today*, 1 (1): 365–76.

——(1984a) 'Poetic metaphor and frames of reference', *Poetics Today*, 5(1): 5–43.

——(1984b) 'Fictionality and frames of reference: remarks on a theoretical framework', *Poetics Today*, 5(2): 227–51.

Hudson, H. H. (ed.) (1935) *Directions for Speech and Style*, by John Hoskyns [1599], Princeton: Princeton University Press.

Hughes, P. (1984) *More on Oxymoron*, London: Jonathan Cape.

Jakobson, R. (1960) 'Closing statement: linguistics and poetics', in T. A. Sebeok (ed.), *Style in Language*, Cambridge, MA: MIT Press, 350–77.

Jameson, Fredric (1984) 'Postmodernism, or the cultural logic of late capitalism', *New Left Review*, 146: 53–92.

——(1987) 'Spatial equivalence', unpublished talk, University of Pittsburgh, Pittsburgh, 19 March.

——(1988) 'Cognitive mapping', in C. Nelson and L. Grossberg (eds), *Marxism and the Interpretation of Culture*, Urbana and Chicago: University of Illinois Press, 347–60.

Jardine, L. (1974) *Francis Bacon, Discovery and the Art of Discourse*, Cambridge: Cambridge University Press.

Johnson, P. and Wigley, M. (1988) *Deconstructivist Architecture*, New York: Museum of Modern Art.

Kedar, L. (ed.) (1987) *Power through Discourse*, Norwood, NJ: Ablex.

Kenner, H. (1973) *A Reader's Guide to Samuel Beckett*, London: Thames & Hudson.

Kertesz, A. (1979) 'Visual agnosia: the dual deficit of perception and recognition', *Cortex*, 15: 403–19.

Kiely, R. (1975) 'The limits of dialogue in *Middlemarch*', in J. H. Buckley (ed.), *The Worlds of Victorian Fiction*, Cambridge, MA: Harvard University Press, 103–23.

Kinkead-Weekes, M. (1980) 'The voicing of fiction', in I. Gregor (ed.), *Reading the Victorian Novel: Detail into Form*, London: Vision Press.

Kishwar, M. (1988) 'Some aspects of bondage', in M. Kishwar and R. Vanita (eds), *In Search of Answers – Indian Women's Voices from Manushi*, London: Zed Books.

Knorr-Cetina, K. (1981) *The Manufacture of Knowledge: An Essay on the Constructivist and Contextual Nature of Science*, Oxford: Pergamon.

Kostelanetz, R. (1982) 'An abc of contemporary reading', *Poetics Today*, 3(3): 5–46.

Kramerae, C., Schulz, M., and O'Barr, W. (1984) *Language and Power*, New York: Sage.

Kress, G. (1985) 'Ideological structures in discourse', in T. Van Dijk (ed.), *Handbook of Discourse Analysis*, vol. 4, London: Academic Press, 27–42.

——(1988) 'Textual matters: the social effectiveness of style', in D. Birch and M. O'Toole (eds), *Functions of Style*, London: Pinter, 126–41.

——and Hodge, R. (1988) *Social Semiotics*, Cambridge: Polity Press.

Kristeva, J. (1986) 'Stabat mater', in S. Suleiman (ed.), *The Female Body in Western Culture*, Cambridge, MA: Harvard University Press.

Kuhn, A. (1982) *Woman's Pictures*, London: Routledge & Kegan Paul.

Labov, W. and Fanshel, D. (1977) *Therapeutic Discourse*, New York: Academic Press.

Lacan, J. (1966) *Ecrits*, trans. A. Sheridan, London: Tavistock.

Lakoff, R. (1975) *Language and Woman's Place*, New York: Harper & Row.

Leach, E. (1970) *Lévi-Strauss*, London: Fontana.

Leech, G. (1983) *Principles of Pragmatics*, London: Longman.

——and Short, M. (1981) *Style in Fiction*, London: Longman.

Levinson, S. (1983) *Pragmatics*, Cambridge: Cambridge University Press.

Lévi-Strauss, C. (1968) *Structural Anthropology*, New York: Doubleday.

Lodge, D. (1990) *After Bakhtin: Essays on Fiction and Criticism*, London: Routledge.

Lundberg, P. (1986) 'George Eliot: Mary Ann Evans's subversive tool', *Studies in the Novel*, 18: 270–82.

Lynch, M. (1985) *Art and Artifact in Laboratory Science*, London: Routledge & Kegan Paul.

McCabe, C. (1981) 'Realism and cinema: notes on some Brechtian theses', in T. Bennett *et al.* (eds), *Popular TV and Film*, London: Open University British Film Institute, 216–35.

McConnell-Ginet, S. (1988) 'Language and gender', in F. Newmeyer (ed.), *The Cambridge Linguistic Survey*, vol. 4, Cambridge: Cambridge University Press.

McGann, J. (1988) 'Contemporary poetry, alternate routes', in *Social Values and Poetic Acts: The Historical Judgment of Literary Work*, Cambridge, MA: Harvard University Press, 197–269.

McHale, B. (1987) *Postmodernist Fiction*, London: Methuen.

McHoul, A. (1982) *Telling How Texts Talk*, London, Routledge & Kegan Paul.

McKenzie, M. (1987) 'Free indirect speech in a fettered insecure society', *Language and Communication*, 7: 153–9.

Mann, W. and Thompson, S. (eds) (1991) *Discourse Analysis: Diverse Analyses of a Fundraising Letter*, Amsterdam: Benjamins.

Marino, M. (1988) 'Puns: the good, the bad and the beautiful', *Humor*, 1(1): 39–48.

Marshment, M. and Gamman, G. (eds) (1988) *The Female Gaze*, London: Women's Press.

Martin, D. (1976) *Battered Wives*, San Francisco: Glide Publications.

Martin, J. R. (1985) *Factual Writing: Exploring and Challenging Social Reality*, Deakin: Deakin University Press.

——(1986) 'Grammaticalising ecology: the politics of baby seals and kangaroos', in T. Threadgold, E. Grosz, G. Kress and M. Halliday (eds),

Semiotics, Ideology, Language, Sydney: Sydney Association for Studies in Society and Culture.

Mehrohtra, R. R. (no date) 'Matrimonial advertisements: a study in correlation between linguistic and situational feeling', *Occasional Papers – Studies in Linguistics*, Simla: Indian Institute of Advanced Study.

Meierus, A. [1589] *Certaine briefe and speciall instructions for gentlemen, merchants, etc.*, trans. P. Jones, London: J. Woolfe (STC 17784).

Mills, S. (1991) *Discourses of Difference*, London: Routledge.

—— et al. (eds) (1989) *Feminist Readings/Feminists Reading*, Hemel Hempstead: Harvester Wheatsheaf.

Modleski, Tanya (1982) *Loving with a Vengeance*, London: Shoestring.

Montgomery, M. (1986) 'DJ talk', *Media Culture and Society*, 8(4): 421–40.

——(1988) 'Direct address, mediated text and establishing co-presence', unpublished discussion paper, Programme in Literary Linguistics, University of Strathclyde, Strathclyde.

Moorjani, A. (1982) *Abysmal Games in the Novels of Beckett*, Chapel Hill: University of North Carolina Press.

Morgan, J. (1975) 'Some interactions of syntax and pragmatics', in P. Cole and J. L. Morgan (eds), *Syntax and Semantics*, vol. 3: *Speech Acts*, New York: Academic Press.

Morris, M. (1989) *The Pirate's Fiancée*, London: Verso.

Mukarovsky, J. (1978) *Structure, Sign and Function*, New Haven: Yale University Press.

Mulvey, L. (1981) 'Visual pleasure and narrative cinema', in T. Bennett *et al.* (eds), *Popular TV and Film*, London: Open University British Film Institute, 206–15.

Myers, G. (1989a) 'The pragmatics of politeness in scientific articles', *Applied Linguistics*, 10(1): 1–23.

——(1989b) *Writing Biology: Texts in the Construction of Scientific Knowledge*, Madison: University of Wisconsin Press.

Nash, W. (1985) *The Language of Humour*, London: Longman.

NCCL (National Council for Civil Liberties) Rights for Women Unit – M. Benn, A. Cook, and T. Gill (1983) *The Rape Controversy*, Nottingham: The Russel Press.

Neumann, A. W. (1986) 'Characterization and comment in *Pride and Prejudice*: free indirect discourse and "double-voiced" verbs of speaking, thinking, and feeling', *Style*, 20: 364–94.

Newman, C. (1984) 'The post-modern arena: the act of fiction in an age of inflation', *Salmagundi*.

O'Barr, W. (1982) *Linguistic Evidence: Language, Power, and Strategy in the Courtroom*, New York: Academic Books.

Palsgrave, J. (1937) *The Comedy of Acolastus*, ed. P. L. Carver, Early English Texts Society 202, London: Oxford University Press.

Pascal, R. (1977) *The Dual Voice*, Manchester: Manchester University Press.

van Peer, W. (1986) *Stylistics and Psychology: Investigations of Foregrounding*, London: Croom Helm.

——(ed.) (1988) *Taming the Text: Explorations in Language, Literature and Culture*, London: Routledge.

Perelman, R. (ed.) (1985) *Writing/Talks*, Carbondale: Southern Illinois University Press.

Perloff, M. (1987) 'The word as such: L=A=N=G=U=A=G=E poetry in the eighties', in *The Dance of the Intellect: Studies in the Poetry of the Pound Tradition*, Cambridge: Cambridge University Press, 215–38.

Petöfi, J. S. and Sözer, E. (eds) (1983) *Micro and Macro Connexity of Texts*, Hamburg: Buske Verlag.

Pospesel, H. (1974) *Propositional Logic: Introduction to Logic*, Englewood Cliffs, NJ: Prentice Hall.

——(1976) *Predicate Logic: Introduction to Logic*, Englewood Cliffs, NJ: Prentice Hall.

Pratt, M. L. (1977) *Toward a Speech Act Theory of Literary Discourse*, Bloomington: Indiana University Press.

Propp, V. (1968) *The Morphology of the Folktale*, Austin: University of Texas Press.

Prynne, J. H. (1982) *Poems*, Edinburgh and London: Agneau 2.

Puttenham, G. ([1589] 1936) *The Arte of English Poesie*, ed. G. Doidge Willcock and A. Walker, Cambridge: Cambridge University Press.

Quirk, R., Greenbaum, S., Leech, G., and Svartvik, J. (1985) *A Comprehensive Grammar of the English Language*, London: Longman.

Rape Counselling and Research Project to the Royal Commission on Criminal Procedure, (1979) *Rape, Police and Forensic Procedure*, London: HMSO.

Raskin, V. (1985) *Semantic Mechanisms of Humor*, Dordrecht: Reidel.

——(1988) 'From the editor', *Humor*, 1(1): 1–4.

Richardson, S. (1804) *The Correspondence of Samuel Richardson*, ed. A. L. Barbauld, 6 vols, London: Richard Phillips.

——(1964) *Selected Letters of Samuel Richardson*, ed. J. Carroll, Oxford: Oxford University Press.

——(1985) *Clarissa or, The History of a Young Lady*, ed. A. Ross, Harmondsworth: Penguin.

——(1986) *The History of Sir Charles Grandison*, ed. J. Harris, London: Oxford University Press.

Ross, A. (1988) 'The new sentence and the commodity form: recent American writing', in C. Nelson and L. Grossberg (eds), *Marxism and the Interpretation of Culture*, Urbana and Chicago: University of Illinois Press, 361–80.

Ross, J. F. (1981) *Portraying Analogy*, Cambridge: Cambridge University Press.

Roth, P. (1968) *When She Was Good*, New York: Bantam Books.

Russel, D. (1982) *Rape in Marriage*, London: Macmillan.

Sacks, H., Schegloff, E., and Jefferson, G. (1974) 'A simplest systematics for the organization of turn-taking in conversation', *Language*, 50(4): 696–735.

Sacks, O. (1983) *Awakenings*, New York: Dutton.

——(1985) *The Man who Mistook his Wife for a Hat*, London: Picador.

Sangari, K. and Vaid, S. (eds) (1989) *Recasting Women: Essays in Colonial History*, New Delhi: Kali for Women.

Sapir, E. (1921) *Selected Writings of Edward Sapir*, ed. D. G. Mandelbaum, Berkeley: University of California Press.

Schieffelin, B. and Ochs, E. (1986) *Language Socialization across Cultures*, Cambridge: Cambridge University Press.

Scholes, R. (1982) *Semiotics and Interpretation*, New Haven, CT: Yale University Press.

Sewell, E. (1952) *The Field of Nonsense*, London: Chatto & Windus.

Short, M. (1988) 'Speech presentation, the novel and the press', in W. van Peer (ed.), *Taming the Text: Explorations in Language, Literature and Culture*, London: Routledge, 61–81.

——(1989) 'Discourse analysis and the analysis of drama', in R. Carter and P. Simpson (eds), *Language, Literature and Discourse*, London: Unwin Hyman, 139–70.

Showalter, Elaine (1971) 'Women and the literary curriculum', *College English*, 32: 855.

——(1979) 'Towards a feminist poetics', in M. Jacobus (ed.), *Women Writing and Writing about Women*, London: Croom Helm, 22–41.

——(1985) 'Shooting the rapids: feminist criticism in the mainstream', paper delivered at the Southampton Conference on Sexual Difference, University of Southampton.

Simpson, P. (1989) 'Politeness phenomena in Ionesco's *The Lesson*', in R. Carter and P. Simpson (eds), *Language, Literature and Discourse*, London: Unwin Hyman, 171–94.

Smit, D. W. (1988) *The Language of a Master: Theories of Style and the Late Writing of Henry James*, Carbondale: Southern Illinois University Press.

Sperber, D. and Wilson, D. (1986) *Relevance: Communication and Cognition*, Oxford: Blackwell.

Spivak, G. C. (1987) *In Other Worlds*, London: Methuen.

Sriniwas, M. N. (1984) *Some Reflections on Dowry*, New Delhi: Oxford University Press.

Stewart, G. (1975) 'Teaching prose fiction: some "instructive" styles', *College English*, 37.

Stewart, S. (1979) *Nonsense: Aspects of Intertextuality in Folklore and Literature*, Baltimore: Johns Hopkins University Press.

Stubbs, M. (1983) *Discourse Analysis: The Sociolinguistic Analysis of Natural Language*, Oxford: Blackwell.

Suleiman, S. and Crosman, I. (eds) (1981) *The Reader in the Text: Essays on Audience and Interpretation*, Princeton,: Princeton University Press.

Tannen, D. (1979) 'What's in a frame? Surface evidence for underlying expectations', in R. O. Freedle (ed.), *New Directions in Discourse Processing*, vol. 2, Norwood, NJ: Ablex, 137–81.

Thomas, J. (1983) 'Cross-cultural pragmatic failure', *Applied Linguistics*, 4: 91–112.

Thompson, A. and Thompson, J. O. (1987) *Shakespeare: Meaning and Metaphor*, Brighton: Harvester Press.

Thorne, B. and Henley, N. (eds) (1975) *Language and Sex: Difference and Dominance*, Rowley, M. A: Newbury House.

Threadgold, T. (1986) 'Introduction' and 'Subjectivity, ideology and the feminine in John Donne's poetry', in T. Threadgold, E. A. Grosz, G. Kress, and M. A. K. Halliday (eds), *Semiotics, Ideology, Language*, Sydney: Sydney Studies in Society and Culture, 3:15–60 and 297–325.

——(1988a) 'Language and gender', *Australian Journal of Feminist Studies*. May.

——(1988b) 'Stories of race and gender: an unbounded discourse', in D. Birch and M. O'Toole (eds), *Functions of Style*, London: Pinter, 169–204.

——(forthcoming) *Feminist Poetics*, London: Routledge.

Todd, J. (1988) *Feminist Literary History: A Defence*, Cambridge: Polity Press.

Toner, B. (1977) *The Facts of Rape*, London: Hutchinson.

Toolan, M. (1985) 'Analysing fictional dialogue', *Language and Communication*, 5(3): 193–206.

——(1988) 'Compromising positions: systemic linguistics and the locally managed semiotics of dialogue', in D. Birch and M. O'Toole (eds), *Functions of Style*, London: Pinter, 249–60.

——(1989) 'Analysing conversation in fiction: an example from Joyce's *Portrait*', in R. Carter and P. Simpson (eds), *Language, Literature and Discourse*, London: Unwin Hyman, 195–211.

——(1990) *The Stylistics of Fiction*, London: Routledge.

Trew, T. (1979) 'Theory and ideology at work', in R. Fowler, R. Hodge, G. Kress, and T. Trew, *Language and Control*, London: Routledge & Kegan Paul, 94–116.

Van den Broeke, M. and Goldstein L. (1980) 'Consonant features in speech errors', in V. Fromkin (ed.), *Errors in Linguistic Performance: Slips of the Tongue, Ear, Pen, and Hand*, New York: Academic Press, 47–66.

Wanner, E. and Gleitman, L. (1982) *Language Acquisition: The State of the Art*, Cambridge: Cambridge University Press.

Ward, E. (1984) *Father–Daughter Rape*, Wellingborough, Northants: The Women's Press.

Weber, J. J. (1982) 'Frame construction and frame accommodation in a Gricean analysis of narrative', *Journal of Literary Semantics*, 11: 90–5.

——(1989) 'Dickens's social semiotic: the modal analysis of ideological structure', in R. Carter and P. Simpson (eds), *Language, Literature and Discourse*, London: Unwin Hyman, 95–111.

West, C. and Zimmerman, D. (1983) 'Small insults: a study of interruptions in cross-sex conversations between unacquainted persons', in B. Thorne and N. Henley (eds), *Language, Gender and Society*, Rowley, MA: Newbury House.

Whorf, B. L. (1952) *Collected Papers on Metalinguistics*, Washington, DC: Department of State, Foreign Service Institute.

Wilkinson, A. (1971) *The Foundations of Language: Talking and Reading in Young Children*, Oxford: Oxford University Press.

Willcock, G. D. and Walker, A. (1936) 'Introduction' to *The Arte of English Poesie* by George Puttenham [1589], Cambridge: Cambridge University Press.

Williams, R. (1983) 'Monologue and *Macbeth*', in S. Kappeler and N. Bryson (eds), *Teaching the Text*, London: Routledge & Kegan Paul.

Williamson, J. (1978) *Decoding Advertisements: Ideology and Meaning in Advertising*, London: Marion Boyars.

Wilson, D. (1975) *Presuppositions and Non-truth-conditional Semantics*, New York: Academic Press.

Wilson, H. S. (1945) 'Introduction', to *Gabriel Harvey's 'Ciceronianus'*, Lincoln: University of Nebraska Press.

Wilson, T. ([1553] 1982) *Arte of Rhetorique*, ed. T. J. Derrick, New York: Garland.

Wodak, R. (ed.) (1988) *Language, Power and Ideology: Studies in Political Discourse*, Amsterdam: Benjamins.

Young, D. (1988) 'Projection and deixis in narrative discourse', in N. Coupland (ed.), *Styles of Discourse*, Beckenham: Croom Helm, 20–49.
Young, R. (ed.) (1981) *Untying the Text*, London: Routledge & Kegan Paul.
Ziz, A. (1988) 'Humor's role in married life', *Humor*, 1(3): 223–9.

Index